Memoirs of
Madame de La Tour du Pin

Memoirs of
Madame de La Tour du Pin

———————◆———————

EDITED AND TRANSLATED BY

Felice Harcourt

WITH AN INTRODUCTION BY

Peter Gay

The McCall Publishing Company

NEW YORK

INTRODUCTION

"When someone writes a book, it is generally with the intention that it shall be read either before or after their death. But I am not writing a book, and as you may wonder what this is, I must explain that it is simply a journal of my life." With this ingenuous disclaimer, Henriette-Lucy Dillon, Marquise de La Tour du Pin, begins one of the most instructive documents to come out of France about the Revolution and Napoleon. Whatever her intentions, she did write a book, and a fascinating one. But we must take her disclaimer, if not literally, at least seriously. Memoirs are a special branch of literature; they reveal not through analysis but through anecdote. And if their author is observant and intelligent—Madame de La Tour du Pin was obviously both—they will reveal more, and other things, than the author intended to reveal. Precisely by being unself-conscious, they furnish valuable, often unduplicable, material to the historian. They give portraits of societies and events from the inside. Even their omissions and distortions are instructive—at least to the instructed. "I do not claim to be qualified to describe the state of society in France before the Revolution," Madame de La Tour du Pin writes in another disclaimer. She might have been unable to write an authoritative history, or offer a sophisticated analysis of the Old Regime, but if there is one thing she *can* do, it is to describe. And even her judgments are not without interest. Writing down her memoirs for the eyes of one of her children, "in old age"—actually she was fifty when she began to write her memoirs, and would live another thirty-three years—she records her impression that "the

Revolution of 1789 was only the inevitable consequence, and, I might almost say, the just punishment of the vices of the upper classes, vices carried to such excess that if people had not been stricken with a mortal blindness, they must have seen that they would inevitably be consumed by the very fire they themselves were lighting." This is by no means the only generalization to arrest the reader's attention; but the charm and value of this book lie in its narration of events and the personality—vivid, alert, powerful—it reveals, almost by the way.

Fortunately for her readers, Madame de La Tour du Pin lived through stirring times. She was born in 1770, during the last years of the long reign of Louis XV; when his grandson, Louis XVI, ascended the throne in 1774, she was a little girl. She witnessed the declining Old Regime as a growing child and a much-wooed heiress. Without embarrassment or resentment, she records the intrigues for her hand and the reasons for her popularity: "Everyone who wanted to marry me was dazzled by my apparently fine expectations"—she had prospects at court, and a great deal of wealth in her family. To be sure, she had a say in whom she would take, and she refused suitors because they had a bad reputation or (as she candidly admits) their "name" was not "sufficiently illustrious." And when, in 1786, at sixteen, she consented to be married, her consent was decisive. But she had never seen her prospective husband. As she would say later: "It was an instinct, a guidance from above. God had destined me for him! And since that decision, which my sixteen-year-old lips uttered almost despite myself, I have felt that I belonged to him, that my life was his. I still bless Heaven for that decision." The theological language should not conceal the simple fact that she was lucky. And her account tells us much about the social style of the French aristocracy in the Old Regime.

That regime did not have much longer to live. When Madame de La Tour du Pin was nineteen, the Revolution broke out. It robbed her of a post as lady-in-waiting to Queen Marie Antoinette, and of a life of idleness punctuated by intrigue, but it supplied her with a succession of adventures which, despite their harrowing quality, she obviously, if intermittently, enjoyed. Nor did they end with the fall of Robespierre; the turbulent world of the Directory, and the even more turbulent world of Napoleon, gave her no peace, and much to write about. But there is no need to anticipate her own account of her life; to summarize it here would be to spoil a remarkable story. Nor is it necessary to give a synopsis of the history she so intensely experienced. Most readers know their way about the French Revolution, and those who do not may turn to the brief Translator's Outline that follows the text.

What deserves comment is the very special personality that emerges from these recollections. That Madame de La Tour du Pin was gay and gallant, energetic and effective, hardly requires notice—it is too obvious. The quality that assumes special importance is actually a striking conjunction of two qualities: a proud caste-consciousness coupled with an ironic detachment. She was an aristocrat completely, instinctively at home in an aristocratic world. Even in exile in remote upstate New York, "resolved" to manage her "house as well as any good farmer's wife," she remained the great lady she had always been. One day, engaged in humble cookery, she heard a voice saying behind her, in French, "Never was a leg of mutton spitted with greater majesty." It was Talleyrand, a good judge of class at all times. She would wash clothes and iron them, but the kind of pride she took in her labors was characteristic of the best that those of her rank had to offer: "My dairy," she records with evident self-satisfaction, "was reputed the cleanest and even the most elegant in the country."

At the same time, she recognized the limitations and saw

Introduction

through the failings of the caste to which she so unmistakably belonged. Her judgment sprang not from the acidulous malice of the gossip or the masochistic self-hatred of the alienated; it was the keen-eyed, un-illusioned detachment of a free spirit. Louis XVI was undignified and paralyzed by illusions; the French nobility in 1789 was "laughing and dancing" its "way to the precipice." And she saw with pitiless lucidity that, while the great upheaval was preparing in the wings, those with property and in power closed their eyes and lived for the moment, without reflection and without compassion. "Never before had people been so pleasure-seeking as in the spring of 1789, before the meeting of the States-General. For the poor, the winter had been very hard, but there was no concern for the misery of the poor." Compared with such aristocrats, old in lineage but obtuse in the management of their responsibilities, Napoleon Bonaparte was a paragon. For Napoleon, Madame de La Tour du Pin has nothing but praise. He is a "great man" who fully deserves "the gratitude of the people." Time-serving? It is true that the Marquis de La Tour du Pin served Napoleon the First Consul, Napoleon the Life Consul, and Napoleon the Emperor after seeing military service in the Old Regime and surviving the Revolution. And it is true that what mattered to her husband mattered to her. He, alone with Napoleon, survives her scrutiny unscathed. But her judgment is something better than the gratitude of a successful and satisfied courtier. The qualities Madame de La Tour du Pin saw in Napoleon were precisely the qualities she thought a fit aristocracy must have, and that the old French aristocracy lacked: the will to do great things, the intelligence to find the means to do them, and the energy to see them through. Is it extravagant to find these qualities in Madame de La Tour du Pin herself, only in more appealing form?

PETER GAY

Principal Characters

THE WRITER
Henrietta-Lucy Dillon, born in Paris in 1770, married in 1787 to the Comte de Gouvernet, later Marquis de La Tour du Pin. They had seven children, only one of whom survived them. Her memoirs, written between 1820, when she was already fifty, and 1853 when she died, cover the period of her childhood, life at the court of Louis XVI, the Revolution and the first year of the Restoration. They were written for Aymar, her only surviving child.

HER FATHER
Arthur Dillon (1750–1794), second son of Henry, 11th Viscount Dillon. He was given the Dillon Regiment in 1766 and commanded it in the service of France until the Revolution. He married, first, Lucie de Rothe, the writer's mother, and secondly the Comtesse de La Touche, first cousin of the Empress Josephine. He was executed by the revolutionaries in 1794.

HER MOTHER
Lucie de Rothe (1751–1782) daughter of General Edward de Rothe and Lucy Cary. Lady-in-Waiting to Queen Marie-Antoinette.

HER GRANDMOTHER
Lucy Cary (?–1804), daughter of Laura Dillon and Viscount Falkland. She married General Edward de Rothe and had one daughter, Lucie, who married Arthur Dillon. After her daughter's death, she brought up her grand-daughter, the writer of the memoirs.

HER GREAT-GREAT-UNCLE
Arthur Dillon (1721–1806), Archbishop of Narbonne. He lived in the house of his niece, Lucy de Rothe and played a considerable part in the writer's life.

HER HUSBAND

Frédéric-Séraphin, Comte de Gouvernet. Born in 1759. Succeeded his
father as Comte de La Tour du Pin de Gouvernet in 1794. In 1815,
Louis XVIII created him a peer of France (an hereditary member of
the upper chamber). In 1820, he was created Marquis de La Tour du
Pin, the title used by his wife in her memoirs in the period after their
marriage.

Until the Revolution, M. de La Tour du Pin was a soldier. In 1791,
he was appointed Minister to the Court at The Hague, but was recalled
by Dumouriez. After a period of hiding in France, exile in America,
a short return to France and renewed exile in England, M. de La Tour
du Pin returned to France and served under the Empire as Prefect in
Brussels (1801–1812). Afterwards he was appointed Prefect in Amiens,
where he was when Louis XVIII returned to France. He then resumed
his diplomatic career and was appointed Minister at The Hague, retain-
ing this appointment while serving as one of the Ambassadors Plenipotentiary of France at the Congress of Vienna. In 1820, he was
appointed Ambassador in Turin, where he remained until he retired
in 1830. He died in Lausanne in 1837, aged 78.

HER CHILDREN

Humbert (1790–1816)
Séraphine (1793–1795)
Alix (Charlotte) 1796–1822, who married Comte Auguste de
    Liedekerke Beaufort and had two surviving children:
        Hadelin (1816–1890) who married Isabelle de Dorff.
        Cécile (1818–1893) who married Ferdinand, Baron de Beeckman.
Cécile (1800–1817)
Aymar (1806–1867) who succeeded to the titles of Marquis de La
    Tour du Pin and Marquis de Gouvernet and who bequeathed the
    memoirs to his nephew, Comte Hadelin de Liedekerke Beaufort
    above.
Of two other children, one was stillborn and one died in infancy.

HER PARENTS-IN-LAW

The *Comte de La Tour du Pin* married an elder sister of the Princesse
d'Hénin. They had two children: Frédéric-Séraphin, Comte de
Gouvernet, who married the writer of the memoirs, and Claire
Suzanne who married the Marquis de Lameth.

The *Comtesse de La Tour du Pin* was guilty of some misdemeanour which resulted in her being confined to a convent, except for the rare visits she was allowed to pay her father, the Marquis de Monconseil.

In July 1789, the Comte de La Tour du Pin became Minister for War, but had to resign in November 1790. In March 1793, he appeared before the Commune of Paris and was executed in April 1794.

The Comtesse de La Tour du Pin survived the Terror.

A COUSIN

The *Marquis de Gouvernet.* Philippe-Antoine-Gabriel-Victor-Charles de La Tour du Pin de La Charce-Gouvernet, Marquis de Montmorin (1723–1794). He used the title of Marquis de La Tour du Pin until 1775, when he succeeded to that of Marquis de Gouvernet. It was his wife who presented Madame de La Tour du Pin to the Queen, on her marriage.

AN AUNT

The *Princess de'Hénin*, an aunt of M. de La Tour du Pin, married to the younger brother of the Prince de Chimay. She arranged the writer's presentation at Court after her marriage and introduced her to her own exclusive circle of friends, all of them of high rank, intelligence and keen followers of the new ideas propounded by Voltaire, Diderot, Rousseau. She emigrated to England during the Terror.

A FAMILY CONNECTION

Trophime-Gérard, Marquis de Lally-Tollendal. Illegitimate son of Thomas-Arthur, Comte de Lally, Baron de Tollendal, Governor-General of French possessions in India, who was executed in 1766 for failure to defend the territory in his charge. His son, the M. de Lally of the memoirs, worked for twenty years to re-establish his father's honour and succeeded in doing so in 1785. The Lally family was of Irish origin and connected by marriage with the Dillons.

A FRIEND

M. de Brouquens, who had been living since 1792 in Bordeaux where he was Director of Food Supplies. In 1793, during the Terror in Bordeaux, he was put under house arrest, but continued in office. He lent the writer a small, secluded house in which to live after the sequestration of Le Bouilh, and helped her and her husband get away to America in 1793. When the war in Spain was over, his job came to an end and he joined the La Tour du Pin family in Belgium.

A FRIEND

M. de Chambeau, a relative of M. de Brouquens, very suspect and in hiding in Bordeaux in an obscure lodging house kept by Bonie (see below). He went to America in the same boat as the La Tour du Pin family, lived with them there and when they returned to France in 1796, he accompanied them as far as Madrid. He lived penuriously there for several years, and eventually returned to France.

A FRIEND

Bonie, a young man with a small apartment house in Bordeaux where he lived alone. He looked after the interests of an émigré, M. de Sansac, sheltered M. de Chambeau and later Madame de La Tour du Pin and her children. At great personal risk he travelled to Tesson to bring M. de La Tour du Pin to Bordeaux to sail with his family to America. He was able to do all this by proclaiming himself an ardent revolutionary, dressing like a sans-culotte, and talking loudly at meetings. When the La Tour du Pin family returned to France from America, he met them at the frontier and arranged their journey back to Le Bouilh.

List of Illustrations

Illustrations of Versailles, Albany and West Point by permission of the British Museum, all other illustrations by permission of Comte Christian de Liedekerke Beaufort.

Principal Members of Mme de La Tour du Pin's

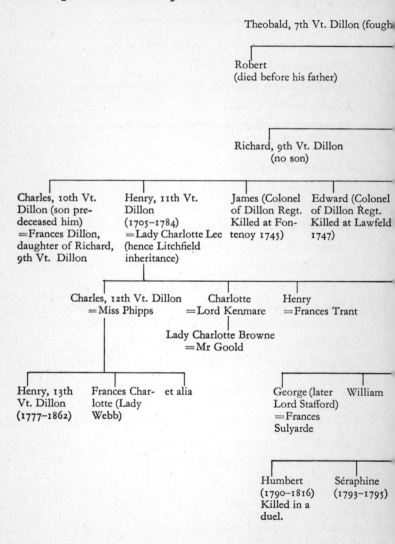

Theobald, 7th Vt. Dillon (fough

Robert
(died before his father)

Richard, 9th Vt. Dillon
(no son)

Charles, 10th Vt. Dillon (son predeceased him) =Frances Dillon, daughter of Richard, 9th Vt. Dillon

Henry, 11th Vt. Dillon (1705–1784) =Lady Charlotte Lee (hence Litchfield inheritance)

James (Colonel of Dillon Regt. Killed at Fontenoy 1745)

Edward (Colonel of Dillon Regt. Killed at Lawfeld 1747)

Charles, 12th Vt. Dillon =Miss Phipps

Charlotte =Lord Kenmare

Henry =Frances Trant

Lady Charlotte Browne =Mr Goold

Henry, 13th Vt. Dillon (1777–1862)

Frances Charlotte (Lady Webb)

et alia

George (later Lord Stafford) =Frances Sulyarde

William

Humbert (1790–1816) Killed in a duel.

Séraphine (1793–1795)

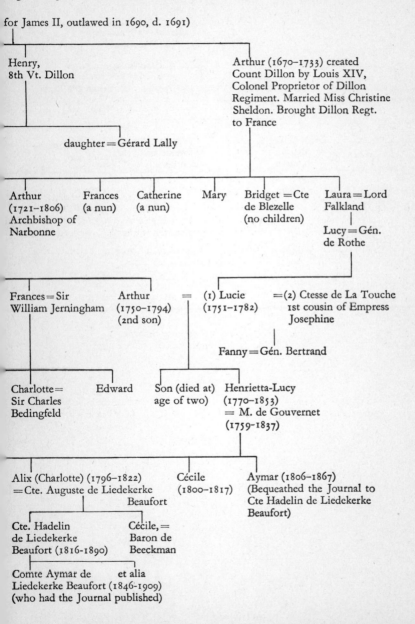

for James II, outlawed in 1690, d. 1691)

Henry,
8th Vt. Dillon

Arthur (1670–1733) created
Count Dillon by Louis XIV,
Colonel Proprietor of Dillon
Regiment. Married Miss Christine
Sheldon. Brought Dillon Regt.
to France

daughter = Gérard Lally

Arthur   Frances   Catherine   Mary   Bridget = Cte   Laura = Lord
(1721–1806)   (a nun)   (a nun)   de Blezelle   Falkland
Archbishop of   (no children)
Narbonne   Lucy = Gén.
                                                                                              de Rothe

Frances = Sir   Arthur   =   (1) Lucie   = (2) Ctesse de La Touche
William Jerningham   (1750–1794)   (1751–1782)   1st cousin of Empress
                                    (2nd son)   Josephine

                                                                              Fanny = Gén. Bertrand

Charlotte =   Edward   Son (died at)   Henrietta-Lucy
Sir Charles   age of two)   (1770–1853)
Bedingfeld   = M. de Gouvernet
                                                                    (1759–1837)

Alix (Charlotte) (1796–1822)   Cécile   Aymar (1806–1867)
= Cte. Auguste de Liedekerke   (1800–1817)   (Bequeathed the Journal to
                        Beaufort   Cte Hadelin de Liedekerke
                                                                    Beaufort)

Cte. Hadelin   Cécile, =
de Liedekerke   Baron de
Beaufort (1816-1890) Beeckman

Comte Aymar de   et alia
Liedekerke Beaufort (1846-1909)
(who had the Journal published)

Immediate family of the Marquis de La Tour du Pin

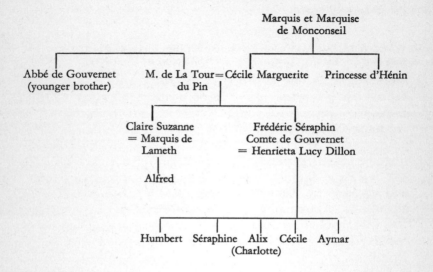

Marquis et Marquise
de Monconseil

Abbé de Gouvernet
(younger brother)

M. de La Tour = Cécile Marguerite
du Pin

Princesse d'Hénin

Claire Suzanne
= Marquis de
Lameth

Frédéric Séraphin
Comte de Gouvernet
= Henrietta Lucy Dillon

Alfred

Humbert Séraphine Alix Cécile Aymar
(Charlotte)

CHAPTER ONE

------◆------

1st of January 1820

I

When someone writes a book, it is generally with the intention that it shall be read either before or after their death. But I am not writing a book, and as you may wonder what this is, I must explain that it is simply a journal of my life. If I set down events alone, a few sheets of paper will suffice for the relatively uninteresting record; if it is to be an account of my opinions and emotions, a sentimental journal, the task will be more difficult, for to describe oneself requires self-knowledge, and fifty years would not be the age at which to begin. Perhaps I shall write of the past and tell the story of my early years, a few episodes only, without any attempt at continuity. I do not intend this to be a confession, but, distasteful as I would find it to reveal my faults, I do nonetheless wish to give a faithful picture of myself as I am and as I have been.

I have never before written anything except letters to those I love. My thoughts ramble. I am not methodical. My memory is already much dimmed. Worst of all, my imagination sometimes sweeps me so far from the subject that I have difficulty in picking up a thread lost so frequently in digressions. At heart, I still feel so young that it is only by looking into the mirror that I am able to convince myself that I am no longer twenty years of age. Let me take advantage, then, of the warmth that is still in me and which may at any moment be chilled by the infirmities of age, to tell something of a troubled and restless life, in which the unhappinesses were caused less, perhaps, by the events known to all the world, than by secret griefs known only to God.

II

In my earliest years, I saw things which might have been expected to warp my mind, pervert my affections, deprave my character and destroy in me every notion of religion and morality. From the age of ten, I heard around me the freest conversations and the expression of the most ungodly principles. Brought up, as I was, in an Archbishop's house[1] where every rule of religion was broken daily, I was fully aware that my lessons in dogma and doctrine were given no more importance than those in history and geography.

My mother had married Arthur Dillon, her second cousin. She had been brought up with him and her affection for him was entirely sisterly. She was as beautiful as an angel and the equally angelic sweetness of her nature made her generally beloved. Men adored her and women were not jealous. Although innocent of coquetry, she was not perhaps sufficiently distant in her relations with the men she liked, and whom the world considered in love with her.

There was one in particular who spent all his time at the house where my mother lived with my grandmother and my uncle, the Archbishop; and he also came with us to the country. It was the Prince de Guéménée, nephew of the notorious Cardinal de Rohan.[2] Because of his attentions to my mother, he was accounted her lover. I do not think he was, for the Duc de Lauzun, the Duc de Liancourt and the Comte de Saint-Blancard were all equally assiduous in their attentions. The Comte de Fersen, said to be Queen Marie-Antoinette's lover, also came to see us every day. The Queen liked my mother. She was always ready to be captivated by glitter and Madame Dillon was very much the rage; it was to this alone that she owed her entry into the Queen's Household and her appointment as Lady-in-Waiting. I was seven or eight years old at the time.

My mother was fond of my grandmother, despite the latter's overbearing nature and the outrageous malice which sometimes mounted to veritable furies of rage. Indeed, my mother was completely in her power and lived, as it were, in thrall to her. She

---

[1] Arthur Dillon, Archbishop of Narbonne, great-great-uncle of the writer, and referred to in the text as her uncle. (T)

[2] Cardinal Prince Louis René Edouard de Rohan, 1734–1803. Rich, worldly and extravagant, dominated by the charlatan Cagliostro. A succession of scandals culminated in the Affair of the Queen's Necklace, when he was duped into sending to Queen Marie-Antoinette a most valuable necklace. He was arraigned but public hostility to the Queen secured his acquittal. He was banished from Court to the provinces and died in exile. (T)

was entirely dependent on my grandmother for money and never had the courage to point out to her that, as the only daughter of her father, the Comte de Rothe, who had died when she was ten, she should by rights have had possession at least of her own fortune. My grandmother, the daughter of an impecunious English peer,[1] had had scarcely a penny from her own parents and had seized by main force the Hautefontaine estate which had been bought with her husband's money. But my mother, married at seventeen to a boy only a year older than herself, who had been brought up with her and who owned nothing in the world but his Regiment, would never have had the courage to talk to my grandmother of money. The Queen pointed out to her the rights which were hers and encouraged her to ask for accounts. My grandmother flew into a passion and maternal affection gave way to one of those incredible hatreds so beloved of writers of romances and tragedies.

III

My first thoughts and my earliest memories are connected with this hatred. I was a continual witness of the appalling scenes which my mother had to face and although obliged to appear unaware, I understood nonetheless, as I played with my doll or studied my lessons, that my situation was a difficult one. Reserve and discretion became essential to me. I acquired the habit of hiding my feelings and of judging for myself the actions of my parents. Now, at the age of fifty, when I look back on those ten-year-old judgements, I find them so accurate that I realise the truth of the statement made by so many philosophers that the mind and judgement we are born with are both reasonably sound and healthy.

I remember being shocked that my mother should complain of my grandmother to her friends; and I thought these friends more inclined to add fuel to the flames than to help them to die down. My father took my mother's part, which seemed to me quite natural. But on the other hand, I already realised that financially he was greatly indebted to our uncle, so that he was in a most difficult position. Indeed, since my uncle took my grandmother's

[1] Viscount Falkland.

part, I thought my father must feel terribly torn between his duty
to him and his affection for my mother.

There was perhaps only one being who sheltered me from con-
tamination, who kept my ideas straight, who helped me to see
evil wherever it existed and who encouraged me in virtue: it was
someone who could neither read nor write! A good country-
woman from the neighbourhood of Compiègne had been found
for me. She was young and she never left me. She was deeply
attached to me and had the heaven-sent gift of healthy judgement,
fairness of mind and strength of soul. Princes and dukes, the
great of the earth, stood arraigned therefore before a girl of
twelve and a peasant woman of twenty-five.

IV

Customs and society itself have so changed since the Revolution
that I want to describe in detail what I can remember of my family's
manner of life.

My uncle, the Archbishop of Narbonne, went rarely or never
at all to his diocese. By virtue of his See, he was President of the
States of Languedoc,[1] but he never visited Languedoc except to
preside over the meetings of the States. These lasted for six weeks
during November and December and as soon as they were over
my uncle returned to Paris on the pretext that the interests of the
Province urgently required his presence at Court, but really in
order to resume his usual life as a 'grand seigneur' in Paris and a
courtier at Versailles.

In addition to the Archbishopric of Narbonne, which was worth
250,000 francs, he also held the Abbey of Saint-Etienne at Caen,
which was worth 110,000 francs, and another smaller one which
he later exchanged for that of Cigny, worth 90,000 francs. When
the States were in session, he received more than 50,000 to 60,000
francs to cover the daily expense of entertaining guests to dinner.
With such a fortune, he might reasonably have been expected to
live creditably, and free from anxiety. But it was not so. He was
always having to resort to expedients. It was certainly not because
he lived in any great luxury. In Paris, he kept noble state, but of a

[1] Each Province had its own States at which the three orders (nobles, Church and
commons) were represented. (T)

simple kind; food was plentiful but it was not extravagant.

In those days, it was not the custom to give great dinner parties, for people dined early: at half-past two or three o'clock at the latest. By dinner-time, the ladies would sometimes have had their hair dressed, but they would still be in *déshabille*. Gentlemen, on the other hand, were nearly always formally dressed,[1] never in a plain town coat or in uniform, but in a dress coat, either embroidered or plain, according to their age and taste. The master of the house or gentlemen who did not intend going into company later in the evening, would wear a town coat or informal dress, for to wear a hat disturbed the fragile edifice of the curled wig, which was always snow-white with powder. After dinner, people conversed; sometimes we played a game of backgammon. Then the ladies would go off to dress and the gentlemen would wait to accompany them to the theatre, if they were to be in the same box. If one stayed at home after dinner, there was a continuous stream of visitors. Supper guests did not arrive until half-past nine.

Socially, that was the really important hour of the day. There were two kinds of supper, those given by people whose supper table was open to guests on every day of the week, so that people could come when they wished, and those to which one was invited, which were numerous and brilliant. I am speaking of the days when I was a child, that is to say, between 1778 and 1784. All the toilettes, all the elegance, everything that the beautiful, fashionable, society of Paris could offer in refinement and charm was to be found at these suppers. In those good days, before anyone had begun to think of national representation, a list of supper guests was a most important and carefully considered item! There were so many interests to be fostered, so many people to bring together, so many others to be kept apart! And what a social disaster for a husband to consider himself invited to a house simply because his wife was invited! One needed a very profound knowledge of convention and the current intrigues.

There were fewer balls than in later years, for the ladies'

---

[1] At Court and on formal occasions, gentlemen wore richly embroidered coats with stiff collars. At other times, they wore coats of plain cloth with a turned-down collar or revers. (T)

fashions of that day made dancing a form of torture: narrow heels, three inches high, which kept the foot in the same position as if standing on tiptoe to reach a book on the highest shelf in the library; a panier of stiff, heavy whalebone spreading out on either side; hair dressed at least a foot high, sprinkled with a pound of powder and pommade which the slightest movement shook down on the shoulders, and crowned by a bonnet known as a 'pouf' on which feathers, flowers and diamonds were piled pell-mell—an erection which quite spoiled the pleasure of dancing. A supper party, on the other hand, where people only talked or made music, did not disturb this edifice.

V

To return to my family. It was customary for us to leave for the country early in the spring and to spend the whole summer there. In the Château of Hautefontaine there were twenty-five guest rooms, and often they were all occupied. But the best visits of all were those of October. By then, the Colonels were back from their regiments where they had spent four months— less the hours it took them to return to Paris—and had scattered to the various châteaux to join their families and friends.

At Hautefontaine, there was a pack of staghounds whose up-keep was shared between my uncle, the Prince de Guéménée and the Duc de Lauzun. I have heard that the expense involved was only 30,000 francs, but you must remember that this did not include the saddle horses of members of the hunt, but only the hounds, the wages of the hunt servants who were English, their horses and food for everyone. Throughout the summer and autumn this pack hunted in the forests of Compiègne and Villers-Cotterets. It was so well run that poor Louis XVI was really jealous, and much as he loved to talk hunting, nothing irritated him more than to hear about the exploits of the Hautefontaine pack.

At the age of seven, I was allowed to ride with the hunt once or twice a week, and when I was ten, I broke my leg while out hunting on the feast of St Hubert. They say I was very brave. They carried me five leagues on a stretcher made from branches, and I did not even murmur.

I remember the time I spent in bed with my broken leg as one of the happiest of my childhood. My mother's friends came in large numbers to Hautefontaine, and we stayed there six weeks longer than usual. People read to me all day, and in the evening a small puppet theatre was wheeled to the foot of my bed, and the marionnettes performed a comedy or a tragedy, the parts being spoken from the wings by the people present. If it was a comic opera, people sang instead. The ladies amused themselves making clothes for the marionnettes. I still remember the cloak and tiara of Ahasucrus and the linen coat of Joash. These amusements were not unprofitable, for it was through them that I became acquainted with all the good plays of the French theatre. The Arabian Nights was read to me from cover to cover, and it was perhaps during this period that I acquired my liking for romances and works of the imagination.

VI

My earliest visit to Versailles was in 1781, when the first Dauphin was born.[1] In later years, when listening to tales of Queen Marie-Antoinette's sufferings and shame, my mind often went back to those days of her triumph. I was taken to watch the ball given for her by the Gardes du Corps in the Grande Salle de Spectacle at Versailles. She opened the ball with a young guardsman, wearing a blue dress strewn with sapphires and diamonds. She was young, beautiful and adored by all; she had just given France a Dauphin and it would have seemed to her inconceivable that the brilliant career on which she was launched could ever suffer a reverse. Yet she was already close to the abyss. The contrast provides much cause for reflection!

I shall make no attempt to trace the Court intrigues which I was too young to fully realise or understand. I had already heard of Madame de Polignac, for whom the Queen had a growing liking. She was very pretty, but not very clever. It was her sister-in-law, the Comtesse Diane de Polignac, an older woman greatly given to intrigue, who guided her along the path to favour. A friend of theirs, the Comte de Vaudreuil, whose pleasant manners made his company much sought after by the Queen, also worked

[1] Louis-Joseph-Xavier-François, 1781–1789.

to further her fortunes, which eventually became very great. I remember that M. de Guéménée tried to make my mother see the danger of the Queen's growing friendship with Mme de Polignac, but my mother was tranquilly content to let the Queen love her and had no thought of profiting from it, either to increase her own fortune or the fortunes of her friends. She was already suffering from the first symptoms of the illness from which she died less than two years later. Ceaselessly tormented by my grandmother, she collapsed under the weight of her unhappiness, for she had not the strength to overcome it. As for my father, he was in America, fighting at the head of the first battalion of his Regiment.

VII

The Dillon Regiment[1] had entered the service of France in 1690 when James II, after the Battle of the Boyne, abandoned all hope of being able to return to his throne. The Regiment was commanded then by my great-grandfather.

CHAPTER TWO

I

My mother had had a son who died when he was two, and his birth had left her delicate and in great pain from a lacteal humour which settled on her liver. As a result, she had no appetite and her blood, thinned by the continual unhappiness inflicted by my grandmother, became inflamed. This violent fever attacked her lungs. She made no attempt to live quietly or to spare herself. She rode, hunted and sang with the famous Piccini, who was enchanted with her voice. But by about 1782, when she was thirty-one, she began to have violent haemorrhages.

My grandmother had been unwilling to believe that her daughter's health was so weak, but she was at last forced to admit

[1] A short history of the Dillon Regiment, written by Mme de La Tour du Pin, will be found in the Appendix. (T)

that she was seriously ill. Nonetheless, her invincible hatred and her suspicious nature led her to see in my poor mother's every action a calculated attempt to free herself from her authority. She was also convinced that my mother had feigned the haemorrhages in order to avoid going to Hautefontaine. Nothing would have prevailed on her to delay her own departure by so much as a single hour. Unfortunately, the doctor my mother consulted—a certain Michel who was much in fashion just then—said that the haemorrhages were from her stomach and ordered her to Spa. It would be difficult to convey the degree of my grandmother's fury at the idea that her daughter should take the waters. She refused to accompany her and gave her no money for the journey. I think it was the Queen who came to my mother's rescue on this occasion, and we left Hautefontaine for Brussels, where we stayed a month.

My uncle, Charles Dillon, had married a Miss Phipps, daughter of Lord Mulgrave. He lived in Brussels, not daring to return to England on account of his numerous debts. At that time he was still a Catholic and it was not until later that he had the unpardonable weakness to change his religion and become a Protestant in order to be eligible for a legacy of £15,000 from his maternal great-uncle, Lord Lichfield, who had made this a condition of the legacy. Mrs Charles Dillon was as beautiful as the day. She had visited Paris the previous year with Lady Kenmare, my father's sister, who was also a very beautiful woman. They had gone with my mother to the Queen's ball and the three sisters-in-law had been greatly admired. Scarcely a year later, they were all in their graves, dying within a week of one another.

II

As I have already said, I had no real childhood. By the time I was twelve, my education was already very advanced. I had read voraciously, but indiscriminately. From the age of seven, I had had a tutor, an organist from Béziers named Combes. He came to teach me to play the harpsichord, for there were then no pianos, or at least, very few. (My mother had one to accompany her singing, but I was not allowed to touch it.) M. Combes was well-educated, and still studying. He has admitted to me since that he purposely slowed down my own studies for fear I should outstrip him in subjects at which he was still working.

I have always been remarkably eager to learn. I wanted to know about everything, from cookery to the experiments in chemistry which I used to watch in the laboratory of a small apothecary at Hautefontaine. The gardener was English and my good Marguerite took me every day to visit his wife, who taught me to read in their language: usually the book was *Robinson Crusoe*, to which I was most attached.

From my earliest days I had a feeling that adventures lay in store for me. My imagination was continuously inventing changes of fortune. I visualised myself in the most unlikely situations. I wanted to know everything that might be useful in any imaginable circumstance. My maid went to visit her mother two or three times each summer, and I made her tell me everything that went on in her small village. For several days on end, I would think of nothing but what I would have to do if I were a peasant, and I envied the lot of those I often visited in the village. They were not forced, as I was, to hide their tastes and ideas.

The continual warring in the house meant that I was perpetually on the defensive. If my mother wanted me to do something, my grandmother would forbid it. Each wanted me to spy for her, but my natural honesty revolted at the idea of such a contemptible rôle. I was silent, and therefore accused of indifference and taciturnity. I was a butt for the moods of all and sundry, and for many an unjust accusation as well. I was beaten or locked in as a punishment for the merest trifles. When I showed emotion at some noble deed in history, I was ridiculed.

When I was eleven, my mother decided that I was speaking English less well and gave me an elegant maid who had been especially brought over from England. Her arrival caused me the deepest grief, for it meant separation from my good Marguerite. She remained in the house, it is true, but hardly ever came to my room. My affection for her increased. I used to escape whenever I could and try to find her, or to meet her about the house, and this became a new source of scoldings and punishments. How careful one should be when bringing up children not to wound their affections, not to be deceived by the apparent shallowness of their natures. Even now, at the age of fifty-five, as I write of the humiliations to which my maid was subjected, my heart is filled again with indignation. Yet the Englishwoman was pleasant. I liked her very much indeed. She was a Protestant, her past had been anything but moral, and she had never read anything but novels. She did me much harm . . .

III

To continue my story. We went to Brussels, to my aunt's house. She was in the last stages of consumption which had in no way affected her quite ethereal charm and beauty. She had two delightful children: a boy of four—the present Lord Dillon—and a daughter who later became Lady Webb. I found these children very amusing and my greatest joy was to look after them, to put them to bed and to nurse them. My maternal instinct was already awakened. I had a presentiment that these poor children were soon to lose their mother, but little did I realise that I was myself so close to the same tragedy.

My mother took me to call on the Archduchess Marie-Christine[1] who, with her husband, Duke Albert of Saxe-Teschen, governed the Low Countries. While my mother and the Archduchess talked, I was taken to a study and shown albums of prints.

At Spa I tasted for the first time the heady poison of praise and success. My mother took me to the ridotto on the days when there was dancing and it was not long before the entire town was talking of the little French girl who danced so well.

The Comte and Comtesse du Nord[2] had just arrived from the depths of Russia and had never seen girls of twelve dancing the gavotte, the minuet and other dances. They were shown the prodigy. Thirty-seven years later, when that same princess was Empress of Russia, she still remembered that young girl of long ago when she met her again as the sedate mother of a family. She said many pretty things to me of her memories of my grace and, above all, of my slender figure.

[1] The Habsburg governor of the Low Countries which belonged to Austria from 1713 until 1790, sister of Queen Marie-Antoinette. (T)
[2] Paul, son of Catherine the Great of Russia, later the Emperor Paul I, and his second wife, Princess Marie-Sophie-Dorothée of Würtemberg.

All this while, everything was combining to corrupt my mind and my heart. My English maid talked to me only of frivolities, of clothes and of success. She told me of her own conquests and spoke of those which I would myself be making in a few years' time. She gave me English novels, but for some strange reason which I find it difficult now to account for, I had no desire to read bad books; I knew there were books that a young lady should not read and that if I did read them, and should later hear them spoken of in my presence, nothing would be able to prevent my blushes. So I found it easier not to read them. In any case, I had no taste for sentimental novels. I have always hated forced sentiment and exaggeration. I do, however, remember a romance written by the Abbé Prévost which made a great impression on me—it was *Cleveland*. The book describes acts of great devotion and that is the quality which appeals to me above all others. I was so anxious to practise it that I longed to give my mother daily proofs of it. I often wept bitter tears because she would not allow me to nurse her, to watch beside her, to bestow on her all the care that I so longed to offer her. But she rebuffed my efforts and kept me at a distance, and I had no inkling of the cause of this strange aversion to her only daughter.

IV

Meanwhile, the waters of Spa were shortening my poor mother's life. She was very unwilling to return to Hautefontaine, being quite sure that my grandmother would greet her, as she always did, with scenes and furious rages. She was not mistaken. But her health was worsening with every minute that passed and she began to long, as does everyone attacked by this cruel illness, for a change of air. She wanted to go to Italy and asked to return to Paris first. My grandmother consented, and it was only then that she began to realise the true state of her unfortunate daughter's health. At least, it was from that moment that she spoke of her state as hopeless, as indeed it was.

When we reached Paris, my grandmother gave up her own apartment to my mother as it was larger, and lavished on her every possible care. This was in such strong contrast with the outrageous manner in which I had seen her treat my mother only a few months before that I could not believe that she was sincere. Years later, when I was older and experienced, I realised that in a passionate nature, such sudden reverses of feeling are quite natural. When one has never exercised self-control and has always satisfied every whim without making the slightest attempt at self-discipline, when one lacks the restraining influence of religion and relies only on oneself, there is no check to prevent a person from abandoning himself to any excess.

During her last days my mother was surrounded with care. The Queen came to see her and every day a groom or page was sent from Versailles to fetch news of her. She grew weaker hourly. But no one spoke of the Sacraments or of bringing a priest to her. As I write these pages forty-five years later, I regret that it should have been so, but at the time I had barely finished learning my catechism. There was no chaplain in that Archbishop's household. The maids, though some of them were undoubtedly devout, were too much in fear of my grandmother to dare to speak out. My mother herself did not realise that her last hours had come. She died of suffocation in my nurse's arms on the 7th of September 1782.

I was told the sad news the following morning by Madame Nagle, a good old friend of my mother's whom I found at my bedside when I awoke. She said that my grandmother had left the house, that I was to get up and go to her and beg her protection and care; she said that my future lay now in my grandmother's hands; that she was on very unfriendly terms with my father, who was in America, and that she would certainly disinherit me if she took a dislike to me, as seemed only too probable. My grieving young heart revolted against the deception which this good lady was imposing on me and she had the greatest difficulty in persuading me to allow myself to be taken to my grandmother. The memory of all the tears I had seen my mother shed, of the terrible scenes she had had to endure in my presence and the knowledge that such treatment had shortened her life, made it utterly repugnant to me to submit to my grandmother's dominion. But my old friend assured me that if I made the slightest difficulty, a strict convent would be my lot; that my father would certainly re-marry in order to beget a son, and would not want to take me to live with him; that I might be forced to take the veil and be sent to the same convent as my aunt,[1] a nun in the Benedictine house at Montargis, who had not left the convent walls since she was seven.

Mme Nagle ended by carrying me off to my grandmother who put on an act of such despair that it froze me with fear and left a most painful memory. I was told that I was cold and heartless, that I felt no sorrow at my mother's death. This charge, which was so very far from true, wrung my heart with indignation. I had a sudden glimpse of all the long years of deceit into which I was being forced. But I would remind you that I was only twelve and that, although my mind was far more developed than is usual at that age, and my education already well advanced, I had never received any moral or religious instruction.

V

I do not claim to be qualified to describe the state of society in France before the Revolution. It would be beyond my skill. But in my old age, as I look back over my memories, I can see for as far back as I can remember, symptoms of the upheaval which broke over us in 1789.

The profligate reign of Louis XV had corrupted the nobility and among the Court Nobles could be found instances of every form of vice. Gaming, debauchery, immorality, irreligion, all were flaunted openly. The hierarchy of the Church, summoned to Paris for those congresses of the clergy which the King, through lack of money and the disordered state of his finances, was obliged to call almost every year in order to obtain the 'don gratuit',[2] had also been corrupted by contact with the dissolute habits of the Court. Almost all the bishops were of noble birth. In Paris they found themselves back among their kinsfolk, in the society into which they had been born, among the friends of their youth and memories of their early days. They had, most of them, studied in the Parisian seminaries of Saint-Sulpice, Saint-Magloire, Vertus and the Oratory. When they were raised to a See, they looked on

[1] The Honourable Catherine Dillon.
[2] A 'voluntary' tax which the clergy imposed on themselves at the request of the King. The Provincial States voted a similar tax (see page 39). (T)

the appointment as honourable exile which separated them from their friends, their families and all the worldly pleasures of society.

The minor clergy, members of the Assembly of the Clergy, were nearly all chosen from among the bishops' vicars-general, or from among the young abbots who owned abbeys and belonged to the same society as the bishops. In Paris they acquired principles and habits which they took back with them to the provinces, where only too often they proceeded to set the worst possible example.

The rot started at the top and spread downwards. Virtue in men and good conduct in women became the object of ridicule and were considered provincial. I cannot quote chapter and verse in support of what I am saying. Many years have passed since the period I am trying to describe and they have transformed it for me into a purely historical generalisation in which the individual has disappeared and I am left with only a broad impression. The older I grow, however, the more sure I become that the Revolution of 1789 was only the inevitable consequence and, I might almost say, the just punishment of the vices of the upper classes, vices carried to such excess that if people had not been stricken with a mortal blindness, they must have seen that they would inevitably be consumed by the very fire they themselves were lighting.

VI

In October 1782, after my mother's death, my grandmother and my uncle went to Hautefontaine, taking with them myself and my tutor, M. Combes, who had entire charge of my education.

I dearly loved that house, which I knew would one day belong to me. It stood in a fine estate between Villers-Cotteret and Soissons, about twenty-two leagues from Paris. It had been built at the beginning of the previous century and stood on a sharply-rising hill, dominating a delightfully green valley, or to be more exact, a gorge opening into the Forest of Compiègne. Meadows, woods, clear lakes stocked with fish lay beyond a magnificent kitchen garden set directly under the windows of the château. The courtyard was a sort of platform which in earlier centuries had undoubtedly been fortified. Architecturally, the château was not at all beautiful, but it was comfortable, roomy, perfectly furnished and very well cared for down to the smallest detail.

My uncle, my grandmother and my mother had accompanied my father as far as Brest when he left in 1779 to fight with his Regiment in the West Indies. On the way back, my uncle bought at Lorient the entire cargo of a ship just arrived from the East Indies. There were porcelains from China and Japan, brightly-coloured glazed chintzes from Persia for hangings, silks, damasks, coloured pekins,[1] and much else beside. To my great joy, all these beautiful things had been unpacked and stored in great warehouses, and the old watchman allowed me to wander there with my maid whenever the weather was bad and we could not go walking. I was often told: 'It will all be yours'. But some presentiment of which I said nothing kept me from dwelling too much on future splendours. My young imagination was more inclined to dwell on thoughts of ruin and poverty. This prophetic instinct was always present in my mind and made me want to learn all the handicrafts necessary to a poor girl, and drew me away from the usual occupations of a young lady and an heiress.

During my mother's lifetime, Hautefontaine had radiated gaiety and brilliance. After her death, all was changed. My father being abroad, it was my grandmother who took possession of all my mother's papers and any letters she had kept.

Just as they had not allowed her to see a priest, so they had not allowed her to concern herself with her worldly affairs: my grandmother had far too great an interest in them to permit any man of business to know how they stood. She had spent my grandfather's fortune and everything we possessed had in some way been altered during my mother's childhood. She was only twelve when her father, Général de Rothe, died suddenly at Hautefontaine. He had bought the estate not long before in the name of his wife, declaring that it was paid for entirely from the dowry of £10,000 given to my grandmother by her father, Lord Falkland.

Grandfather de Rothe had had inheritances from his mother, Lady Catherine de Rothe, and from his aunt, the Duchess of Perth. These sisters were the daughters of Lord Middleton, the minister of James II of whom historians have written so diversely. Another relative had left him the house in the Rue du Bac where

---

[1] Coloured silk material originally from China. Similar to taffetas. (T)

we lived when we were in Paris, together with 4,000 francs in bonds on the Hôtel de Ville of Paris.[1] But when M. de Rothe died, only the house and the bonds remained, and they were given to my mother.

My uncle, the Archbishop, had lived in the house in the Rue du Bac for twenty years without paying his niece, Mme Dillon, a farthing in rent. On the excuse that she lived there herself, he had not even paid for repairs. Yet my uncle even then had more than 300,000 francs in Church benefices. It is true that he had paid some gambling debts of my father's, for he was afflicted with that wretched passion, as were his two brothers, Lord Dillon and Henry Dillon. I have never known how much my uncle paid, but have heard it said that the debts were considerable. However, that may be, after my mother's death all that remained to me was the house in the Rue du Bac—rented for 10,000 francs to the Baron de Staël, who later married the famous Mlle Necker— and 4,000 francs in bonds on the Hôtel de Ville of Paris. From my father I could expect nothing. He had already run through his inheritance of £10,000, which was given to him with the Dillon Regiment, of which he was the hereditary owner, heir to the last of his uncles killed at Fontenoy.

I therefore had to humour my grandmother who, on the slightest provocation, threatened to send me into a convent. Her despotism ruled my entire life. Never had I seen anyone with such a strong need to dominate, to wield power. She began by separating me entirely from my childhood friends and she herself broke with all her daughter's friends. It is probable that in the correspondence she seized, she had found replies to well-grounded complaints which my mother had every right to make about the cruel state of dependence in which she had to live during the last years of her life, and also some very unflattering comments on my grandmother's iniquitous behaviour. My grandmother insisted that I should no longer see or communicate with the Mlles de Rochechouart, the Mlles de Chauvelin, or Mlle de Coigny. By a refinement of cruelty, my grandmother made the break with my young friends appear to come from me. I learned that I was

[1] In 1522, Francois I authorised the Hotel de Ville in Paris to issue the first public loan known in France. Interest on stock was payable in perpetuity. (T)

accused of ingratitude, of fickleness and lack of feeling, and was not allowed to explain.

My good tutor, who knew my grandmother better than I did myself, was the only being to whom I could talk of my sorrows. But he pointed out to me most forcibly that it would be best to humour my grandmother, that my future life depended on her, that if I crossed her and she were to put me in a convent, she would still be clever enough to make it appear that the decision was my own; that, separated from my father, of whom I might at any moment be deprived by the fortunes of war, I would be entirely alone if my grandmother and my uncle should withdraw their protection. And so I had to resolve to endure the daily trials which were the inevitable consequence of the terrible nature of this woman on whom I was dependent. I can truthfully say that for five years, not one day passed without my shedding bitter tears.

But as I grew older, I suffered less, either because I had become used to ill-treatment, or because my mind, which was mature beyond my years, the strength of my character, the calm with which I endured my grandmother's passions and the imperturbable silence with which I met the calumnies she spread in every direction, and particularly to the Queen, forced her to hold me in a certain degree of respect. Perhaps, also, she feared that when I entered society I would talk of all that I had had to endure. However that may be, by the time I was sixteen and she had noticed that I was taller than she, my grandmother was exercising a certain restraint in her rages. But she certainly made up for it in other ways, as you will see later.

VII

In 1782, towards the end of autumn, my uncle set out for Montpellier to preside over the States of Languedoc, a prerogative of the Archbishops of Narbonne which he had exercised for the past twenty-eight years.

We remained at Hautefontaine, where my grandmother soon grew very bored. Her bad temper became frightening in its intensity. She realised that in losing my mother, she had also lost the friends who until then had surrounded her and humoured her.

They had done so in an attempt to secure peace for my mother, and by giving my grandmother the impression that it was she who was the centre of their attentions, they had perhaps effectively lessened my mothers' sufferings. But after her death, when my grandmother took possession of my mother's papers and found the letters of these so-called friends, she realised the truth about their behaviour, and in her heart burned hatreds of which only she was capable.

And so, when she grew lonely at Hautefontaine, in that great house which had been the scene of such activity and of so many brilliant gatherings, when she saw the stables empty and no longer heard the voices of the hounds or the horns of the huntsmen, when from the windows she saw the long rides stretching away in vistas of unbroken emptiness, she realised the need to change her way of life and to persuade the Archbishop, until then concerned exclusively with his own pleasures and upholding the dignity of his rank, to cultivate ambition and occupy himself with the affairs of his province and those of the clergy.

The office of President of the Clergy[1] was in the King's gift and my uncle applied for it. The President at that time was the Cardinal de la Rochefoucauld, who was advised and much influenced by his nephew, the Abbé de Pradt. My uncle doubtless promised to smooth the passage of the 'don gratuit' at each Assembly of the Clergy to a greater extent than did the strictly honest Cardinal.

To accomplish her purpose, my grandmother decided to persuade my uncle, whom she dominated completely, to change his manner of living and his place of residence. When he returned from Montpellier, where he never stayed longer than absolutely necessary, we went to see him in Paris. I think that, in the absence of my father, who had been Governor of St Kitts since its capture—his regiment having contributed gloriously to the success of the French troops on that expedition—my guardians had pointed out to my uncle that he could not continue to live in my house, as he had been doing, without paying rent or undertaking the repairs. He therefore decided to move, and most iniquitously borrowed 40,000 francs to pay for the most urgent

[1] President of the Assembly of the Clergy, which was concerned mainly with temporal and administrative matters, including the 'don gratuit'. (T)

of the repairs. He did this by mortgaging the house where he had lived for twenty years without once loosening his own purse strings. It was not until the Revolution, when he left France, that this debt was discovered, and I had to pay it when I sold the house in 1797. Until then, he had paid the interest on the loan, which was not mentioned in my marriage contract.

My uncle moved to the house at the corner of the Rue St Dominique and the Rue de Bourgogne. He bought it on a life-lease, in his own name, although his architect, M. Raimond, who was most careful of my interests, advised him that the house should be bought outright in my name, my uncle to have the use of it for his life. But this arrangement, which would have increased my fortune without depriving my uncle of any of his, did not appeal to him and, despite his age—he was seventy-seven— he persisted in buying it in his own name. Raimond next suggested that he should buy, this time for me, a pretty little house in the square in front of the Palais Bourbon, which was just being built. But again he refused. He had recently obtained the commendatory abbey of Cigny, which represented nearly 100,000 francs in revenue. He gave this addition to his income as a reason for indulging his taste for building and furnishing, a pastime which had taken the place of an earlier recreation—horses and hunting— which he could no longer enjoy. He spent large sums on the arrangement of his new house, which was very dilapidated when he took it over. At the same time, my grandmother, who had taken a dislike to Hautefontaine after spending two such boring months there, bought for 52,000 francs a house at Montfermeil, near Livry, five leagues from Paris. The price was modest, for it stood in 90 acres of ground. The house, called the Folie Joyeuse, was charmingly situated. It had been built by a M. de Joyeuse who had begun the construction at what is normally the final stage, namely, the wings, After tracing the outline of a fine courtyard and enclosing it with palings, he built two wings, one to the right and the other to the left, each terminating in a pretty, square pavilion. But by then, he had no money left for the main part of the house, so that the only link between the two pavilions was a corridor at least one hundred feet long. The creditors stepped in, took possession of the house and sold it. The park was delightful.

It was enclosed by a wall, every path led to a gate and all the gates opened into the Forest of Bondy, which at that point is very beautiful.

Cart-loads of furniture were brought from Hautefontaine and by the Spring of 1783 we were more or less comfortably settled in. No repairs were undertaken during the first year, for there existed in those days a manorial right of withdrawal by which every lord of the manor on whose land a house was sold could, during one year from the date of sale, to the very hour of the signing of the contract, substitute himself for the buyer and, by simple notification, prevent him completing his purchase. Although there was no danger that M. de Montfermeil would do this, for he had recently inherited a legacy from his father, Président Hocquart, my uncle and my grandmother thought it prudent to let the statutory year pass. They therefore limited their activities to planting and putting the garden in order.

The summer was spent in drawing up plans with architects and draughtsmen, which I found extremely interesting. My uncle enjoyed telling me about all he intended to do. He spoke to me of buildings, of gardens, of furniture, of every kind of improvement. He had confidence in my intelligence. He asked me to calculate and measure with his gardeners, the slopes and other surfaces. He made me go through every detail of the estimates, checking the measurement figures.

I was very tall for my age, enjoyed excellent health and was very active, both in mind and body. I wanted to see everything and to know everything; to learn all the handicrafts from embroidery and making of flowers, to laundry work and the smallest kitchen tasks. I found time for everything, losing never a moment, storing away in my mind all that I was taught and never forgetting it. I set myself to learn from the specialised knowledge of all the visitors who came to Montfermeil, and it was thus, with the aid of a good memory, that I acquired the vast range of knowledge which has proved so extremely useful throughout my life.

One day, when there were a number of very grave-looking bishops to dinner and the conversation was of astronomy and the period of certain discoveries, one of the bishops could not recall the name of the learned man who had been persecuted for a truth which is today accepted without question. As I was only thirteen, I was most careful not to say a word, for I have always hated putting myself forward. But I was so tired of seeing that none of these prelates could remember the name, that it slipped out. Very low, I mumbled: 'It was Galileo'. My neighbour, who may not have had a very good memory, but who was certainly not deaf, heard me and cried: 'Mademoiselle Dillon says that it is Galileo'. I was so terribly embarrassed that I burst into tears, fled from table and was not seen again that evening.

CHAPTER THREE

I

In November 1783, or thereabouts, I learned that my grandmother intended in future to accompany my uncle, the Archbishop, to the States of Languedoc. In those days, the annual session of the States was a very brilliant affair and I was overjoyed at her decision. A treaty of peace had recently been concluded with the English, and after three years during which they had been unable to visit the Continent, they were once more crossing the Channel in large numbers, as they were to do again a few years later, in 1814. At this period, visits to Italy were less common than they are now. The fine roads through the Mont Cenis and Simplon passes were not yet built, there were no steamships and the road along the Mediterranean coast was almost unusable. The climate of the south of France, especially of Languedoc and of Montpellier above all, was still exceedingly fashionable.

The whole idea of this journey enchanted me, for it would be virtually my first. I was still very disappointed at not having been taken to Brittany and the only journey I had ever taken was to Amiens, where I went to bid farewell to my father at the beginning of the war.

I will tell you here about one of our journeys to Montpellier. It is typical of them all, for until 1786, when I went there for the last time, they all followed much the same pattern.

Our preparations, the shopping and the packing were an occupation and a pleasure but one of which I was to weary during the course of a frequently uprooted existence. We travelled in a large *berline* with six horses: my uncle and my grandmother in the back, myself on the seat in front of them next to a secretary or one of the priests on my uncle's staff, and two servants on the front seat. At the end of the journey, these servants were usually far more tired than those who had ridden all the way, for the seats of that day were not set on springs. They rested on two wooden posts which rested, in their turn, on the transom and were therefore as hard as any wagon. A second berline, also drawn by six horses, carried my grandmother's maid and mine, Miss Beck, two footmen and, seated on the cross-bench, two servants. The butler and the chef travelled in a postchaise.

There were also three couriers, one riding half-an-hour ahead of us and the other two with the carriages. M. Combes, my tutor, always left several days before us, travelling either in the *diligence*, then called the 'Turgotine',[1] or in the mail-coach, which carried only one passenger, and was rather like an elongated wagon on shafts.

Each year, the Ministers detained my uncle so long at Versailles as to leave him scarcely time to reach Montpellier for the opening of the States, which took place on a set date. This meant that he had to travel with the greatest possible speed, a very trying necessity at that season of the year.

We travelled with eighteen horses, and an order would be sent through the administration to reach the posting stages several days ahead of us to ensure that fresh horses would be ready. We drove for long hours every day, leaving at four o'clock in the morning and stopping only for dinner. The postchaise and the first courier would arrive an hour ahead of us to ensure that the table was ready, the fire lit and some good dishes prepared, or given at least a finishing touch by our own chef. He travelled with bottles of meat jelly and sauces prepared in advance, as well as everything else needful to make the bad inn meals palatable. The postchaise and the first courier would leave again as soon as we

[1] The first *diligences* were established in 1775, during the ministry of the economist and reformer, Turgot. (T)

arrived, and when we stopped for the night, we would find, as in the morning, everything in readiness for us.

When we travelled, I had to share my grandmother's room, which I did not like at all for she always took the best bed and a good half of mine as well. She took up most of the fire, too, and had so many toilet articles that there was no room for mine. I was scolded on the slightest pretext, and never allowed to go to bed on arrival despite the fact that each evening I was exhausted with weariness, for she would not allow me to sleep in the carriage, or even to lean back. Once, I think it was in 1785, I was so ill at Nîmes from over-tiredness that she was obliged to stay there with me for two days for I had not the strength to go on to Montpellier.

We used to spend a few hours at Lyons when the Archbishop was there. But my uncle did not consider him very highly. He did not stand well at Court and seldom went to Paris. I do not remember ever having seen him there, not even during Assemblies of the Clergy. He had once had an affair with the famous Duchesse de Mazarin, but that was no reason for disgrace in those dissolute days when virtuous living was the exception among the highest clergy. On the contrary, I believe it was a good action which caused his fall from favour. It may have been prompted by ostentation, but was none the less a useful deed: the city of Lyons had asked that the hospitals should be provided with iron bedsteads. The Ministers refused, or were unwilling to authorise the expenditure, and the Archbishop of Lyons, M. de Montazet, gave 200,000 francs from his own purse for the purpose. The Ministers disliked the lesson they had been given, but the King was far from disapproving. That excellent prince was always well disposed towards all good works, but from weakness or timidity was too often led into rejecting ideas which he had at first found good. It was this exaggerated modesty and mistrust in his own judgement which was so fatal to us.

The generosity of the Archbishop of Lyons had made him very popular in the city and this had aroused the jealousy of his peers. They preferred to use their revenues to build palaces or fine country houses, not to found charitable institutions. But it was in just such dioceses as theirs, where fine episcopal palaces had arisen, large enough to house thirty guests at a time, that many parish priests were forced to live on straitened incomes, in presbyteries which were not even weather-proof.

II

To return to our journey to Languedoc. At that time, the road which followed the Rhône to Pont-Saint-Esprit was so bad that there was continual danger of overturning. Postilions demanded extra fees at each relay stage, claiming that they had not brought us by the main highway, but by small roads that wagoners could not use. We generally spent a night at Montélimar, where there was a very well-kept inn which had a high reputation among English people travelling to the south of France. They all put up there for the night. It sometimes happened that the torrent which flows through this little town, and which has to be crossed at a ford, was so swollen by rain or, in spring, by the melting of the snow, that it was necessary to wait several days for the waters to subside.

The walls of the corridors and the staircase of this inn were entirely covered with medallions bearing the names of persons of note who had stayed there. It was a favourite pastime of mine to read them, especially those of the most recent arrivals, whom we hoped to meet at Montpellier.

One year, we were in great peril when we crossed the ford. The water was high enough to float the carriage, so the doors had to be opened to allow it to pass through. My grandmother and I climbed on the cushions and tucked up our skirts. The men were on the cross benches. To the springs had been fastened small pieces of wood on which stood men with long pointed sticks to prevent the carriage from turning over. All this was amusing to a young, adventurous person like myself, but my poor grandmother, a terrible coward, suffered cruelly. Unfortunately, her fear expressed itself in bad temper which was naturally directed at me. When I see the fine bridges by which one crosses the rivers today, the steamboats and all that industry has contrived, I find it difficult to believe that it is only fifty-five years ago that I encountered all the difficulties and obstacles which so greatly lengthened our journeys to Montpellier. If sentiments and virtue had made as

much progress as industry, we would now be angels, worthy of
Paradise. But we are still far from that.

At the La Palud stage, the traveller entered the territory of the
Comtat Venaissin,[1] which was Papal territory. I liked to see the
boundary signs painted with the tiara and the keys. I felt as if I
were arriving in Italy. We left the highway to Marseilles at this
point and took the excellent road which the Papal government
had allowed the States of Languedoc to build, and which was the
most direct route to Pont-Saint-Esprit.

At La Palud, my uncle stopped to change. He put on country
clothes of purple cloth—and when it was cold, added a quilted
redingote lined with silk of the same colour—stockings of purple
silk, shoes with gold buckles, his insignia of the Order of the
Holy Ghost and a clerical tricorne hat with gold acorns.

As soon as the carriage had passed the last arch of the bridge
at Saint-Esprit, the cannon of the small citadel which still stood
at the head of the bridge, fired a 21-gun salute. There would be a
ruffle of drums and the garrison would turn out, the officers in
full dress. All the civil and religious authorities would be waiting
and would come to the door of the berline to pay their respects to
my uncle. If the weather was fine, he would climb down from his
carriage while eight horses were harnessed to it.

He listened to the addresses and replied with the utmost
affability and grace. My uncle was a stately figure, tall, with a fine
voice and an air of elegant assurance. He would enquire the needs
of the local people, say a few words in reply to the petitions presented to him, and never forgot any detail of the petitions which
had been addressed to him the year before. All this took nearly a
quarter of an hour and when it was over, we would set off like
the wind, for not only had the postilions' traces been doubled,
but the honour of driving the coach of so great a personage was a
source of much pride.

In the minds of the people of Languedoc, the President of the
States was a far more important personage than the King. My
uncle was extremely popular, despite his very haughty manner.
In fact, this manner only became evident when he was dealing

[1] This area was under Papal rule from 1274 to 1791. Today, it forms part of the
Department of Vaucluse. (T)

with those who were, or thought they were, his superiors. That is how it happened that when he was Archbishop of Toulouse, Cardinal de la Roche-Aymon who was then Archbishop of Narbonne, gave up his presidency of the States on the ground that since it was impossible to be superior to Monsieur Dillon, one had perforce to make way for him.

We used to spend a night at Nîmes, where my uncle always had business to attend to. One year we stayed several days with the bishop and I had time to visit in detail the ancient monuments and the factories. Although the monuments were not so well cared for as they are today, they had already begun to clear the Arena and had pulled down recent buildings to free the 'Maison Carrée'.[1] They had also found the inscription 'C. CAESARI AUGUSTI F. L. CAESARI AUGUSTI F. COS DESIGNATO PRINCIPIBUS JUVENTUTIS'.[2] It was a M. Séguier, a distinguished archaeologist, to whom the city of Nîmes is much indebted, who found this inscription. He traced it from the marks of the nails which had originally held the bronze letters in place.

My uncle so arranged the journey as to arrive in Montpellier after sunset. By doing this, he avoided receiving a salute of guns and so spared the susceptibilities of the Comte de Périgord, Commander of the Province and the King's Commissioner at the opening of the States, who was not entitled to this privilege. It was deplorable that so great a gentleman should betray such weakness over a trifling matter of protocol entirely without personal significance. As it happened, the Archbishop of Narbonne was by birth the equal of M. de Périgord, but had he been only a peasant, this privilege would still have been his due.

III

The business before the States amounted, essentially, to deciding what financial contributions could be levied, and the Court always hoped for an increase in the 'don gratuit', which it lay within the power of the States to withhold entirely if any of its privileges

[1] A small temple dating from 16 B.C.—one of the most perfect of the Augustan period. (T)
[2] 'To Caius Caesar, son of Augustus, to Lucius Caesar, son of Augustus and Consul-designate, Princes of Youth'. Caius and Lucius were the sons of Agrippa and the grandsons of Augustus who adopted them as his heirs.

had been infringed. The King's Commissioner would discuss the
interests of the Province with the Syndics of the States, of whom
there were two. In my time, they were M. Romme and M. de
Puymaurin, both men of great ability. They took it in turn to go
to Paris each year, accompanied by a delegation from the States,
to deliver to the King the 'don gratuit' voted by their Province.

So far as I can remember, this delegation was composed of a
Bishop, a baron, two deputies from the Third Estate, one of the
mayors and the Archbishop of Narbonne, who presented the
delegation to the King. Everyone from Languedoc who was at
Court and in Paris at the time—it always took place in the
summer—accompanied the delegation. After a dinner given by
the First Gentleman of the Bedchamber, they were all taken for a
walk in the gardens of Trianon or Marly and the fountains would
be set in play. On one occasion, I accompanied the deputation
and my grandmother and I were taken around the grounds in
armchairs on wheels. drawn by 'suisses' (footmen). Those very
same armchairs had served the Court of Louis XIV. After being
taken through the fine groves at Marly, and having admired the
magnificence of the fountains and waterfalls, we found an
excellent collation prepared for us in one of the principal salons.
I think this was in 1786. It was the only time I ever saw Marly in
all its splendour, though I have been there many times since.
That fine château no longer exists.[1] It has disappeared without
trace and the suddenness of its destruction makes it easier to
understand how Rome can be today surrounded by a wilderness.

After journeying 160 leagues over wretched, bumpy roads,
crossing swift rivers without bridges and in real danger of his
life, the traveller came at last to the passage of the Rhône and
on the far bank lay a road as fine as any path in a well-kept
garden. He crossed superb bridges, perfectly built; he drove
through towns where industries flourished and countrysides
that yielded rich harvests. The contrast was striking, even to a
fifteen-year-old.

The house in which we lived at Montpellier was very fine and
very large, but terribly gloomy for it stood in a dark, narrow

[1] This Château, built by Mansart for Louis XIV as a retreat where he could escape
from ceremonial, was sold and destroyed during the Revolution. (T)

street. My uncle rented it furnished and it was excellently fitted
out in red damask. He occupied the first-floor apartment which
had very fine Turkish carpets everywhere. They were common
in Languedoc in those days. The apartment enclosed a square
courtyard. Along one of its four sides was a dining-room for
fifty covers, and along another side an equally large drawing-
room with six windows. In this room the furniture and hangings
were of beautiful crimson damask, and it had an immense fireplace of a very ancient style which would be much admired
today.

My grandmother and I occupied the ground floor, where it was
always dark by three o'clock in the afternoon. We never saw my
uncle during the morning. We breakfasted at nine o'clock and
afterwards I went for a walk with my English maid. For three
years, I had been going three times a week to the fine physics
laboratory belonging to the States, and the Professor in charge,
the Abbé Bertholon, was kind enough to give me private lessons.
This meant that I could study the apparatus, help him with his
experiments, make some of my own and put as many questions
as I liked, learning far more than would have been possible at
open lectures. Physics interested me tremendously. I studied it
most diligently and Abbé Bertholon expressed himself satisfied
with my capability. My maid came with me, and as she understood
hardly a word of French, she busied herself cleaning and drying
the apparatus, to the very great satisfaction of the Professor.

We had to be in full dress, even wearing jewels, by three o'clock
exactly, ready for dinner. We would go up to the drawing-room
where, except on Fridays, we always found about fifty guests.
On Saturdays, my uncle dined out, either with the Bishop, or
with some other important member of the States. My grandmother
and I were always the only ladies present and the most important
of the guests would be placed between us. When there were
foreigners, especially Englishmen, they were put beside me. It was
training for me in the art of conversation and behaviour, in
learning to decide which subjects would most interest my
neighbour, often a person of importance and sometimes of
learning, too.

In those days, everyone with a decently dressed servant was

waited on by him at table. No decanters or wine glasses were put on the table. At big dinners, there were silver buckets on a sideboard to hold the wine for the various courses. There was also a stand of a dozen glasses and anyone wishing for a glass of one of the wines sent his servant to fetch it. This servant always stood behind his master's chair.

I had a servant of my own who also dressed my hair. He wore my livery which, since our braidings exactly resembled those of the Bourbons, had to be in red. The dark blue used by my family in England would have made our livery resemble that of the King, which was not allowed.

After dinner, which did not last more than an hour, we went to the drawing-room where there would be a gathering of members of the States come to drink coffee with us. We all remained standing, and after half an hour, my grandmother and I would go downstairs to our own apartments. Afterwards, we often went visiting, carried in sedan chairs, which were the only possible means of transportation in the streets of Montpellier. The fine new parts of the city did not exist then. The Place Peyrou was still outside the town and the great ditches which surrounded the city were laid out in gardens, well sheltered from the cold.

Montpellier society centred around the wives of the Presidents and Councillors of the Cour des Comptes (Audit Office). and those of the nobles who lived all the year on their estates and for whom the session of the States was the main annual diversion. There were also foreigners of note, relatives of the Bishops who were attending the States, and officers from the garrisons of the Province who had leave to come and join in the festivities. There was a theatre to which my grandmother took me once or twice, and balls—one given by the Comte de Périgord, another at the Intendance,[1] and others in private houses, but never at my uncle's or at the houses of any of the Bishops.

IV

When we returned to Paris at the beginning of 1784, we found that my father was back from America. Until the signing of the peace treaty, he had been Governor of St Kitts and after handing

[1] The seat of the administration of a Province. (T)

the island over to the English, had remained for a while in Martinique where he had become much attached to the Comtesse de La Touche, the thirty-year-old widow of a naval officer who had left her with two children, a son and a daughter. She was very pleasant and exceedingly rich. Her mother, Mme de Girardin, was a sister of Mme de La Pagerie. The latter had just married her daughter[1] to the Vicomte de Beauharnais, who had brought his wife to France with him. Mme de La Touche also came to France, bringing her two children. My father followed her and the possibility of a marriage between them immediately became much talked of. My grandmother was furiously angry at the idea and nothing would pacify her. Yet it was very natural that my father should wish to marry again in the hope of having a son: he was thirty-three and Colonel of one of the finest regiments in the Army. Unlike the other regiments of the Irish Brigade, it had retained its name, and had a proud warrant giving it the right to leave France with drums beating and colours flying whenever its owner wished. It was natural, therefore, that my father should want a son. It would, of course, have been preferable for him to choose his wife among the titled Catholic families of England, but he did not like Englishwomen and he did like Mme de La Touche. She was amiable and good, though weak, with the careless good nature of all Créoles.

The marriage took place in spite of my grandmother. My father wished me to be presented to my stepmother, but the only visit I managed to pay her was in 1786, when my father was leaving to take up an appointment as Governor of Tobago.

He was very upset at not having been made Governor of Martinique or San Domingo, as he had earned a right to one of these two posts. He had served throughout the war with the greatest distinction. His Regiment had won the first successful battle of the campaign, taking the island of Grenada by assault and capturing the Governor, Lord Macartney. His intervention had contributed greatly to the capture of the islands of St Eustace and St Kitts. He had governed St Kitts for two years and when it was ceded to the English by the Peace Treaty of 1783, the people

[1] Josephine, a first cousin of Mme de La Touche who, after the death of her first husband married the Emperor Napoleon.

of the island had showered on him tokens of their esteem and gratitude. Echoes of all this had found their way even to England, as my father discovered when he visited that country on his return to Europe. He was given a most flattering welcome there.

But our uncle, the Archbishop, was so dominated by my grandmother that, at her instigation, he refused to support his nephew's candidature for the governorship of Martinique or San Domingo. However, though he did not support him, he put no obstacle in his way. My father had to accept the governorship of Tobago and he lived there until he was appointed to represent Martinique in the States-General.[1] He left France with his wife, my small sister, Fanny, and my tutor, M. Combes, whom he was taking out as registrar of the island. This was a great grief to me. Mlle de La Touche entered the Convent of the Assumption with a governess and her brother was sent to school with a tutor.

Before leaving, my father spoke to my grandmother of a marriage he very much wished for me. During the war, he had met in Martinique a young man, aide-de-camp to the Marquis de Bouillé, who was much liked by the Marquis and whom he himself esteemed highly. My grandmother refused even to consider this marriage, although the man in question was of high birth and an eldest son. She declared that he was a bad lot, that he was in debt and that he was short and ugly. I was so young that my father did not insist. He gave my uncle, the Archbishop, a power of proxy to marry me as he saw fit. But I myself often thought of the man whom my father had suggested. I asked about him. My cousin, Dominic Sheldon, who had been brought up by my grandmother and who lived with us, knew him and often spoke to me about him. I learned that he had, indeed, been wild in his youth and determined to think no more about him.

V

In 1785, we remained in Languedoc much longer than usual. After the States, we went to Alais to spend a month with kindly Bishop de Bausset, at that time Bishop of Alais

[1] A powerful assembly of the three estates of the realm: clergy, nobility and third estate. It met only at the summons of the King, and dealt with matters affecting the Kingdom as a whole, e.g., war and finance. The first States-General met in the 14th century and the last in 1789. (T)

and later a Cardinal. I found this journey very interesting.

My uncle was very well liked in the Cevennes, where he had done much to encourage the development of industry. He took me to the coal and copper sulphate mines, and thanks to my studies in chemistry with M. Chaptal, later Minister of the Interior, and my lessons in experimental physics at which I had been so diligent, I was able to understand something about the processes used. I often talked with the engineers, who frequently dined with my uncle and the knowledge I thus acquired helped me to understand the plans being discussed in the drawing-room.

It is to my stay in Alais that I attribute my love of mountains. This small town is deep in the Cevennes, set in a charming valley surrounded by cool meadows, shaded by chestnut trees that must be centuries old. Every day there were delightful excursions. The young men of the district formed themselves into a guard of honour for my uncle and wore the English uniform of the Dillon Regiment—red with yellow facings. All belonged to the best families in the district. Every day, the Bishop invited some of them to dinner. Their wives or sisters came in the evening. We made music together or danced. It was a very happy visit.

I was sad when we had to leave Alais to spend two months at Narbonne.

From Narbonne, we went to Toulouse, travelling by way of Saint-Papoul where we stayed for several days. My uncle went to visit the beautiful college at Sorèze, directed at the time by a very able Benedictine, Dom Despaulx. I did not go with him, and my grandmother and I were taken only as far as the lake of Saint-Ferréol, the source of water for the Languedoc Canal.

It was at Saint-Papoul that I met the Vaudreuil family, who lived nearby. They had three daughters and one son. The latter, whom I met again in Switzerland fifty years later, was at that time seventeen or eighteen and would have been well pleased to marry the elegant niece of the powerful metropolitan archbishop.

On that journey, providence seemed to have strewn my path with suitors: near Toulouse, M. de Pompignan; at Montauban, M. de Fénélon who was suggested by the Bishop, M. de Breteuil. But my moment had not yet come, and if you believe in presentiment or predestination, then I would say that I did have a very marked presentiment of it at Bordeaux, as I will tell you later.

VI

I do not know why Bordeaux should have interested me more than the other towns through which we passed. The fine theatre had just been opened and I went there several times with my grandmother, sitting in the Jurats' box. The Jurats of Bordeaux held the same position in the town as the Mayor of today. There were evening parties in various houses; a splendid luncheon on board a ship of six hundred tons belonging to a Mr MacHarty, an Irish merchant. This superb vessel, which was about to leave for India, was named after me: the *Henrietta-Lucy*.

In Bordeaux I also saw Mme Dillon, the mother of all those Dillons who have always claimed, though mistakenly, to be related to me. This lady, who was of a good English family, had married an Irish merchant named Dillon, whose forefathers had probably come from the part of Ireland known since the days of Queen Elizabeth, as Dillon's Country, where, as in Scotland, many of the people took their lord's name. However that may be, this particular Dillon's affairs went badly, and he raised a certain sum of money and came to settle in Bordeaux, where he went into trade. He bought a property at Blanquefort and established his wife there. She was a superbly handsome woman, and her extraordinary beauty soon became famous throughout the Province. She spent the winters in Bordeaux. Since she had distinguished manners, was intelligent, very well-bred and had a baby every year, she interested everyone. Her husband died, leaving her pregnant with her twelfth child. She had very little money, but possessed every charm and great courage.

Maréchal de Richelieu took her under his protection and recommended her to my uncle, who was about to visit Bordeaux. He promised to see that the children were given a good start in life, and kept his word. The three eldest were girls. Thanks to their beauty, they made good marriages: the first married Président Lavie, who had a fine fortune; the second married a financier, M. de Martinville, by whom she had a son who later edited, I believe, the new paper called *Le Drapeau Blanc*; the third married the

Marquis d'Osmond, who saw her in Bordeaux one day when his Regiment was garrisoned there and fell in love with her. The last two were extremely calculating, and greatly furthered the fortunes of their brothers. My uncle and my grandmother fell completely under their spell, and were induced to promote their interests by means which I have often heard described as questionable.

For instance, my uncle's brother, Edward Dillon, had been a Knight of Malta. After a brilliant and adventurous career, he was killed at the head of his Regiment at the Battle of Lawfeld. Means were found to use the patents of nobility he had had to produce before being admitted to the Order of Malta, to further the fortunes of three of these Dillon boys: the third, Robert, the fourth, William, and the fifth, Frank.

Theobald, the eldest, went into the Dillon regiment, after finishing his service as a page, and married in Belgium. I met him there, very well established in a picturesque château near Mons.

Edward, the second son, owed his fortune to his handsome face. It is he who was nicknamed 'Beau Dillon'. His patrons were the Queen and the Duchesse de Polignac, and he was given a place in the Household of the Comte d'Artois. He remained in favour until his death. His only daughter was married in Germany to M. de Karoly, and died very young. She was a charming girl. Two other sons became priests and would doubtless have become bishops if it had not been for the Revolution. All these Dillons, without exception, were very steady and it was as rare as it was honourable that of the nine brothers holding some form of employment in France, not one should have fallen into the errors or excesses which were the curse of so many families during that troubled period.

To return to my presentiment, I must tell you that a few days before leaving Bordeaux, perhaps only the day before, my servant asked me, as he dressed my hair, if he might go that same evening to a château not far off the highway. He had once been in service there and wanted to meet some of his old friends. He said he could rejoin the carriages at the halt nearest to the château, namely at Cubzac, where our road crossed the Dordogne. I asked him the name of the château, and he told me it was 'Le Bouilh' and belonged to the Comte de La Tour du Pin, who was living there. His son was the young man whom my father had wanted me to marry and whom my grandmother had refused. I was far more troubled by my servant's reply than seemed reasonable: it was, after all, only a reminder of someone to whom I had until then been indifferent and whom I had never seen. I enquired the whereabouts of the château and was annoyed to learn that it could not be seen from the road. However, I made a note of the point along our route when we would be nearest to it, and of the appearance of the countryside nearby.

I was deep in my thoughts as we crossed the stream at Cubzac, a crossing which I knew belonged to M. de La Tour du Pin. As we stepped ashore, and all the way to Saint-André, I told myself over and over again that I might have been châtelaine of all that beautiful countryside. But I was very careful to keep such thoughts hidden from my grandmother, who would have been far from pleased with them. Nonetheless, they remained in my mind, and I often spoke to my cousin, M. Sheldon, of M. de Gouvernet whom he used to meet out hunting with the Duc d'Orléans— Philippe Egalité.

CHAPTER FOUR

I

By the time we returned to Paris, I was sixteen and my grandmother told me that negotiations were in progress for my marriage to the Marquis Adrien de Laval. Through the death of his elder brother, Adrien had recently become heir to the family honours. His mother, the Duchesse de Laval, had been a very close friend of my own mother. She was in favour of our marriage and it was equally pleasing to me. The name of Laval-Montmorency sounded well in my aristocratic ears. The younger Laval had left his seminary when his brother died and entered the army. Our fathers were closely connected, but what pleased me most in the proposal was that marriage would enable me to leave my grandmother's house. I was no longer a child, my education had begun so early that by the time I was sixteen, I was as mature as most girls are at twenty-five, and my grandmother was making my life miserably unhappy. But, accustomed as I was to thinking about my position, I had firmly resolved not to accept from resentment a marriage out of keeping with my station.

It was known that I would inherit my grandmother's entire fortune, and she herself did everything possible to foster the idea that she was most devoted to my interests, and that they were her sole pre-occupation. There were two diametrically opposed qualities in her character: violence and duplicity. She was reputed rich, and there is no doubt that she was so. There was not only the fine estate at Hautefontaine, but the charming house only five leagues from Paris which she had just bought and which my uncle was having re-decorated, the income from the Hôtel de Ville de Paris which she was to give me on my marriage, and an enormous quantity of furniture and furnishings. It was certain that I would inherit it all, for when I was sixteen, my grandmother was already sixty.

Who would have suspected that my uncle, with an income of 400,000 francs, was having to resort to expedients and had persuaded my grandmother to borrow in order to come to his rescue? Everyone who wanted to marry me was dazzled by my apparently fine expectations. It was known that on my marriage I would be appointed a Lady of the Queen's Household and in those days that was a weighty factor among the highly-born when considering possible alliances. 'To be at Court' was a magic phrase. There were only twelve Ladies of the Household. My mother had been one because the Queen had a tender personal affection for her, because she was the daughter-in-law of one English peer and the grand-daughter of another and also because my father, a distinguished soldier, was one of the very few men eligible to become a Marshal of France.

Of the three regiments composing the Irish Brigade, only those of Dillon and Berwick had retained their names. The Duchesse de Fitz-James, a Mlle de Thiard, was, like my mother, a Lady of the Household and they were also of about the same age. But the Duke, her husband, was a grandson of the Maréchal de Berwick, whose father had also been a Marshal of France. His military reputation, however, was mediocre whereas my father had served with great distinction in the war which had just ended. He had been appointed Brigadier General when only twenty-seven. This rank, later abolished, was an intermediate one between Colonel and Lieutenant-General.

I will tell you a story about ranks which will show you just how ridiculous some of the Court etiquette could be. When the island of Grenada was captured, the fort was carried by a grenadier company from Dillon's Regiment. My cousin, Mr Sheldon, who was only twenty-two, so distinguished himself that M. d'Estaing, the Commander-in-Chief of the Army, gave him the task of bringing back to France and presenting to the King the first standards to be captured during the war. It was a very great honour. When he landed at Brest, he hired a postchaise, and on arriving at Versailles, went straight to the Minister for War. It so happened that my uncle, to whom my cousin had sent a courier, was with the Minister when he arrived. He had stopped at the last posting-house to make a soldierly toilet and had changed into his best captain's uniform. But when the Minister wanted to take him straight to the King, he learned with amazement that 'Mr Sheldon could not be received in uniform'! The dress in which he had captured the standards was not acceptable for their presentation to the King! The Gentlemen-in-Waiting would not give way and Mr Sheldon found himself obliged to borrow from one and another, a suit of Court dress, a tricorne and a dress sword. It was only when he had assumed a thoroughly civilian appearance that he was permitted to lay at the King's feet the colours he had risked his life to help capture. Yet people are surprised that the Revolution should have destroyed a Court where such childishness prevailed. Uniform was only permitted at Court on the day officers took leave, before the 1st of June, to rejoin their Regiments.

II

But let us come back to me. I was, as I have told you, a good match from every point of view, and since this chapter is devoted to my personal attributes, I think the moment has come to describe myself. On paper, the portrait will not be flattering, for my reputation for beauty was due entirely to my figure and my bearing, not at all to my features.

My greatest beauty was my thick ash-blond hair. I had small grey eyes and my eyelashes were very thin, partly destroyed when I was four by a bad attack of smallpox. I had sparse, fair eyebrows, a high forehead and a nose often described as Grecian, but long and too heavy at the tip. My best feature was my mouth, for my lips were well shaped and had a fresh bloom. I also had very good teeth. Even today, at the age of seventy-one, I still have them all. I was said to have á pleasant face and an attractive smile, yet in spite of that, my appearance might have been considered ugly. I am afraid a number of people must have thought so, for I myself considered hideous certain women said to resemble me. But my height and my good figure, my dazzlingly clear and transparent complexion made me outstanding in any gathering, particularly by day, and I certainly overshadowed other women endowed with far better looks than mine.

I have never expected to be thought beautiful and have therefore never suffered that demeaning jealousy which I have seen tormenting so many women. Thus it was in the most entire good faith that I praised the looks, the wit or the talents of others, and that I advised them concerning their dress. I will not say that I was indifferent to my own advantages or unaware of them, but in my earliest youth I set myself a code, and I have never departed from it.

As my uncle was President of the Assembly of the Clergy, we often spent the summer in Paris and at the big dinners he gave during the session, I used to meet the Maréchal de Biron, the last great gentleman of the period of Louis XIV, or at least, the last to preserve the traditions of that day. He was eighty-five when I was only fifteen. He took a liking to me and said that I resembled some lady of his own time. He sat me beside him at table and was kind enough to talk to me. One day he told me that from his earliest youth he had given much thought to the various difficulties of old age in society and that having himself when he was my age been extremely bored and badgered by certain of his elders, he had resolved if he should himself live to a great age to avoid inflicting the same suffering. He advised me to do the same. I have always remembered that piece of advice. I have followed it also in matters of dress, and have often congratulated myself on having done so, for there is nothing so ridiculous or so ugly as an elderly woman wearing flowers or ornaments which do but emphasise the ravages of the years.

The Maréchal de Biron was Colonel of the Gardes Françaises and they adored him. There was nothing military about them except their uniforms. I had seen him when I was a child, parading before the King at the head of his men in the review held every year on the little plain of Sablons near the bridge at Neuilly.

He owned a magnificent and very beautiful house in Paris—it belongs nowadays to the Order of the Sacred Heart[1]—set in a splendid garden of three or four acres, with hot-houses filled with rarest plants. The Maréchal lived in magnificent style and did the honours of Paris in the grand manner. He owned boxes in all the principal theatres and although he never went himself, his boxes were always occupied by foreigners of distinction, particularly the English, whom he preferred above all the others, and among whom he selected the most notable. It was a much coveted honour to be received at his house.

He never gave balls, but there would be a concert at his house whenever some foreign singer or great musician visited Paris. He gathered about him everyone of distinction, always with the greatest courtesy and in the grand manner, but with unsurpassable ease amid all the splendour, for that was his natural setting. One day, speaking to my uncle and rolling his r's as had been the fashion when Louis XV was young, he said: 'Monsieur l'Archevêque'—for Marshals of France did not accord bishops the customary 'Monseigneur'—'if I should have the misfortune to lose Madame la Maréchale de Biron, I should beg Mlle Dillon to take my name and to allow me to place my fortune at her feet.' But this misfortune, for which he would have been so easily comforted, did not befall him. His wife, from whom he had been living separately for fifty years on account of some misdemeanour of which I know nothing, survived him and died on the scaffold with her niece, the Duchesse de Biron.

The Maréchal de Biron died in 1787 or 1788, and his funeral

[1] Today the Musée Rodin (T).

was the last splendour of the monarchy. Never had there been anything so magnificent.

The Maréchal was not succeeded in the Regiment by his nephew, the Duc de Biron, as the Regiment had hoped, but by the Duc du Châtelet, who made himself unpopular the moment he took up his appointment by setting immediately about the task of restoring military discipline which had been so sadly neglected in that particular corps. Many of the soldiers did not even live in quarters and appeared in barracks only when they were on duty. As a result, they had mixed a great deal with the middle and lower classes, and so became an easy prey to the revolutionaries. M. du Châtelet, a hard and difficult man, looked on the Régiment des Gardes Françaises as an ordinary regiment in need of reform. He started by making himself odious and the revolutionaries turned it to their own account.

III

The proposal to marry me to Adrien de Laval came to nothing because the Maréchal de Laval, his grandfather, decided he should marry his cousin, Mlle de Luxembourg. I was sorry, for I should have liked to bear his name.

My grandmother suggested that I should marry the Vicomte de Fleury, but I did not wish to do so. His reputation was bad, he was neither intelligent nor distinguished and he belonged to the cadet branch of a not very illustrious family. I refused him.

The next suitor for my hand was Espérance de l'Aigle, of whom I had seen a great deal when we were children. I did not consider his name sufficiently illustrious. It was perhaps not a very sensible decision, as he was indeed an excellent young man, with a very pleasant home. He was connected with the Rochechouart family, whom I was to meet again when I entered society, for we moved in the same circles. Tracy, his father's estate, was six or seven leagues from Hautefontaine. My grandmother did not want to continue her visits to Hautefontaine and would no doubt have agreed to partly hand over this property to me, to allow me at least to live there. This marriage seemed to have everything to commend it and I heard nothing but good of it, yet I refused.

Marriages are made in heaven. My thoughts still turned to

M. de Gouvernet. I was told unfavourable things about him. I had never seen him. I knew that he was short and ugly, that he had contracted debts, that he had gambled and so on, all those things which in any other man would immediately have repelled me. But my mind was made up; I told Sheldon that he was the only man I would marry. He tried endlessly to argue me out of what he called an obsession, but I refused to be convinced.

One morning in November 1786, when we were preparing to leave for Languedoc, my grandmother told me: 'This M. de Gouvernet is back again with his offer of marriage. Mme de Monconseil, his grandmother, is hemming us in on all sides. His father is Commander of a Province and will eventually be a Marshal of France. He is held in the highest esteem in military circles. His cousin, the Archbishop of Auch, is bringing to bear on your uncle all the influence he can muster. His cousin, Mme de Blot, sees that her nephew, the Abbé de Chauvigny, speaks to us of him every day. The Queen herself wishes it, for Mme de Monconseil's daughter, the Princesse d'Hénin, has spoken to her about it. Think it over and make your decision.' I replied without any hesitation: 'My mind is already made up. There is nothing I should like better.'

My grandmother was astounded. I think she had hoped that I would refuse him. She could not understand how I could prefer him to M. de l'Aigle. Frankly, I could not have explained it myself. It was an instinct, a guidance from above. God had destined me for him! And since that decision, which my sixteen-year-old lips uttered almost despite myself, I have felt that I belonged to him, that my life was his. I still bless Heaven for that decision.

The Abbé de Chauvigny acted as intermediary between Mme de Monconseil and my uncle. As was proper, he never spoke to me of this matter, no more did I to him in the conversations we had together. But I spoke with him whenever I could, for he had a pretty wit. One evening in the drawing-room, he was twisting in his fingers the envelope of a letter I had just seen him pass to my uncle. He looked at the seal, admiring the design, but when I unthinkingly held out my hand to see it, he kept hold of it, and looking hard at me, said: 'No, not yet.' I realised immediately that the letter was from Mme de Monconseil, or at least from someone who was writing about my marriage. The Abbé was maliciously amused at my blushes and confusion and we did not speak to one another again that evening.

The next morning, my grandmother told me that my uncle had received a charming letter from Mme de Monconseil; that she was extremely anxious for me to marry her grandson, of whom she was very fond; that she would do all in her power to bring it about, but that she did not possess any great influence with her son-in-law, the Comte de La Tour du Pin, with whom she had had some very unpleasant differences of opinion. It was then that I learned that Mme de Monconseil's daughter, Mme de La Tour du Pin, who was fifteen years older than her sister, the Princesse d'Hénin, had conducted herself very badly and for twenty years had been shut away in a convent, which she seldom left. Her husband made her a small allowance, but refused to see her. They were not legally separated. Every effort had been made to avoid the scandal of legal proceedings, partly in order not to embarrass her sister who, not long before, when she was fifteen, had married the Prince d'Hénin, younger brother of the Prince de Chimay, and partly out of consideration for her own daughter,[1] who was three years older than her brother, M. du Gouvernet, and had been sent to board in a Paris convent. Later, I will tell you more about this charming woman.

At that time, Mme la Marquise de Monconseil was eighty-five years of age, and I have often been told that even at that great age, she was still beautiful. M. de Monconseil had married her when she was very young. He was a soldier, like most gentlemen of that period, and had spent a very gay and dissipated youth. He had been a page to Louis XIV. He used to tell how, when lighting the way for the King one evening as he left Mme de Maintenon's house, he had been carrying two torches in one hand, as was then the custom, and had set fire to the King's wig. Telling the story to his daughter, seventy years later, he trembled again at the memory of the fear he had felt at that moment.

M. de Monconseil fought in all the wars of the later years of the reign of Louis XIV, and in all those of the reign of Louis XV.

[1] Claire Suzanne, Marquise de Lameth.

His wife, who was beautiful, witty and a mistress of intrigue, had greatly furthered his fortune. I think they forgave one another many faults. They often lived far apart. M. de Monconseil was quickly promoted to the rank of Lieutenant-General, and commanded the forces in Upper Alsace. He lived always in Colmar, and came rarely to Paris, where his wife spent most of her time and where she was assiduous in fostering his interest. I have heard it said that she never let a mail leave without sending him a letter, very short but full of interesting news. As there were no news sheets in those days, personal letters were highly prized. What a pity that collections of such letters should have been destroyed!

When he was forty, for some reason which I greatly regret not knowing, M. de Monconseil left the King's service and retired to his estate of Tesson in Saintonge. He settled there and did not leave it again until he died, aged ninety. He led a most edifying life and when he died, his bequests to charity were on a far larger scale than might have been expected from the size of his fortune. Though comfortable, it was not immense. He had a fine house at Saintes and spent three months there every winter. The rest of the year, he lived at Tesson which he built himself and whose park and gardens he had planted. He rarely went to Paris to see his wife, who lived in a good, pleasant house there. It was at his request that his son-in-law, M. de La Tour du Pin, sometimes allowed his own wife to leave her convent and spend a few days with her father at Tesson. But in forty-five years, this had happened on only two or three occasions.

M. de Monconseil was much attached to his grandson,[1] who visited him often at Tesson.

IV

And so it happened that the journey I made to Montpellier in 1786 was my last.

Through some intrigue whose details I now forget, M. de Calonne, then Comptroller-General and powerfully protected by the Queen, had obtained the removal of M. de Saint-Priest from his post as Administrator (*Intendant*) of Languedoc, and had

[1] M. de Gouvernet, later Marquis de La Tour du Pin, and husband of the writer. (T)

appointed in his stead a M. de Belinvilliers, his niece's husband. This change was very unpopular in the Province, where the Saint-Priest family was much loved and esteemed. The newcomers tried to please by their extravagance and splendour. Workmen were brought from Paris, even from the Plaisirs du Roi ou des Menus[1] itself, to build a fine ballroom in the garden. There, the new *Indendant* and his wife brought together people from all classes of society. It was the first time such a mingling of classes, later known as a 'fusion', had been attempted. Mme Riban, wife of the famous perfumer, a bottle of whose pomade or perfume was to be found on every dressing-table, was there in all the radiance of her beauty. There were also other outstanding members of the bourgeoisie, to the great horror of the elderly wives of the Presidents of the Cour des Comptes, the only tribunal we had in Montpellier.

CHAPTER FIVE

I

You will understand how eager I was to return to Paris where my future was to be decided. We set out even sooner than I expected.

A courier arrived with news that the First Assembly of Notables[2] had been summoned. My uncle was a member, so we had to leave for Paris the day after the closing of the States. I myself date the Revolution from that day.

My uncle decided, that as he was not too well, we would spend a night at Fontainebleau. It would prevent him from being overtired when we reached Paris and he would be able to go the following morning to Versailles. We always found the house looking as if we had never left it. Whether tired or not, the

[1] A name given to the department charged with administering the King's expenditure on out-of-the-ordinary amusements of any kind. (T)

[2] An extraordinary council composed of leading citizens chosen by the King from the three estates. By convening this Assembly, the King could avoid summoning the powerful States-General, but without departing from the liberal tradition. In 1787 it met to deal with the financial confusion and to reform abuses. (T)

servants had to be in their places, dressed, powdered and trim
as ever. I had to do the same. We arrived at two o'clock, and at
three, my grandmother and I were in the drawing-room ready to
dine, taking no account at all of the 210 leagues we had just
covered.

In the evening, people came to call. The first visitor was an
elderly Comte de Bentheim, a stout German whose wife, always
referred to as 'The Sovereign', was one of my grandmothers'
friends. After the usual opening remarks about the bad weather,
weariness and the state of the roads, my uncle asked the Comte
what news there was in Paris. 'Oh,' replied the stout German,
'there's one piece of social news—Mme de Monconseil is dead.'
It would be impossible to describe my feelings on hearing those
few words. I became pale and my uncle, fearing that my agitation
would betray me, said that I was tired and that it would be better
for me to retire, which I did immediately. But when I took his
hand to kiss it, as I did every evening, he said to me in English
that it would not change our plans.

For a few days, the only topic of conversation was the death of
Mme de Monconseil, the grief of her daughter, Mme d'Hénin,
who had lived with her, and the admirable care given to her by
M. de Gouvernet.[1] It all concerned me closely, but I had to
appear indifferent. Fortunately, I was able to talk about it to my
cousin, Charlotte Jerningham, who had just left the Ursuline
Convent in the Rue Saint-Jacques, where she had spent three
years without once going out. Her mother had come to Paris to
fetch her, but they stayed until after my marriage.

II

In the absence of his father, who was not in Paris just then, M. de
Gouvernet quickly made it known to my uncle that his grandmother's death in no way changed his own wish for an alliance
with my great-uncle's family, and he asked for a private interview.
He came one evening, and my uncle was very favourably impressed with him. M. de Gouvernet insisted that he should be
permitted to go and tell his father personally that the request he
intended to make for the hand of Mlle Dillon would be granted

[1] Her grandson, and future husband of the writer. (T)

by her and by her grandmother. My uncle agreed and M. de Gouvernet took his leave. I tell you this in such detail so that you may see the ways of good society in a period so far removed from that in which I am writing. My uncle went up to see my grandmother and, finding me alone with her, embraced me, saying: 'Goodnight, Madame de Gouvernet.'

Several days passed, but before the week was over, my uncle was one day informed that M. de Gouvernet was waiting in his study. 'But that is impossible,' he exclaimed. It was, however, true. He had been to Le Bouilh, spoken to his father, persuaded him to write the formal request for my hand, asked his wishes concerning the arrangements and then, climbing back into his carriage, had returned to Paris. This haste seemed to me in the very best taste. It was agreed that he would wait on my grandmother the following morning, but that he would not see me until the marriage contract had been signed. Such was the custom of the day, unless there happened to be some chance meeting. In my case, that was very unlikely, for I never went out on foot, never walked in any public place and never went to the theatre.

The following day, such a memorable one for me, I hid behind a curtain and watched M. de Gouvernet descend from a very pretty cabriolet drawn by a fine and very spirited grey. If you remember that I was not yet seventeen, you will understand why this arrival pleased me far more than if he had come in a fine carriage escorted by a groom who offered his arm as he climbed out. In two bounds, he was at the top of the steps. He was very correctly dressed: a town coat which was either black or very dark grey, for he was still in deep mourning; a military collar and a military hat, the latter usually not worn by anyone except a colonel. This suggestion of high rank combined with such a youthful appearance was really very dashing. I had been told that he was ugly, but did not find him so. His assurance and air of decision pleased me immediately. I had stationed myself where I could see him when he went in to see my grandmother. She offered him her hand, which he kissed with the greatest deference. I could not hear their conversation, so I tried to imagine it. He remained with her for a quarter of an hour and it was agreed that the contract would be signed as soon as it had been drawn up by the lawyers.

After that, M. de Gouvernet would be free to come every day to my uncle's house.

It took eight days to prepare the contract, but before it was complete, Mme d'Hénin called on my grandmother. She asked for me, and as I had thought she might do so, I was prepared. The elegance and assurance of this very beautiful woman who, I knew, would examine me from head to foot, so frightened me that my legs would hardly bear me forward into the room and I literally could not see where I was going. She stood up, took my hand and embraced me. Then, with the outspokenness of ladies of her day, she stood me at arms' length and cried: 'Ah, what a pretty figure. She is charming. My nephew is very lucky.' It was torture for me. She sat down again and asked me a lot of questions to which I am sure I must have made the most stupid replies. As she left, she embraced me again and made me a number of pretty compliments on the pleasure it would give her to take me into society.

This visit took place, I believe, the day before the signing of the contract. It was not customary for the young lady to be present at this preliminary ceremony, the contract being signed only by the families and the lawyers. But when the lawyers had gone, I was sent for. My grandmother came to the door to take my hand and I crossed the salon in a state bordering on unconsciousness. I felt everyone's gaze upon me, especially that of M. de Gouvernet, at whom I was very careful not to look. I was put beside Mme d'Hénin and my aunt, Lady Jerningham, who had pity on my embarrassment.

I was very simply dressed. I had begged my grandmother to leave the choice to me. At that time we wore very straight gowns laced at the back, drawn in very tightly at the waist. Mine was of plain white muslin, with a waistband of dark blue ribbon ending in a fringe of brilliantly-coloured silk and came from England. They said I was as pretty as a picture. They looked at my hair, which was really very beautiful. Such scrutiny in the presence of the 'high and mighty lord, the future husband', as he had been named twenty times during the reading of the contract, was quite unbearable.

From then on, M. de Gouvernet came every day to dine or

spend the afternoon, or to take supper with us, either in Paris or at Versailles, where my uncle had been living since the opening of the Assembly of Notables.

My grandmother and I had remained in Paris and every day of the week, at half-past one, we set out for Versailles. We arrived there in time for dinner at three o'clock. My uncle scarcely left his office, which, if I remember rightly, was presided over by Monsieur, the King's brother, later Louis XVIII. He would appear just as we were about to sit down to table, always bringing with him several guests. M. de Gouvernet, as I have said, came out from Paris every day to dine with us. He always wore formal dress and sword, for it had not yet become the custom, especially at Versailles, to wear town dress and a round hat to dinner. No gentleman wishing to be correctly dressed would have been seen otherwise than in formal dress with a sword, unless he were about to ride to Paris or drive there in his cabriolet. And in that case, he would take care to reach the courtyard by way of the back stairs, avoiding the apartments, galleries and guard rooms. Men had not yet lost their sense of respect. Failure to observe, I do not say the etiquette, but even the slightest nuance in the courtesies of society would have been in the worst possible taste.

During this Assembly of Notables, which I found unbearably boring, politics were the sole topic of every conversation. All who entered the drawing-room had some infallible remedy for the treasury deficit as well as for the abuses which had been allowed to grow within the state. My uncle wanted the entire country governed by States, as in Languedoc. M. de Gouvernet often joined in these conversations. His remarks were intelligent and forceful, and I enjoyed listening to him.

He had presented his brother-in-law, the Marquis de Lameth to my uncle and two of the latter's brothers, Charles and Alexander. Alexander was a Knight of Malta and a great friend of M. de Gouvernet. There was a fourth brother, Theodore, who survived all the others, but I did not meet him until later.

The Marquis de Lameth was a handsome man of thirty, tall, well-built, serious and even solemn in manner. He nearly always lived either in the country, at his lovely château of Hénéncourt, near Amiens, or with his regiment, the Régiment de la Couronne.

He was a good soldier, but with a passion for detail. He was a strict disciplinarian, saw that orders were carried out with scrupulous promptitude, kept aloof from his subordinates and was very just in his estimate of their duties. M. de Gouvernet resembled him in this.

III

I seem to remember that this Assembly of Notables ended its session towards the middle of April. I had found it tiring from every point of view, and so had M. de Gouvernet, who came every day to Versailles, driven by gallantry, or perhaps by a more tender feeling. We had found means to talk a great deal together and to become increasingly certain that we were made for one another. Later we often found pleasure in recalling the charm of those first conversations, in which we were both trying to understand and to know one another, in which each of us was studying the opinions and tastes of the other and from which we both always emerged so well satisfied. What pleasant plans we made for our future, and not one of them has come true! We were too happy in the present to foresee the storms we would have to face and yet we were aware of a deep conviction that however heavy the reverses we might have to endure, we would find in our mutual affection the strength to withstand them unfalteringly.

M. de Gouvernet had not yet quite understood my grandmother's character. He had accepted Mme d'Hénin's impression, and she knew only what was known to all the world, for she had not entered the Queen's Household until after my mother's death. The sadness of life is quickly forgotten at Court. The Queen mourned my mother for twenty-four hours, and the very next day was expressing a wish to visit the Comédie Française. The Duchesse de Duras, who was in waiting that day, said to her: 'It would perhaps be better for Your Majesty to go to the Opéra, otherwise, in passing before Saint-Sulpice, Your Majesty will meet the funeral procession of Mme Dillon'. The Queen accepted the rebuke and remained at Versailles. The Duchesse de Duras, née Noailles, was a woman of the greatest virtue, and the Queen was in awe of her. She had dearly loved my mother and later extended this affection to me.

IV

I first met my future father-in-law a few days before the signing of the contract. He was a short man, of upright carriage, very well built who in his youth had been handsome. He still had the finest teeth one could wish for, fine eyes, an air of assurance and a charming smile which showed all his essential goodness and kindliness. He made no attempt to overawe me and I did my utmost to appear pleasing to him. He was a man of simple ways, scrupulously attentive to his duties as Commander of the Provinces of Saintonge and Poitou and of the district of Aunis. He devoted every minute he could spare to the building and planting he had undertaken at Le Bouilh, which was his favourite residence. As he was separated from his wife and came to Paris only on short visits, either to wait upon the King or to consult Ministers on public matters, he kept no establishment there. He was not ambitious: his son thought he should have been more so and that a man of his ability should not have remained so much in the background. He belonged to an earlier age, to the days of St Louis. He had served in the Seven Years' War as Colonel of a regiment composed of the cream of all the other regiments and known as the Grenadiers de France. He had greatly distinguished himself, and all his promotions, including that to the rank he then held, had been given without any soliciting on his part. His intrigue-loving mother-in-law, Mme de Monconseil, could not understand such detachment. She did not like him. She found him unnecessarily severe towards his wife, whose misbehaviour had been so public that, although the gentlest of men, he had thought it necessary to treat her with the utmost strictness. He was very just and very good, rightly considering it his duty to remove her from a world in which she set such a scandalous example. He permitted her to appear sometimes at her father's house and wished her to be present at his son's marriage. M. de Gouvernet and Mme de Lameth treated her with great deference and respect.

The Queen, who approved of my marriage, expressed a wish to see me. She openly declared her kind intention to take me under her protection and asked my uncle to bring me to see her, together with Mme d'Hénin, of whom I already stood in such great awe. I was very shy, which made me awkward and sometimes almost incapable of movement: my legs would not bear me up, every limb felt paralysed. In vain did I reason with myself and try to overcome it; each attempt ended in failure. In addition to this form of cowardice, which is probably very similar to that which paralyses a soldier who disgraces himself in battle, there was another quirk in my character which has remained with me throughout my life: an unconquerable horror of insincerity and false professions of sentiment. I knew instinctively that the Queen would make a show of emotional pity and I knew also that she had not missed my mother for longer than a day. My whole heart rebelled at the thought of being obliged, in my own interest, to help her play this part. As I walked through the apartments on my way to that bedchamber which I have since entered so often, Mme d'Hénin was tactlessly telling me all over again that I had to be very amiable to the Queen, that I must not be unresponsive, that the Queen would be very emotional and so on, advice which only served to increase my embarrassment.

I found myself in the Queen's presence, but without any recollection of how I arrived there. She embraced me and I kissed her hand. She told me to sit beside her and asked me a thousand questions about my education, my accomplishments and so on, but despite the prodigious effort I was making, I could find no voice to reply. Eventually, seeing the large tears welling from my eyes, she took pity on my embarrassment and talked to my uncle and Mme d'Hénin. My shyness left her with a bad impression which she perhaps never quite forgot. I have since had reason to regret very much that, having doubtless judged me wrongly then, she never thought to put my devotion to the test in circumstances when my youth, and let me say it, my courage might perhaps have changed the destinies of France.

V

We went to Montfermeil towards the 8th or 10th of May 1787. As it was contrary to custom for a future husband to sleep under the same roof as his bride, M. de Gouvernet came from Paris every day to dine with us and stayed until after supper. On the evening of the 21st of May, he slept at the Château of Montfermeil, which the kind owners had put at the disposal of my family. A number of the gentlemen were lodged there and the ladies stayed in my grandmother's charming house.[1] I myself was given a delightful apartment, furnished in perfect style. The hangings were of Indian cloth or calico, patterned with trees, flower-laden branches, fruits and birds against a buff-coloured ground, and lined throughout with fine green silk.

In the enormous wall closets was the beautiful trousseau my grandmother had given me. It consisted entirely of household linen, lace and gowns of muslin. It had cost 45,000 francs. There was not a single silk gown. M. de Gouvernet's wedding presents to me included jewels, lengths of ribbon, flowers, feathers, gloves, blonde lace, lengths of cloth—shawls were not then in fashion—many hats and elegant bonnets, as well as mantles of black or white muslin trimmed with blonde lace.

Mme d'Hénin had given me a charming tea table and tea service. The teapot, sugar bowl and other pieces were in silver gilt and the porcelain was of Sèvres. Her gift was the one which gave me the greatest pleasure. I believe it cost 6,000 francs. The Abbé de Gouvernet, an uncle of M. de Gouvernet, gave me a fine dressing-case which had its own special place in my travelling coach. My grandfather[2] gave me a fine pair of ear-rings worth 10,000 francs.

When I entered this pretty apartment, I found a charming plant stand in the middle of my bedroom, filled with rare plants and vases of flowers. In the small room next door, where I usually sat, had been placed a small book-case filled with English books, including a pretty collection of English poets in seventy volumes and also some Italian books. On the walls were beautiful English prints in good frames. All these were from M. de Gouvernet and I thanked him very warmly.

I tell you of all this splendour and elegance only in order to show the contrast with the remainder of my story.

[1] La Folie Joyeuse.
[2] Henry, 11th Viscount Dillon.

CHAPTER SIX

I

On my wedding day, everyone gathered in the salon at noon. On my side, the company included my grandmother, Mme de Rothe; my uncle, Mgr. Dillon, Archbishop of Narbonne; my aunt, Lady Jerningham; her husband, Sir William Jerningham; her daughter, Miss Charlotte Jerningham, who later became Lady Bedingfeld; her eldest son, George William Jerningham, the present Lord Stafford; the Sheldons; their elder brother, Mr Constable, who was my first witness; Sir Charles Jerningham, Sir William's brother, who had been my mother's friend and was mine also, and who acted as my second witness. All these were members of my family. The guests included all the Ministers of the Government, the Archbishops of Paris and Tolouse, some Bishops from Languedoc who were in Paris, M. de Lally-Tollendal, of whom I will tell you later, and many others whose names I do not remember.

M. de Gouvernet's family was represented by his father and mother; his uncle, the Abbé de Gouvernet, Canon of the Noble Chapter of Macon; his sister, the Marquise de Lameth, with her husband and his brothers; his aunt, Mme d'Hénin; the Chevalier de Coigny and the Comte de Valence, who were his witnesses; the Comtesse de Blot and a number of other distinguished persons, about fifty or sixty in all.

We went in procession across the courtyard to the chapel. I walked first, giving my hand to my cousin, the younger Jerningham. Then came my grandmother with M. de Gouvernet. The others followed, I do not know in what order. At the altar stood my uncle and M. de Juigné, the Archbishop of Paris. The Curé of Montfermeil, a gentleman from Picardy named M. de Riencourt, celebrated a Low Mass and my uncle, with the permission of the Archbishop of Paris who assisted him, gave us the nuptial blessing. Bur first he preached a charming sermon in that fine vibrant voice of his which never failed to touch the heart. The canopy was held by young Alfred de Lameth, who was seven, and by my sixteen-year-old cousin Jerningham, to whom I gave a fine sword when we returned to the salon.

All the ladies embraced me, in order of kinship and age. Then a footman brought in a large basket of green and gold sword knots, favours, fans and cords for the Bishops' hats, to be distributed among the guests. This was a very costly custom. Sword favours of the finest ribbon cost between twenty-five and thirty francs each. Military sword knots in gold and the tasselled cords for the Bishops' hats cost fifty francs, and the fans for the ladies cost between twenty-five and one hundred francs each.

Nor must I forget to describe the bride's dress. It was very simple: a gown of white crêpe and fine Brussels lace, and pinners[1], for in those days one wore a bonnet, not a veil. I had a cluster of orange blossoms in my hair and another at my waist. For the dinner, I wore a fine turban trimmed with tall white plumes, to which was pinned the cluster of orange blossom.

Dinner was at four o'clock, and we stood about talking until then, feeling rather bored. Afterwards, we went to visit the servants and the peasants. There was a table of one hundred places for the livery servants, whose variously coloured coats and trimmings looked very picturesque, and another table for the peasants and workmen. They drank my health with a will. I was very much liked by them and they had the greatest confidence in me. Many of them had known me all my life and on many occasions I had looked after their interests and their wishes; I had many times forgiven their faults or softened my grandmother's displeasure, which was frequent and usually unfair. They wished me happiness in the union into which I had just entered and their goodwill touched me more than all the compliments that had been offered me in the salon. The evening ended with an excellent concert.

II

The following day, most of the guests took their leave. I wore elegant half-mourning, as there was still a month of mourning for

[1] Two long streamers of material pinned to either side of a lady's coif or bonnet. They were worn especially by ladies of rank in the 17th and 18th centuries. (T)

Mme de Monconseil. Mme d'Hénin told us that the Queen wished me to be presented the following Sunday. I had been married on Monday, and it was on Tuesday that my aunt told my grandmother of the Queen's wish. My grandmother had not been consulted. Mme d'Hénin added that I would have to go with her to Paris on the morning of Thursday so that my dancing master could give me two lessons in the curtsey. There was also my presentation dress to be fitted and a visit to be paid to Mme de La Tour du Pin,[1] who, as my mother-in-law no longer went to Court, was the only member of my new family eligible to present me.

My grandmother had not been able to hide her fury when she heard that my presentation was arranged, but there could be no question of disputing it. She realised that her empire over me was finished. She trembled with rage at the realisation that the Queen would henceforth have me at her service and that Mme d'Hénin, who was to introduce me into society, would in future determine my conduct. She said nothing before my new family, but I took care not to be alone with her that day.

The next day, I accordingly left for Paris with my aunt, Mme d'Hénin, and spent the next two mornings with M. Huart, my dancing master. It is impossible to conceive of anything more ridiculous than those rehearsals of the presentation. M. Huart, a large man, his hair very well dressed and white with powder, wore a billowing underskirt and stood at the far end of the room to represent the Queen. He told me what I had to do, sometimes taking the part of the lady who was to present me and sometimes that of the Queen. Standing at the far end of the room, he showed me just when to remove my glove and bow to kiss the hem of the Queen's gown. He showed me the gesture she would make to prevent me. Nothing was forgotten or overlooked in these rehearsals, which went on for three or four hours. I wore a train and the wide paniers of Court dress, but above and below was my ordinary morning dress, and my hair was only very simply pinned up. It was all very funny.

---

[1] Louise-Charlotte de Béthune, wife of a cousin, Philippe-Antoine-Gabriel-Victor-Charles de La Tour du Pin de La Charce-Gouvernet, Marquis de Montmorin (1723–1794), who used the title Marquis de La Tour du Pin until 1775, when he succeeded to the title Marquis de Gouvernet.

I was presented on Sunday morning, after Mass. I was 'en grand corps', that is to say, wearing a special bodice without shoulders, laced at the back, but narrow enough for the lacings, four inches wide at the bottom, to show a chemise of the finest lawn through which it could easily be seen if the wearer's skin were not white. This chemise had sleeves, but they were only three inches deep and the shoulders were uncovered. From the top of the arm to the elbow fell three or four flounces of blonde lace. The throat was bare. Mine was partly covered by the seven or eight rows of large diamonds which the Queen had kindly lent me. The front of the bodice was as if laced with rows of diamonds and on my head were more diamonds, some in clusters and some in aigrets.

The gown itself was very lovely. On account of my half-mourning, it was all in white and the entire skirt was embroidered with pearls and silver.

Thanks to M. Huart's good coaching, I made my three curtseys very well. I removed my glove and put it on again not too awkwardly. Then I went to receive the accolade from the King and his brothers, the Princes,[1] from the Duc de Penthièvre,[2] the Princes of Condé, Bourbon and Enghien.[3] By a fortunate chance, for which I have many times thanked Heaven, the Duc d'Orléans was not at Versailles that day, and so I avoided being embraced by that monster. However, I have often seen him since, even in his own house, at the famous suppers he gave in the Palais Royal.

The day of one's presentation was very embarrassing and exceedingly tiring. It meant being stared at by the whole Court and being torn to shreds by every critical tongue. On that day, one became the topic of every conversation and on returning to the 'jeu'[4] in the evening—I cannot remember if it was at seven or at nine o'clock—every eye was upon you.

The following Sunday, I returned to Versailles, still wearing

---

[1] The Comte de Provence, later Louis XVIII, and the Comte d'Artois, later Charles X.
[2] Son of the Comte de Toulouse.
[3] The Prince of Condé, his son the Duc de Bourbon, and his grandson, the Duc d'Enghien.
[4] Games of cards, chess, backgammon and so on were played at Court every evening. (T)

mourning, and from then on I went there with my aunt nearly every week. The Queen had decided that I should not take my place as a Lady of her Household for another two years, but I was considered as such from the beginning and on Sundays I entered her bedchamber with the ladies who were in attendance.

III

Since the ceremonial is no longer the same, it would perhaps be of interest to describe the Sunday Courts over which that unfortunate Queen presided so brilliantly. Such details have now acquired an historical value.

A few minutes before midday, the ladies entered the salon next to the Queen's bedchamber. They all stood, except the elderly ones, who in those days were treated with great deference, and those of the younger ladies who were thought to be pregnant. There were always at least forty people present, often more. Sometimes, we were very closely packed, for our paniers took up a great deal of room. Ordinarily, when the Princesse de Lamballe, Mistress of the Household, arrived, she went straight into the bedchamber where the Queen was dressing. She usually arrived before the Queen had begun her toilette. The Princesse de Chimay, a sister-in-law of my aunt d'Hénin, and the Comtesse d'Ossun, the first a Lady-in-Waiting and the second the Mistress of the Robes, also went in. A few minutes later, a footman advanced to the door of the bedchamber and called in a loud voice for 'Le Service'.[1] The four ladies on duty that week, and all those who had come, as was customary, to wait on the Queen between their periods of duty, would then enter the bedchamber, together with younger ladies such as the Comtesse de Maillé (née Fitz-James), the Comtesse Mathieu de Montmorency and myself, who were eventually to be appointed to the Household.

As soon as the Queen had greeted each of us in her charming, kindly way, the door was opened and everyone admitted. We stood to the right and left of the room in such a manner as to leave a clear space at the door and in the centre of the room. Often when there were many ladies in attendance, we stood in rows two

[1] i.e., those in waiting. (T

or three deep. But the first arrivals would withdraw skilfully towards the door leading to the card-room, through which the Queen had to pass on her way to Mass. To this salon a few privileged gentlemen who had either been received earlier in private audience, or who were to present visitors from abroad were often admitted.

Thus it happened one day that the Queen, stopping unexpectedly to say a word to someone, saw me in the corner of the doorway shaking hands with the English Ambassador, the Duke of Dorset. She had never seen this English form of greeting before and found it very amusing. As jokes do not die easily at Court, she never failed to ask the Duke on the many occasions when we were both present, 'Have you shaken hands with Mme de Gouvernet?'

This tragic Queen still betrayed, even then, a few trifling and very feminine jealousies. She had a very lovely complexion and a radiant personality, but she showed herself a little jealous of those young ladies who could bring to the hard light of noon a seventeen-year-old complexion more dazzling than her own. I was one of them, and once when she was passing through the door, the Duchesse de Duras, who was always very kind and helpful to me, whispered in my ear: 'Do not stand facing the windows.' I understood what she meant and followed her advice. But this did not prevent the Queen from sometimes passing remarks which were almost cutting about my liking for bright colours and for the poppies and brown scabious which I often wore. However, she was usually very kind to me, sometimes paying me those forthright compliments which princes have a habit of casting at young women down the whole length of a room, making the unhappy persons concerned blush to the very roots of their hair.

These Sunday morning audiences lasted until forty minutes past noon. Then the door opened and the footman announced: 'The King!' The Queen, who always wore Court dress, would go to meet him with a charming air of pleasure and deference. The King would incline his head to the right and the left, and speak to a few ladies whom he knew, though never to the young ones. He was so short-sighted that he could not recognise anyone at a distance of more than three paces. He was stout, about five foot six or seven inches tall, square-shouldered and with the worst possible bearing. He looked like some peasant shambling along behind his plough; there was nothing proud or regal about him. His sword was a continual embarrassment to him and he never knew what to do with his hat, yet in Court dress he looked really magnificent. He took no interest in his clothes, putting on without a glance whatever was handed to him. His coats were made of cloths suited to the various seasons, all very heavily embroidered, and he wore the diamond star of the Order of the Holy Ghost. It was only on his feast day, or on days of gala or great ceremonial that he wore the ribbon over his coat.

Preparations for attending Mass began at a quarter to one o'clock. The First Gentleman of the Bedchamber for the year led the procession, and behind him came the Captain of the Guard who was on duty and many other officers, either of the Guard or holding high office, the Captain of the Guard himself walked immediately in front of the King. The King and Queen walked together, slowly enough to be able to say a word as they passed, to the large numbers of courtiers who lined the gallery. Often, the Queen would speak to the foreign ladies who had been presented to her in private, to artists and to writers. An inclination of the head or a gracious smile was noted and carefully stored against future need. The ladies followed in order of rank. We walked four or five abreast, the young ones trying to be on the outside and those who were considered to be in fashion—among whom I had the honour to be included—taking great care to walk close enough to the line of courtiers to be able to catch the pretty things whispered to them as they passed.

It took great skill to walk through that vast room without treading on the long train of the lady in front. Feet were never raised from the ground, they glided over the gleaming parquet until the Salon of Hercules was safely crossed. Then, each lady threw her train over one of her paniers and, making sure she had been seen by her servant who would be waiting with a large, gold-fringed, red velvet bag, she rushed to one of the side galleries of the Chapel, trying to find a place as close as possible to the gallery occupied by the King and Queen and the Princesses, who had joined them either in the card-room or in the Chapel. Mme

Elisabeth¹ was always there, and sometimes Madame² as well. Each servant put the red velvet bag on the floor in front of his mistress, who took out a missal, but hardly ever read it, for by the time she had found herself a place, arranged her train and searched through her immense bag, the Priest would have already reached the Gospel.

At the end of Mass, the Queen curtseyed deeply to the King and we left again in the same order in which we had arrived. The only difference was that the King and Queen would stop longer to speak to people. We returned to the Queen's room, the ladies who were at Court remaining in the card-room until it was time to attend the Queen to dinner. Before dining, the King and Queen always spent a quarter of an hour talking to the ladies who had come out from Paris. We of the younger set irreverently called them the 'traineuses'³ because they wore longer skirts to their Court gowns and their ankles were hidden.

Dinner was in the first salon, where a small rectangular table was laid with two places, and two large green armchairs were placed side by side, so close that they touched. The backs of these chairs were high enough to screen completely the persons seated in them. The table-cloth reached the ground. The Queen sat on the King's left. They sat with their backs to the fireplace, and about ten feet in front of them, was arranged a semi-circle of stools for the duchesses, princesses and other ladies whose office entitled them to this privilege. Behind them stood all the other ladies, facing the King and Queen. The King ate heartily, but the Queen neither removed her gloves nor unfolded her napkin, which was a very big mistake. As soon as the King had drunk his wine, everyone curtseyed and left. The ladies who had come to pay their court did not need to remain any longer.

Many people who, although they had not been presented, were nonetheless known to the King and Queen, and to whom Their Majesties were very gracious, remained until dinner was over. The Gentlemen of the King's Household usually did the same.

Then began a veritable race to pay court to the royal princes

¹ Sister of Louis XVI.
² Marie-Josephine-Louise of Savoy, wife of the Comte de Provence.
³ A play on words. Literally, the stragglers. Used here because of the unusually long trains worn by these ladies. (T)

and princesses, who dined much later. Everything depended on getting there as quickly as possible. The first visit was to Monsieur,[1] later Louis XVIII, the next to the Comte d'Artois,[2] then one to Mme Elisabeth and others to the King's aunts and even to the little Dauphin[3] who was in the charge of his tutor, the Duc d'Harcourt. Each visit lasted three or four minutes only, for the princes' salons were so small that they had to dismiss the first comers to make room for the next.

For a young lady, the pleasantest of these visits was that to the Comte d'Artois. He was young and had that charming appearance which he was never to lose. Great efforts were made to please him, for to succeed was a guarantee of fame. He was on friendly terms with my aunt, whom he always greeted as 'Chère Princesse'.

By the time we returned to our own apartment, we were rather weary, and as we had to be at the 'jeu' at seven o'clock in the evening, we stayed quietly in our rooms in order not to disarrange our hair, especially if it had been dressed by Léonard, the most famous of all the coiffeurs. We ourselves dined at three o'clock, the fashionable hour in those days. After dinner, we talked until six o'clock and a few gentlemen whom we knew very well would come to tell us the latest news, the gossip and the intrigues they had heard during the morning. Then, once again arrayed in Court dress, we returned to the same salon of the Palace where we had waited during the morning. But this time, the gentlemen were also there.

We had to be there before seven, for the Queen entered before the chiming of the clock. Beside her door would be one of the two Curés of Versailles. He would hand her a purse and she would go around to everyone, taking up a collection and saying: 'For the poor, if you please.' Each lady had her 'écu'[4] of six francs ready in her hand and the men had their 'louis'.[5] The Curé would follow the Queen as she collected this small tax for her poor people, a levy which often totalled as much as one hundred 'louis' and never less than fifty.

[1] The Comte de Provence.
[2] Later Charles X.
[3] The first Dauphin, Louis-Joseph-Xavier-François, who died in 1789.
[4] A silver coin. (T)
[5] A gold coin. (T)

I often heard some of the younger people, including the most spendthrift, complaining inordinately of this almsgiving being forced upon them, yet they would not have thought twice of hazarding a sum one hundred times as large in a game of chance or of spending in a morning, to no purpose at all, a sum much larger than that levied by the Queen.

It was the fashion to complain of everything. One was bored, weary of attendance at Court. The officers of the Garde du Corps, who were lodged in the Château when on duty, bemoaned having to wear uniform all day. The Ladies of the Household in attendance could not bear to miss going two or three times to Paris for supper during the eight days of their attendance at Versailles. It was the height of style to complain of duties at Court, profiting from them none the less and sometimes, indeed often, abusing the privileges they carried. All the ties were being loosened, and it was, alas, the upper classes who led the way. The Bishops did not live in their dioceses and seized on any pretext to visit Paris. Colonels, obliged to serve with their regiment for only four months of the year, would not have dreamed of staying five minutes longer than the minimum period. Unnoticed, the spirit of revolt was rampant in all classes of society.

IV

The Minister of War, the Maréchal de Ségur, who had been a guest at my wedding, had given my husband a month's leave. So, instead of leaving for Saint-Omer, where his Regiment was garrisoned, he remained with me at Montfermeil.

It was my love for riding and driving that gave him his first insight into my grandmother's character. Mme de Montfermeil, of whom I saw a great deal, suggested that I should ride with her. As she had a very quiet horse, and as those of M. de La Tour du Pin[1] were very lively, she put hers at my disposal. When I mentioned this to my grandmother, she was by no means pleased, but when she knew that my husband, anticipating my wish, had given me a charming riding dress and wanted me to accompany him when he went riding, her displeasure turned into lively

[1] From now on, Mme de La Tour du Pin always refers to her husband by this title, and the translator has followed her practice.

anger. My uncle no longer rode himself, but he, too, had instructed his groom to train a fine grey he had bought in England for my use. He made me a present of it, together with a pretty little carriage of a kind known today as a tilbury. I used to drive this equipage myself in the beautiful lanes of the Forest of Bondy. My cousin, Mme Sheldon, was spending the summer with us and usually accompanied me.

During the month's leave which M. de La Tour du Pin spent at Montfermeil, he often took me hunting. All these youthful pastimes were utterly displeasing to my grandmother, whose character grew daily more disagreeable. She did not yet feel sufficiently at ease with my husband to dare, in his presence, to attack those he loved. But as soon as he went out of a room, she began to criticise my aunt d'Hénin and all her friends, and to talk of the inconvenience it was for elderly people to have young ones staying in their house, the difficulties it caused and so on. She delighted in all kinds of painful, hurtful remarks. Seeing that I so often arrived in our room with reddened eyes, M. de La Tour du Pin made me tell him the trouble. I tried not to betray the full extent of it, but he soon guessed. He talked to his aunt, who had been at Versailles with my mother, and to many others of her contemporaries, and soon knew of my grandmother's disgraceful conduct towards her daughter. He determined there and then that she would not behave in the same fashion to me, and seeing this determination, I lived in continual dread that his vehemence would one day provoke him into rash outspokenness.

However, he managed to restrain his feelings and returned to his Regiment at the end of June. I was very sad to see him go. I remained at Montfermeil with my family, the butt of my grandmother's bad temper and in daily fear of scenes. Whenever my aunt wrote asking me to join her in Paris so that she could take me to Versailles or into society, I never knew how best to make the announcement that I was to be away for two or three days. I realised very clearly that my grandmother's character would make it impossible for us to live in my uncle's house. His very affection for me did him a disservice. My grandmother also feared that my husband would gain too much influence over the Archbishop, who had taken a great liking to him. From the time of my marriage, therefore, she determined to settle again at Haute-fontaine with my uncle in order to remove him more surely from the dangers of his own affections, which might set him too firmly on our side.

Towards the middle of August, M. de La Tour du Pin came to spend another week at Montfermeil, the Maréchal de Ségur permitting this on condition that he did not show his face in Paris. Owing to the troubles in Holland, Colonels who commanded garrisons in Flanders were at that time being threatened with having to spend several months of the autumn and winter with their regiments. It looked as if we might have to intervene, which would have been a very wise move. However, the King's indecision and the Government's weakness made it impossible to take a stand—a stand which, by giving the people of France something else to think about, might perhaps have diverted them from the ideas of revolution which were ripening so fast in their minds.

CHAPTER SEVEN

I

As I am not writing history, I will not enter into the causes of the dissensions which first split the United Provinces of the Netherlands into two parties: the supporters of the House of Orange-Nassau and the Patriots. The former wanted increased power for the Stadtholder, the senior official of the Republic. The second wanted to restrict his power, and to keep it within the limits imposed by the families of de Witt and Barneveld.

The Stadtholder, William V, was a nonentity. But his wife—a niece of Frederick the Great, and sister of his successor, Frederick William II—was ambitious. She wanted crowns for her husband and herself. The aristocracy of Guelder and the provinces of Over-Yssel and Utrecht watched with some uneasiness the wealth of the merchants of Holland. The Princess of Orange did what she could to fan this discontent, or at least to keep it seething. She was assured of the support of England and Prussia, and had no fear

at all of intervention by France, despite the very decided views of
our ambassador, the Comte de Saint-Priest, who was continually
asking his feeble Court to support the Patriot party, since it was
conservative. At the urging of Prussia, which had assembled
troops at Wesel, the Princess of Orange incited rebellion in
Amsterdam and the Hague: the Stadtholder was insulted by so-
called Patriots and his supporters exacted reprisals. The French
Embassy was sacked and M. de Saint-Priest withdrew to the
Austrian Netherlands. To give the Prussians an excuse for intervening, the Princess of Orange pretended a fear she was very far
from feeling, and openly left The Hague to retire into Prussian
territory—to Wesel, in fact. The Patriots were maladroit enough to
fall into the trap. The Princess, pretending to be unaware that
they had forward posts on the Utrecht road, took that route, in
the hope of being stopped. She succeeded beyond her hopes. She
was captured and taken to Amsterdam. The Orangists straight-
way rushed to arms and called on the Prussians for help. The
latter set out immediately and advanced as far as The Hague. Their
passage was marked by the firing and sacking of all property
belonging to Patriots. In vain did M. de Saint-Priest send courier
after courier to Versailles urging his government to send troops
to Holland and not to abandon the party he was supporting; in
vain did M. Esterhazy, the commander of the army corps which
had been promised to the Patriots, go to Versailles to implore
help from the Queen. Nothing could overcome the indecision of
the King and the weakness of his ministers.

The affair dragged on. M. Esterhazy, whom the Queen treated
as a friend and called 'mon frère', continued to hope that she would
eventually obtain the intervention of the French Government in
favour of our allies and sent M. de La Tour du Pin to Antwerp
to arrange with M. de Saint-Priest what action should be taken
if French troops arrived.

But the Ambassador knew his Government far too well to
expect anything generous or decisive from it. We ignobly
abandoned the Dutch Patriots to their unhappy fate and contented ourselves with recalling our Legation, or rather the
Ambassador, leaving a Chargé d'Affaires who was authorised to
wear the orange cockade on the grounds that he would be

assaulted if he went out without it. M. d'Osmond, Minister to The Hague, was ordered not even to consider joining his post.

Many Dutch Patriots took refuge in France, where they were not backward in spreading their very understandable discontent. Their accusations were of the liveliest interest to all those who were already discontented with the Government, but still had some hope of reforming it. And so, many good Frenchmen were drawn into the movement, still patriotic and loyal, which was doing all it could to bring about the changes which, to all thinking men of good will, seemed essential.

II

In 1787, my sister-in-law and very dear friend, Mme de Lameth, had to stay in Paris until October owing to the serious illness of her youngest son, who had almost died. The Colonels of M. Esterhazy's Division had been ordered to remain with their regiments and since M. de La Tour du Pin had in consequence received similar instructions, my sister-in-law suggested that I should go with her when she left for the country on the 1st of October. Her brother would then be able to join us as his Regiment was garrisoned at Saint-Omer, only a short day's ride from Hénéncourt.

I have such very happy memories of that journey. I had been so accustomed to the constraint which my grandmother's terrible character imposed on all the household at Montfermeil, that to live with my husband and his amiable sister seemed to change my whole existence. They were both very witty and gay. We went to Lille to see my brother-in-law, the Marquis de Lameth, who was there with his Régiment de la Couronne. Never had I enjoyed myself so much.

We returned to Hénéncourt, and there found the good Curé, an old man of ninety who lived in the château. He had celebrated his first Mass in the presence of Mme de Maintenon and remembered Saint-Cyr[1] in great detail. In my childhood, I had myself visited this admirable establishment with Mme Elisabeth,[2] who had had

[1] A boarding school for daughters of the nobility, founded by Mme de Maintenon. Now a military academy. (T)
[2] Sister of Louis XVI.

the kindness to take me on walks or to the hunt when I was with
my mother at Versailles.

When the Colonels were eventually allowed to return to Paris,
my husband and I went back to Montfermeil. My sister-in-law
was to remain in the country until the beginning of winter. It was
very fashionable then for Colonels to travel in uniform redingotes,
with two epaulettes, and for the ladies to wear very elegant riding
dress, the skirt slightly shorter than that normally used for riding.
It was essential that this dress, including the hat, should come
from London, the vogue for English fashions being just then at
the height of its extravagance. As a result I looked quite English.

III

Shortly afterwards, I found that I was pregnant and therefore
could not go with my uncle and my grandmother to Montpellier,
as we had planned. We had intended returning by way of Bordeaux
and Le Bouilh in order to visit my father-in-law. It was arranged
instead that while my family was away, I should stay with our
aunt, Mme d'Hénin. As she took me out into society, this was
both pleasanter and more convenient, for it was not customary in
those days for a young lady to go alone into company during the
first year of her marriage. Going out in the morning to visit
young friends or to the shops, she had to take a maid in the
carriage with her. There were even some of the older ladies who
carried their strictness to the point of disapproving that a young
lady should walk with her husband on the Champs Elysées, or
to the Tuileries, insisting that they should be accompanied by a
liveried footman. My husband found this convention intolerable
and we never observed it.

Once I was settled in my aunt's house, we went nearly every
day to the theatre. The plays finished early enough for people to
go out to supper afterwards. My aunt and I had permission to sit
in the Queen's boxes, a favour accorded to only six or eight of the
youngest ladies of her Household. The Queen had boxes at the
Opera, the Comédie Française and at the theatre known then as
the Comédie Italienne, where light operas were sung in French.
All we had to do was to look at the 'Journal de Paris' and choose
our theatre.

In each of these three theatres, the Queen's box was a stage one, furnished like a very elegant salon, with a large, well-heated and well-lit ante-room. The furnishings included a fully equipped dressing-table with everything necessary for repairing one's coiffure, should it be necessary, a writing table and so on. Stairs led to another ante-room where the servants waited. At the entrance was an usher in the King's livery. It was never necessary to wait a single minute for one's carriage. Usually, one arrived at the Comédie Italienne in time for the first piece, always the best, and at the Opera in time for the ballet. I record these rather trifling details only to emphasise the contrast with my present situation when, at the age of seventy-one, I cannot afford even forty 'sols'[1] to hire a miserable sedan chair to take me to mass on a wet Sunday.

As I was staying with my Aunt, this would seem to be the place to tell you something about the people in her circle. It was the most elegant and most highly-considered coterie in Paris and it received me into its midst during my very first winter in society. It consisted of four very distinguished ladies: Mme d'Hénin; the Princesse de Poix (née Beauvau); the Duchesse de Biron, who had recently lost her grandmother, the Maréchale de Luxembourg; and the Princesse de Bouillon (née Princesse de Hesse-Rothenbourg. They had all been linked since their youth in a friendship which was to them almost an article of faith, unfortunately perhaps the only one they had. They upheld one another, defended one another, adopted one another's ideas, friends, opinions and tastes. They protected any young woman connected with any one of them against all comers. By birth, they were all of importance and high rank, and they were all what we then called 'philosophes', or free-thinkers. Voltaire, Rousseau, d'Alembert, Condorcet, Suard and their like were not of this circle, but their principles and ideas were eagerly adopted by it and many gentlemen of these ladies' acquaintance did frequent this group of literary men which in those days was quite separate from the world of the Court.

It was M. Necker's ministry which was mainly responsible for

[1] An old form of the word 'sou'. (T)

the mingling of different classes which until then had kept themselves apart. When Mme Necker, that pedantic, priggish Genevan, moved with her husband into the lodgings of the Contrôleur-Général,[1] she brought with her a double following: those who admired her wit and those who admired her cook. Her daughter, Mme de Staël, was married to an Ambassador and therefore moved in Court circles. She, too, drew to M. Necker's house a number of people with intellectual leanings, including my aunt and her friends. The Maréchal de Beauvau, father of Mme de Poix, was on friendly terms with M. Necker, and his wife was one of the arbiters of Parisian society. It was essential, if you wished to acquire distinction, to have her approval and to be received by her. She gathered at her house and afforded a somewhat aloof patronage to a swarm of M. Turgot's[2] followers known as the 'Economists'.[3]

But let us return to my aunt. At the time of my marriage, Mme d'Hénin was thirty-eight. At the age of fifteen, she had married the seventeen-year old Prince d'Hénin, younger brother of the Prince de Chimay. They were much admired as the handsomest couple ever seen at Court. During the second year of her marriage, Mme d'Hénin caught smallpox and this illness, for which there was then no effective treatment, left on her face weeping scars which were never cured.

When I first met her, she was still very beautiful, with lovely hair, charming eyes, teeth like pearls, a magnificent figure and a most aristocratic bearing. Her marriage contract had stipulated separation of property and she lived with her mother until the latter's death. Although M. d'Hénin had an apartment in Mme de Monconseil's house, and was not separated in law from his wife, he none the less lived with an actress of the Comédie Française, a Mlle Raucourt, who ruined him.

Unfortunately for morals, such a situation was only too frequent and the Court, by its very indifference, did nothing to mend

---

[1] Minister of Finance, and in effect, the Prime Minister. (T)
[2] Anne-Robert-Jacques Turgot, Baron de l'Aulne (1727-1781). At one time Contrôleur-Général des Finances (Prime Minister). A great administrator and reformer, and one of the earliest economists, in the modern sense of the word. (T)
[3] A group of 18th-century writers concerned with economic problems. They were the first to make a study of this science. (T)

matters. It was considered amusing and quite unimportant. The first time I went to Longchamp with my aunt, our carriage often overtook or was overtaken by the carriage of this actress, which resembled our own in every detail. Horses, trappings, liveries all were so exactly alike that it was like looking at ourselves in a mirror. When society is so corrupt that corruption itself seems natural, and when no one is shocked at anything, why should anyone be astonished at excesses among the lower classes, who have been set such a bad example? Among the common people there are no shades of feeling: as soon as they have reason to despise or hate something above them, they abandon themselves to their feelings and know no restraint.

The shamelessness with which the ladies of high society flaunted their love affairs was notorious. Liaisons were known almost as soon as they began and if they lasted acquired a measure of acceptance. In the circle of the 'princesses combinées' as they were known, there were, however, certain exceptions to these scandalous ways. Mme de Poix, deformed, lame, helpless for a large part of the year, had never been accused of any intrigue. When I met her, she still had a charming face, despite her forty years. She was the most amiable person in the world.

Mme de Lauzun, who became Duchesse de Biron after the Marshal's death, was an angel of sweetness and kindness. After the death of her grandmother, the Maréchale de Luxembourg, who had owned the largest house in Paris and with whom she had lived, she bought a house in the Rue de Bourbon overlooking the river. She furnished it with a simple elegance that was as much in keeping with her considerable fortune as with the modesty of her nature. She lived there alone, for her husband followed the example of M. d'Hénin and lived with an actress of the Comédie Française. After the death of my mother, whose friendship and good influence had kept him in good company, he had become caught up in the set which surrounded the Duc d'Orléans— Egalité—who corrupted everything within his reach.

The Duchesse de Lauzun had a library of rare works, including many of Rousseau's manuscripts. Amongst them was that of *La Nouvelle Héloïse*, written entirely in his own hand, as well as a quantity of letters and notes written by him to Mme de Luxembourg. I particularly remember the letter he wrote to her explaining and justifying his incredibly cruel decision to send his children to a foundling home. In the same letter, were the most sympathetic, sensitive condolences on a misfortune which had just befallen Mme de Luxembourg: she had lost her dog! I believe that after Mme de Biron's sad death, all these precious manuscripts, as well as the rare editions in her collection were taken to the King's Library.

Mme la Princesse de Bouillon had been married very young to the last Duc de Bouillon, who was both half-witted and legless. She lived with him in the Hôtel de Bouillon on the Quai Malaquais. Naturally, he was never seen in public, remaining always in his apartments with his attendants. But he was brought every day to dine with his wife and I have sometimes seen the two places laid opposite one another. Thank Heaven, I never had the misfortune to meet this deformed piece of humanity, who had to be carried in his servants' arms. In the summer he went to his home in Navarre, that beautiful place which has since belonged to the Empress Josephine, but I believe that Mme de Bouillon went there rarely or never at all.

She was a woman of prodigious wit and charm: to my mind the most distinguished person I have ever met. She had never, at any time, been pretty. She was excessively thin, almost a skeleton, with a flat, Germanic face, a turned-up nose, ugly teeth and yellow hair. She was tall and ungraceful, would sink into the corner of a sofa, draw her legs up under her, cross her long skinny arms under her mantle and then, from that collection of fleshless bones, there would sparkle forth so much wit, originality and amusing conversation that one was carried away on the wings of enchantment. She showed me very great kindness and of this I was extremely proud. She was forty and I was eighteen, but she allowed me to visit her as if I had been her contemporary. My intense interest in her conversation pleased her and she would say to my aunt: 'The young Gouvernet came to be amused at my expense this morning.' I was very well aware that, at a quarter to two, one had to disappear in order to avoid meeting her 'cul de jatte'.[1]

---

[1] A person without legs or unable to use them.

Such a meeting would have distressed her greatly, for even after twenty years, she had never been able to accustom herself to his condition.

Yet this ugly, brilliant princess had had at least one lover. She even brought up a small girl who bore a striking resemblance both to herself and to Prince Emmanuel de Salm-Salm. He was generally accepted as her permanent lover, but at that time he was certainly no more than a friend. He was a very tall man, as thin as his mistress, and he always seemed to me rather insipid. He was considered learned. Perhaps he was, but if so, he kept the treasury of his knowledge very well locked and after a conversation with him, it was always impossible to remember what he had said.

Until the time of my marriage, the Chevalier de Coigny,[1] a brother of the Duc de Coigny and principal Equerry to the King, was my aunt's accredited lover. Such at least, was his reputation, and it might once have been true, but it was quite certain that for a very long time only the reputation had persisted, for he had formed another tie with Mme de Monsauge, widow of a 'fermier-général'[2] and mother of the charming Comtesse Etienne de Durfort. He later married her.

I was much attached to this stout, gay and amiable knight. He was fifty, so I talked to him as often as I could and he told me hundreds of anecdotes which I still remember and which would, perhaps, be amusing if I were to re-tell them here. Since I was destined to live in the highest ranks of society and at the Court, I listened with interest to his tales. A knowledge of the past would be very useful to me.

IV

I counted among my friends many people of the same age as the Chevalier de Coigny, the Comte de Thiard and the Duc de Guines, for they appreciated my evident pleasure in talking with them. My aunt's friends had decided that I ought to be 'a la mode'. I, on the other hand, had decided not to listen to any unbecoming

[1] Marie-François-Henri de Franquetot, Marquis and later Duc de Coigny, a peer and marshal of France. 1737–1821.
[2] Someone who leased from the Crown the taxes collected in a given area.

conversation from a young man, an easy decision since I was so
deeply in love with my husband. There was no severity or prudish-
ness in my attitude to young men, only that easy friendliness which
is so disconcerting to the flirtatious. Archambault de Périgord
used to say: 'Mme de Gouvernet is impossible; she treats all
young men as if they were her brothers.'

Women did not dislike me. As I envied no one, I drew attention to the good qualities of others, to their intelligence and their
clothes. This exasperated my aunt who, despite her superior
mind, had suffered many petty jealousies in her own youth and
was now suffering them all over again on my behalf.

I also knew how important it was to make friends among the
older women, who in those days were all-powerful. Before my
grandmother retired from society, or rather, before society
abandoned her, she had made many enemies and it was a handicap
to me to have grown up in her charge. I had to win my way back
into the favour of many who had loved my mother and who
looked on my grandmother's charge of me as a misfortune, almost
a fault.

I had renewed my childhood friendship with the Rochechouart
family. They moved in a quite different circle from that of my
aunt, but she was not unwilling that I should also frequent theirs.
I also saw many of my sister-in-law's friends, for although she
frequented, as I did, the company which surrounded my aunt,
she also had certain friendships of her own.

One house where we all visited and where I was received with
the most affectionate friendship was that of Mme de Montesson.
She loved M. de La Tour du Pin like a son. He had gone to live
with her after Mme de Monconseil's death and had remained
there until his marriage. She welcomed me with the greatest
kindness and I was very friendly with her great-niece, Mme de
Valence, daughter of Mme de Genlis. She was three years older
than me and was considered the model of everything that a young
lady should be. Her first child had died and she was expecting
another shortly.

Spiteful tongues suggested that Mme de Montesson, carried
away by a strong attachment to M. de Valence, had persuaded him
to marry her niece in order to have an excuse for devoting herself

entirely to him. I do not know what the truth was. She was old enough to have been his mother, but it cannot be denied that it was his influence which ruined her, for he advised her badly over the administration of the fine fortune left to her by the Duc d'Orléans.[1]

It was well known that she was the perfectly legitimate wife of the Duc d'Orléans. They had been married by Loménie, Archbishop of Toulouse, in the Church of Saint-Eustache, in Paris, in the presence of the Curé of the Church. However, the King refused to recognise the marriage and Mme de Montesson no longer went to Court. The Duc d'Orléans left his apartments in the Palais Royal and went to live in the Rue de Provence, in a house communicating with one which Mme de Montesson had just bought in the Chaussée d'Antin. All the inside dividing walls had been pulled down and the two gardens made into one. However, the Duc d'Orléans had his own entrance in the Rue de Provence, with a porter in his livery, and Mme de Montesson had hers with a porter in grey livery. But they shared the same courtyard.

When I entered society, Mme de Montesson had just put off her widow's mourning and emerged from retirement in the Convent of the Assumption. This retirement had been forced on her by the Court's refusal to allow her to wear mourning in public or to dress her servants in black. Invitations to her house were much sought after, for she entertained the best company in Paris, also the most distinguished, from the very oldest ladies to the very youngest. She no longer gave fêtes or entertainments, as she had done while the Duc d'Orléans was alive, and this I much regretted. She adopted me immediately as if I had been a daughter.

Such was my introduction to society while staying with Mme d'Hénin. My family had prolonged their visit to Languedoc and when they returned, in about February 1788, I in my turn found myself in circumstances which prevented me leaving my aunt to rejoin them.

As the result of a miscarriage, I was confined to my bed. It had been caused by an excess of blood, I believe, or perhaps it was only the consequence of an imprudence at Versailles. Hearing

[1] Louis-Philippe, Duc d'Orléans, 1725–1785. Father of Philippe Egalité.

nine o'clock strike as I passed through the gallery one Sunday evening, and fearing that the Queen would already have entered, I started to run. But my paniers caught in a doorway and I was considerably shaken. At the time, I felt no ill effects and returned to Paris. But two days later I became ill. This accident caused me a two-fold grief—my own personal grief and the disappointment I knew it would cause my excellent father-in-law.

When my grandmother returned to Paris, she came to see me. Extreme weakness still forced me to remain in bed, but she pretended to think it was an excuse for not leaving my aunt's house. From our conversations, she soon learned of my success in society, of the warm welcome I had received from a large number of people whom she detested and of the attentions and kindnesses of my mother's friends. This roused in her a deadly spite and I think it was then that she resolved to seize upon the first pretext that offered to oblige us to leave my uncle's house. I did return, nevertheless, to the Hôtel Dillon. A charming suite of rooms had been arranged for me on the mansard floor, but unfortunately the only entrance was by way of a small, ugly, winding stair which passed close to my grandmother's dressing room.

I cannot remember the exact sequence of the events which led to the break with my relatives, but the major causes of this domestic catastrophe were my grandmother's unyielding hatred of M. de La Tour du Pin, her boundless jealousy of my uncle's liking for him and a fear that my uncle might be led into speaking to my husband of his affairs, thereby divulging her own and all the liabilities she had undertaken on his behalf. After many months of repeated clashes, and incited by bad counsellors, my grandmother asked us to leave her house. Despite my tears and the pleading of my uncle, the Archbishop, whose affection we had won but who was too frightened of my grandmother to oppose her, we had to leave the Hôtel Dillon and were never to return. It was in June 1788.

My aunt most kindly took us into her house. But despite all the unhappiness which my grandmother's character had caused me, I felt a very deep grief at separating from my family. Society was divided in its sympathies. Some attributed to me wrongs of which I was innocent. Former friends of my mother defended me

warmly. The Queen was among them. Nor did M. de La Tour
du Pin escape criticism. He was accused of violence, of hastiness
and so on. In short, it was one of the most painful incidents of my
life. I knew then my first real grief and the memory of it still
causes me a very lively regret. but I cannot reproach myself for
any fault which might have caused it.

CHAPTER EIGHT

I

My aunt, Mme d'Hénin, gave us an apartment in her house in the
Rue de Verneuil, a ground floor apartment looking out on to a
small and exceedingly dismal garden. We did not want to be
dependent on her and had a cook of our own to prepare meals
for our servants and for ourselves when my aunt dined out or
was in waiting at Court.

My good Marguerite, who had never left me, withstood all my
grandmother's offers, promises of promotion, even her pleading,
and remained with me. I had a very great affection for this good
woman and my trust in her was limitless.

We spent the summer of 1788 at Passy, in a house which Mme
d'Hénin, Mme de Poix, Mme de Bouillon and Mme de Biron
rented together. My aunt and I lived there all the time; the others
came to stay in turn. I was again expecting a baby and took the
greatest care to avoid another mischance. But for the first three
months of my pregnancy, I continued to attend the Court at
Versailles; it was not customary to do so beyond that period.

The Queen was kind enough to excuse me from accompanying
her to Mass, fearing I might walk too fast and slip on the parquet.
I remained in her room while she was in Chapel and so came to
know in detail the routine of the waiting women. It consisted in
making the bed, removing every trace of the Queen's toilet, and
wiping the tables and other pieces of furniture. To anyone used
to the ways of today, it would seem very odd that their first
action was to open the immense double curtains which surrounded

the bed. The next was to remove the bed linen and pillows, tossing them into immense baskets lined with green taffetas. Four footmen in livery then came to turn the mattresses, which were too heavy for women to lift. The footmen then withdrew and the four women put on white sheets and arranged the covers. The whole task took five minutes, so that although Mass, including the walk to and from Chapel, did not last more than twenty-five to thirty minutes, I was there alone for a fairly long time, sitting in an armchair near the window. When there were large numbers of people present, the Queen, who was always thoughtful, would tell me as she passed, to go and sit in the card-room so that I would not have to stand too long and get tired.

These precautions prevented me from attending the reception given for the ambassadors of Tippoo-Sahib, which was a very splendid affair. They had come to ask the support of France against the English. But we gave them only words, as we had done to the Dutch. These three Indians stayed several months in Paris, at the King's expense, taken everywhere in a carriage drawn by six horses. I often saw them at the Opera, and in other public places. They were all of fine, light, Hindu colouring, with white beards to their waists, and very richly dressed. At the Opera, a fine stage box was reserved for them. Seated in large armchairs, they often propped their yellow, babouche-shod feet on the edge of the box, to the delight of the public who, let it be said, had no fault to find with this custom.

II

M. de La Tour du Pin had just been appointed Colonel of the Régiment de Royal-Vaisseaux. Discipline in this Regiment was very slack, not among the soldiers and non-commissioned officers, where it was excellent, but among the officers, who had been spoiled by their former Colonel, M. d'Ossun, husband of the Queen's Mistress of the Robes. My husband was very strict in matters of discipline and when he took command of the Regiment, he found that despite the fact that there were twenty-two Knights of Malta in their ranks, these gentlemen were not carrying out their duties. Noticing that the Regiment's daily drill was taken by the non-commissioned officers and the Lieutenant-Colonel,

M. de Kergaradec, M. de La Tour du Pin announced that he himself would attend the drill every day at sunrise and that he expected all the officers to be present. This roused a storm of fury.

There was to be a camp that year at Saint-Omer, under the command of the Prince de Condé. The Régiment de Royal-Vaisseaux had been chosen to demonstrate certain new tactical groupings which had just been issued. The officers were annoyed rather than flattered at being chosen for this distinction. It meant an end to the lazy, negligent ways into which they had been allowed to fall. They felt no shame at combining together to resist all the reproofs of their commanding officer. Punishments, arrests, imprisonments —nothing would induce them to carry out their duties. The officers even passed a resolution not to see their Colonel, except on official occasions, when it could not be avoided. All his invitations to dinner were refused. It was almost open mutiny and it lasted right through the summer; then the camp was set up and the Regiment reported there for duty. The first manoeuvre at which it was to demonstrate the new methods was a failure. M. de La Tour du Pin was furious. He informed the Prince de Condé of the bad spirit in the Regiment, or rather, among its officers, and the Prince said that if they had not improved by the next manoeuvres, he would have them all put under arrest for the entire duration of the camp. Command of the companies would be given to the non-commissioned officers. This threat was effective. When the camp broke up, the Inspector, the Duc de Guines, also made it known that there would be no awards to officers of the Royal-Vaisseaux, neither Crosses of Saint-Louis nor the customary six months' leave. The Colonel would spend the whole winter in garrison. At that, these fine gentlemen submitted and made their apologies to M. de La Tour du Pin. Their conduct became irreproachable, but the damage had already been done. They had set an example which a year later was to prove only too effective.

III

While all this was happening at Saint-Omer, I was leading a pleasant existence at Passy with my aunt and one or two of her friends. I went often to Paris and also spent some time at Berny

with Mme de Montesson, who continued to show me much
kindness. At Berny, I very often met the aged Prince Henry of
Prussia, a brother of Frederick the Great. He was a man of considerable military and literary ability, a great admirer of all the
'philosophes' whom his brother had made so welcome at his
Court, and in particular of Voltaire. He had a more thorough knowledge of our literature than any Frenchman. He knew all our
plays by heart and would recite whole speeches in an incredibly
bad German accent and with a foreign intonation so ridiculous
that we found it very difficult not to laugh.

IV

As I am not writing a history of the Revolution, I will not speak
of all the conversations, discussions, or even of the arguments
which differing opinions gave rise to in society. At eighteen, I
found all these arguments very tedious and tried to find distraction in going as often as possible to a charming house to which
I was drawn by childhood friendships which had deepened,
particularly since the day I had to leave my family. This was the
Hôtel de Rochechouart, one of those patriarchal houses, whose
like will not be seen again, in which many generations mingled
without any sense of strain, without tedium and without making
exacting claims on one another.

Mme de Courteille, a very rich widow, had married her only
daughter to the Comte de Rochechouart. She lived with her
daughter, her son-in-law and their two daughters in a fine, and
very large house they had built in the Rue de Grenelle. Mme de
Rochechouart had been my mother's closest friend and I had
spent my childhood with her two daughters, one of whom was
four years older than me and the other two years older. The elder
had been married, at the age of fifteen, to the Duc de Piennes,
later the Duc d'Aumont. She was amiable and agreeable to look
at without being exactly pretty. M. de Piennes followed the
custom of the highest society in those days and was the acknowledged and declared lover of Mme de Reuilly, which made his wife
very unhappy. She loved him and was very grieved by his bad
behaviour, trying to keep it carefully hidden, she never uttered a
complaint. By this ill-assorted marriage there were two children,

two boys, the younger—the only one still alive—being an albino. His hair, his eyebrows and his eyelashes were like white silk. His eyes, light blue and red, like those of an angora rabbit. He could not stand the light and had a little green taffetas shade which, as a child, he wore continuously. The elder, charming in appearance and very witty, was killed in the Crimea.

Of the two Rochechouart sisters, it was the younger, Rosalie, who was my closest friend. She had been married at the age of twelve years and one day to the grandson of the Maréchal de Richelieu, the Comte de Chinon, himself only fifteen. The wedding dinner was held at the Hôtel de Richelieu and all generations were represented, from that of the Maréchal whose first marriage had taken place during the reign of Louis XIV, to that of the bride's friends, little girls of my own age. Immediately after this dinner, the bridegroom left with his tutor to travel throughout Europe. It was early in 1782 when he set out and when he returned to France during the winter of 1788 or 1789, he was a tall, handsome young man of excellent character.

There were rejoicings in the Hôtel de Rochechouart on his return, but his poor wife was far from sharing the general joy. At fourteen she had become completely hunchbacked, and was afraid that her husband would find this deformity distasteful. She had no illusions that her musical talent, her lovely voice, her wide knowledge, her adorable nature and her lofty mind would make her husband, almost unknown so far as she was concerned, forget such an infirmity.

Misfortune was heaped on misfortune, and the poor young man found on his return that his two sisters, born of his father's second marriage, were also as misshapen as his wife. One later became Mme de Montcalm, and the other Mme de Jumilhac. This trio of hunchbacks gave him a horror of France.

At the first sign of the coming Revolution, he emigrated and went to Russia where he served as a volunteer in the armies of the Empress Catherine II, covering himself with glory in the Russian war against the Turks. He was with the army which captured Ismail and distinguished himself very highly. After the deaths of his grandfather and his father, he was appointed First Gentleman of the Bedchamber.

He returned to France during the Consulate, but later went back to Russia, and did not return for good until the Restoration. He spent many of the intervening years as Governor of Odessa.

V

My baby was born in December 1788, but with such difficulty that I very nearly died. After twenty-four hours of terrible pain, I brought into the world a child who was stillborn, strangled during its birth. I was not immediately aware of this, for I was unconscious and two hours later was suffering the agony of puerperal fever.

Towards the end of the winter, I began to pick up the threads of my social life and went once again to sing at the Hôtel de Rochechouart.

The musical gatherings there were very distinguished. They were held once a week, but if a piece called for several players or singers, there were rehearsals as well. Mme Mongeroux, a famous pianist of the day, played the piano; an Italian singer from the Opera sang the tenor parts; Mandini, another Italian, sang the bass; Mme de Richelieu was the prima donna; I sang the contralto; M. de Duras the baritone; the choruses were sung by other good amateurs. Viotti accompanied us on the violin. We executed the most difficult finales in this way. Everyone took the greatest pains and Viotti was excessively severe. Another critic at our rehearsals was M. de Rochechouart himself, a born musician, who let no fault pass unremarked.

When dinner time came, we would often be in the middle of a finale. As soon as we heard the bell, everyone took up their hat and then Mme de Rochechouart would come in saying that there was enough for us all. And so we would stay and continue the rehearsal after dinner. It was not really a morning's music, but a day's music.

On the evening of the final performance, there would always be an audience of about fifty people of all generations. Mme de Courteille would be in her sitting-room playing trictrac with her old friends, but from time to time she would come to the music room to watch what was known as 'la belle jeunesse'.

Nowadays I live out of the world, and cannot judge today's

society. But from what I am told, I doubt if there exists anywhere the ease, harmony, good manners and absence of all pretention which was to be found then in all the great houses of Paris. Usually, three generations lived together in the same house, but they did not irk one another or clash in any way. It seems that these gatherings of all the generations are now things of the past and that, to M. de Talleyrand's great regret, old ladies are no longer to be met in society.

It must have been in about the spring of that year that the Duke of Dorset was succeeded as English Ambassador by Lord Gower and his charming wife, Lady Sutherland. Before the Duke left Paris, he gave a grand ball, the supper being so arranged that we sat at small tables in a gallery whose walls were entirely hidden by foliage. At the bottom of the invitation cards was the blunt instruction: 'Ladies will wear white.' This kind of command annoyed me and in protest I ordered a charming dress in blue crepe, with flowers of the same colour. My gloves were trimmed with blue ribbons, my fan was of a similar shade and there were blue feathers in my hair, which was dressed by Léonard. This small revolt earned me a certain success and people did not omit to quote 'Blue bird, blue skies'. Even the Duke of Dorset was amused and observed that the Irish had always been an unruly race.

VI

Amid all these pleasures, we were drawing near to the month of May 1789, laughing and dancing our way to the precipice. Thinking people were content to talk of abolishing all the abuses. France, they said, was about to be re-born. The word 'revolution' was never uttered. Had anyone dared to use it he would have been thought mad. In the upper classes, this illusion of security misled the wise who wanted to see an end to the abuses and to the wasting of public money. That is why so many upright and honourable people, including the King himself, who fully shared the illusion, hoped that they were about to enter a Golden Age.

Now that I have lived through so many events in the course of a long life, I am amazed at the utter blindness of the unfortunate King and his Ministers. There is no possible doubt that the Duc d'Orléans had his secret preparations well in hand long before the meeting of the States-General. But the proclamation he sent to all the bailiwicks where he owned property appeared, on the surface, to be a most patriotic document professing the loftiest intentions. The proclamation was carried by a number of people of the highest birth who represented him in the local assemblies of nobles. These representatives were candidates for nomination as deputies to the States-General. M. de La Tour du Pin went to Nemours with the Vicomte de Noailles, brother of the Prince de Poix; but M. de Noailles won more votes than my husband, who also failed to get himself elected at Grenoble, where he went to represent his father. His father was elected in Saintonge.

I remember that some presentiment made me very glad that M. de La Tour du Pin was not elected to that Assembly which was to prove so disastrous to us. But my gladness really sprang from being released from the long, tedious hours of never-ending political conversations to which I had had to listen every day. People who frequented my aunt's company and my aunt herself were never short of ideas for reforming abuses and for establishing a fairer distribution of taxes. People were particularly insistent on the need to base the new French Constitution on that of England, which very few people knew anything about. M. de Lally[1] himself, despite his claim to know it thoroughly, was unaware of its details. Yet he was consulted as an authority. He spoke so well that he charmed the ladies, who listened to him with delight. He had completely turned my aunt's head and she had no doubt at all that he would be a great success in the States-General.

He had just been elected a deputy to the Assembly of Nobles in Paris. I was present at one of the first of this Assembly's meetings. We were twenty or thirty ladies, hidden behind the curtains of the galleries arranged in the windows of the hall. An odd coincidence drew everyone's attention to M. de Lally. When the officials were being appointed, the two names drawn first from the ballot box to fill the posts of the two Secretaries to the Assembly, were those of M. de Lally and M. d'Epremesnil, President of the Parlement de Paris.[2] Now, M. d'Epremesnil had been the judge-

[1] Trophime-Gérard, Marquis de Lally-Tollendal.
[2] The High Judicial Court of Paris. There was one in each province.

advocate at the tribunal which had sent M. de Lally's father, General de Lally, to the scaffold in 1766. In all the various courts where M. de Lally had tried to have his father's honour cleared, M. d'Epremesnil had opposed his plea, doing everything in his power to uphold the condemnation. His opposition was marked with such passionate animosity that a strong hatred had sprung up between the two men. They were as fire and water. Therefore, when the two secretaries were nominated, and left their places at the back of the hall to sit side by side at the desk, a very noticeable murmur of sympathy for M. de Lally arose. He was applauded wildly when, in a few short words of thanks to the Assembly for his nomination, he declared that all private dissensions must disappear in face of the public good.

The nomination of the President also caused something of a sensation. M. de Clermont-Tonnerre, a young man as distinguished by his charming appearance and his eloquence as by his rare qualities of intelligence and the strength of his character was appointed to this high office. He made a good speech, certainly extempore, for he could not have expected to be appointed President of an Assembly in which he was the youngest member. His fine figure, his speech and his eloquence produced an effect on the young and beautiful Princesse Lubomirska, who was sitting beside me, which was to end by causing her death. They evoked in her such a violent passion for M. de Clermont-Tonnerre that she refused to leave Paris and so became one of the first victims of the Terror.

In the early spring of 1789, after a terrible winter which caused much suffering among the poor, the Duc d'Orléans—Egalité— was extremely popular in Paris. The previous year he had sold many paintings from the fine collection in the palace and it was generally believed that the eight millions raised by this sale had been devoted to relieving the sufferings of the people during the hard winter which had just ended. In contrast, whether rightly or wrongly, there was no mention of any charitable gifts from the royal princes or from the King and Queen. That unfortunate princess had fallen entirely under the influence of the Polignac family. She no longer went to the theatre in Paris. The people never saw her or her children. Nor did the King ever show himself.

Hidden away at Versailles, or busy hunting in the nearby forests, he suspected nothing, foresaw nothing and believed nothing he was told.

The Queen hated the Duc d'Orléans, who had spoken ill of her. He had wanted his son, the Duc de Chartres, to marry Madame Royale. The Comte d'Artois also wanted the hand of this princess for his son, the Duc d'Angoulême, and this was the marriage favoured by the Queen. The Duc d'Orléans' request was therefore refused, and he took it as a mortal affront. His visits to Versailles were rare and I do not remember ever having seen him in the Queen's apartments at the hour when all the princes came, that is to say, just before Mass. Since he was never in his apartments at Versailles, I had not been officially presented to him and whenever he met me at the house of Mme de Montesson, he always jokingly asked Mme d'Hénin my name. I none the less attended the suppers at the Palais-Royal, which were very brilliant that winter.

I attended the one given to christen the fine silver service which the Duc d'Orléans had ordered from Arthur, the great silversmith of the day. I remember that it seemed to me too light and too English in shape, but that was the fashion. Everything had to be copied from our neighbours, from the Constitution to horses and carriages. Some young men, like Charles de Noailles, went so far as to affect an English accent and made a study of all the awkwardnesses of manner, the style of walking, in fact, all the outward signs of an Englishman, so that they could adopt them for their own use. They envied me because people in public places would often exclaim when they saw me: 'There's an Englishwoman!' They thought it a compliment.

VII

Since I have mentioned M. de Lally at the moment when he had become a man of some note, it is right that I should tell you something of his origins, for he, his father and grandfather had all been born bastards—a strange coincidence in a family, and probably unique.

Gerard Lally, great-grandfather of the Lally of whom I am speaking, was a poor Irish gentleman who supported James II.

I think he came from somewhere on my great uncle's[1] estate. He seduced Lord Dillon's daughter and after the birth of their son Lord Dillon insisted on their marrying and legitimising the child. This first bastard distinguished himself in the wars of James II, who created him a baronet and gave him permission to raise troops on his grandfather's land. He accompanied James II to France and died, if I am not mistaken, at Saint-Germain. Although he never married, he left a natural son, born to him by a lady in Normandy whose name I have never known. This son became Général de Lally, who was condemned to death and executed in 1766.[2] He first went to war at the age of twelve, distinguished himself in all the wars of the reign of Louis XV, and accompanied Prince Charles-Edward on his glorious campaign of 1745 which ended in the disastrous defeat at Culloden in 1746.

It was said that on his return to France he fell very much in love with my grandmother. What is certain is that he had a most tender friendship with Miss Mary Dillon, the Archbishop's eldest sister. Miss Dillon never married and died at Saint-Germain-en-Laye in 1786. For a very long time she was on bad terms with the Archbishop. Their quarrel, caused originally by a clash of interests, was prolonged by the unfortunate meddling of Mme de Rothe, my grandmother, who hated Miss Dillon and feared her influence over the Archbishop. For this reason, I did not see Miss Dillon until the year before her death. She had become reconciled to my uncle and we often went to see her at Saint-Germain. But let us return to the Lally family and the third case of bastardy, to which they seemed to be condemned. Before Général de Lally went to India as Governor of the French possessions there, he had had an affair with a Comtesse de Maulde, the wife of a Flemish gentleman, and a son was born to them. He was sent, under an assumed name, to the Jesuit college in Paris.

Miss Mary Dillon was in Général de Lally's confidence and looked after the child. After the General's execution—in which the Jesuits played a dastardly part—it was decided to move the child. When he was told who he was, he determined to do everything

[1] Henry, 8th Viscount Dillon.
[2] French Governor defeated by the English at Pondichéry, and executed as a traitor on his return from India. (T)

possible to restore his father's honour. When he was eighteen, he began his appeals and for twenty years this cause was his sole occupation and he thought of nothing else. He inherited little from his father and lived with Miss Dillon. When I met him there in 1785 he had recently won his case, after pleading in person before three High Judicial Courts. He was then 35, a fine looking man but with something of effeminacy about him which I did not like.

Much of the credit for his success must go to Miss Dillon. Her influence over him was complete, and she had devoted herself to his interests. He lost her in 1786, and she left him everything of which she was free to dispose. This amounted only to furniture. But she had also arranged that he could continue to live in the apartment she had occupied at Saint-Germain, the one given by Louis XIV to her father when he arrived at the Castle with James II. She had been born there, as had also been her ten brothers and sisters, of whom the Archbishop of Narbonne was the youngest. When my father came back from the West Indies, he was very sorry that the apartment had not been kept in the family, for it was the cradle of the Dillons in France. It would have been more tactful, too, if M. de Lally had refused to accept from among the things left to him the many family souvenirs. They were of no interest to him, but they had great value for my father and me by reason of their origin.

CHAPTER NINE

———————◆———————

I

About that time, that is to say, in 1789, I happened to make a strange acquaintance: Mme de Genlis, tutor[1] to the young Princes

---

[1] The Duc d'Orléans (Egalité) insisted on Mme de Genlis being called, rather unusually, a 'tutor'—it implicitly emphasised his children's royalty. Royal children had a 'gouverneur' (tutor), others a 'gouvernante' (governess). When he asked the King's permission to do so, Louis XVI shrugged his shoulders and replied, as he walked away: 'Tutor or governess, you are entitled to call her as you please. In any case, the Comte d'Artois has children'.

of Orléans[1] and their thirteen-year old sister, Mademoiselle.[2] She lived with Mademoiselle at the Convent of Belle-Chasse, in a very small pavilion which had been especially built for her. Also living in the pavilion were Paméla, later Lady Edward Fitz-Gerald, of whom I will tell you more, and Henriette de Sercey, both of whom were educated with the Princess. Mme de Genlis was responsible for the Princes' education also, but they did not sleep at the pavilion. They came very early each morning and stayed until after supper, when they went back with their assistant-tutor to the Palais Royal. As I had often met them, and was extremely friendly with Mme de Valence, the daughter of Mme de Genlis, Mme de Montesson used to invite me sometimes to her house when the two young Princes were there. Mme de Genlis took a great liking to me and wanted me to come to the small evening dances which were held once a week that winter. They always ended before eleven o'clock and were not followed by a supper.

The Duc de Chartres was beginning to go out into society, that is to say, he was sometimes present at the Palais Royal suppers. He had entered the Army and been admitted to the Order of the Holy Ghost. He was heavily built, very ungraceful and awkward, with pale, heavy cheeks and a sly expression, a solemn, shy boy. Some considered him cultivated, even learned, but in those frivolous, carefree days, it was very easy to appear more learned than was really the case. But it must be admitted that the system of education adopted by Mme de Genlis, strange though it may then have seemed in a world so full of affectations and absurdities, did in fact have advantages, particularly when compared with the education given by the Duc de Sérent to the two children of the Comte d'Artois. They were never seen and knew as little of France as if they had been heirs to the throne of China. The Princes of the House of Orléans, on the other hand, devoted their walks and their leisure to everything improving and instructive. They knew something of the various trades, of machines,

---

[1] The Duc de Chartres (1773–1850), later King Louis-Philippe of the French; the Duc de Montpensier (1775–1807) and the Comte de Beaujolais (1779–1808). (T)
[2] Louise-Eugénie-Adélaide d'Orléans, whose influence over her eldest brother was considerable, even in matters of government, after he became King. (T)

libraries, restaurants, public monuments and the arts. They became known to the people, and in the case of the one Prince who lived to grow up,[1] events have shown this to have been an advantage. In the days of which I am speaking, the two younger Princes were still children. I was often present at their supper on the evenings when there was dancing. The other guests had supper at home or with friends, for there was never any question of eating at Belle-Chasse or of drinking anything there except water. The Princes' supper was extremely frugal, perhaps exaggeratedly so. Mme de Genlis did not have supper with them, and Henriette de Sercey and Paméla found the greatest satisfaction in making their soup go further by adding a large glass of water and then breaking pieces of dried bread into it.

Since I have mentioned Paméla, I will tell you something of her origin. Mme de Genlis said that she had adopted the child in England, but everyone was perfectly certain that she was her own daughter by the Duc d'Orléans. I have, however, reason to believe that Mme de Genlis was telling the truth. My aunt, Lady Jerningham, was closely acquainted with a clergyman in Shropshire who, in his turn, was a very close acquaintance of Mme de Genlis. One day he received a letter from her saying that 'for reasons of particularly great importance' she wished to undertake the education of a little girl of five or six. She went on to describe the child in great detail. A large sum was to be paid to the parents, on condition that they kept the whole affair absolutely secret. They were not even to know the name of the person to whom the child's education was entrusted, only that her education would be in every way superior to her station and that she was destined to very great fortune.

The clergyman found a child exactly answering to the description given by Mme de Genlis and sent her to the place in London that had been arranged. Lady Jerningham was certain that this child was Paméla. Nothing could have been more charming than the child's appearance when I first knew her. Her face was quite flawless, her every movement graceful, her smile angelic and her teeth pearly white. When she was eighteen, that is to say, in 1792, Lord Edward Fitz-Gerald, fifth son of the Duke of Leinster, fell

[1] Later King Louis-Philippe.

madly in love with her, married her and took her to Ireland, where he was the leader of the Rebel United Irishmen. When her husband died,[1] she returned to the Continent and settled at Hamburg, where she married the American consul, Mr Pitcairn. The really strange part of the whole story is that Mme de Genlis did, in fact, have an illegitimate daughter whose father was Philippe Egalité. But she hated her from the very beginning and when her legitimate daughter married M. de Valence, she gave her this illegitimate child, Hermine, who was then eight or ten years old, saying that in educating her, Mme de Valence would be serving an apprenticeship for the education she would later have to give her own children. Hermine married a stockbroker named Collard and one of her many daughters—Mme Cappelle—was the mother of the notorious Mme Lafarge.[2]

II

Never had people been so pleasure-seeking as in the spring of 1789, before the meeting of the States-General.[3] For the poor, the winter had been very hard, but there was no concern for the misery of the people. There were races at Vincennes, where the horses of the Duc d'Orléans ran against those of the Comte d'Artois. It was after the last of these races, as we were driving home along the Rue Saint-Antoine with Mme de Valence, that we found ourselves in the midst of the first riot, the one which destroyed the worthy Réveillon's wallpaper factory. It was not until long afterwards that I realised the true significance of that mob, which was a hired one.

M. de Valence was at the time First Equerry to the Duc d'Orléans and as we passed through the crowd of four or five hundred people which filled the street, the sight of the Orléans

[1] Having arranged French assistance for an Irish rising, he returned to Ireland in 1798 to organise it. Trying to evade arrest he was wounded and died on the 4th of June, 1798. (T)
[2] Born in 1816, and married against her will, she was eventually accused of murdering her husband. After twelve years' hard labour, she was pardoned but died a year later, in 1853. (T)
[3] The oldest and most important of the nation's assemblies. It consisted of representatives of the three estates of the realm and each order had a collective vote. The States-General could be summoned only by the King, and represented the King's real power against factional interests. (T)

livery roused their enthusiasm. For a few minutes they held up
the carriage shouting 'Long Live our Father! Long Live King
d'Orléans!' At the time, I paid little attention to these cries, but
a few months later, when I had certain knowledge of the activities
of the scheming Duc d'Orléans, they returned to my mind. The
popular movement which ruined Réveillon had been organised,
I have not the slightest doubt, with the purpose of getting rid
of him. He was a good man who employed three to four hundred
workers and enjoyed an excellent reputation in the Faubourg
Saint-Antoine.

Here is the story as he used to tell it himself. In his early youth,
he worked—at which trade I cannot remember—in that same
Faubourg where he always lived. On his way to work one day,
he saw a fellow workman, a poor man and the father of a family,
being taken off to gaol for some petty debt. The man was desperate
at having to leave his wife and children in such terrible poverty,
knowing that his own imprisonment would only increase their
wretchedness. Convinced that Providence had intended this
meeting, Réveillon rushed to a second-hand shop, sold his tools,
his clothes, everything he possessed, paid the debt and restored
this father to his family. 'From that moment,' he used to say,
'everything I have done has prospered. I have made a fortune, I
employ four hundred workers and I can amply afford gifts of
charity'. He was simple, just and adored by his workmen. I do
not know what became of him after that dreadful evening when
his printing blocks, his machines and his warehouses were burned
and destroyed.

III

As soon as the elections were over, everyone prepared to move to
Versailles. All the members of the States-General set about finding
apartments in the town, those who were attached to the Court
transferring their family and household to the apartments reserved for them in the Château. At that time, my aunt had an
apartment there and I lodged with her. It was on an upper floor,
above the Galerie des Princes.[1] The room which I occupied

---

[1] In the wing of the Château overlooking the south garden and the Orangery
terrace, between the terrace and the Rue de la Sur-Intendance.

looked out over the roofs, but my aunt's room overlooked the terrace and had a very fine view. It was only on Saturday nights that we slept there. As Governor of Versailles, M. de Poix had a charming small house with a pretty garden at the Ménagérie,[1] and this he lent to my aunt who established herself there with all her servants, her cook, her horses, my own saddle-horses and my English groom. It was a very pleasant house. Everyone was at Versailles and we all awaited, amid much gaiety and without the slightest feeling of anxiety—visible anxiety, at any rate—the opening of that Assembly which was to give birth to a new France.

Looking back at our blindness, I can understand it in young people like myself, but find it inexplicable in men of the world, in Ministers and above all, in the King.

I have forgotten why I did not accompany the Queen and all her Household to the procession after Mass on the Feast of Pentecost. I went to watch it cross the Place d'Armes, as it always did, on its way from one parish of Versailles to the other.[2] We were with Mme de Poix in one of the windows of the Grande Ecurie. The Queen looked sad and cross. Did she, perhaps, have some presentiment of what lay before her?

M. de La Tour du Pin was so annoyed at not being elected to the States-General that he did not even wish to attend the opening session. It was a magnificent spectacle but has been described so often in memoirs of the period that I shall forbear to do so. The King wore the robes of the Order of the Holy Ghost, as did all the Princes, with the difference that the King's were more richly embroidered and very thickly encrusted with diamonds. This good prince was not dignified in appearance. He stood badly and walked with a waddle; his movements were abrupt and lacking in grace; his sight was very poor, and since it was not customary to wear spectacles, he used to screw up his face. His speech was short, and he delivered it in a fairly firm voice. The Queen's great dignity was much commented on, but it was plain from the almost convulsive way in which she used her fan that she was very agitated.

[1] A house standing alone in the Great Park, at the end of one arm of the canal, facing the Trianon.
[2] Saint-Louis in the Rue Satory and Notre Dame in the Rue de la Paroisse.

She often looked towards that part of the Chamber where the Third Estate was sitting and seemed to be trying to seek out a face in the ranks of that mass of men among whom she already had so many enemies.

A few minutes before the King entered, there was an incident which I saw with my own eyes, and it was seen by everyone present, but I cannot remember ever having seen it mentioned in accounts of that memorable session. Everyone knows that the Marquis de Mirabeau, having failed because of his dreadful reputation to get himself elected to the Provençal Assembly of Notables, was afterwards elected by the Third Estate. He entered the Chamber alone and took his place towards the middle of the rows of backless benches which stretched one behind the other. There arose a very low, but widespread murmur—a 'sussurro'— and the deputies already seated in front of him moved one bench forward, while those behind him removed to a distance. He thus remained isolated in the middle of a very marked space. Smiling contemptuously, he sat down. This situation lasted several minutes and then, as the crush of members increased, those who had moved away were forced nearer and the empty space became gradually filled.

The Queen had probably been told that there would be such an incident, one which was perhaps to influence her fate more than she suspected at the time, and this is the probable explanation of her curious glances at the benches of the Third Estate.

The speech of M. Necker, Minister of Finance, seemed to me unbearably dull. It lasted more than two hours and, to my nineteen-year-old ears, seemed never-ending. The ladies were seated on fairly wide benches which rose in tiers and had nothing to lean against except the knees of the person behind. The first row was naturally reserved for the ladies of the Court who were not in attendance, a fact which obliged them to maintain an impeccable attitude throughout the entire proceedings, and which they found exceedingly tiring. I think I have never felt so weary as during that speech, though M. Necker's supporters praised it to the skies.

All the opening stages of that Constituent Assembly are well known. They are recorded in history and it is not a history that I am writing. On the 1st of June, my husband, like the other Colonels, joined his Regiment. He was garrisoned at Valenciennes and was therefore not with the troops assembled at the gates of Paris under the command of Maréchal de Broglie, the troops which, as a result of that fatal hesitancy whenever a firm decision was essential, were not used when the crucial moment came. The Queen knew only how to show displeasure, not how to act. She merely retreated It must also be admitted that encroachments on the royal authority were so novel that neither the King nor the Queen realised that there was any real danger. It did not occur to them that there was anything worse to fear than some small revolt like that against the shortage of food—the 'flour war', as it was called—at the beginning of their reign.

It was soon realised that the Constituent Assembly would go further than had at first been expected, but no one doubted that it would be easy to check the spirit of change which was creeping in everywhere. When the King went to the Assembly on the 23rd of June, he had no idea, poor Prince, that his presence only drove the innovators underground. If anyone had tried to tell him that his army was corrupted, that the entire Régiment des Gardes Françaises had been won over, that foodstuffs were being purposely held up to create hunger in Paris and drive the people to revolt, he would have been dismissed as mad. It is very easy now, fifty years later, after suffering all the consequences of this feebleness at Court, to say what should have been done! But at the time, when no one even knew what a revolution was, a course of action was less easy to decide.

There was no great change in the web of Court ceremonial. There were discussions in the salons, people were beginning to exchange sharp remarks, that was all. The first event to strike me as serious was the resignation of M. Necker. It was his manner of leaving rather than the likely consequences which seemed extraordinary to me. I had called at the Contrôle-Général the day before my aunt and I left to visit the Maréchal de Beauvau at Le Val, his country house at the end of the terrace at Saint-Germain. His daughter, Mme de Poix, was there with an extremely select company, all of them 'philosophes'.[1] I was only nineteen and did not find such company very amusing. Mme la Maréchale de Beauvau was serious, learned and unbending. She terrified me. One had to conform to her standards in everything, from dress to conversation. Charles de Noailles, the son of Mme de Poix, and his cousin, Amédée de Duras, both only one year older than me, were there and we would all three have liked to escape into the garden to enjoy our own light-hearted company. But the strict observance of the time-table and the proprieties would never have permitted this. However, in the evening, we made music, accompanied by Mme de Poix who was an excellent musician. Mme la Maréchale amused herself by making me take a small negress, Ourika, on my knee and admiring the contrast between the child's ebony-black skin and my own fairness.

While we were at lunch in a summer-house in the garden, a footman arrived in a state of great anxiety to ask the Maréchal if he knew where M. Necker was. He said that on the previous evening, after returning from the Council, the Minister and Mme Necker had gone out in the carriage, saying that they were going to supper at Le Val. They had not been seen since and no one knew where to find them. The news was beginning to become known and crowds were collecting in front of the windows of the Contrôle-Général in Versailles. A mounted groom had been sent to all the places to which M. and Mme Necker were likely to have gone, but nowhere was there any news of them. This was extremely disquieting and my aunt wanted to return to Versailles —or rather, to the Ménagérie, where we were staying. When we reached home, the mystery was explained. M. Necker's horses had been sent back to Versailles after taking their owners to Le Bourget. There the Neckers had taken a postchaise to return to Switzerland by way of the Low Countries. M. Necker's purpose in leaving his Ministry in this way was to avoid the popular demonstrations which his departure was certain to arouse. I have heard this manoeuvre attributed to excessive pride. Personally, I think

[1] Lit. 'philosophers'. A name given in France at this period to followers of the new intellectual movement led by Voltaire, Montesquieu, Diderot and Rousseau. Its principles were humanitarian, universal and not national, and it was critical of established religions. (T)

M. Necker was acting in good faith and that, realising that the country was racing towards catastrophe, he did not want to excite the people who were already beginning to make themselves feared.

Mme de Montesson was in Paris, preparing to leave for Berny where she was to spend the summer. Loving the social whirl as she did, she would doubtless have preferred to establish herself for the season in Versailles, which was then the centre both of social life and of business affairs. Everyone who could, tried to live as near to it as possible. But her relations with the Court made this unthinkable. On the other hand, it was becoming impossible to remain in Paris, on account of attempts to stir up doubt and anxiety about the supply of food. This anxiety was one of the weapons used by the revolutionaries to unsettle the people. As Berny was not very far from Versailles, and could be reached in two hours by the road to Sceaux, Mme de Montesson decided to stay there with Mme de Valence and made me promise to spend a month or six weeks with her there.

IV

On the 13th of July, I therefore sent off my saddle horses in charge of my English groom, who spoke very little French, telling him to go by way of Paris to get certain things he needed. I tell you this very minor circumstance to show that we had not the slightest presentiment of what was to happen in Paris the next day. All the talk was of a few isolated disturbances at the doors of certain bakers whom the people had accused of adulterating the flour. The Court put its entire trust in the small army gathered on the Grenelle plain and the Champs de Mars. Not even the daily desertions from this force clouded this confidence.

When you think that I was so situated as to hear about all that went on, that M. Lally, an influential member of the Assembly, lived with my aunt and me in the small house at the Ménagérie, that I went every day to Versailles for supper with Mme de Poix, whose husband was the Captain of the Guard and a member of the Assembly, and who saw the King every evening, you will be amazed at what I am about to tell you.

Our feeling of security was so complete that at midday, and

even later, on the 14th of July, neither my aunt nor I had any
suspicion that there had been the slightest disturbance in Paris.
I set out in my carriage, with a maid and a manservant on the
box, to drive to Berny by the main Sceaux road, which runs
through the Forest of Verrières. It is true that this road, the one
from Versailles to Choisy-le-Roi, does not pass through a single
village and is very lonely. I can still remember that I had dined
early at Versailles in order to arrive at Berny in time to be settled
into my apartment before supper which, in the country, was at
nine o'clock. That fact alone shows the degree of our extraordinary unawareness. As we entered the outer courtyard at
Berny, I was surprised to see no signs of activity, to find the
stables deserted and the doors shut. The courtyard of the château
had the same deserted air. The concierge, who knew me well,
came out on to the steps when he heard the carriage and called
to me in a frightened voice: 'Oh Madame, Madame is not here.
No one has been able to leave Paris. They have fired the cannon
of the Bastille. There has been a massacre and it is impossible to
leave the city. The gates are barricaded and guarded by the
Gardes Françaises who have risen with the people.' You can
imagine my astonishment—it was even greater than my anxiety.
But although I was very young, I was never upset by the unexpected so I ordered the carriage to return by the way it had come
and take me to the staging post at Berny. I knew the owner was a
good man, devoted to Mme de Montesson and her friends. I told
him that I was very anxious to return immediately to Versailles.
He confirmed the concierge's story, which had been based entirely
on supposition since no one had been able to leave Paris. But the
city banners were flying from the barricades and, inside, could
be seen the sentinels wearing tri-coloured cockades in their hats
and shouting 'Long Live the Nation!'

My livery coachman said that nothing would persuade him to
return to Versailles, so I had four post horses harnessed up, and
taking two postilions recommended by the postmaster, set out for
Versailles at a fast gallop. I reached there at about 11 o'clock.
My aunt had a migraine and was in bed. She had not been to see
Mme de Poix. M. de Lally had not yet returned. She knew nothing.
As for me, I admit that the fate of my English groom and my three

horses was my over-riding anxiety. I had a terrible fear that they might have been offered in holocaust to the nation.

The next morning, my aunt and I went early to the Château. My aunt went to collect what news she could and I went to visit my father-in-law for the same purpose. From him I learned what had happened: the capture of the Bastille,[1] the revolt of the Régiment des Gardes Françaises, the deaths of M. de Launay, M. de Flesselles and many other less well known people, the badly-timed and pointless charge on the Place Louis XV[2] by a squadron of the Royal-Allemand commanded by the Prince de Lambesc. The following day, a deputation from the people forced M. de La Fayette to put himself at the head of the newly-formed Garde Nationale. A few days later came the news that M. Foulon and M. Bertier had also been murdered. The Régiment des Gardes expelled all officers who refused to recognise the new organisation and their places were taken by the non-commissioned officers. This act of insubordination, which was imitated throughout the French Army, did at least have one advantage for Paris: it ensured the existence, at the very beginning of the revolt, of an organised body capable of restraining the worst of the rabble from the excesses they would otherwise have committed.

The small army in the Plain of Grenelle was disbanded. The regiments, their ranks already thinned by desertion, were sent to garrisons in the provinces where they spread that same fatal spirit of insubordination that they had learned in Paris and which, thereafter, could not be stamped out.

V

Seven or eight days after the 14th of July, M. de La Tour du Pin arrived secretly at Versailles from his garrison, unable any longer to endure the anxiety he felt for both his father and myself. At Valenciennes, where his Regiment was confined, fresh rumours were arriving all the time, all of them false and contradictory. This minor breach of orders was condoned and, at his father's

[1] This ancient fortress and prison, though no longer of any military significance, represented in the eyes of the people, the old royal despotism. Its capture confirmed the power of the people over the King and marked the real beginning of the Revolution. (T)

[2] Present-day Place de la Concorde. (T)

request, my husband was granted leave. My father-in-law realised that he would probably soon be offered a high office. He was too modest to desire such a responsibility and was very glad to have his son at hand. My husband did not want his father to accept the post of Minister for War which was offered him and, after the King's visit to Paris at the demand of the Commune and the return of M. Necker, who was recalled in the hope that he would be able to restore calm, he wanted to leave Versailles in order to avoid influencing his father's decision.

I had been ordered to take the waters at Forges, in Normandy. It was thought that they would strengthen me, for my illness after the birth of our last child had so weakened my kidneys that it was even feared I might not be able to have any more children, a possibility which reduced me to despair. We went, therefore, to Forges and the month we spent there is one of the periods of my life that I most enjoy recalling. Every day we took long rides in the beautiful woods near the town. We had taken a wide choice of books with us and my husband, an indefatigable reader, used to read to me while I worked, for I already had that keen pleasure in handwork which remains with me still, even at the advanced age at which I am writing these memoirs.

On the 28th of July, there occurred one of the most extra-ordinary phenomena of the Revolution, one which has never yet been properly explained. It is, in fact, incomprehensible unless one accepts the existence of some gigantic network stretching to every corner of France permitting any action anywhere to communicate its own state of revolt, agitation and terror to every commune in the kingdom simultaneously. I will describe to you what I saw that day at Forges, and the same thing was happening simultaneously everywhere else.

We had a modest apartment on the first floor, overlooking a small square on the high road to Neufchatel and Dieppe. It was morning and seven o'clock was striking. I was dressed and ready to go riding, and was waiting for my husband who had gone alone to the Spring. For some reason which I have forgotten, I had not wanted to go with him. I was standing at the window watching the road by which he would return when, along it, but from the opposite direction, I heard a mass of people rushing into the square under my window—our house stood on a corner—all of them showing every sign of desperate fear. Women were weeping and wailing, men were raging, swearing, threatening, some were raising their hands to Heaven crying 'We are lost!' In their midst, haranguing them, was a man on horseback. He wore a disreputable, torn green coat and had no hat. His dapple-grey was covered in lather and its cruppers were cut and bleeding slightly. He stopped under my window and began a sort of harangue in the style of quacks in public places, saying: 'They[1] will be here in three hours; they are pillaging everything at Gaillefontaine;[2] they are setting fire to the barns . . .' and so on. After a few sentences in this vein, he clapped spurs to his horse and galloped off towards Neufchatel.

Since I am not by nature fearful, I went out, mounted a horse and rode at a walking pace along the street which was filling with people who thought their last day had come. I talked to them and tried to convince them that there was not one word of truth in what they had been told, that it was impossible for the Austrians, with whom we were not at war, to have arrived, as the impostor had been saying, in the heart of Normandy without anyone having heard that they were on the march. As I reached the door of the Church, I found the curé arriving to sound the tocsin. At that moment, M. de La Tour du Pin rode up, fetched from the fountain by my groom. They found me still mounted and holding on to the curé by the collar of his cassock, trying to explain to him what folly it would be to alarm his flock by sounding the tocsin, instead of joining his efforts to mine to prove to them that their fears were groundless.

My husband then took charge and told the crowd that there was no vestige of truth in what they had been told. To reassure them, he said we would go over to Gaillefontaine and bring back news from there. Meantime, they were not to sound the alarm, but return to their homes. We set off at a canter, followed by my

[1] The Austrians. Many royalists, led by the émigré princes, hoped and worked for the intervention of Queen Marie-Antoinette's brother, the Emperor Leopold II of Austria, to save the monarchy and restore order. Since Austria governed the Low Countries on the northern border of France and controlled the principalities to the east, it would not be difficult to start rumours of invasion. (T)

[2] A small town two leagues from Forges.

groom who, since the 14th of July when he had happened to be in Paris, was convinced that all Frenchmen were mad. He came respectfully up to me and, raising his hat, asked 'Please, milady, what are they all about?'

It took us about an hour to reach the country town where the Austrians were supposed to be. As we rode down the sunken path leading to the main square, a man armed with a rusty pistol stopped us with the challenge: 'Who goes there?' Coming out in front of us, he asked if the Austrians were not at Forges and when we replied that they were not, he took us to the square and shouted to all the people gathered there: 'It isn't true! It isn't true!' At that moment, a large, rather prosperous-looking citizen came up to me and cried: 'Eh, citizens, 'tis the Queen!' From all sides came the shout that I should be taken to the Commune,[1] and although not at all frightened by my predicament, I was greatly frightened by the danger to a crowd of women and children who were thrusting themselves in front of my horse, a very excitable animal. Luckily, a locksmith's apprentice who had come out of his shop to see me, started to laugh like a madman, saying that the Queen was at least twice as old as that young lady and twice as large, that he had seen her only two months before and that I was not she. This assurance gained me my liberty, and we left immediately to return to Forges, where the rumour was already rife that we had been captured by the enemy. We found the men armed with anything they had been able to lay hands on and the Garde Nationale was standing by. And that was the sole purpose of the scare: to ensure that, throughout France, on the same day and almost at the same hour, the entire population should resort to arms.

[1] A territorial area administered by a mayor and municipal council. By extension, the municipality. (T)

CHAPTER TEN

I

A few days after these events, my husband learned that his father had been appointed Minister for War, so we left immediately for Versailles. It was the beginning of my public life. My father-in-law gave us a fine apartment on the first floor of the Ministry for War,[1] put his household in my charge and entrusted the honours of his house to my sister-in-law and to me. My sister-in-law also had lodgings in the Ministry, but had to leave us two months later. At Montpellier and in Paris, I had been so accustomed to big dinners that my new position did not worry me. I took the greatest care to confine my activities strictly to the honours of the house. Each week there were two dinners for twenty-four people, and all the members of the Constituent Assembly were invited in turn. Their wives did not come. Mme de Lameth and I sat opposite one another and placed next to us the four most important guests, taking care to choose them from all the parties. So long as we were at Versailles, the men always wore formal dress at these dinners and I remember M. de Robespierre in an apple-green coat, with his thick white hair wonderfully dressed. Mirabeau alone never called on us and was never invited. I often went out to supper, either to the houses of my colleagues, or to those of people who were staying in Versailles for the session of the National Assembly, as it had been re-named.

On the 14th of July,[2] the Comte d'Artois left France to visit his father-in-law[3] in Turin, taking his children with him. He was also accompanied by many members of his Household, including M. d'Hénin, the Captain of his Guard. The Queen feared that popular agitation might endanger the safety of the Polignac family and made them, too, promise to leave France. Mme de Polignac

[1] In the south wing of the Cour des Ministres.
[2] The Comte d'Artois actually left Paris on the night of the 16/17th of July 1789.
[3] Victor-Amédée III, King of Sardinia.

resigned her appointment as governess to the Children of France and took with her her daughter, the Duchesse de Gramont.

France is a country much given to fashions and just then emigration became all the vogue. People started raising money on their estates so that they would have ample funds to take out of the country and very large numbers of them welcomed this new fashion as a means of escape. The younger ones looked on it either as a heaven-sent excuse to travel, or as a pretext for setting off to join their friends and companions. No one realised what the consequences of such a decision were to be.

Yet the happenings of the night of the 4th of August when, on the motion of the Vicomte de Noailles, it was decreed that feudal rights should be abolished, ought to have convinced even the most incredulous that the National Assembly was unlikely to stop at this first measure of dispossession. This decree ruined my father-in-law and our family fortunes never recovered from the effect of that night's session. It was a veritable orgy of iniquities. The value of the property at La Roche-Chalais lay entirely in feudal dues, the income from invested money and leases or from the mills. There was also a toll river-crossing. The total income from all these sources was 30,000 francs a year, and the only charge on this sum was the salary paid to the agent who, on an appointed day, received payments in grain or the money equivalent of the grain at current market price. This type of property where there were, in effect, two proprietors to each piece of land, was very common in south-western France. The decree did not at first order complete seizure of the land, it merely fixed a rate at which it could be redeemed. But before the day fixed for this payment had come round, it had been decided that no payments would be accepted. And so everything was lost.

We also lost the toll crossing at Cubzac, on the Dordogne, which was worth 12,000 francs, and the income from Le Bouilh, Ambleville, Tesson and Cénévrières, a fine property in the Quercy which my father-in-law was forced to sell the following year. And that was how we were ruined by the stroke of a pen. Since then we have been forced to contrive a living, sometimes by the sale of some of the few possessions remaining to us, sometimes by taking salaried posts—though the salaries rarely covered the expense the posts involved. And so, inch by inch, over a long period of years, we have gradually slid to the bottom of an abyss from which we shall not emerge in our generation.

I was far from thinking, then, that my grandmother, who had removed six months earlier to Hautefontaine with my uncle, the Archbishop, was to deprive me of her fortune, on which I had every right to count. I could not foresee that my uncle, who had not been appointed to the States-General, whose income had been reduced by only five or six thousand francs and who therefore still enjoyed a yearly revenue of 420,000 francs from Church appointments, whose quiet life at Hautefontaine could not have cost him even a quarter of that amount, would leave behind him when he emigrated the following year, debts amounting to 1,800,000 francs in which my grandmother's fortune would be heavily pledged.

We did not immediately feel the full extent of our ruin. As a Minister, my father-in-law received a salary of 300,000 francs, in addition to his pay as Lieutenant-General and Commander of a Province. But he had, in fact, to maintain considerable state and as well as the two weekly dinners for twenty-four people, there were also every week the two lavish and elegant supper parties to which I invited twenty-five to thirty ladies of all ages. Only my sister-in-law and I were able to enjoy these supper parties for my father-in-law usually retired to bed at the end of the council meetings as he rose very early in the morning. This however, did not prevent his colleagues and their wives from calling on us.

In spite of my youth, all these ladies treated me with kindness. The Comtesse de Montmorin, wife of the Minister for Foreign Affairs, was particularly good and amiable to me, and I enjoyed a close friendship with her daughter, the Baronne de Beaumont. The Comtesse de Saint-Priest and her excellent husband, the Minister of the King's Household, claimed me as an old acquaintance, remembering that they had seen me in Languedoc when I was very young and had even met me when I was a child at my uncle's house in Paris. The same applied to the Archbishop of Bordeaux, M. de Cicé, the Keeper of the Seals.

On her mother's side, Madame de Saint-Priest was Greek. She

was the daughter of a Prussian Minister in Constantinople and a
lady from that part of the city known as the Fanar,[1] a district she
had never left until she married M. de Saint-Priest, French Ambassador to the Sultan. Although her salon was thoroughly
French, the remainder of her house was Greek and she often
wore Greek dress, which I found very amusing. She had several
children and at the time of which I am writing, was expecting
another. She had arrived from Constantinople only a year before
and was not only still enjoying all the charm of her new sur-
roundings but had not yet lost her feeling of surprise at even the
very slight independence allowed to Frenchwomen.

I rarely saw Mme de La Luzerne whose husband[2] was Minister of
Marine. She was the daughter of M. d'Angran d'Alleray, the
'Lieutenant Civil'[3] and felt very out of it at Versailles, which had
never been frequented by the 'noblesse de robe'.[4]

Mme Necker, the wife of the Contrôleur-Général (Prime
Minister), lived more or less in the same style as we did. But as she
rarely went out, she gave daily suppers to which she invited
deputies, men of learning and her daughter's admirers. In this
salon, her daughter reigned over a group of intellectuals; she was
then at the full height of her youthful enthusiasms, interested alike
in politics, science, learning, intrigue and love. Mme de Staël
lived with her parents at the Contrôle-Général in Versailles and
went to Court only on Tuesdays, the day when the Ambassadors
were received. She was at that time more than friendly with
Alexander de Lameth, who was still a friend of my husband, a
friendship which dated from their childhood and caused me some
anxiety. I had a very poor opinion of this young man's morals and
was particularly anxious in case he should obtain any political
influence. My sister-in-law shared my opinion of him and when,
a few months later, my husband openly dissociated himself from
him and his brother, Charles, we were delighted.

I have never pretended to be a woman of intellect, I have only

[1] A part of Constantinople peopled by descendents of the Greeks who remained in
the city after its capture by Mahomet II in 1453.
[2] César-Henri, Comte de La Luzerne.
[3] The second law officer of the Crown in the provostship of Paris. (T)
[4] Those ennobled by reason of their office, as opposed to the 'noblesse d'épée' or
feudal nobility. (T)

tried to use with wisdom the common sense which Providence has given me. I knew Mme de Staël intimately, but not to the point of exchanging confidences with her. But she had sufficient trust in my husband to confide everything to him and he had told me in the greatest detail about her life. I profited from this to remain on a footing of familiarity, but not of friendship with her. We sometimes had conversations which are amusing to recall. Mme de Staël could not understand why I was not enthusiastic about my looks, my colouring, my figure and when I admitted that I did not attach more importance to these personal attributes than they warranted, for they would disappear with age, she exclaimed naïvely that if she had had them, she would have wanted to rouse the world. Her greatest pleasure, and a very odd one it was, too, was to imagine a set of circumstances and then ask me: 'Would you do this or that?' And as my answers always showed that I was happy and ready to act in accordance with the ideals of devotion, self-sacrifice, abnegation and courage which her ready imagination had conjured up, she declared that I thought like a romantic. What she found most difficult to understand was my readiness to make every possible sacrifice for my husband, and she could only describe it in the following terms: 'It seems to me that you love him as a lover'.

That woman was an odd mixture and I have often tried to understand the mingling of virtue and vice in her. Vice is too strong a word. Her great qualities were no more than tarnished by the passions to which she abandoned herself the more easily because she felt a pleasant surprise whenever a man sought from her pleasures from which her unfortunate looks seemed to have excluded her for ever. Indeed, I have every reason to believe that she surrendered without the slightest struggle to any man who showed himself more aware of the beauty of her embrace than of the charms of her mind. Yet you would be wrong to conclude that I considered her shameless, for she did insist on a certain delicacy of feeling and she has shown herself capable of passions that were very deep and devoted while they lasted. For instance, she deeply loved M. de Narbonne, who deserted her, so far as I can remember, in a most shameful manner.

II

Groups of Gardes Nationales were organising themselves throughout the kingdom, taking as their model the Garde Nationale of Paris commanded by M. de La Fayette. The King wanted a similar Garde formed at Versailles from among the messengers and employees of the Ministries, partly because he hoped that such a step would improve the spirit of the corps and partly in the hope that a Garde which included so many people who depended on the Court for their livelihood would be less likely to desert it. But the commanding officer was badly chosen: he was the Comte d'Estaing, who had acquired a reputation he was far from meriting. I knew from my father what to think of that appointment. M. Dillon had served under him at the beginning of the war in America and had the most positive proof that M. d'Estaing lacked not only skill, but even courage. Yet, when he returned to France, favours were heaped upon him while my father, to whom he owed his first victory, since it was Dillon's Regiment which captured Grenada, had only the frustration and disappointment of seeing others promoted over him. It was due to the Queen's influence that M. d'Estaing was appointed Commander-in-Chief of the Garde Nationale at Versailles; my father-in-law, in an attempt to retain some measure of control over the force, appointed his son as second-in-command. This meant, in fact, that his son commanded the force, for M. d'Estaing's arrogance and disdain gave him the greatest distaste for dealing with such a middle-class force and he avoided doing so on every possible occasion. He therefore had no part in the organising of the Garde, or in the appointment of its officers. Berthier, who has since become the Prince de Wagram and a very distinguished staff officer, was made Chief of Staff. He was a good man with a talent for organisation, but his weakness of character left him a prey to intriguers. He recommended as officers certain merchants of Versailles who already belonged to the revolutionary party and who were eventually to sow discord in the force.

Even before the end of August, it had been discovered that schemes existed to create a shortage of food, and many of the plotters were surprised and arrested. Two of them were brought to trial, admitted their guilt and were condemned to be hanged. On the day of their execution a crowd gathered in the square. The mounted police, not numerous enough to keep order and prevent the crowd from freeing the condemned men, thought it best to take the two men back to prison. The execution was put off until the following day. The mob pulled down the gallows and pillaged the bakeries, accusing the bakers of denouncing those who had tried to subvert them. But the law had to be upheld. On the day of the execution, M. d'Estaing being unwilling to come to Versailles, it was M. de La Tour du Pin who assembled the Garde Nationale and ordered it to ensure, by force of arms, the execution of the condemned men. There were strong protests, but his unshakeable firmness had its effect. He told the Garde that he himself would lead them and that any who refused to march would be immediately struck from the roll. After that, they no longer dared to resist. Seeing that the chief of the Garde was not a man to be alarmed by threats, the people no longer opposed the execution. The men were hanged and the Garde Nationale was left with the feeling that it had emerged from a campaign covered in glory. M. de La Tour du Pin had never before had anything to do with the carrying out of the death penalty and he returned home very much distressed by the sad spectacle at which he had had to be present.

On the feast of St Louis, it was customary for the magistrates and municipal authorities of the City of Paris to wait on the King and offer him their good wishes. This year, the Garde Nationale wanted to share this privilege and the General-in-Chief, M. de La Fayette, brought his entire staff to Versailles at the same time as M. Bailly, the Mayor of Paris and all the municipal authorities. The fishwives came too, as was their custom, to carry a bouquet to the King. The Queen received them all in state in the green salon next to her bedroom. The usual procedure was followed. The Queen was not in Court dress, but sparkled with many diamonds and other precious stones. She sat in a large chair with a back, her feet on a small stool. To the right and left of her, a few duchesses in Court dress were seated on their stools and behind her stood the entire Household, both Ladies and Gentlemen.

I had managed to be fairly near the front in order to be able to see and hear. The usher announced: 'The City of Paris!' The Queen waited for the Mayor to go down on one knee, as was customary, but M. Bailly made only a very deep bow as he entered. The Queen replied with an inclination of the head which was not sufficiently friendly. M. Bailly then made a little speech, very well written, in which he spoke of devotion, attachment and also a little of the fears of the people at the daily threat of a food shortage.

Next came M. de La Fayette, who presented his staff officers of the Garde Nationale. The Queen's colour rose and I could see that she was under the stress of some very strong emotion. She stammered a few words in a shaking voice and nodded her head in dismissal.

They all left, feeling—as I heard later—very annoyed with her, for that unfortunate Princess was incapable of gauging the importance of an occasion; she allowed her feelings to be seen without reflecting what the consequences might be. These officers of the Garde Nationale, who could have been won by a gracious word, went off instead in a very bad humour and spread their discontent throughout Paris, increasing the ill-will which was being stirred up there against the Queen, mainly at the instigation of the Duc d'Orléans.

The fishwives were also very badly received and resolved to take their revenge.

The Garde Nationale, at Versailles as elsewhere, wanted its own standards and it was decided to have them solemnly blessed at Notre Dame de Versailles. A group of senior officers, headed by M. d'Estaing, came to ask me to take the collection at this ceremony. It had previously been arranged that I would agree to do so. But my gravity was sorely shaken when, in the middle of my polite words of acceptance, I saw behind M. d'Estaing a servant from the Château, armed to the teeth. He was Simon, and he had charge of my aunt's apartment and had often prepared our supper. These incidents were still new and, to the young, merely amusing. If I had been told that Berthier, the modest chief of staff, whose father was in charge of the offices of the Ministry for War, would one day be sovereign prince of Neuchâtel and marry a

German princess, I would have laughed at such a fairy tale; but we have since seen others far stranger.

I went, therefore, to this very brilliant and solemn ceremony, which was attended by representatives of all the military corps in Versailles. During the very long High Mass, I had plenty of time to meditate on the course of events. Scarcely fourteen months before, on the Feast of Pentecost, I had taken the collection in the Chapel of Versailles at a Chapter of the Order of the Holy Ghost presided over by the King and attended by all the Princes of the blood, many of whom had by now left France.

A very handsome young man whom I did not recognise came up to give me his hand, obviously much embarrassed at his rôle. Perhaps he too, like Simon, was some servant from the Château or a shopkeeper from Versailles. I did not ask his name. The collection was good and the Curé and his poor very pleased with it, which was all I needed to know. My aristocratic notions were somewhat confused by having to play this kind of rôle. But my father-in-law had wanted it so and the King wished it. And that was sufficient to make me accept with good grace. I had put on a pretty toilette which brought me many compliments, and afterwards we had to entertain to dinner the staff of the Versailles Garde. Perhaps due to presentiment, I did not like them.

The summer wore on. I was again pregnant, and it seemed possible that this time there would be a happy outcome. My health was good and as my father-in-law had twelve carriage horses which he never used, my sister-in-law and I used them to go driving in the beautiful forests near Versailles.

Every day news came of small riots in Paris. The cause was always the same: the increasingly difficult food situation, for which there seemed to be no convincing explanation. There is no doubt that the shortage was contrived by the revolutionaries.

The Court, stricken sublimely blind, could not see disaster approaching. The Garde Nationale of Paris was behaving quite well. It had a nucleus of soldiers—no officers—from the former Régiment de Gardes Françaises and they had, as it were, inoculated the citizens who joined its ranks with certain military traditions. The former sergeants and corporals of the Gardes Françaises had been appointed to officers' duties and it was they who trained the Garde Nationale. Almost immediately, it was at full strength. M. de La Fayette paraded about on his white horse and, in his foolishness, had not the slightest suspicion that the Duc d'Orléans was dreaming of a throne and plotting to seize it. It is absurdly unjust to believe that M. de La Fayette was the instigator of the events of the 5th and 6th of October 1789. He thought himself the ruler of Paris, but his reign ended on the day the King and the Assembly returned to that city. He was then given a charge he did not want, was overwhelmed by the tide of revolution and carried along with it despite himself. I will tell you later what I remember of those days, when the weakness of the King was at the root of all the trouble.

III

The Régiment de Flandre-Infanterie, whose Colonel, the Marquis de Lusignan, was a Deputy, had been summoned to Versailles. The Gardes du Corps wished to give a dinner for the officers of the Régiment de Flandre and the Garde Nationale. For the occasion they asked to borrow the great theatre of the Château, which lies at the end of the Chapel gallery. This magnificent hall could be transformed into a ballroom by laying a floor to raise the pit level with the boxes. There was a splendid, heavily-gilded screen which fitted in front of the stage to continue the design of the other walls. The dinner began quite late and the theatre was brilliantly lit—this was always necessary, as there were no windows.

Towards the end of dinner, my sister-in-law and I went to watch the scene, which was magnificent. Healths were being drunk and my husband, who had come to meet us and take us to one of the stage boxes, had time to whisper that people were getting very heated and that some rash things had been said.

Suddenly it was announced that the King and Queen were to appear at the banquet: an imprudent step which produced a very bad effect. The sovereigns did indeed appear in the centre box, accompanied by the young Dauphin, who was nearly five years old.[1] Enthusiastic cries of 'Vive le Roi!' could be heard. I myself heard no others, despite declarations that such there were. A

[1] The second Dauphin, Louis-Charles, born in 1785.

Swiss officer approached the box and asked the Queen's permission to take the Dauphin around the banqueting room. She consented, and the small boy was not in the least afraid. The officer put him on the table and he walked boldly round it, smiling, quite undismayed by the shouting all about him. The Queen was less confident and when he was taken back to her, she embraced him tenderly. We left after the King and Queen had gone. Everyone was leaving and my husband, worried for me in such a crush, came to join us. During the evening, we heard that certain ladies in the Chapel gallery, including the Duchesse de Maillé, had distributed white ribbons from their hats to some of the officers. It was a most foolish thing to do, for the next day the disaffected papers, of which there were already many, did not omit a description of the 'orgy' at Versailles, which ended, they said, with a distribution of white cockades to all the guests. I have since seen this absurd story printed in serious history books, yet in reality this thoughtless prank consisted of one bunch of ribbons which Mme de Maillé, a heedless chit of nineteen, had taken from her hat.

IV

On the 4th of October, many of the Paris bakeries had no bread and a great outcry arose. One unfortunate baker was hanged on the spot, despite the efforts of M. de La Fayette and the Garde Nationale. But at Versailles there was no alarm. The riot seemed no different from earlier ones when the Garde Nationale, on which the Court thought it could depend, had been sufficient to control the people. Many messages sent to the King and the President of the Chamber had been so reassuring that on the 5th of October, at ten o'clock in the morning, the King went hunting in the Forest of Verrières and after lunch I went to visit Mme de Valence who had come to Versailles for the birth of her child. We went driving in Madame Elisabeth's garden at the end of the main avenue and as we were leaving the carriage to cross the side avenue, we saw a man ride past at full gallop. It was the Duc de Maillé, who shouted to us: 'Paris is marching here with guns'. We were greatly alarmed and returned immediately to Versailles, where the news had already spread.

My husband had gone to the Assembly knowing nothing of all this. Everyone was aware that there was a great deal of unrest in Paris, but no one had been able to get any precise details, for the people had rushed to the barricades, shut the gates and refused to allow anyone to leave the city. M. de La Tour du Pin hurried to his father, who was already in conference with other Ministers. Their first step was to send messengers in every direction which the hunt might have taken, to warn the King to return. A number of people who had come to Versailles about their own affairs, offered their services as aides-de-camp and my father-in-law accepted their offer. My husband busied himself assembling his Garde Nationale, in which he felt little confidence. The Régiment de Flandre was ordered to stand to and to occupy the Place d'Armes. The King's Guard saddled their horses. Couriers were sent to summon the Swiss Guards from Courbevoie. People were sent every other minute to the high road to gather news of what was happening. It was learned that a huge mob, with women outnumbering men, was marching on Versailles. Behind this advance guard was the Garde Nationale of Paris, armed with cannons and followed by a large mob of people marching in complete disorder. It was too late to try to close the bridge at Sèvres. The local Garde Nationale had already handed it over to the women and was fraternising with the Garde from Paris. My father-in-law wanted to send the Régiment de Flandre and some workmen to block the Paris road, but the National Assembly had declared itself in session, the King was not there and no one had the authority to initiate a hostile act.

My father-in-law and M. de Saint-Priest were desperate, the former saying: 'We are going to allow ourselves to be taken here, perhaps massacred, without doing anything in our defence.' Meantime, the recall to arms was being sounded for the Garde Nationale. It assembled on the Place d'Armes and put itself in battle order, facing outwards from the iron gate leading into the Cour Royale. The Régiment de Flandre stationed itself between the Grand Ecurie on its left and the gate on its right. The positions inside the Cour Royale and in the Chapel arch were held by the Swiss Guard, a strong detachment of this Corps being always stationed in Versailles. All the gates were closed. All the entrances to the Château were barricaded and doors that had not turned on their hinges since the days of Louis XIV were shut.

Eventually, towards three o'clock, the King and his suite arrived at full gallop up the Grande Avenue. This ill-starred prince, instead of stopping for a moment to say something heartening to the fine Régiment de Flandre, which was shouting 'Vive le Roi!' passed them without a word. He went straight to his apartments, shut himself in and did not reappear. The Garde Nationale of Versailles, which was getting its first taste of war, began to grumble and say that it would not fire on the people of Paris. There were no cannons at Versailles.

The advance guard of three to four hundred women began arriving and spread along the avenue. Many of them entered the Assembly, saying that they had come for bread and to take the deputies to Paris. Some of them, drunk and very weary, took possession of the rostrums and benches inside the Chamber. Night fell and a number of pistol shots could be heard: they came from the ranks of the Garde Nationale and were aimed at my husband, their commanding officer. He had ordered them to remain in position and they were refusing to obey. One shot hit M. de Savonnières and broke his arm at the elbow. I saw the unfortunate man taken to the apartments of Mme de Montmorin,[1] for I refused to leave the window and watched it all. My husband escaped by a miracle, and seeing that his troops were deserting him, he took up a position before the King's Guard, where it stood in battle order near the Petite Ecurie. But they were so few in numbers—only de Gramont's company—that it was decided in council that any attempt at defence was impossible. My husband had reported the disaffection of the Garde Nationale and it was agreed that since it would inevitably fraternise with the Garde Nationale of Paris as soon as the latter appeared on the scene, it would be best to make no attempt to re-assemble it.

At this point, my father-in-law and M. de Saint-Priest proposed that the King and his family should withdraw to Rambouillet and there wait to see what conditions the Paris rebels and the National Assembly would propose. At first, the King accepted this suggestion. At about eight or nine o'clock, the company of

[1] Wife of the Foreign Minister.

the Garde du Corps was therefore summoned to the Cour Royale, which it reached by way of the gate from the Rue de l'Orangerie. The Garde marched along the terrace,[1] crossed the small park[2] and reached the Saint-Cyr road by way of the Ménagérie. There remained at Versailles only enough men of this troop to assure a continuous guard in the apartment of the King and that of the Queen. The Swiss Guard[3] and the 'Cent Suisses'[4] stayed at their posts.

At this juncture, two or three hundred women who had been wandering from gate to gate for about an hour discovered a small door that opened on to a secret stair leading to the Cour Royale, just under the part of the building where we were. The entrance was probably revealed by someone who knew of these stairs. The women rushed through and, taking by surprise the Swiss Guards on duty at the top, spread into the courtyard and entered the apartments of the four Ministers lodged in that part of the building. So many came into our apartment that the entrance, the ante-rooms and the staircase were packed. My husband arrived at that moment to bring my sister and me the latest news. Worried at finding us so surrounded, he decided to take us to the Château itself. My sister-in-law had taken the precaution of sending her children to the house of a deputy who was a friend of ours and had lodgings in the town. Following M. de La Tour du Pin, we went up to the gallery[5] where a number of people who lived in the Château had already gathered, mortally anxious at the turn events were taking. They had come to the royal apartments in order to be as close as possible to the source of news.

While all this was happening the King, still hesitating over the best course of action, decided not to go to Rambouillet. He consulted everyone. The Queen, just as undecided as he, could not bring herself to undertake a flight by night. My father-in-law besought the King on his knees to place his person and his family

[1] Orangery Terrace, under the windows of the Queen's apartments.
[2] The gardens to the west of the Château.
[3] A corps of Swiss soldiers who served in foreign armies, particularly the French Army. (T)
[4] A corps of Swiss infantry attached to the King's personal guard. (T)
[5] The great gallery of the Château.

in a place of safety, telling him that the Ministers would remain to deal with the rebels and the Assembly. But this good Prince, repeating over and over again 'I do not want to compromise anyone', lost precious time. At one moment, it was thought he would give way and orders were given to bring round the carriages which had been standing ready for two hours in the Grande Ecurie. It is doubtless very difficult to believe that it did not occur to a single equerry in the King's entourage that the people of Versailles might oppose the royal family's departure. Yet this was just what happened. As soon as the mob of citizens from Paris and Versailles that had collected on the Place d'Armes saw the courtyard gates of the Grande Ecurie opening, there was a terrified, angry shout of 'The King is leaving'. They fell immediately upon the carriages, cut the traces and led the horses away. Word had to be sent to the Château that departure was impossible. My father-in-law and M. de Saint-Priest then offered our own carriages, which were standing ready outside the gate of the Orangerie, but the King and Queen would not accept this suggestion. Discouraged, alarmed and fearful of the direst misfortunes, they both remained there in silence, waiting.

Silently too, people walked up and down that gallery which had seen all the splendours of the monarchy since the days of Louis XIV. The Queen remained in her room with Madame Elisabeth and Madame. The card-room, which was almost in darkness, was filled with women who spoke in whispers, some sitting on the tabourets, others on the tables. As for myself, I was so agitated that I could not remain still a minute. I went constantly to the 'Oeuil de Boeuf'[1] where it was possible to see the comings and goings of visitors to the King's apartments, hoping to meet my husband or my father-in-law there and to learn the latest news from them. The waiting seemed unbearable.

It was midnight when my husband, who had been in the court-yard for a long time, eventually came to tell me that M. de La Fayette had arrived with the Garde Nationale of Paris. They were

[1] The long inner room lit only by a round window above a door, which led directly to the King's bedroom. It was there that the courtiers waited for the King, discussing intrigues and the latest news. The name of this room thus became synonymous with gossip and intrigue in high places. (T)

at the gate of the Cour Royale[1] and M. de La Fayette was asking to speak to the King. My husband said that the section of the Garde which was made up of former members of the Régiment de la Garde was showing great impatience and the slightest delay might cause difficulties, if not danger.

The King commanded that M. de La Fayette be admitted. M. de La Tour du Pin hurried to the gate and M. de La Fayette, so tired that when he dismounted he could hardly stand, took not more than seven or eight officers of his staff and went up to see the King. He was very agitated and told the King: 'Sire, I thought it better to come here and die at the feet of Your Majesty than to die uselessly on the Place de Grève'. Those were his exact words. The King then asked him what they wanted and M. de La Fayette told him: 'The people are asking for bread and the Garde wants to resume its former duties at Your Majesty's side'. To which the King replied: 'Well, then, let it do so.'

This conversation was reported to me at the time. My husband went down again with M. de La Fayette and the Garde Nationale of Paris, whose ranks were almost entirely composed of former Gardes Françaises, resumed their former duties there and then. Some immediately replaced the Swiss Guards on sentry duty at each outer gate and the remainder, numbering several hundreds, formed a main guard and bivouacked, as they had always done, on the Place d'Armes in a long building composed of several great rooms built in the shape of tents and painted to resemble them.

While all this was going on, the people of Paris began to wander away from the Château towards the town and the wine-shops. A multitude of people, dropping with weariness and soaked to the skin, found shelter in the stables and coach-houses. The women who had invaded the Ministry ate everything it was possible to find for them, and then went to sleep on the floor of the kitchens. Many of them wept, saying that they had been forced to march and that they did not know why they were there. Their leaders seemed to have taken refuge in the Chamber of the National Assembly, where they spent the night among the Deputies who were taking it in turn to keep the session open.

[1] More exactly, of the Cour des Ministres.

The King, being assured that the most complete calm reigned in Versailles, as indeed it did, dismissed all those still in attendance in the Oeuil de Boeuf or in his cabinet. The footmen came to the gallery to tell those ladies who were still there that the Queen had retired. The doors were closed, the candles put out and my husband accompanied us back to my aunt's apartment.[1] He did not wish us to return to the Ministry on account of the women sleeping in the ante-rooms, who were a most revolting sight.

As soon as he had seen us safely to this apartment, he went back to his father and begged him to go to bed, saying that he himself would stay up all night. He went home to put a riding coat over his uniform—for the night was cold and damp—and then, taking his round hat, went down to the courtyard, visited the various posts and made a tour of the courtyards, passages and garden to make sure that all was quiet. He did not hear the least sound, either about the Château or in the nearby streets. The various sentry posts were being diligently relieved and the Garde, reinstalled in the big tent on the Place d'Armes, had put its cannons in battery formation before the entrance and was carrying out its duties with the same precision as before the 14th of July.

Such is the real story of what happened at Versailles on the 5th of October. M. de La Fayette's fault, if fault there was, was not the much-criticised hour of sleep which he snatched, fully dressed, on a sofa in the salon of Mme de Poix, but his total unawareness of the Duc d'Orléans' plot. The Duke's fellow-conspirators came to Versailles at the same time as M. de La Fayette, but unknown to him. The traitor Duke took his seat in the Assembly a number of times during the day of the 5th of October and in the evening, left for Paris—at least, that is what he gave people to understand. But as you will see, I later learned beyond any possibility of a doubt that he was present at Versailles when the attempt was made to assassinate the Queen.

V

After making his night inspection without hearing anything which

---

[1] Above the Galerie des Princes, right at the top of the buildings which form the south wing of the Château, overlooking the Orangery terrace on one side and the Rue de la Sur-Intendance on the other.

might indicate the least danger of disorder, M. de La Tour du Pin returned to the Ministry of War. Instead of going to his study, or to his room, which opened, as mine did, on to the Rue du Grand Commun, he stayed in the dining-room by the open window, for fear of falling asleep. It might be well to explain here that the Cour des Princes was, in those days, enclosed by an iron railing and that a sentry of the Garde du Corps was posted nearby because this was the point at which the King's personal guard took over—a duty undertaken principally by the Garde du Corps and the Cent Suisses. Inside this small courtyard was a passage communicating with the Cour Royale. It enabled the sentries at the post in the Cour Royale, near the Chapel arch at the corner of the Cour de Marbre, to relieve one another without having to pass out through the middle gate of the Cour Royale and to return by that of the Cour des Princes. You will see later how necessary a knowledge of this passage was to the assassins.

Dawn was just breaking. It was after six o'clock and the deepest silence still reigned over the courtyard. As he leaned against the window, M. de La Tour du Pin thought he heard the sound of many feet, as if a large number of people were climbing the slope from the Rue de l'Orangerie[1] to the forecourt.[2] To his amazement, he saw a ragged crowd armed with axes and sabres, entering through a gate usually kept locked, whose key could only have been got through treachery. At the same moment, my husband heard a pistol shot. In the time it took him to rush down the stairs and have the door of the Ministry opened, the assassins killed M. de Vallori,[3] the guard on duty at the gateway to the Cour des Princes, crossed the passage I have just mentioned and were advancing on the main body of the Garde in the Cour Royale. Part of the mob, not more than two hundred of them, rushed up the marble staircase, and the remainder threw themselves upon the sentry on duty.[4] His comrades had shut themselves into the guardroom, leaving him outside, quite defenceless. The assassins did not attempt to force the door, yet ten or twelve of the

[1] Author's error. Instead, read Rue de la Sur-Intendance.
[2] i.e., the Cour des Ministres.
[3] In most contemporary papers, he is called M. de Varicourt.
[4] His name was Deshuttes.

Garde du Corps were inside. They could have attacked the mob with firearms or sabres in an attempt to defend their companion, but they did nothing and the unfortunate man, after firing his musket and killing the nearest of his assailants, was torn to pieces by those behind. This cowardly deed completed, the invaders hurried to rejoin the remainder of the mob which had just managed to force its way into the guardroom of the Swiss Guards at the head of the marble stairs. These giants have been much blamed for not defending this stair with their long halberds, but it is probable that only one of their number was on duty at the stair. That was the usual custom and people had been convinced that nothing would happen and that the strong iron railings and gates, all securely closed, would withstand attack long enough to permit the defenders to take up their positions.

A proof that no unusual precautions had been taken was the fact that the murderers, once at the head of the stairs, and guided, without a doubt, by someone who knew the way, turned into the Queen's Guardroom and came suddenly upon the only Garde on duty there. He rushed to the door of the bedroom, which was locked on the inside, and knocking again and again with the butt of his musket, shouted 'Madame, you must flee, there are men here who have come to kill you'. Then, resolved to sell his life dearly, he set his back to the door, fired his musket and then defended himself with his sabre. But he was soon cut down by those wretches who, fortunately, had no firearms. He fell against the door and as his body prevented the murderers from forcing it open, they bundled him into a window recess. This saved his life. He lay there unconscious until after the King had left for Paris and then his friends came to collect him. This brave man—Sainte-Marie[1] by name—was still alive at the time of the Restoration.

While all this was going on, my sister-in-law and I were asleep in a room in the apartment of my aunt, Mme d'Hénin. I was exceedingly tired and my sister-in-law had difficulty in waking me to tell me that she thought she could hear a noise outside. She asked me to go and listen at the window which looked out over the leads, for the noise seemed to be coming from that direction.

[1] M. de Miomandre de Sainte-Marie.

I shook myself, for I had been very fast asleep, and then climbed on to the window and leaned out over the leads. But they jutted out too far for me to be able to see the street.[1] I could distinctly hear a number of voices shouting: 'Kill them! Kill them! Kill the Garde du Corps!' I was terrified. Neither my sister-in-law nor I had undressed, so we rushed into my aunt's room, which overlooked the park, and from which she could hear nothing. Her fear was as great as ours. We immediately sent for her servants, but before they had been roused, my good, devoted Marguerite came in, pale as death. She collapsed on the first chair within reach, crying: 'Oh, Heaven, we shall all be murdered'. This was not exactly reassuring. The poor woman was so out of breath that she could scarcely speak. However, after a minute or two, she told us that she had left my room in the Ministry in order to find me and ask if I would need her, for my husband had told her on the previous day that I would remain at the Château. On her way down the outside stair, she had come upon a large mass of people, the dregs of the town, and had seen a man with a long beard, a well known model[2] at the Academy, in the act of beheading the body of a Garde du Corps who had just been killed.[3] As she passed the gate in the Rue de l'Orangerie,[4] she had also seen a gentleman arriving, his boots splashed with mud and a riding whip still in his hand. It was none other than the Duc d'Orléans, whom she knew very well by sight. She told us also that, at sight of him, the wretches had cried joyfully: 'Long Live our King d'Orléans!', he meantime signing to them with his hand to be quiet. My good Marguerite added that, realising that her white apron and very clean gown might make her conspicuous among such a bedraggled mob, she had fled, stepping across the body of a Garde[5] who had fallen across the gate to the Cour des Princes.

Hardly had she finished this exciting tale when my husband arrived. He told us that when he had seen the assassins entering

[1] The Rue de la Sur-Intendance.
[2] Nicolas Jourdan, an artist's model, referred to elsewhere in this text as 'coupe-tête' (the beheader).
[3] i.e., Deshuttes.
[4] Rue de la Sur-Intendance.
[5] M. de Vallori, or de Varicourt.

the Cour Royale, he had immediately rushed to the main Garde, on the Place d'Armes, to have the call to arms sounded. We also learned from him that the Queen had managed to escape to the King's apartment by the little passage under the Oeuil de Boeuf, which linked her bedchamber with the King's. He persuaded us to leave my aunt's apartment, which he thought too close to those of the King and Queen and advised us to join Mme de Simiane at a house near the Orangerie belonging to one of her former waiting women. M. l'Abbé de Damas came to escort us. I left in a state of despair and great anxiety at all the dangers threatening my husband. He had had to order me to go to this woman's house, but promised to keep me informed of everything that happened to him.

At the end of two hours, which to me seemed centuries, my husband sent his servant, as he had promised, to tell me that the King and Queen were being taken to Paris, that the Ministers and members of the Administration and the National Assembly were leaving Versailles and that he himself had been ordered to remain there to prevent looting in the Château after the King had left. He said that he had been given for the purpose a battalion of the Swiss Guard, the Garde Nationale of Versailles—whose commanding officer, M. d'Estaing, had resigned—and a battalion of the Garde Nationale from Paris. He strictly forbade me to leave my shelter for the time being. I remained there alone for several hours, as my aunt had gone to join Mme de Poix, who was also leaving for Paris, and my sister-in-law had had to go and fetch her children and then re-join her husband. He had just arrived from Hénéncourt and wanted her to leave straight away for the country. I do not think I have ever in my life—certainly never until then—passed such cruelly anxious hours as during that morning. The cries of people being murdered which had awakened me still rang in my ears. The slightest noise made me tremble. My imagination conjured up all the dangers which my husband might be running. Even my good Marguerite was not there to give me courage. She had gone back to the Ministry to help my servants pack our belongings, which were to be sent off to Paris in my father-in-law's waggons.

I had no news of Mme de Valence, except that on the previous evening she had had the first labour pains. But she was unlikely to be in any danger as she lived in the Orléans coach houses, and that livery was a protection in itself. But what fears might she not be enduring at such a moment! My presentiments were justified. A member of the Garde du Corps was killed under her very window, a low mezzanine one. She was so frightened that the labour pains stopped completely, and it was as if they had never begun. She left for Paris by way of Marly and her daughter, Rosamonde, was not born until three days later.

Towards three o'clock, Mme d'Hénin came back and told me that the sad procession had left for Paris, the heads of the murdered guards being carried by their murderers on pikes immediately in front of the King's carriage. The Garde Nationale of Paris, which surrounded the carriage, had discarded their own hats and crossbelts in favour of those of the Garde du Corps and the Swiss Guard, and they tramped along with the women and the people. This horrible masquerade made its way slowly to the Tuileries, followed by a stream of carriages of all kinds conveying the National Assembly.

Meanwhile Louis XVI, as he climbed into his carriage, had said to M. de La Tour du Pin: 'You are in complete charge here. Try to save my poor Versailles for me.' This was a command my husband was firmly determined to carry out. He made his arrangements with the officer commanding the battalion of the Garde Nationale of Paris that had been left with him, a very determined man who showed the utmost good will—none other than Santerre![1]

Accompanied by my aunt, I left my shelter and went back to the Ministry. A terrible solitude already weighed heavily over Versailles. The only sound to be heard in the Château was the fastening of doors and shutters which had not been closed since the time of Louis XIV. My husband made his preparations for the defence of the Château, certain that as soon as night fell, the

[1] Antoine-Joseph Santerre (1752–1809), owner of an ale-house in the Faubour Saint-Antoine and known for his kindness and generosity. As an officer in the Parisian Garde Nationale, he did all in his power to restrain the violence of the mob. At the moment of Louis XVI's execution, he ordered a roll of drums to ensure silence, but this was misconstrued into an attempt to drown the King's voice. (T)

strange sinister figures to be seen wandering about the streets and inside the still open courtyards would band together to pillage it. Fearful for me in the rioting he expected, he obliged me to leave with my aunt.

We did not want to go to Paris in case the gates should be closed and I should be separated from my husband and unable to rejoin him. My wish was to remain at Versailles; near my husband, I was not afraid of anything that might befall. But he feared the dangerous consequences to my health of any further terrors like those we had just experienced. He said that my presence paralysed the effort which it was his duty to make to justify the King's trust in him. In the end, he persuaded me to go to Saint-Germain and to await developments in the Château there, in the apartment of M. de Lally.

We made the journey in a miserable little carriage, my aunt and I, accompanied by a maid whose home was in Saint-Germain. My father-in-law's horses and carriages had gone to Paris, and in Versailles it would have been impossible to find a means of transport, no matter how large the fee offered. The journey lasted three long hours. The bumpy paving of the road and the hundred and eighty steps I had to climb to reach the apartment—where the old concierge was amazed to see me—completely exhausted me. I became very ill and before the night was over, all the symptoms of a miscarriage threatened. A drastic cupping prevented this misfortune, but left me so weak that it took me several months to recover.

CHAPTER ELEVEN

I

A fortnight later, I left for Paris and stayed with my aunt in the Rue de Verneuil until the Hôtel de Choiseul, which had been taken over by the Ministry of War, was ready for occupation.

My father-in-law lodged temporarily in a house near the Louvre.

It belonged, I believe to the Menus Plaisirs.[1] I went there every day to dine with him and to receive for him in the salon. But although I suffered scarcely at all, I had remained so frighteningly pale that people who did not know me were shocked at my appearance. I had quite lost my appetite and my husband and father-in-law were distressed that nothing could be found to restore it. But my pregnancy continued nonetheless, though so unnoticeably that there was much discussion as to whether it really existed at all.

After the revolution of the 6th of October, my aunt had persuaded M. de Lally, who was completely under her domination, to desert the National Assembly. She also forced him to leave France with M. Mounier. They both withdrew to Switzerland. It was a mistake; it was deserting one's post in the face of the enemy and although their two voices in the Assembly would probably not have prevented any of the events which followed, they must have reproached one another bitterly for having acted in a manner which could be interpreted as arising from fear. However that may be, my aunt followed M. de Lally to Switzerland and at that point he decided to marry his former mistress, Miss Halkett, a niece of Lord Loughborough, Lord Chancellor of England.

At the beginning of the winter, we moved into the Hôtel de Choiseul, a fine house where I had a charming apartment quite separate from my father-in-law's, but communicating with it by a door opening into one of his salons. There was a pretty, separate stair which led only to my apartment. It was just like having a charming house of our own and our windows opened on to gardens, which today are entirely built over. As my father-in-law entrusted many important matters to my husband, he was kept very busy and I seldom saw him except at luncheon, which we ate alone, and at dinner.

In Paris, my father-in-law no longer gave big dinner parties, but each day we were twelve to fifteen at table, the guests being deputies, foreigners or persons of note. We dined at four o'clock. Afterwards, my father-in-law spent about an hour in the salon

[1] A special department to defray entertainment expenses incurred by the King outside the formal routine of the Court. (T)

talking to those visitors who still followed the Versailles custom of coming for coffee. He then went off to his study and I returned to my own apartment or went out visiting.

When the Queen returned to Paris, she gave up her boxes at the theatre, an expression of resentment which, though very natural, was most unfortunate. It made the people of Paris more hostile than ever towards her. This ill-starred princess either did not know how to consider people's feelings or was not prepared to do so. When she was displeased, she allowed it to be evident, regardless of the consequences, and this did great harm to the King's cause. She was gifted with very great courage, but little intelligence, absolutely no tact and, worst of all, a mistrust—always misplaced —of those most willing to serve her. She refused to recognise that the terrible danger which had threatened her on the night of the 6th of October was the result of a plot by the Duc d'Orléans, and from then on vented her resentment on all the people of Paris and avoided appearing in public.

I greatly missed being able to use the Queen's boxes at the theatre and as I feared the crowds, did not go to any plays during the winter of 1789–1790. I often arranged small supper parties of eight or ten people in my apartment. My father-in-law never joined us on these occasions as he went early to bed and rose correspondingly early in the morning.

It was during the first months of 1790 that the demagogues set out to corrupt the army. Every day some piece of disturbing news reached us: one regiment had seized its funds; another had refused to change garrison; in one place, the officers had emigrated; in another a town sent a deputation to the Assembly asking for the transfer of the regiment stationed there on the grounds that the officers were aristocrats and did not fraternise with the citizens. My poor father-in-law was worked to death trying to deal with all these reports. Many officers absented themselves without leave, intending to go abroad, and the lack of discipline, of which the non-commissioned officers took every advantage, encouraged revolt.

On the 19th of May, I gave birth to a healthy son who was to be my joy for twenty-five years. His godparents were my father-in-law and Mme d'Hénin, who had come from Switzerland to be

with me when he was born. We called the baby Humbert-
Frédéric. Priests were still free to exercise their office without
taking the oath,[1] and my son was baptised in the parish of Saint-
Eustache. When he was born, he seemed to be only skin and bone,
but a good foster-mother took charge of him and he soon gained
weight.

In Paris, the Court followed the same routine as at Versailles,
except that we no longer went to Mass after the publication of the
Decree requiring priests to take the oath. The dinner ceremonial
remained the same as at Versailles. When I had recovered from
my son's birth, I waited on the Queen in full Court dress. She
welcomed me most amiably. Mme d'Hénin had resigned when
she went to Switzerland and there was some question of my taking
her place. However, the Queen was unwilling. There was already
talk of appointing my husband to be Minister in Holland and
since I would naturally accompany him, the Queen thought it
was not worth while for me to begin my service if it was to be
interrupted so soon. 'And also,' she added, 'who knows if I
might not expose her to further dangers like those of the 5th of
October?'

II

I cannot remember now how the idea arose that all the military
organisations in the country should 'fraternise', as it was called
then, by sending the senior member of every rank to Paris for
the 14th of July, anniversary of the capture of the Bastille. The
'Moniteur' gives an account of the session at which this decision
was taken.

The Garde Nationale, which had been organised throughout
the kingdom during the previous year, also sent deputations of the
highest-ranking officers and the oldest of the guardsmen. Preparations started at the end of June.

The Champ de Mars, in front of the Ecole Militaire, was in
those days a very smooth green on which the students from the
school carried out their exercises and where the Régiment des
Gardes Françaises held their manoeuvres.

At that time, there was no garrison either in Paris or in the

---

[1] of obedience 'to the King, the Law and the Nation'. See Translator's Note, p. 438.
(T)

neighbouring districts. The Gardes Françaises were the only troops in town and they numbered, I believe, about two thousand at the most. They provided a detachment for Versailles, and relieved it every week. The Regiment of the Swiss Guards, which was never seen in Paris, was stationed at Courbevoie. The Gardes du Corps included four companies: only one was on duty at Versailles and the remainder were garrisoned in the neighbouring towns of Chartres, Beauvais and Saint-Germain. No other regiment ever appeared at Versailles or in Paris. The only uniforms to be seen in those two towns were those of the recruiting sergeants of the different regiments. They were usually based either under the Pont-Neuf or on the Quai de la Ferraille, watching their chance to enlist some discontented young workman or ne'er-do-well, whom they proceeded to remove from the city.

My father-in-law gave my husband the task of checking all the deputations, seeing to their accommodation, their food and even their entertainment, for all the theatres had been ordered to reserve free places for the old soldiers and boxes for the officers. Many were lodged in the Invalides[1] and the Ecole Militaire.[2] The people of Paris set to with enthusiasm on the work which had to be done on the Champ de Mars. In a fortnight, everything was ready. The great semi-circle or amphitheatre of earth which you see there today was raised by two hundred thousand people of every age and station, both men and women. Such an extraordinary spectacle will never be seen again. The first step was to mark out the semi-circle, and then the level had to be raised by four feet, using the earth from the centre of the arena. But that proved insufficient, so more was brought from the Plain of Grenelle and from the area between the Ecole Militaire and the Invalides, where the slightly raised ground was levelled down. Thousands of barrows were pushed by people of every quality. In Paris there were still some monasteries where the monks continued to wear their habits, and you would see Capuchin monks and friars pulling beside the ladies of the town, clearly recognisable by their dress, both harnessed to small tip carts

[1] Founded in 1670 by Louis XIV to house officers and soldiers wounded in his wars. (T)
[2] Founded in 1752 as a military academy. (T)

known as 'camions'. Laundresses and Knights of St Louis worked side by side in that great gathering of all the people; there was not the slightest disorder or the smallest dispute. Everyone was moved by the same impulse: fellowship. Everyone who owned a carriage horse sent it for a few hours every day to pull earth. There was not a single shop boy in Paris who was not busy on the Champ de Mars. All other work was suspended, all the workshops were empty. People toiled until midnight and at daybreak were back again. Many of the workers camped in the nearby streets. The reinforced ditches surrounding the Champ de Mars were filled with small travelling taverns, tables laden with coarse food and barrels of wine. Finally, on the evening of the 13th of July, I went with my sister-in-law, who had just arrived back in Paris, to stay in a small apartment in the Ecole Militaire overlooking the Champ de Mars, so that we would be on the spot the following morning. My father-in-law had an excellent meal sent over, with everything necessary to provide a large luncheon for the military who might come to see us during the ceremony. This precaution was more than usually appreciated since the servants at the Tuileries had forgotten to send any food for the King's children. The misleading spectacle, planned to mark indissoluble unity between the King and his people, went on long after the royal children's usual dinner hour, and Monsieur le Dauphin was very glad to be able to share our luncheon.

The poor little Prince was wearing the uniform of the Garde Nationale. As he passed a group of officers of the Garde standing at the foot of the stairs to receive the King, the Queen said graciously to them as she showed them her son: 'He has not got the cap yet.' 'No, Madame,' replied one of the officers, 'but he has many at his service.' It is true that this first Garde Nationale included all the more balanced elements of the population of Paris. It was considered a rampart against the spirit of revolution. All the shop-keepers, the great merchants, the bankers, proprietors and members of the upper classes who had not yet left France were enrolled in it. In society, every man under fifty was a member, and duties were scrupulously carried out. M. de La Fayette himself, who has been so greatly criticised, did not dream at that time of a republic for France, whatever the ideas he might have brought back from America concerning that particular form of government. He was as fervent as any of us in his desire for the establishment of a wise freedom and the disappearance of abuses, but I am certain that neither then nor later did he have the slightest inclination or desire to overthrow the monarchy. The Queen's unbounded hatred of him, which she showed whenever she dared, did however embitter him as much as his gentle, almost foolish good nature permitted. But he was not weak, and his conduct during the Empire amply proved it. He resisted all Napoleon's approaches, bribes and cajolery. The Restoration has been unjust towards him. Mme la Dauphine[1] inherited the Queen's hatred of him. She listened to all the absurd tales told about him, from that of his having fallen asleep on the 6th of October 1789 to that which reproached him for having acted as the King's gaoler after the royal family's flight to Varennes. But let us return to the Fédération[2] of 1790.

An altar was set up on the Champ de Mars and Mass was celebrated there by that least estimable of all French priests, the Abbé de Périgord. When M. de Marboeuf was raised to the See of Lyon, the Abbé de Périgord was appointed Bishop of Autun, and later became the Prince de Talleyrand. Although he had been the Representative of the Clergy, which assured him of a bishopric after five years in office, the King was so displeased, and rightly so, with his unpriestly behaviour that he refused to grant him a See. This refusal had about it a firmness which was far from usual in the King, but his decision was stiffened on this occasion by his conscience in matters of religion. However, when the Abbé's father, the Comte de Talleyrand, was dying, he asked as a last favour that his son should be raised to a bishopric and the King, who until then had withstood his petitions, could no longer stand firm in his refusal and the Abbé de Périgord became Bishop of Autun.

It was he who celebrated Mass at that Fédération of 1790. His

[1] Marie-Thérèse-Charlotte, Duchesse d'Angoulême, daughter of King Louis XVI and Marie-Antoinette.
[2] The name given to the celebrations on the Champ de Mars on the 14th of July 1790 to celebrate the first anniversary of the fall of the Bastille. (T)

brother, Archambauld, served the Mass for him and although later, when he joined the Princes at Coblentz, he strenuously denied this, I saw him myself, with my own eyes, at the steps of the altar, wearing an embroidered coat and a sword.

There is nothing in the world exactly comparable with this assembly which might give you some idea of what it was like: the troops drawn up in good order in the middle of the arena; the multitude of different uniforms mingling with those of the Garde Nationale, which were dazzlingly new; a closely-packed crowd standing on the embankment surrounding the arena, the thousands of umbrellas of every conceivable colour which opened suddenly when there was a fairly heavy shower of rain. All this made the most amazing spectacle and I enjoyed it all from my place at a window of the Ecole Militaire.

In front of the middle balcony, a very ornate stand had been erected. It jutted out almost to the entrance of the amphitheatre, so that the Royal Family was close both to the altar and the spectators. Among the members of that unfortunate Family who were present were the King, the Queen, their two children, Mme Elisabeth, Monsieur and Madame.[1] It was only two months since my confinement and I was still very weak, so I did not go down to the stand. The Queen, however, had to pass close to me and, being accustomed to her various expressions, I could see that she was making a tremendous effort to hide ill-humour. But she was not succeeding sufficiently well for her own good or the King's.

III

Towards the end of July 1790, I had fairly well recovered from my son's birth. My aunt wanted to return to Lausanne and my husband, knowing how much I wished to visit Switzerland, let me go with her for six weeks. Mme de Valence, whose conduct in those days was still exemplary, was at Sécheron, near Geneva, with Mme de Montesson, who was there for the summer. She was to have her three-year-old elder daughter, Félicie, (later Mme de Celles) inoculated. Her other daughter, born a few days after the 5th of October, was still too young for this operation. It was agreed that she should take a small house separate from her aunt's

[1] The Comte and Comtesse de Provence.

and that I should go and spend some time with her there. I agreed to this small journey, leaving my son with his good foster-mother and Marguerite at the Ministry of War, little thinking that by leaving Paris I was to incur grievous anxiety. My maid, who was about to have a baby, did not accompany me. I took only one servant and a small postchaise with shafts, for there were in those days no barouches.

My aunt took with her a young cousin who had just left her convent, Pauline de Pully. Her mother, a first cousin of my aunt and my mother-in-law, had behaved very badly and it was an excellent thing that my aunt should take charge of this fifteen-year-old girl, who was outstandingly intelligent and well educated. She had a thorough knowledge of Latin and told us quite simply that she read Tacitus while her hair was being dressed. Until then her life had been divided between the convent in Orléans and an old uncle, a priest, who lived in the town. She knew nothing whatsoever about contemporary life. She expected to find in Lausanne the equestrian colony described by Caesar, and if she looked forward to seeing the Alps, it was in the hope of finding some trace of Hannibal's elephants. She knew so little of the present day and had such a lively wit and imagination that she was both amusing and original. Seated in the carriage between my aunt and me, she kept us well entertained. But by the end of the second day, she was certain we must have reached the furthest confines of Europe. However, circumstances soon convinced her that she was still in France, and in the midst of a revolution.

We had armed ourselves with every possible kind of passport, both for the civil authorities and the Gardes Nationaux, as well as for the various other military authorities. But a careless remark of my aunt's nearly cost us very dear. The relay stage at Dole was outside the town, on the Besançon road. We crossed the town by a rather deserted road and except for a few shouted insults from passers-by, such as: 'There go some more on the way out, those dogs of aristocrats', we managed to leave the town without incident. We had already met similar behaviour in other places and had become accustomed to it.

When we reached the staging post, my aunt asked the postmaster if we were on the right road for Geneva. He told her that if she wanted the Geneva road, she would have to go back through the town. Vainly did I point out to her that our passports stated that we had to leave France by Pontarlier. She said that didn't matter, and when the horses were harnessed, gave instructions to re-trace our steps and return through the town to pick up the Route des Rousses. Her excuse was that she had told M. de Lally to meet her in Geneva and that she would find M. Mounier there too.

So back we went into the town. But what we had not realised was that our road would oblige us to cross the crowded market in the main square. We were forced to go at a walking pace because of the press of baskets and people, and were at first greeted with insults; then the storm increased as we advanced, and a voice suddenly shouted: 'It's the Queen!' We were stopped, the horses were unharnessed, the courier was dragged from his horse and there were shouts of 'A la lanterne!' The door was opened and we were told to get out, which we did, but with many misgivings. I said I was the daughter of the Minister for War and demanded to be taken before the local commander or that he should be fetched. My aunt said she had a letter from M. de La Fayette for M. de Malet, the commander of the Garde Nationale. 'There's his house,' shouted someone, and indeed we could see two sentries at a door over which floated a large tricolour flag. It was only a few steps away, so I dragged my aunt and Pauline with me and we went into the house. The mass of people did not dare to follow, out of respect for the commander who was a popular man. I must add, however, that he did not exactly rush to our defence. We went into a waiting room. It was empty. We went on into a dining-room, where a very well-laden table was set for seven or eight people and showed every sign of having been abandoned in a hurry. Two or three over-turned chairs showed the haste in which the guests had left and a table napkin on the floor near a door showed the direction they had taken. My aunt refused to go any further, but said loudly, towards the door in question, that she had a letter from M. de La Fayette which she wished to deliver to M. de Malet. No reply. Not a sound. After a quarter of an hour, my aunt rang a bell she had noticed, in the hope that some-one would appear. To leave again was out of the question, for

we could see that our carriage in the square outside was still surrounded by the mob, although we could not see what they were
doing. Pauline and I had not had any lunch. Seeing that my aunt
had seated herself resignedly, saying 'We'll just have to wait', we
sat down too, close to the table and began to eat the abandoned
dinner. An excellent stew, some meat paté and choice fruits soon
satisfied our young appetites and we laughed heartily at our ad-
venture and the cowardice of the chief of the national militia.

We waited three hours and then, having seen from the window
that our carriages had been taken away, we heard steps in the
room above us, though no one had ever answered the bell which
we had rung so often. Soon a solemn-faced man came in, a solid
middle-class citizen, accompanied by two or three other men of
respectable age. He asked my aunt her name and then, indicating
me, said: 'And this is your daughter?' She told them that I was
the daughter-in-law of the Minister for War, that I knew there
was a cavalry regiment in garrison at Dole and that I wished to
speak to its commander, who would doubtless be able to persuade
the President of the Commune—for such was the title of the
official nowadays known as the Mayor—to set us at liberty. The
man to whom she was speaking then announced that he was
himself the President of the Commune. He added that the people
were very excited, that my aunt's name sounded false, that many
thought she was the Queen, and a hundred other stupidities of
the kind. My aunt, realising that they wanted to hold us prisoner,
suggested that verification should be obtained by sending one of
her servants to Paris, and asked that we should meantime be
permitted to move to an inn. One member of the Commune
suggested taking us to his house. It would be safer than the inn,
where we might have to put up with further insults. We agreed
to this, and he offered me his arm—for the possibility that the
officers might decide to intervene on my behalf had made a considerable impression on him, and may perhaps even have
frightened him a little.

Our host took us to his house and lodged us in rooms that were
very ordinary, but very good. Our maid and the three menservants joined us there. While we were writing to Paris to
describe what had happened, my aunt to M. de La Fayette and I to

my husband, and just as our cook, who was a fast horseman, was
preparing to leave, the Commune assembled to make out a passport for our messenger which would serve also as a safe-conduct.
At the same time, they drew up a declaration praising the 'high
civic spirit of the people of Dole who had been unwilling to allow
to leave their boundaries persons who were suspected of being
other than they claimed to be. A man who had been to Paris had
declared that the eldest of the three was the Queen, that the
youngest might well be Madame Royale and the tall one was
Mme Elisabeth'. This fine story was believed throughout the
town.

Our host made us promise that we would not try to go out.
We were, in fact, forbidden to do so and resigned ourselves to
remaining in our cheerless ground-floor lodging, which opened
on to a minute garden where the light of day scarcely penetrated,
even at noon.

The next morning, two members of the Commune came to
question us. They asked hundreds of questions, looked at our
papers, our escritoires, our wallets. They asked me to give them an
account of everything I had in the postchaise, wanted to know
why I had so many new shoes if I was to spend only six weeks in
Switzerland, as I had stated, and a hundred similar absurdities.
And then, suddenly, it occurred to me that the officers from the
town who had been sent to Paris for the Fédération would
probably have returned to their Regiment. There was a possibility that they had dined with my father-in-law and would
recognise me. This was acclaimed as a brilliant idea and someone
set out in search of them.

And so, towards the end of our first day's imprisonment, the
officers of the Royal-Etranger arrived and offered me their
services and their protection. The youngest were all ready to
draw their sabres in defence of a woman of twenty who was the
daughter of their Minister. The older ones wanted to take me to
the garrison quarters. They said there was a very fine apartment
there where we would be very comfortable while we waited for
our messenger to return.

I begged them to hide their anger, assuring them that my father-
in-law would be furious with me if I allowed them to embark on

my behalf on measures which might endanger the public peace. But I could not stop them coming to visit me throughout the day, one after another, to such an extent that by the end of the fourth day even the members of the municipality realised that it had been stupid to arrest us, and gave us permission to leave. It took a few hours to re-load our carriages, and as we wanted to reach Nyon by night, we decided not to set out until the following morning at five o'clock. The carriages were not brought to the house where we had been detained but waited for us outside the town and I hoped that we would be able to leave on foot, un-recognised, at that early hour. But as I was putting on my hat I heard the sound of sabres on the tiles in the hall. All the officers were there, and whether we liked it or not, we had to accept their escort to our carriages. Fortunately, we met none of the towns-people. I was terrified, for some of the young men were so excited that the slightest hostile glance would have sent their hand to their sabre-hilt. I felt the greatest relief when, after many words of thanks and polite exchanges, we were at last on our way to the Jura.

Our vindication arrived that very evening. The President of the National Assembly had written to the President of the Commune by the courier we had sent, reprimanding him in strong terms for arresting us. M. de La Fayette sent a message to the commander of the National Guard who had so prudently re-mained invisible. My father-in-law recommended our safety to the Lieutenant Colonel of the area and we congratulated ourselves on having managed, by such a prompt flight, to escape all the very tedious honours that would have been showered upon us to recompense in some measure for our unjustifiable detention.

We arrived at Nyon at midnight, passing the frontier without any difficulty. My aunt did not find M. de Lally there. He was at Sécheron where it was agreed that we would go the following morning. Pauline and I were given a small room, and I woke at dawn in my eagerness to see that beautiful lake of which I had read so many descriptions. I ran to the window and cannot find words to describe the wonder and emotion I felt on opening the shutters and seeing that lovely stretch of water shining in the rising sun.

IV

The next day we arrived at Sécheron, where we found both M. de Lally and M. Mounier. There were also letters from my husband who sounded anxious about the revolt of numerous garrisons in Lorraine, and particularly about that of Nancy which included the Régiment du Roi-Infanterie and the Régiment de Châteauvieux-Suisse. But that did not worry me then. M. Mounier advised my aunt to make an expedition to Chamonix, so we left the following day and were away nearly a week.

On our return, I found a letter from my husband which had been sent on from Lausanne, where he thought I was staying with my aunt. He told me he was leaving for Nancy with orders from the King to M. de Bouillé to group some of the French and Swiss regiments and then to march on Nancy where the Régiment du Roi and the Régiment de Châteauvieux had barricaded themselves in, having first seized their funds and arrested M. de Malseigne, the commandant of the town. A cavalry regiment belonging to the garrison, the Régiment Mestre, had gone over to the rebels, and it had been decided that the strongest measures must be taken against them by way of example. This news worried me and I asked to go to Lausanne, where my letters were being addressed. My aunt, equally worried, readily agreed and we left with hired horses for there were then no posting stages between Geneva and Lausanne.

At Rolle, where we stopped to rest the horses, we learned at the inn that M. Plantamour of Geneva was there on his way to Nancy. My aunt asked to have a private word with him. She returned a few minutes later to the room where I had remained with Pauline, looking very troubled, which increased my anxiety. She told me that there had been fighting in Nancy, but that details were not yet known, that M. Plantamour was going there in order to take the equivalent of the money that the Régiment de Châteauvieux had stolen from its regimental funds, a sum which the old General whose name the Regiment bore, wished to replace from his personal fortune. But she was most careful not to tell me of the rumour that the Minister of War's son had been killed before Nancy. It seemed to her most unlikely. If it had indeed been so, a courier would have been sent to tell me. However, she was extremely anxious, and we left for Lausanne. She told me later that never in her life had she suffered so intensely as during that journey.

When we arrived, M. de Lally—who had gone on ahead of us— gave me a number of letters written by my husband after his return to Paris. He told me what had passed at Nancy. The facts belong to history, but I will tell you about those which concern M. de La Tour du Pin. He had left Paris with an order from the King to act with the utmost severity towards the mutinous garrison in Nancy if, after being summoned more than once to submit, it persisted in its revolt.

M. le Marquis de Bouillé, who had acquired a great reputation as a soldier during the war in America, was commander-in-chief in Lorraine and Alsace. He was instructed to assemble those infantry and cavalry regiments on which he could depend and move towards Nancy. M. de La Tour du Pin, whom he sent into the town to parley, went to the house of the local commander, M. de Malseigne, whom the mutineers were holding prisoner, along with all the other officers who had remained faithful to their duty. When my husband had exhausted every means of conciliation, he left Nancy to inform the General of the obstinate resistance of the three regiments. They did not dare to prevent his departure, either because his presence as a prisoner would have been an embarrassment, or because, being prudent, they hoped to persuade him to intervene on their behalf should they lose their struggle and be forced to submit. M. de La Tour du Pin rejoined M. de Bouillé at Toul and preparations were made to march on Nancy, though it was realised that this would very gravely endanger the safety of M. de Malseigne. But the latter managed to have his horse saddled without his gaolers being aware of it and appeared so calmly at the gate that the sentinel mistook him for someone setting out on a peaceful ride and let him pass. Once outside, he took a short cut he knew of and reached the highroad from Nancy to Luneville, where his former regiment of cuirassiers was stationed. Nancy was five post leagues distant from Luneville. M. de Malseigne covered the first three leagues at a canter, but realising that he was being followed, set spurs to his horse. When

he arrived near Luneville, he began to fear he might be stopped
on the bridge. However, at that moment he saw the cuirassiers on
the manoeuvre field on the opposite side of the river along which
he was galloping, so he forced his horse into the water and swam
across. His pursuers did not dare to follow and returned, looking
rather foolish, to Nancy.

M. de Bouillé, relieved of the fear that he would be endangering
the life of M. de Malseigne, marched the next day on Nancy. A
Swiss regiment, that of Salis-Samade, was in the van. As it drew
near the entrance to the city, a single arch with a gate, the leading
troop saw a company of the Régiment du Roi guarding a cannon
set in the middle of the gateway. In front of it stood a young
officer shouting to his men not to fire and making signs to them
that he wished to speak. M. de La Tour du Pin rode forward,
but as he did so, the rebel soldiers fired and the gunners lit the
fuse of their cannon, which was loaded with grape-shot. This shot
hit the van of the Swiss regiment and killed many, especially of
the officers, who were nearly all towards the front of the ranks.
M. de La Tour du Pin's horse was killed and he himself had a
terrible fall. Until his servant, who was there as a volunteer,
managed to reach him in the field where his horse had carried
him before collapsing, it was thought that he was dead. Meantime,
the remainder of the column had forced the gate and entered the
town. Young M. Désilles, the officer who had tried to stop the
rebels from firing, was riddled with the shot his own men had
fired. He lay there, wounded in seventeen places, but he lived for
another six weeks, dying eventually from the effects of only one
wound, from which it had been impossible to extract the lead.

After making its submission, the Régiment de Châteauvieux
asked permission to hold its own trials and pass its own sentences,
a privilege accorded to Swiss regiments. The day after the affair,
officers from three of these corps formed themselves into a council
of war, held an open-air session and condemned twenty-seven of
the ringleaders to death. They were executed on the spot. The
two French regiments were disbanded and their troops dispersed
among other units. Some of the French mutineers were shot and
an even larger number were sent to penal servitude, but none of
these measures curbed the spirit of revolt. The army was lost to

the throne on the day that its officers, instead of facing the storm, decided to emigrate, imagining that they could abandon their standards without dishonour. The non-commissioned officers were there, ready to take their place, and it was they who formed the kernel of the army which later conquered Europe.

As soon as the Nancy garrison had laid down its arms, my husband returned to Paris with the news. His father took him, travel-stained as he was, directly to the King and for once the rule prohibiting the wearing of uniform at Court was laid aside.

V

While all this was going on, I was in Lausanne, where I spent a very gay fortnight. There were many English people staying there and they gave dances. I also met a very famous man, Mr Gibbon, whose appearance was so grotesque that it was difficult not to laugh. There were many émigrés, too. I did not enjoy their company, for they were much given to exaggeration and as soon as Mme de Montesson arrived at Paquis, near Geneva, I went to join her. Mme de Valence and I shared a small house.

The inn at Sécheron was then greatly in fashion. Many émigrés whom I knew had come to stay there for the summer: the Duc de Guines with his daughter, the Duchesse de Castries, the old Comte de Pons and his wife who understood not the first thing of what was happening in France, and many others beside. A number of the young people who had accompanied the Comte d'Artois to Turin had already tired somewhat of Piedmont and they, too, came to Switzerland. Archambauld de Périgord was among them. He had emigrated straight from the foot of the altar after the Fédération. They all brought the airs and the insolence of Paris society into the midst of Swiss customs, which were then even simpler than they are today; they mocked at everything, and were everlastingly amazed that there should exist in the world anything besides themselves and their ways; they referred to the people of the country, who were offering them a safe and honourable asylum, as 'those people'; they were convinced that the Swiss were only too pleased to have them in their midst, and pitied those who did not rush to imitate them.

I hope that I, personally, was not so ridiculous, but cannot be certain that I did not sometimes fall into the same errors. They were, after all, the manners of all the people I knew and among whom I had always lived.

Fortunately, I remained only three to four weeks in Geneva, or, more exactly, at Paquis. My husband then came to fetch me and took me back to Paris. As he was in a hurry, and wanted to return by way of Alsace in order to see M. de Bouillé, we left Geneva very early in the morning so as to have a few hours of daylight in which to visit Berne, Soleure and Bâle.

M. de Bouillé came to meet us between Huningue and Neuf-Brisach, and I waited patiently in the carriage while my husband talked with him as they walked up and down in the road. After spending a morning in Strasbourg, we stopped for the night at Saverne and from there went on to Nancy. As we crossed that town in the moonlight, we passed in front of the lodging of the unfortunate M. Désilles, who was dying. A sentinel had been placed at the door to prevent people stopping to talk under his window. He died a few days later. We travelled from Nancy to Paris without any further stops and there I found again my dear child, in excellent health and much improved in looks. He had an excellent foster-mother and my good Marguerite watched over her and the baby with incomparable, unfailing care.

CHAPTER TWELVE

I

At the Ministry of War, I resumed the life I had always led in Paris. Nearly every morning I went riding with my cousin, Dominic Sheldon. I often went to the theatre with young Mme de Noailles whose mother, Mme de Laborde, did not go into society. In any case, the pride of the families of Poix, Mouchy and de Noailles would never have been satisfied with such a chaperon. The fortune of Mlle de Laborde had been most welcome, her family much less so. Her father-in-law, the Prince de Poix, was very fond of me and delighted that I should accompany his daughter-in-law, whose sixteen years deferred with a certain respect to my twenty. The Princesse de Poix also showed me much friendship and kindness and was very glad for her son's wife to accompany me in society. I have never suffered from that smallness of mind which makes some women jealous of the success of other young women and I rejoiced sincerely in the success of Mme de Noailles. I looked on Nathalie as a younger sister, and we often wore matching dresses and had our hair dressed in a similar style.

I cannot remember why I never went to Méréville, M. de Laborde's magnificent house in Beauce, but I often went with Mme de Poix to supper at the Hôtel de Laborde in the Rue d'Artois. One could be sure of hearing very good music there, played by some of the finest musicians in Paris. As for my friends of the Hôtel Rochechouart, it was always late in the season before they tore themselves away from their lovely Château de Courteilles.

My father-in-law's distaste for his Ministry increased daily. Nearly all the regiments in the Army were in a state of revolt. Most of the officers, instead of meeting the efforts of the Revolutionaries with steady firmness, sent in their resignations and left France. To emigrate became a point of honour. Those who remained with their regiments or in their province, received letters from the émigré officers reproaching them for cowardice and lack of loyalty to the royal family. Elderly gentlemen who had retired to their manors received through the post small parcels containing a white feather or an insulting caricature. It was an attempt to convince them that it had become their duty to abandon their sovereign. They were promised the intervention of innumerable foreign armies. The King, as good as he was weak, scrupled to stem this torrent and so, day by day, he was able to note the departure of yet another supporter, sometimes even of some member of his Household.

My father-in-law was powerless before the intrigues of the Assembly and not finding in the King the firmness he had a right to expect, decided to resign his office.[1] It was suggested to my husband that he should take his father's place. He had just finished working out a plan for the reorganisation of the whole

[1] He did so on the 15th of November 1790.

Army and the King himself thought that the originator of the plan was capable of putting it into effect. But my husband refused, fearing that if he took his father's place it might be wrongly interpreted.

It was then during the last days of December 1790, that he was appointed Minister Plenipotentiary in Holland, but it was agreed that he would not take up his new duties until the King had accepted the Constitution.[1] The National Assembly was expected to complete it before the end of the winter.

We left the Ministry of War and went to live in Mme d'Hénin's house in the Rue de Varenne. She had had all her furniture sent over there from the Rue de Verneuil, which she had given up. This house was most convenient. We moved in there with my sister-in-law, Mme de Lameth, her two children and my father-in-law. My husband kept the saddle horses and another for his cabriolet. My father-in-law no longer wanted a carriage. He kept only two carriage horses for my sister-in-law and me. My sister-in-law de Lameth hardly ever went out in the evening. But she went every morning to the meetings of the Assemblée, sitting in a box which one of the King's equerries had had arranged in the Chamber. His own apartment in the riding school of the Tuileries was against one of the Chamber walls. As you know, when the Assembly moved to Paris, it was housed in the Tuileries.

I went sometimes to the sessions which interested me, but not regularly, as my sister-in-law did. My mornings were more usefully employed. I had a drawing master, a singing master, an Italian master and, if there was time, I also rode from three o'clock until nightfall. When my cousin Sheldon could accompany me, I went to the Bois de Boulogne, but usually, I went by way of the Plain of Grenelle to the Bois de Meudon. In those days I rode a very lively thoroughbred, whose step and manner I enjoyed tremendously; but he was a great trouble to me in the Bois de Boulogne for he could never bear another horse in front of him, and on such occasions was always ready to seize the bit.

[1] In July 1789, the National Assembly started work on a new Constitution for France. It issued the Declaration of the Rights of Man, abolished Feudalism, reformed the judiciary, the system of local and provincial government, the government of the Church, entrusted legislative power to a single chamber of 145 members. The Constitution was completed in September 1791 and accepted by the King.

I was returning home one day in the Spring of 1791 from a solitary ride, with only my English groom for company. It was about half-past four. As I was about to enter the Rue de Varenne to reach our house, I found the road barred by a picket of the Garde Nationale. In vain did I explain that I lived in the street and ask why it was barred, a measure likely to deprive me of my dinner. I was merely told that there had been a little trouble at the Hôtel de Castries and that no one was allowed to pass. I tried to pass by the Rue de Grenelle, in the hope that the picket there, which I had seen from the distance, would be less intransigent. But they were equally firm. The guards at the Rue Saint Dominique were no better. Eventually, at the Rue de l'Université, I found the way clear and managed to make my way up the Rue de Bourgogne by telling a sentinel at the corner of the Rue de Varenne that I was on my way from the house of M. de La Fayette.

When I reached the Hôtel de Castries, I learned that a riot had been organised by Charles and Alexandre de Lameth, and directed by their secretary, a good-for-nothing Italian called Cavalcanti, as a consequence of the duel which had been fought that very morning between M. de Castries, a Deputy of the Right and Charles de Lameth. The latter had been slightly wounded in the arm. The two Lameth brothers, in an attempt to show that they were the idols of the people, had organised this popular manifestation at a cost of some thousand francs and a few barrels of Brie wine. The rioters reached the apartment of the Duc, who was living alone in the house. Fortunately, he was not at home. All the furniture in the apartment was thrown out of the windows, mirrors were shattered, windows lifted from their hinges and thrown down into the courtyard. In fact, only the walls remained.

This disaster could have been avoided if it had not been for the laziness of M. de La Fayette, for I would not like to think that his inactivity was due to any other motive. An Englishman of my acquaintance, Captain (later Admiral) Hardy, met the Lameth faction in the Rue de Sèvres. Out of curiosity, he asked the reason of the expedition and then thought it best to run to M. de La Fayette's house in the Place du Palais Bourbon where the headquarters of the Garde Nationale had been set up. He arrived 'au grand galop' and rushed up to see the generalissimo, only to be terribly taken aback by the calm with which he took the news of the danger threatening M. de Castries' house. He was so very slow in giving orders for the suppression of the riot that the Garde Nationale did not arrive until all was over, and the posting of sentries at all the doors when the enemy had already left was greeted with nothing but scorn. From her window, my sister-in-law had seen Cavalcanti urging the people on, and from what she saw was firmly convinced that her brothers-in-law were the instigators of the disorder. Like us, she no longer had any dealings with them, and we did not even greet one another when we met.

In the Spring of 1791, my husband began preparing to leave for Holland. We packed our belongings and the cases were sent by sea to Rotterdam. We sold our saddle horses and I set out with my son and his foster-mother for Hénéncourt, where my sister-in-law was already staying. M. de La Tour du Pin joined us there for a while and then returned to Paris to complete his arrangements. However, M. de Montmorin told him that the King did not wish him to leave until the day after that on which the Constitution, so soon to be presented, had received the royal assent. M. de La Tour du Pin therefore remained in Paris. I joined him for a few days to see the unseemly splendour of Voltaire's funeral procession on its way to the Pantheon, where he was to be buried.

I was living quietly at Hénéncourt with my sister-in-law when, one morning at about nine o'clock, my blackamoor, Zamore, came to my room in a state of great agitation. He told me that two unknown men had just passed the gate and had said that during the evening of the previous day the King, his two children, the Queen and Mme Elisabeth had left Paris and that no one knew where they had gone. This news worried me greatly and I wanted to speak to the men. I ran to the courtyard gate, but they had already disappeared and no one knew what had become of them. I have always thought that they hid in the village, for it was set in the midst of one of the great Picardy plains and they certainly could not have left it unseen. They must have remained hidden until evening at least.

My anxiety was considerable. I was afraid my husband might be involved and decided to send Zamore to Paris to get reliable news of what had really happened. He left an hour later, but before his return I had received a letter by post from M. de La Tour du Pin and knew that the news we had heard was true. My brother-in-law came back from Amiens, where he had been, and we spent two days in a state of indescribable anxiety. We had no news of the outcome of this attempt and the days seemed centuries long. My brother-in-law would not allow us to go to Amiens, for fear that the gates might be shut and make it impossible for us to return to the country. We hoped that the King had managed to cross the frontier, but did not dare to imagine the consequences his escape might provoke in Paris. I was in the greatest anxiety for my husband, but did not dare to join him as he had forbidden me to do so. On the evening of the third day, a man coming from Amiens told us that the King had been arrested and that he had returned to Paris a prisoner.[1] An hour later, Zamore arrived with a long, desperate letter from my husband.

I will not describe here the details of that unfortunate flight, which was so clumsily organised. Memoirs of the day have described it in all its aspects. But what I did learn from Charles de Damas was that, at the moment of the arrest, he had asked the Queen to let him take the Dauphin up on his horse, that he could in this way have saved him, but that the Queen would not consent. Unhappy princess, mistrustful of even the most faithful among her servants!

Before the King left Paris, it had been suggested to him that it might be better to take two trustworthy young men used to riding post, rather than the two soldiers of the Garde du Corps who did, in the event, accompany him and who had never ridden anything but troop horses. The King refused. The entire flight, organised by M. de Fersen, who was a fool, was a succession of blunders and imprudences.

Monsieur and Madame travelled by another route, guided by M. d'Avaray. Louis XVIII has published an account of it in all its burlesque detail.[2]

It was only after two months of imprisonment that the King

[1] The reasons leading up to the flight, and its consequences, are described in the Translator's Note, pp. 435-444.
[2] *Relation d'un Voyage a Bruxelles et a Coblentz, 1791* and *Mémoires sur l'Emigration 1791-1800*.

decided to accept the Constitution[1] presented to him. My husband
drew up a long memorandum advising him not to accept it. This
note was all in my husband's own hand, but unsigned. M. de La
Tour du Pin handed it to the King himself. After the 10th of
August, it was found in the famous iron cupboard and the King
had written at the top 'Handed to me by M. de G. to persuade me
to refuse the Constitution'. Friends spread the tale that the initials
were those of M. de Gouvion, who was killed in the first engage-
ment of the war, and I believe it was under his name that the
memorandum appeared when it was published with the other
documents from that iron cupboard.

The Constitution was accepted during the second Assembly,
known as the Legislative Assembly,[2] and for a few months
afterwards there was a lull. I am convinced that if war had not
been declared[3] and if the émigrés had returned, as the King seemed
to wish, the excesses of the Revolution would have been over.
But the King and Queen believed that the European powers
would keep their promises. There was misunderstanding on both
sides, but France lived on and won glory in the defence of her
territory. As Napoleon said to Siéyès:[4] 'If I had been in La
Fayette's place, the King would still be sitting on his throne and',
he added, tapping Siéyès on the shoulder, 'you, Abbé, would be
only too glad to say Mass for me.'

II

We left for The Hague at the beginning of October 1791. My
sister-in-law went with us, together with her two sons and their
tutor. Her health was very poor and the consumption from which
she was to die the following year already very advanced. As she
greatly loved fashionable company, the thought of spending the
winter alone at Hénéncourt was unbearable.

---

[1] The King accepted it on the 13th of September 1791 and signed it the following
day at a Session of the National Assembly.
[2] The first session was held on the 1st of October 1791.
[3] The circumstances are described in the Translator's Note, p. 440.
[4] A member of the Third Estate in the States-General of 1789, an authority on constitutional forms; later, a member of the Directorate and an ally of Napoleon in his
coup d'état of 1799.

Since 1787, when the French Embassy was practically driven out of Holland, the Comte de Saint-Priest withdrawing to Antwerp, France had been represented at The Hague by a Chargé d'Affaires, M. Caillard. He was an experienced diplomat, and very useful to my husband who had never before concerned himself with diplomacy, except through the reading of history, which was his favourite study. But in character, M. Caillard and M. de La Tour du Pin were poles apart. M. Caillard was prudent to the point of timidity and had kept his post only by sending despatches exaggerating the difficulties. He had managed in this way to convince M. d'Osmond who, thanks to his standing with the King's aunts, had for the previous two years been Minister in Holland, that any French envoy who appeared at The Hague did so at the peril of his life. From the day when the Stadtholder's Party, with the help of English gold and Prussian soldiery, had dominated the Patriots' Party, both conquerors and conquered had worn a piece of orange ribbon in either their buttonhole or their hat. Women attached a small piece to the end of their belt or to their fichu, and servants wore it as a cockade. Only the Spanish Minister, acting on instructions from his Court, refused to wear this favour—or, to be more correct, this badge of servitude. My husband told the Minister that he would follow the example of the House of Bourbon. In any case, ever since the Decree abolishing liveries in France, Ministers to foreign countries had had permission to use the King's livery and we had adopted it for our household. It was quite out of the question for the royal livery of the Bourbons to be cluttered with the insignia of a private person, for such, after all, was the Stadtholder's true standing.[1] He was no more than the senior military officer of the Republic, though certainly of excellent family and married to a Royal Highness. It may even have been lingering resentment which prevented the Court of Spain from wearing the insignia of the House of Orange. However that may be, the Spanish Legation was the only one which had not adopted it. When M. de Montmorin, our excellent but weak Minister of Foreign Affairs, was

[1] William V, Prince of Orange, was the Stadtholder. By the Treaty of Utrecht, Holland had been ceded to France. Only the title, Prince of Orange, survived. William VI, brother of William V, became first King of the Netherlands in 1805. (T)

consulted, he told my husband: 'Oh well, try it, but at your own risk!'

We arrived at The Hague, at nine o'clock in the evening and after supper my husband went with M. Caillard to call on the Spanish Minister. He told him that he would follow his example in not wearing the orange ribbon and that his household would certainly not wear it. The household, he added, would not even wear the French cockade, for its resemblance to the colours of the Dutch Patriots' Party might irritate the people of The Hague, who were all supporters of the House of Orange.[1] This decision pleased the Spanish Minister, the strong-willed Comte de Llano.

The following morning, my son was taken for a walk by his nurse. At the courtyard gate stood a group of people watching to see if she would wear the orange ribbon. When they saw that she did not, they began shouting insults in Dutch, which the nurse did not understand for she knew not a word of the language. But she was frightened and came straight back. When the carriages arrived to take M. de La Tour du Pin to call on the Grand Pensionary, a small crowd of some fifty people soon collected, but mainly to admire the fine clothes and elegance of our blackamoor, Zamore. Until then, M. Caillard had worn the Orange colours. That day he was half dead with fright and accused my husband of imprudence. His fears greatly amused M. de La Tour du Pin.

The credentials were presented to the Grand Pensionary who, according to the constitution of the country, was the first minister of the States. He then carried them to the States-General to be registered by the Recorder. This office was held by M. Fagel, a member of an illustrious family which had filled the office since its foundation, in other words, since the establishment of the Republic. He was the eldest of five brothers and later became an Ambassador of the King of the Netherlands, who looked on him as his friend.

When we reached The Hague, the Stadtholder was in Berlin where he had just married his eldest son to the young Princess of

---

[1] There were two main parties in Holland: the Orange, or Stadtholder's, Party and the Patriots' Party, the latter being liberal and politically inclined to France.

Prussia. They all returned to The Hague a few weeks later, and then there began a series of fêtes, balls, suppers and amusements of every kind, which suited my twenty-one years to perfection. I had brought many elegant toilettes with me from France and soon became very much the fashion. People sought to copy me in everything. I danced very well and was a great success at balls. No thought of the morrow ever troubled my head. I was the acknowledged leader at all society gatherings. The Princess of Orange herself did not disdain to dress like me and to have her hair dressed by my manservant. In short, I was dazzled by my success, little realising how short a time it would endure.

In March 1792, Dumouriez was appointed Minister of Foreign Affairs and his first thought was to avenge some personal grudge he bore my father-in-law for something the latter had done during his Ministry. He dismissed my husband on the false ground that he had not put sufficient firmness into a demand for reparations for an alleged insult to the French flag. M. de La Tour du Pin heard the news in an odd manner: Dumouriez had appointed to succeed him a certain M. Bonnecarère, French Resident at the See of the Sovereign Bishop of Liège. The Minister told him of his appointment in a note which was worded: 'Well, my dear Bonnecarère, we have shown M. de La Tour du Pin the door and I have appointed you in his stead.' By an error on the part of some secretary, this note was not sent to the man in Liège for whom it was intended, but to my husband at The Hague. Opening other despatches that had arrived by the same courier, he found his official notice of recall and immediately had the news conveyed to Grand Pensionary van der Spiegel.

We hurriedly rented a small, unfurnished and very pretty house for ourselves, my sister-in-law and her children. My sister-in-law did not want to return to France and preferred to remain with me at The Hague. That very day, all the furniture we did not wish to sell, was transferred to this house. The remainder of the furnishings, including the wines, services of porcelain, horses and carriages, remained at the Hôtel de France, to be sold after the arrival of the new Minister, should he not wish to keep them. As my husband did not have a Secretary of Legation, M. Caillard having shortly before been transferred to St Petersburg as Chargé d'Affaires, he entrusted the archives to his private secretary, none other than M. Combes, my old tutor, who looked after our interests better than we could have done ourselves.

M. de La Tour du Pin then went to England to visit his father, who had just arrived there, intending to persuade him to join us at The Hague. From England, he travelled to Paris and from there sent me by every courier letters which became more and more alarming.

III

M. Bonnecarère, whom Dumouriez had appointed Minister at The Hague, did not take up that post. Instead came M. de Maulde, who arrived on about the 10th of August, and was very badly received. His calls were not returned, except by the English Ambassador whose country was not yet at war with France. He did not want any of our things and sent his secretary to tell me that he refused to allow them to be auctioned in the salons on the ground floor of the Hôtel de France, although he himself was occupying only a mezzanine floor, and had with him only one servant who was also his housekeeper. This secretary, though certainly very common, did not then arouse that feeling of horror which his name later inspired; he was the brother of Fouquier-Tinville.[1]

The weather being very fine, I obtained permission to hold the sale of our possessions on the small Voorhout, a charming promenade right in front of the Embassy. It was an event. All our friends came; even the smallest objects fetched the wildest prices; not the tiniest piece remained unsold and I collected a sum of money which certainly amounted to more than double the original cost of the objects. These funds were put into the keeping of M. Molière, a reputable Dutch banker, who looked after them for me and later sent them to me in America.

My aunt, Mme d'Hénin, had emigrated to England and often urged me to join her there. But my sister-in-law's health was

---

[1] Antoine Quentin Fouquier-Tinville (1746–1795). Became Public Prosecutor of the Revolutionary Tribunal in 1793. He was notorious for his pitiless zeal in accusing his victims, who included the Queen, and even his own cousin, Camille Desmoulins. He was, in his turn, accused and guillotined in 1795. (T)

worsening so visibly that I was unwilling to leave her. My father-in-law, too, was thinking of joining us in Holland. My husband spent a few days in The Hague between the 10th of August and the time of the September massacres,[1] and then his father summoned him to London.

As I was in a position to know a great many details of the flight of the wretched émigrés in Belgium after the Battle of Jemappes,[2] I will tell you about it here.

The Prince de Starhemberg, Austrian Minister at The Hague, was a close friend of mine. He was a young man, only twenty-eight, and so irresponsible that he gave more thought to his dress and his horses than to the affairs of his Legation. Nearly every day, a messenger arrived from Brussels bringing him despatches from Prince de Metternich—father of that Prince de Metternich who today reigns over Austria—who was accredited to the Archduchess Marie-Christine, Governor of the Netherlands. M. de Starhemberg sent these despatches on to England by way of Hellevoetsluis. This young diplomat unsuspectingly confided to me everything he learned. His wife, Mlle d'Arenberg, took me to the Court of the Princess of Orange every time there was a Drawing-Room and the diplomatic corps treated me with as much friendliness and courtesy as if I had still been a member of it. As I had kept a large wardrobe, I could go everywhere without incurring much expense. I had kept with me only my good Marguerite, who looked after my son, and my faithful Zamore, who dressed my hair as best he could, for it was difficult to do it oneself. As for my poor sister-in-law, she went early to bed and after dinner would go straight up to her rooms with her children and their tutor.

One day, then, there was a Drawing-Room and the Starhembergs were to fetch me. I was in my room, dressed and ready, when Prince de Starhemberg arrived, looking quite distraught and saying: 'Everything is lost. The French have defeated us completely. They are occupying Brussels'. He told me the news as we climbed into his carriage and advised me to reveal nothing

[1] See Translator's Note, p. 441. (T)
[2] In this battle of 1792, the French defeated the Austrians, who fled towards Brussels. (T)

of this at Court, where no one as yet knew anything of these grave events. But when the Princess of Orange came in and walked towards me, I realised that she knew. Resting her fan on my hand, she asked me what news I brought, and our eyes, as they met, were full of meaning. She already foresaw the fate awaiting her.

The flight of the émigrés, more than a thousand of whom had taken refuge in Brussels, was the saddest, most lamentable thing imaginable. Reassured by the declarations of the Ministers of the Archduchess, who had promised to give them warning of any French approach, they lived there without the slightest misgiving. With that heedlessness and lack of foresight which so often brought disaster upon them, they thought themselves perfectly safe in Brussels, despite the Prussian retreat in Champagne. M. de Vauban, from whom I have these details, was returning home across the Place Royale at about midnight when he thought he heard the sound of many horses in the courtyard of the Palace, which stood where the Museum stands today. He waited, hidden in a recess, and after a moment, saw all the carriages of the Court setting out, the waggons and drays piled high with luggage, and all heading in silence towards that gate of the city known as the Namur Gate. Convinced that the Archduchess was leaving Brussels secretly, he rushed to warn the nearest Frenchmen. Those who had been that very evening at Court, refused at first to believe in such a breach of faith, but it took only a few minutes to make them realise that it was so. It is difficult to convey an idea of the tumult and panic which then overtook all those poor people in their haste to get away. The whole night was spent packing the few belongings they had with them and at daybreak every available boat, carriage and waggon was hired at an extortionate price to carry them to Liège and Maestricht. The wisest, and those most plentifully provided with funds, decided to cross to England. I had numerous acquaintances among those who fled. Many of them still persisted in the attitude formerly fashionable in Paris and Versailles and presented a sorry spectacle of the most shocking heartlessness towards their companions in misfortune. I hastened to offer my services to the most heavily stricken, but paid very little attention to the richer people, not concealing from them that those who had the means to help themselves and thought not at all of others need not count on my assistance. This criticism was directed in particular at M. and Mme de Chalais, who have never forgiven me for it.

IV

During the last days of November 1792, the Convention passed a decree against émigrés, ordering them to return within a given period—a very short one—under pain of confiscation of their property. My good father-in-law was in England and thinking of rejoining us at The Hague, where his daughter and I eagerly awaited him. When he heard of this Decree, he changed his plans. He wrote to us that not for any personal consideration would he act against his children's interests and that he was therefore returning to Paris. This very fatherly letter expressed a melancholy so profound that if it had been possible even then, after the massacres of September, to conceive the excesses to which the Revolution was to lead, it might have been thought inspired by presentiment.

I do not know why I have not spoken yet of the flight of M. de La Fayette, M. Alexandre de Lameth and M. de La Tour Maubourg.[1] All three secretly left the army division commanded by M. de La Fayette, intending, with a confidence so inconceivably foolish that it is inexplicable, to cross the frontier into foreign territory. When they arrived at the Austrian outposts, they were arrested immediately. The Austrian authorities wanted to hold them as hostages for the safety of the King and his family, who had been shut away in the Temple since the famous 10th of August. M. Alexandre de Lameth was allowed to write to his sister-in-law, who was with me at The Hague, to ask her to send money. M. de La Fayette, too, wrote to Mr Short, the American Minister at The Hague. I saw Mr Short the very same day and suggested he should use the good offices of a man whom I knew to be both able and discreet. This man was Dulong, and he had

[1] When the Monarchy was suspended in August 1792 after the capture of the King at Varennes, M. de La Fayette tried to raise armed protest among the troops of his Army Division. Finding them unwilling to support the King, and given the prevailing atmosphere—it was just before the September massacres—he felt himself in danger, left the Army and crossed the northern frontier into Austrian-held territory. (T)

been for many long years in the employment of the French Legation, to which he was still attached. He was very devoted to me and from him I was able to learn all the news sent to the new French Minister, almost to the contents of the despatches. M. de La Fayette was held in Liège and Dulong undertook to organise his escape. The essentials were speed, secrecy and money. Dulong thought that at least 20,000 francs would be needed to carry it out. Mr Short refused to provide this money. My own interest in M. de La Fayette was, as you know, limited, but I knew him to be a friend of Mme d'Hénin and Mr Short's refusal to intervene on behalf of a man who was a friend of Washington made me most indignant. Mr Short was himself a very rich man and could have used his own money. He refused all the plans suggested and was later strongly blamed by his own Government.

M. de La Fayette and his two companions were transferred to the prisons of Olmutz, where they remained until the Treaty of Campo-Formio.[1]

When the Terror was over, Mme de La Fayette went to Vienna with her two daughters, and persuaded the Emperor of Austria to allow her to be imprisoned with her husband at Olmutz, sharing all the rigours of his confinement. It was something of a miracle that she herself had escaped death, for so many of her family had perished under the guillotine: her grandmother, Mme la Maréchale de Noailles; her mother, the Duchesse d'Ayen; her sister, the Vicomtesse de Noailles, mother of Alexis, on the 22nd of July 1794, and the Maréchal de Mouchy and his wife earlier in the same year, on the 27th of June. In her self-sought captivity, she showed a resignation and a courage which drew strength from religion alone, for her husband had never treated her with anything but the most cruel indifference and she could certainly not have forgotten the numerous infidelities to which she had had to accustom herself.

My father, who was in command of the army division at de Famars, between Quesnoy and Charleroi,[2] did not follow M. de La Fayette's example. When he learned of all that had happened in Paris during August 1792, that is to say, of the attack on the

1 Treaty of peace between France and Austria in 1797.
 The camp was, in fact, between Quesnoy and Valenciennes.

Tuileries and the overthrow of the monarchy, he addressed an Order of the Day to his troops in which he renewed his own oath of loyalty to the King, and he recommended them to do likewise. The result of this gallant declaration was his removal from command on the 23rd of August 1792, and an order to return to Paris. In vain did I beg him not to go, and my fears were only too justified. I have always reproached myself for not going to him and compelling him to return with me to The Hague. God willed it otherwise. Poor father![1]

V

As I owned a house in Paris occupied by the Swedish Ambassador, as well as certain State or City of Paris bonds, my husband was afraid I would be included in the list of émigrés that had just been published. He sent a very trustworthy servant to The Hague to fetch me and accompany me back to Paris, charging him to tell me that at the Belgian frontier, a few leagues from Antwerp, I should find M. Schultz, one of my father's former aides-de-camp who had become aide-de-camp to Dumouriez. This officer had orders to see that I was treated with respect and even furnished with an escort, if necessary. I bade farewell to my poor sister-in-law, who died two months later, and set out with my son, aged two and a half, my faithful Marguerite, a manservant and Zamore. The winter was becoming very severe and this made the journey most difficult. At that time, I was still no campaigner, but as delicate, as much a fine lady and as spoiled as it was possible to be. Flattered and fêted during my stay in The Hague, I still thought that I had accepted the greatest sacrifice that anyone could require of me when I agreed to do without the services of my elegant maid and my footman-hairdresser. I realised, it is true, that I might not be able to have a carriage in Paris, that I might no longer go to balls, that I might even find myself obliged to spend the winter in the country. I had resolved to bear all these reverses with courage and determination, unlike the émigrés from Paris with whom I had just spent two months and who, after spending, as they admitted, a most amusing time in Brussels, counted on having the same in London, their final destination. I am recording these weaknesses

[1] He was guillotined on the 13th of April 1794.

and illusions so that my son[1] may judge, now that he knows my beginnings, how far I have risen above them.

I left The Hague on the 1st of December 1792, buried in the depths of an excellent berline, well covered in pelisses and bear-skin rugs, with my small Humbert bundled up like a little Eskimo, and my good Marguerite. So far as I can remember, we travelled to Gorkum and spent the first night there. Throughout the day we could hear guns. My footman said it must be the French laying siege to the citadel of Antwerp, but that it would take them a long time to capture it for the garrison was very strong and the city well-provisioned. The next day, at Breda, a town still in Dutch territory, there was the same sound of cannon. Since no alarming news had been published, I set out without any fear and on the frontier of the Austrian Netherlands, found M. Schnetz, a brave soldier and a friend of my father's. I was very glad to see him.

On arriving there the previous day, he had been astonished at the absence of news from Antwerp. He said laughingly that perhaps the town had been captured, not for one moment thinking that this might really be the case. But when, towards midday, the sound of gunfire ceased, he said in rather military language that that outpost of the Austrian power had . . . capitulated. It had. In fact, a French sentry posted at the outer gate of the city confirmed that we were masters of the great fortress and when we stopped at the 'Bon Laboureur' Inn[2] on the immense Place de Meir, we had the greatest difficulty in obtaining a room. It was thanks to the intervention of a general whose name I have forgotten that an officer gave up to me the room in which he was already installed, and from which he rather unwillingly had his baggage removed. As I went up the stairs, I met a crowd of officers, both young and old, who made the most improper suggestions concerning the general's reasons for intervening.

My good Marguerite and I, once in our room, and with the door safely locked, tried to get little Humbert to sleep. He was very frightened by the noise he could hear in the inn. M. Schnetz

[1] Frédéric-Claude-Aymar, Comte de La Tour du Pin de Gouvernet, later Marquis de La Tour du Pin and Marquis de Gouvernet, the only child to survive his parents.
[2] Known today as the 'Grand Laboureur'

came to suggest that I should go down to supper and declared that I had nothing to fear as the general, a friend of my father's, had put a guard in the corridor. The fact that he had thought this precaution necessary frightened me still more. M. Schnetz, seeing that I was not tempted by the proposal of supper, went off. Marguerite got Humbert to sleep, and I barricaded the door with the bed and everything else I could find in the room.

Just then my attention was drawn to the window, which gave on to the Place, for there was a great glow which I thought must come from some illuminations. I will never be able to forget the sight which met my eyes. In the midst of that vast Place had been lit a fire whose flames were leaping as high as the roof tops. Numbers of soldiers, drunk, reeling, unsteady, swayed about it, flinging in any furnishings they could find: bedsteads, chests of drawers, sideboards, screens, clothes, baskets full of papers and then a mass of chairs, tables and armchairs with gilded wooden frames, all of which made the fire blaze higher minute by minute. Dreadful looking women, their hair loose and their dress in disorder, mingled with this gang of madmen, giving them wine, perhaps vintage wine from the cellars of Antwerp's rich citizens. Wild laughter, foul oaths and obscene songs added to the general horror of this diabolic fling. For me, it was the embodiment of all that I had ever read about the capture of a town by assault, of the pillaging and terrible disorders which resulted. I stood at the window throughout the night, fascinated and terrified, unable to tear myself away despite my horror.

Towards morning, M. Schnetz told me that we would have to leave for Mons. As we left Antwerp, I was struck by the rare spectacle spread before us. Between the forward line of the fortifications and the first sentry post, that of Contich, we drove through the entire French army which was camping there. These conquerors, who were already making the fine armies of Austria and Prussia quake in their shoes, had all the appearance of a horde of bandits. Most of them lacked a uniform. After requisitioning everything in all the cloth shops in Paris and other big cities, the Convention had hurriedly had cloaks made from materials of every imaginable hue. This medley, a vast human rainbow, stood out curiously clearly against the snow which covered the ground:

the camp looked like some gigantic and very vivid flower-bed. It would have been a sight to enjoy had it not been for the red bonnets which most of the soldiers were wearing and which reminded us of all that we had to fear from them. Only the officers were in uniform, but with none of the brilliant embroideries which Napoleon has since scattered so liberally.

Forced to drive at almost a walking pace, the way seemed long. The roads, cut up by the artillery, were cluttered with waggons, ammunition carts and guns. We advanced slowly, amid the shouts and oaths of the drivers and the rough pleasantries of the soldiers. It was obvious that Schnetz was worried and regretted not having brought an escort. Eventually, at nightfall, we reached Malines where we spent a calmer night than at Antwerp, though there were still many troops about.

The following morning we set out for Brussels, where we had not intended to stop, but M. de Moreton de Chabrillon, the local commander decided otherwise. The horses had already been put to and M. Schnetz had had my passport franked when there arrived an order from the General that I was not to be allowed to pass. The horses were unharnessed, but I was not allowed to leave the carriage. After a while, my son and his nurse were permitted to go into the postmaster's house, and I waited alone.

Eventually, three hours later, M. de Chabrillon authorised my departure without any explanation of his odd display of officious authority. He was of good family and I had met him hundreds of times, though I had never spoken to him. He was very short-sighted and had strong revolutionary sympathies.

That was not the last of my alarms. It was late when we arrived at Mons and we had the greatest difficulty in finding somewhere to stay. All the inns were full. In the end, one of them offered us two small rooms for my maid and me, on a very low first floor, overlooking the street. They told me the officers who had been occupying these rooms had only just left. M. Schnetz and my two menservants would have to sleep on the far side of a very large courtyard, an arrangement which meant that my maid and I would be quite separated from them. It was far from satisfactory, but there was no alternative. My son was tired. I put him into my bed and decided not to undress. But I was growing sleepy nonetheless when a noise in the street, near my windows, awakened me. There was loud knocking on the door of the house, and terrible swearing. I soon heard the inkeeper shouting that a general's wife was sleeping in the room and that an aide-de-camp who was accompanying her was also in the inn. A drunken voice replied that he was coming to see if it was true. He had with him a number of other men in the same state, and as I threw myself under the bed, I saw two hands grasp the balcony, as someone tried to haul themselves up. I was frozen with terror, but did not lose my head. Calling loudly for my maid, I prepared to throw at the intruder a great log that was burning in the hearth. At that moment, I heard him fall back into the street, and he either hurt himself in the fall or his comrades were afraid of punishment, for they carried him off and my fears were quietened.

The next day, M. Schnetz went to lodge a complaint, a step which was far from my thoughts, but he insisted that he had to do so in order to discharge his responsibility.

As we left, we met a squadron entirely composed of negroes, all very well mounted and perfectly equipped. The Duc d'Orléans' fine negro, Edward, was in command. As he was a great friend of Zamore, the latter asked my permission to spend the day with his fellow negroes. I rather feared that they would enlist him in their ranks and that I wouldn't see him again. But I was wrong. That good boy was given a wonderful time by his comrades, but in the evening he was back with me, telling me in his simple way all that had been done to try to persuade him to stay. His loyalty to me had won the day and I was most grateful.

The rest of my journey passed without any incident worthy of note. M. Schnetz left me, I think, at Péronne and I took the road to Hénéncourt where I found my brother-in-law, the Marquis de Lameth.

CHAPTER THIRTEEN

I

In Holland, I had been spoiled, admired and flattered. Returning to France, I had scarcely crossed the border when the Revolution was all about me, dark and menacing, laden with danger.

I returned, it is true, to the very same room from which I had set out so light-heartedly only fifteen months before, but the light-heartedness had gone.

Looking critically at my past life, I reproached myself for its futility. Some presentiment of other fates in store made me resolve very firmly to put away for ever the thoughts of carefree youth, the far from disinterested flatteries of the world and the vain successes to which I had aspired.

A bitter sadness gradually filled my heart as I realised the frivolity of the life I had led until then. Still, I felt that I possessed qualities which fitted me for more useful things, and so I was not discouraged, but felt rather that in such disastrous times I should refresh and strengthen the springs of my being.

It pleased me to invent all the situations in which I might be called on to show very great courage. In my mind, I conjured up every conceivable loyalty, every kind of hazardous undertaking. I dismissed none of the possibilities, esteeming that if they came to pass, they could but better my life by permitting me to devote it to the carrying out of my duty, however painful or dangerous that might be.

I felt that by this means I would find my way back to the path which Providence had ordained for me. In those troubled times, and without my being aware of it, God had enlightened me. But later, when He gave me the grace to draw closer to Him and to know Him, I remembered the change brought about by those hours of serious thought. From that day forward, my life was different, my moral outlook transformed.

II

It was very late when we arrived at Hénéncourt. My brother-in-law told me he felt very gloomy about his own chances and was very thankful that his wife and children had left France. It had been arranged that I would stay twenty-four hours at Hénéncourt in order to get the necessary papers to take me safely to Paris. These included a certificate stating that I had been living at Hénéncourt since the recall of M. de La Tour du Pin. My hope that he would be there to meet me was disappointed, for travel within France had already become as difficult as it was dangerous. A traveller not only needed a passport, but in order to obtain it had to be accompanied by two guarantors who, on their personal responsibility, undertook that he would not travel in any direction other than that indicated. To visit the outlying parts of Paris, a special pass was necessary, and every post of the Garde Nationale had the right to demand a sight of it. In short, to the really important difficulties had been added a thousand petty vexations and life in France had become intolerable.

I had to set out from Hénéncourt alone and arrived the following day in Passy, though not without some difficulty. The man in charge of the posting stage at Saint-Denis at first flatly refused to take me to Passy, my destination, saying that my passport was for Paris and he was bound to take me there by the shortest route. After an hour of argument and explanation, throughout which I was terrified in case I compromised myself, being little accustomed to such situations, my servant had the idea of showing his own pass for Passy, and then, on payment of two or three supplementary stages, we were allowed to leave.

At Passy, I was at last reunited with my husband, who was living in a house belonging to Mme de Poix. It was too big for our household, so we were able to leave all the windows on the street front shut and give the impression that the house was unoccupied. We used the concierge's small entrance. There were two or three other entrances as well, which made it a good hiding-place. Another advantage was that, being the last house on the Auteuil side of the village, we were easily able to keep in touch with my father-in-law who, since his return from England, had been living in Auteuil in a house belonging to a relative and friend of his, the Marquis de Gouvernet. The latter's house, 'La Tuilerie', stood in an isolated position between Auteuil and Passy. Fortunately, we could reach it by paths on which there was no danger of meeting anyone. An old cabriolet with a fairly broken-down horse, whose real owner I never discovered, used to take us to Paris and we were therefore able to avoid sharing the secret of our hiding-place with all the cab-drivers of the city.

After luncheon, my husband and I went every day to 'La Tuilerie' for my husband had to look after his father's affairs and his own. We usually dined in Paris, either with my father or with Mme de Montesson, whose house was always open to us.

My father was living in a furnished house in the Chaussée d'Antin, doing all he could to help the King, calling on his judges, inviting them to meet in his own house and trying to organise the party which was later to be known as that of the Girondins, explaining to them that it was in their own interest to safeguard the life of the King by getting him away from Paris and keeping him as a hostage in some stronghold in the interior of the country where he could communicate neither with foreign powers nor with the royalists who were just beginning to organise themselves in La Vendée. But the Terrorist party, whom my father had no hope of being able to convince and, above all, the Commune of Paris, which was completely Orléanist, were too powerful for any human effort to turn them from their terrible purpose.

My poor father appealed most urgently to Dumouriez, who came to Paris in the middle of January, but was not deceived by his empty promises. Dumouriez was a strong supporter of Orléans and his son and boasted of being the latter's mentor in all military matters. His journey to Paris had been made entirely in their service.

I shall not tell you of all our terrible anxieties and disappointments during January 1793. The events of those days belong to history and every historian has described them according to his own views. But I wish here to vindicate my father's honour and refute the hateful aspersions which people have not hesitated to cast upon it. His interviews with the judges of Louis XVI had but one purpose: to save, if not the freedom, at least the life of the King. On the very morning of the trial, he was still convinced that the vote would be for imprisonment until peace was restored. And indeed that is the resolution which would have been passed had it not been for cowardly changes of mind when the moment of voting came. Throughout that memorable session, we were at my father's house, suffering an anxiety it is quite impossible to convey. When we left, we knew the King had been condemned, but still hoped for the revolt my father so confidently expected. Everyone in Paris who was of the same mind had planned, each one independently, to mingle with the Garde Nationale and to try to direct it into some action which would help the unfortunate King; but this plan, if it was put into effect, certainly did not succeed.

On the morning of the 21st of January, the gates of Paris were closed and orders were given that no reply was to be made to those outside who asked the reason why. We guessed the reason only too well, my husband and I, and from a window of our house overlooking Paris, we listened for the rattle of musketry which would give us some hope that so great a crime would not be committed unchallenged. We stood there in a shocked silence, hardly daring to say a word to one another. We could not believe that such a price would be exacted and my husband was greatly distressed at having left Paris and at having refused to believe such a tragedy conceivable. Alas! The deepest silence lay like a pall over the regicide city. At half-past ten, the gates were opened and the life of the city resumed its course, unchanged. A great nation had that day soiled its history with a crime for which the future would hold it guilty. Yet not the smallest detail of the daily round had changed.

We walked towards Paris, trying to keep our faces calm and our thoughts unspoken. Avoiding the Place Louis XV,[1] we went first to see my father, then to visit Mme de Montesson and Mme de Poix. People scarcely spoke, so terrified were they. It was as if each carried the burden of his share in the crime which had just been committed.

Returning early to Passy, we found Mathieu de Montmorency

[1] Where Louis XVI was guillotined. Now the Place de la Concorde. (T)

and the Abbé de Damas waiting at our house. Both had been at
the place of execution with their battalion of the Garde Nationale.
They had made certain remarks which would now endanger their
safety and had therefore left Paris to avoid arrest and had come to
ask us to hide them until they could either leave or return to their
homes. They feared a house search, that first infliction which
usually preceded by several months a person's actual arrest.
During such a search, all papers of every kind were seized and
carried off to the offices of the 'section',[1] where even the most
private correspondence served to while away the time for the
young Gardes Nationales on duty.

III

Towards the middle of March, my father-in-law was arrested at
'La Tuilerie' and brought, with the Maréchal de Mouchy and the
Marquis de Gouvernet, before the Commune of Paris. It seems
that the similarity of name had caused the Marquis to be mistaken
for my husband. And they did indeed question him about the
affair at Nancy, blaming him for the death of good patriots. After
a good deal of questioning, they were all released, but my father-
in-law, more anxious for his son than for himself, decided that
we ought to go to Le Bouilh because from there my husband could
make his way to La Vendée or leave with us for Spain. The
second of these alternatives seemed the wiser, as our good friend,
M. de Brouquens, had been living in Bordeaux for a year. He had
been allowed to continue as Director of Food Supplies and was in
charge of supplies to the army fighting in Spain under General
Dugommier's command.

We therefore decided to leave. It grieved me profoundly to
leave my father, though I was still very far indeed from imagining
that I was embracing him for the last time. The difference in our
ages was so slight, barely nineteen years, that I looked on him
more as a brother than a father. He had an aquiline nose, a very
small mouth, large black eyes and light chestnut hair. Madame de
Boufflers declared that he resembled a parrot eating a cherry.
Owing to his height, his handsome face and fine bearing, he had

---

Local popular assemblies whose resolutions could be sent as high as the national
assembly itself. (T)

remained very youthful in appearance. No one was ever nobler in manner or more aristocratic in bearing. His originality of mind and evenness of temper made him a most agreeable companion. He was my best friend, and a comrade also to my husband who never managed to break the habit of addressing him with the familiar 'thou'. Of my father's aristocratic appearance, M. de La Tour du Pin used to say laughingly that Edward Dillon's[1] nickname, 'Beau Dillon' was a double usurpation: of name and of personal good looks.

My father-in-law was impatient to see us well away from Paris and made us promise to leave as soon as possible. We set out on the 1st of April 1793. Not one of the petty vexations of the day was spared us, though we had passports covered in visas, renewed at almost every stage. But we travelled post, and that aristocratic manner of travel did us great disservice among all good patriots. It had been decided that we would cover only a short distance each day, for I was two months' pregnant and having been ill the previous year at The Hague from a miscarriage, I was afraid of injuring myself again.

We eventually arrived at Le Bouilh towards the middle of April, and it was a great joy to me to be in a place so beloved of my poor father-in-law. His attachment to it had even diminished his fortune, for he had made many inprovements and added a number of buildings. At the time, his fortune had been such as to permit embellishments in the place where he expected to spend in tranquillity the last days of his very good, honourable life. But on the very day he was appointed Minister, he had given instructions to dismiss the workmen, instructions so definite that we found the masons' scaffoldings and the diggers' wheelbarrows just where they had been left when the order arrived.

The house did not please me the less for that. The four months we spent there have remained in my memory, and particularly in my affection, as the most precious of my life. There was a fine library to occupy our evenings and my husband, who read for hours at a time without wearying, devoted them to giving me a course in history and literature which was as amusing as it was

---

[1] Second son of the Bordeaux Dillons and therefore not, according to Mme de La Tour du Pin, a true Dillon. (See page 47)

instructive. I also worked at clothes for the baby and realised then the value of having learned in my youth all the feminine accomplishments. There was no flaw in our domestic happiness, it was more complete than it had ever been. My husband's perfect good humour, his adorable nature, his pleasant wit, combined with the mutual trust which bound us and our complete devotion to one another, ensured our happiness despite the dangers which surrounded us. None of the disasters which threatened had power to alarm us so long as we could bear them together.

This happy period of my life was to be succeeded by many vicissitudes. Terrible misfortunes have afflicted us. At the moment of writing, I am old and my situation as wretched as ever, perhaps worse. But my sufferings will not continue much longer. I pray most fervently that God will grant me one grace: to descend peacefully into the tomb.

IV

Thanks to the Girondins, who had not voted for the death of the King, the town of Bordeaux was in a state of partial revolt against the Convention. Many royalists joined in, hoping thus to persuade the Departments of the south, particularly that of the Gironde, to join the movement which had recently been organised in the Departments of the west. But Bordeaux was very far from having the energetic courage of the Vendée.[1] However, an armed troop of eight hundred to a thousand young men from the town's leading families had been formed. They drilled on the slopes of the Château-Trompette and made a great deal of noise at the theatre in the evenings. But not one of them shouted 'Long Live the King!' The organisers of this party had only one aim: to become independent of Paris and the Convention and to establish for the south of France a federal government similar to that of the United States. M. de La Tour du Pin went to Bordeaux. He saw the leaders of the proposed federation but was so disgusted by his

---

[1] An area south of the River Loire where the nobles lived on their estates, and the peasantry were devoted to the Church and not inimical to the nobles. The revolution was not resisted until it demanded military service. Rebellion broke out in February 1793 and was a serious threat until October of that year. Brutal repressions followed, but the war did not end until February 1795. (T)

talks with them that he refused to join a movement which was to include such regicides as Fonfrède and Ducos.

At the end of the summer, while we were waiting for my baby to be born, we began to feel anxious about the municipality of Saint-André-en-Cubzac. A rascally lawyer named Surget, who had been called in before the Revolution to put my father-in-law's papers in order when the old château was being pulled down and everything transferred to the new one, spread the tale that the barony of Cubzaguès had been subject to a lien since the time of Edward III and that the instrument was among our papers. The story was correct, but it was not a royal domain. The barony had, in fact, been exchanged for the town of Saint-Bazeille on the Garonne, the English considering the position of the latter town a military threat to their new conquest. The Sire d'Albret, to whom Saint-Bazeille belonged, had made an excellent bargain when he ceded it against the barony of Cubzaguès, the premier barony of Guyenne, with the finest seigneurial rights in nineteen adjoining parishes.

Surget wrote a memorandum on the subject and we had reason to believe he sent it to Paris, for two months later, when the Representatives of the People arrived in Bordeaux, they immediately ordered the sequestration of Le Bouilh.

My husband was worried at the possibility of a house search or the stationing of a garrison in the Château at the time of my baby's birth. He was also anxious for me to have the care of a good accoucheur and nurse from Bordeaux. My father-in-law had been arrested shortly before. Seals had been put on the Château of Tesson, near Saintes, and the Department of Charente-Inferieure had taken possession of the fine house we owned in Saintes itself and intended using it for its offices.

We therefore thought it prudent to accept the suggestion of our excellent friend, M. de Brouquens, that we should stay in a small house of his about a quarter of a league from Bordeaux. This house, named Canoles, offered every advantage from the point of view of safety. It was isolated, in the middle of a vineyard, surrounded on three sides by small local roads leading in different directions and on the fourth side by a fair stretch of sandy heath. There was no village in the neighbourhood and all the country thereabouts—known as Haut-Brion—consisted of a number of fairly large estates, planted with vines and nearly all adjoining. We moved there on, I think, the 1st of September 1793, and M. de Brouquens, who was himself obliged to remain in Bordeaux to superintend the administration of his food supplies, came to dine with us daily.

One day, he arranged a meeting at Canoles of all the officials of the municipality and the Department. They talked of nothing but the valiant deeds they were going to accomplish against the revolutionary army, whose passage was marked by a trail of severed heads. Lost in confused theories, these officials wanted to be neither royalist, like the people of La Vendée, nor revolutionary, like the Convention. Oblivious to what was happening on their very doorstep, they still clung to the belief that Tallien and Ysabeau would give them time to sort out their ideas. In the event, Tallien and Ysabeau arrived only to sever more heads, and that but three days later.

This army of butchers, dragging a guillotine along with them, had already reached La Réole and claimed many victims there. I will tell you about one of them, so that you will have an idea of what it was like. The incident was so horrible that it ought to be recorded. M. de Lavessière, an uncle of Mme de Saluces, was an inoffensive man who had retired to the country after the destruction of the Parlement of Bordeaux, of which he had been a member. His wife was the most beautiful woman in Bordeaux, and they had two young sons. All four were arrested. The husband was condemned to death and, during his execution, his wife was put in a pillory, facing the guillotine, her two sons bound on either side of her. The executioner, more humane than the judges, stood so that she could not see the fall of the fatal knife. It was to such people as those judges that we were about to become subject.

If I had not been then in the ninth month of my pregnancy, we might perhaps have left for Spain. But even if such a journey had been possible, it would still have been necessary to make our way through the entire French army. Besides, who could have expected a city of eighty thousand people, its gates defended by a large battery and reinforced by an élite troop recruited from the leading

families of the town, to submit without resistance to seven
hundred criminals with only two guns between them?

Having taken refuge in Canoles, I awaited the baby's birth with
some impatience, for my husband refused to leave me until it was
over and the danger he incurred by remaining increased with
every day that passed. The revolutionary army entered Bordeaux
on the morning of the 13th of September. Less than an hour later,
all the federalist leaders were arrested and imprisoned. The revolutionary tribunal was set up immediately and remained in session
for six months, not one day passing without the execution of
some innocent person.

The guillotine was set up permanently in the Place Dauphine.
The small group of fanatics who escorted it had met with no
opposition when they brought it into Bordeaux, though a few
cannon shots fired into their close ranks as they passed along the
Rue du Faubourg-Saint-Julien would certainly have put them to
flight. But the people of Bordeaux who, only the previous day,
had been declaring with true Gascon flourish their intention to
resist, did not even show themselves in the deserted streets. The
boldest shut their shops, the young men hid or fled and by
evening terror reigned in the city. So great was this terror that
when an order was published directing every holder of arms,
under pain of death, to take them before midday the next day to
the lawns of Château-Trompette, barrows could be seen passing
along the streets and people furtively throwing into them every
weapon they possessed. It was noticed that some of these had
probably not been used for at least two generations. All these
arms were piled up at the place indicated. It does not seem to have
occurred to anyone that it would have been far braver to use them
in self-defence.

V

While all this was going on, I gave birth during the night to a
daughter whom I named Séraphine, after her father, who stayed
just long enough to give her his blessing. At the moment of her
birth, we learned of the arrest of many people in neighbouring
country houses. My doctor's maidservant had come out from the
town to tell him that they were looking for him in order to arrest

him and that seals had been put on his house. That night, we posted a trustworthy woman on the road leading to Canoles, telling her to give us warning of any sound of people approaching so that, if danger threatened, my husband and the doctor would be able to escape through the vineyards. I suffered more from fear than from the actual pain of my daughter's birth. An hour afterwards, her father left us, neither of us knowing what fate held in store or when we would see one another again. It was a terrible moment, and at such a time might have been fatal to me. However, my health fortunately did not suffer at all. I had only one wish: to get well again as quickly as possible so that I would be ready to deal with whatever might arise. The poor surgeon, not daring to return to his own house, hid in the room of the newborn baby. A small bed was put there for him, in the depths of a kind of alcove which was not used, and was hidden by the maid's bed and Humbert's cradle.

Three days later, our friend and host, M. de Brouquens, returned to Bordeaux, where he usually lived. He was greatly distressed by the death of M. Saige, Mayor of Bordeaux, who had been guillotined the previous day. M. Saige, the town's leading citizen, both in wealth and in the respect accorded to him, was also the first to suffer in the massacre of municipal authorities.

I must tell you here about a father and son, by name Dudon, who had formerly been Procureurs and Avocats-Généraux to the Parlement. It had been decided that they would be taken to Paris for execution. Madame Dudon, the son's wife, confident in her powers of persuasion and in her great beauty, went with her two young sons to throw herself at the feet of Representative Ysabeau, an ex-Capuchin friar, to beg that her husband should not be taken to Paris with his father, but should be allowed to escape and cross over into Spain. The wretch promised to allow this, on condition that she paid him, within a few hours, the sum of twenty-five thousand francs in gold. It was not easy in those days to collect so large a sum in the space of one day. The Republic had at that time minted very little gold and it was forbidden under pain of death to keep louis and, above all, to use them. Mme Dudon, distraught and in despair, rushed to all the people she knew, regardless of class, and managed to collect the stipulated sum. She returned to Ysabeau with her treasure. He received her and undertook that her husband would that night be freed from prison. It was a cruel mockery: he had left prison half-an-hour previously, but on his way to the scaffold. To hear such news while powerless to move from my bed, with only my terror-stricken doctor for company, was, as you will easily understand, very distressing.

VI

I have said that M. de Brouquens returned to his Bordeaux house. Hardly had he entered it than they came to arrest him and take him to prison. He pointed out that, since he had entire charge of all food supplies to the army which was being sent to fight in Spain,[1] his arrest would gravely hamper its administration and would therefore be strongly disapproved of by the Commander-in-Chief. These good reasons, or rather, the fear that M. de Brouquens' colleagues in Paris would complain to the Convention, caused the Representatives to decide to put him only under house arrest. It was imprisonment nonetheless, for he could not go out, but he did retain his freedom within the house, which was large and well provided with means of escape should danger become too imminent. The twenty-five men of the Citizen Guard stationed at his door were nearly all of the district and beholden to him in one way or another. His kindness and willingness to help were, in fact, unbounded and the people of Bordeaux adored him.

He had to feed these twenty-five men during the whole period of his arrest, which lasted most of the winter.

At about midnight on the night following his arrest, just as he was going to bed, an officer of the municipality, followed by the Chef de la Section and a number of Gardes, presented themselves at M. de Brouquens' house and summoned him to accompany them to Canoles where they wanted to go through his papers. In vain did he tell them that he only spent a few minutes of each day there in order to visit his garden and see that his wine-cellar was taken care of, that he did not really live there. He had to go with them. His anxiety and worry were acute. He knew that my

[1] Spain, ruled by a cadet branch of the French Bourbons, joined the First Coalition against the French Republic, but withdrew in 1795.

name, my rank in the world, the position of my father-in-law who had so recently been confronted with the Queen during the latter's trial, would inevitably mean imprisonment for me. He did not see how I could escape death and he was desperate when he thought of my husband who had entrusted me to his care and whom he loved dearly, for he could think of no way to save me from the dangers which threatened. However, there could be no question of avoiding the visit. Fortunately, one of his guards who was particularly attached to him and guessed the trouble, took the matter into his own hands and came to give the alarm.

I was sleeping peacefully, for at twenty-three one sleeps even at the steps of the scaffold. Suddenly I found myself being shaken by an old servant who had been left in charge, a trustworthy woman who, in tears and pale as death, was crying: 'And now those cut-throats are coming to look through everything and put on the seals. We're lost!' As she spoke, she slipped a fairly large packet under my pillow and disappeared by the way she had come. I felt the packet and realised that it held a little bag containing five to six hundred louis. M. de Brouquens had told me of it and that he was saving it against some sudden need, either his own, or M. de La Tour du Pin's or mine. It was scarcely reassuring to find it there and when I took it from its hiding place, I had to take the greatest care to keep it hidden from the girl who looked after my child. I had never trusted her, and not long before, the doctor, M. Dupouy, had also discovered that she was there to spy on me. As the woman was under a great obligation to him, he nonetheless had hopes that she would not betray me.

My good Marguerite had tertian fever and was not sleeping in the children's room. She was in quite a different part of the house. So I had my small three-day-old daughter put into my bed. The maid pushed her own bed and Humbert's against the alcove where poor Dupouy was making himself as small as possible, feeling more dead than alive and convinced that his last hour had come. Having made these preparations, I went back to bed, for although it was only three days after my baby's birth, I had been up, and we all waited resolutely for the arrival of the enemy. M. de Brouquens declared later that I had put all my faith in the effect of a certain kerchief of rose-coloured batiste which I was wearing on my head. However, despite this quip, I was probably looking fairly ill.

My room was on the ground floor and impossible to miss. It opened into the drawing-room, where my faithful Zamore was hurriedly setting out some paté and, above all, wine and liqueurs to put our persecutors in a good humour. Half-an-hour later, though it seemed a century, they arrived. First, they examined the house from outside. Then they came into the salon. I heard the clatter of their sabots—to wear shoes or boots would have denoted lack of patriotism—and then their terrible talk of what they were going to do. My blood froze in my veins when I thought of the dangers about me. Every minute, I expected them to open my door. I clasped my poor baby to me and my eyes were fixed in horror on that door which might suddenly open to admit those fierce men. Eventually, I clearly heard the question: 'Who is in that bedroom?' followed by M. de Brouquens' reply: 'Hush!' I couldn't hear what happened. M. de Brouquens told me later that he had suddenly thought to tell them that 'the young daughter of some friends had been entrusted to him so that her baby could be born in secret in his isolated house. That she had only been there three days and that she was very delicate and very ill.'

How could such blood-thirsty hearts feel pity? But they did, and the very men who, during the morning, had watched the severing of twenty innocent heads without a thought of mercy, took off their sabots so that they should not make a noise as they searched the first floor above my room. After two hours, which for me were hours of anguish, after drinking and eating everything in the house, they went away, taking their prisoner with them and sending the new mother their crude congratulations.

I stayed on at Canoles with my good doctor, who was beginning to feel slightly reassured, although the danger had not entirely passed—far from it. But I have always noticed that people who take fright easily are equally easily reassured. And so, once the house search, with all its dangers, was over, he recovered his calm. He was a man of wit, and a good and religious person. He was very skilled in his profession and following my rule of never disregarding any opportunity to learn, I profited from his presence to learn much about medicine and surgery. As we had no books on these subjects, he himself gave me a short course in midwifery and surgery. In return I gave him lessons in dressmaking, embroidery and knitting. He was very adept and his progress in these accomplishments was rapid. We continued thus for more than six months, for he lay hidden with us all that time and he has told me that when he left Canoles shortly afterwards to live among the peasants of the Landes, where there were no books or other interests to occupy him, he would have died of boredom if, thanks to my teaching, he had not been able to occupy his days in making stockings and shirts for the family which sheltered him.

VII

In the evenings, the good doctor read the gazettes to me. I had asked him to do so, though just then they made terrible reading. They became even more painful to me one day when we found an account of my revered father-in-law being 'confronted' with the Queen. The gazette described Fouquier-Tinville's anger when M. de La Tour du Pin continued to refer to her as 'The Queen' or 'Her Majesty' instead of 'The Woman Capet' as the Public Accuser[1] wished. My fears reached their peak when I heard that my father-in-law, being asked the whereabouts of his son, had replied truthfully that he was on his estates near Bordeaux. The result of this only too frank reply was an order the very same day to Saint-André-en-Cubzac to arrest my husband and send him to Paris.

He was at Le Bouilh and had only an hour in which to make his escape. Fortunately, he had made his preparations and, on the pretext of having to visit his farms, he had kept a fairly good horse ready in the stables. Disguising himself as best he could, he left for his estate at Tesson, near Saintes, intending to hide in the château. True, it had been requisitioned, but an excellent concierge and his wife were still there. He had plenty of funds with him: ten to twelve thousand francs in bills. He travelled all night. The weather was terrible, rain fell in sheets, the thunder

---

[1] An officer of the law charged during the Revolution with prosecuting those thought to have acted against the good of the State. Fouquier-Tinville was the most notorious of them. (T)

was continuous and the lightning dazzled and frightened his excitable horse.

As he left Saint-Genis, a posting stage on the road from Blaye to Saintes, a man standing in front of a small house shouted to him 'Terrible weather, citizen! Would you like to stop here a while to let the worst of the storm pass?' M. de La Tour du Pin accepted his invitation, dismounted and tied his horse under a small shed placed, luckily for him as you will shortly see, right beside the door.

'You yoke your oxen very early,' he remarked to the old peasant. 'Yes, I do,' replied his chance host. 'It isn't three o'clock, but I want to get there early in the morning.' 'Ah, you're going to the fair at Pons?' asked my husband with much presence of mind —'So am I. I am going to buy grain for Bordeaux'. As he was saying this, they entered the house. A very old man was sitting in the chimney corner and seemed to be waiting for the peasant. A quarter of an hour passed in talk about the high cost of grain and cattle. Then the man near the fire left the house and when he came back some ten minutes later, he was wearing a sash. He was the Mayor. 'Naturally, you have a passport, citizen?' he asked my husband. 'Oh yes,' was the answer, 'one doesn't travel nowadays without that.' So saying, he showed him a false passport in the name of de Gouvernet, which he had been using all the summer during his journeys between Saint-André and Bordeaux. 'But,' said the Mayor, looking at it, 'your passport has no visa for the Charente-Inférieure. You must remain here until morning. I shall have to consult the Municipal Council'. And he returned to his former seat by the fire.

My husband felt he was lost unless he acted boldly. During the exchange, the master of the house had been showing signs of annoyance and he now moved nearer to the open door and said aloud, as if talking to himself: 'Ah, the weather has completely cleared.' My husband rose very calmly. In those days, my dear son, your father was not as you remember him. He was thirty-four, very agile and at vaulting could have competed with the best. Imperceptibly, talking all the time of the lull in the storm, he drew nearer to the open door, stretched out a hand into the darkness and unhooked his horse's bridle. With one leap, he was in the saddle, and spurring hard was already well away before the poor Mayor had had time to leave his seat near the hearth and get to the door. The passport, it is true, remained with him as evidence, but he never mentioned it, which was perhaps the wisest course at a time when every action roused suspicions.

M. de La Tour du Pin did not dare to ride through Pons, on account of the fair. He stopped in Mirambeau at the house of a former groom of his father's, a man whom he trusted completely and who belonged to the district. This man kept a small inn and drove a stage-waggon to Saintes once a week. His name was Tétard and he offered to hide my husband, but he had young children and was afraid they might unwittingly betray him. He therefore suggested that it would be safer to seek refuge with his brother-in-law, a good, well-to-do locksmith named Potier, who was married, but childless. This man was quite willing to shelter my husband, though for a handsome consideration, and the deal being concluded, he put him in a safe place in his house, in a small window-less room leading off the bedroom, which was also the kitchen.

Years later, I visited this dreadful hole. It was separated by only a thin plank from the shop where the boys worked and where the forge and bellows were installed. When the locksmith and his wife left their room, always taking the key with them, my husband had to lie quite still on his bed in order not to make the slightest noise. He was also strongly urged not to have any light, in case it was seen from the workshop below. But once the shop was shut, he came out and had supper with the man and his wife. The groom often brought him news and sometimes gazettes or books that he had fetched from Tesson.

That is how my husband passed the first three months of our separation. The postmaster of Saintes, on whose devotion he could rely, advised him not to make his way into the Vendée for not only was it extremely difficult to pass through the lines of the republican troops who patrolled the countryside to the south, but royalist feelings had reached such a pitch of exaggerated fervour that it was no longer certain that they would admit to their ranks someone like M. de La Tour du Pin who had remained in the King's service after he had accepted the Constitution. Nor could my husband travel to the Vendée in his own name. To join the royalists openly would have been to sign death warrants for his father and for me.

CHAPTER FOURTEEN

I

As I said earlier, the house search at Canoles did not have any bad effect on my recovery. On the contrary, it made me the more determined to regain my full strength as soon as possible. Eight days afterwards, I was out walking in the garden with my Aesculapius. We passed a large heap of vine shoots piled against a hedge between Canoles and the property next door and noticed that some of the branches nearest to the ground had been cleared away and thrown against the hedge and that in the hole thus formed, the earth was freshly trodden. There were also a few crusts of bread, which led us to suppose that someone was hiding in the hole by day and that he was probably in need of food. We decided to bring some and in the evening we set out a well-filled plate, a loaf of bread and a bottle of wine. The following evening, M. Dupouy went back after dark and found the bottle empty and the food gone. But only a week later, when we went as usual one evening to collect the plate and the bottle, we found the food untouched. We were very upset, knowing all that might have befallen our unknown boarder.

As I mentioned earlier (p. 181), Surget, the lawyer, had presented a memorandum to the municipality of Saint-André-en-Cubzac claiming to prove that the Bouilh estate was a royal domain received in exchange. To show its zeal, the municipality passed the information on to the Representatives of the People who ordered its immediate seizure. They came to Le Bouilh without warning and affixed seals so generously that not a single door escaped. But the excellent woman I had left in the château had by then hidden the most precious of the linen and portable objects and she used to send them to me in Bordeaux every week, a small parcel at a time.

II

I was beginning to worry in case my prolonged stay in M. de Brouquens' house should attract too much attention. Above all, I feared that sooner or later my presence there would compromise him and I knew that he would never tell me if this should become the case.

I discussed this difficulty on a number of occasions with a relative of M. de Brouquens, M. de Chambeau, who was himself under suspicion and obliged to remain in hiding. He had found a very well concealed refuge in the house of a man named Bonie, who kept a small, dark apartment house in the Place Puy-Paulin. This man was young and very active; his wife was dead and he had put his only child into the care of his mother-in-law. He lived absolutely alone in this house with one old servant. He looked after the affairs of M. de Sansac, an émigré who had been declared dead and whose estate had ostensibly been inherited by an unmarried sister. Bonie gave himself out to be a fervent demagogue, and wore the rough frieze jacket known as the 'carmagnole',[1] sabots and a sabre. He frequented the local 'section' and the Jacobin Club and addressed everyone with the familiar 'thou'.

M. de Chambeau told Bonie of my difficulties: that I did not know where to go, that my husband was in hiding, my father and my father-in-law imprisoned, my house seized and my only friend, M. de Brouquens, under house arrest in his own home. At twenty-four years of age, with two young children, what was to become of me?

Bonie came to see me at Canoles. He was touched by my unhappy circumstances and suggested I should take refuge with him. His house was empty and M. de Brouquens advised me not to refuse the offer. I accepted. Bonie gave me a very gloomy, dilapidated apartment overlooking a small garden and I moved there with my two children, their nurse and my dear Marguerite, who was still suffering from a fever which nothing seemed to cure. My blackamoor, Zamore, passed for a liberated Negro waiting to join the army. My cook went to work for the People's

[1] Named after a song and dance of the Revolutionaries. (T)

Representatives and was able to lodge in Bonie's house and prepare my dinners and suppers. Two couriers who carried despatches to Bayonne and might prove very useful in case of need, also lived in the house. In short, the situation was, if not the best, certainly the least bad that could be hoped for.

The apartment was so situated that I could practise my music without any fear of being heard. Since I spent nearly all my time alone, this was a great comfort. I knew a very good singing master named Ferrari, an Italian by birth, who had sworn to me and shown me proofs that he was one of the Princes' agents. He was very witty and original and had great talent.

My room was fairly large and the entrance to it was through a kind of wood store where I had laid up large quantities of logs brought secretly from Le Bouilh, unknown to the official caretakers. They had been stolen and brought to me by our own peasants. A woman from those parts who sold vegetables for a living, and who was wholly devoted to our interests, came to Bordeaux twice a week to take produce to market. She led a donkey with panier baskets, the bottom half filled with clothes and linen and the top with cabbages and potatoes. She very cleverly succeeded in making the men at the toll-gate believe that these objects had been stolen from the enemies of the people. Sometimes she gave them a few pieces and brought the rest to me.

My husband managed to send me a letter every week by a young boy who came to Bordeaux. These letters, which bore no address, were hidden in a loaf which the child brought to the Hôtel Puy-Paulin, ostensibly for the wet-nurse. As he always came on the same day of the week the cook used to go at high-tide to meet him. This poor fifteen-year-old child was quite unaware of the subterfuge. He had merely been told that there was a wet-nurse in the house who had been forbidden by the doctor to eat 'section bread'. This is perhaps the place to tell you what that term meant.

On the very day they arrived in the town, the People's Representatives published what they called a 'maximum' and had it posted up. It was an order imposing a small tax on produce of every kind and the penalty for infringing this order was death. The result was an immediate breakdown in the supply of goods.

Merchants owning grain hid it rather than sell it at a lower price than they had paid for it, and the famine which resulted was blamed on the merchants' lack of civic spirit. To meet the difficulty, each 'section' appointed one or more bakers to ensure the bread supply for their area and they were officially instructed to distribute it only to those in possession of a card issued by the 'section'. Many bakers refused and were executed; others closed their shops. A similar card system was put in force for the butchers. A tax was imposed on the quantity of meat to which people were entitled, regardless of its quality. Fishmongers and sellers of eggs, fruit and vegetables no longer went to market. Grocers hid their goods and it was only through influence that one could find a pound of coffee or sugar.

To avoid all fraud in the distribution of cards, an order was issued that a notice should be posted up at the entrance to every house giving the names of all the people living there. A copy of this notice had to be filed at the 'section'. The notices were on paper with a tricolour edging and at the top was written: 'Liberty, Equality, Fraternity or Death'. Everyone tried to fill in the required details as illegibly as possible. Ours was written in an excessively fine hand and posted up very high so that it was difficult to read. Many were written in an ink so pale that the first rain made the names illegible. The bread cards were personal, but one person could take to the shop the cards of an entire household. Men received a pound of bread, children under ten only half a pound. Wet-nurses were entitled to two pounds and I was able to take advantage of this privilege to increase my poor Zamore's ration. It will be difficult for you to believe that we reached such a degree of absurdity and cruelty, and above all that a whole great city should have submitted docilely to such a régime.

The 'section' bread, made from all types of flour, was black and tacky and people today would hesitate to give it to their dogs. It was delivered straight from the oven and people stood in queues, as they used to call them, to buy it. It is a very odd fact that people found a kind of pleasure in those gatherings. The terror in which we lived prevented us from exchanging more than a word or two when we met in the street, and the queue represented, as it were, a lawful assembly where the timid could talk to their neighbours or learn the latest news without exposing themselves to the imprudence of asking a question.

Another characteristic of the French is the ease with which they submit to authority. For example: two or three hundred persons, each waiting for his pound of meat, would be gathered before the butchers' shop; then their ranks would open without a murmur or a single protest to make way for men who carried off fine pieces of appetising meat destined for the tables of the People's Representatives and this despite the fact that most of the waiting crowd would only be able to get scraps. My cook sometimes had to fetch the provisions for these monsters, and he told me one evening that he could not understand why the people had not murdered him. The same thing happened at the baker's, and if envious eyes dwelt for a moment on a basket of small white rolls intended for our masters, complaints were not audible.

I cannot remember the political reasons behind the arrest of all the English and American merchants living in Bordeaux. They were sent to prison, as were all other nationals of those two countries—workmen, servants and others on whom the authorities managed to lay hands. This measure gave me good reason to fear being taken for an Englishwoman, which had often happened in the past. Bonie became seriously alarmed. He advised me not to wear a hat when I went out in the daytime, but to dress like the women of Bordeaux. I rather liked the idea of disguising myself. I ordered the waistcoats, which suited me admirably, for I was then very slight, and which, with one red kerchief on my head and another knotted about my neck, changed me so completely that I sometimes met people I knew without being recognised. This gave me greater courage when I went out. M. de Brouquens, still confined to his house, was greatly amused at the bold guesses of his twenty-five guards concerning the daily visits of 'la belle grisette'.[1]

III

Despite all this, my situation in Bordeaux became daily more dangerous. Looking back, I cannot see how I escaped death. I was advised to try to have the sequestration on Le Bouilh removed,

[1] 'The pretty jade.' (T)

but it seemed to me that it would be fatal to draw attention to myself. I was in a state of most anxious uncertainty when Providence sent me a special protector.

Mme de Fontenay, then known as Citizeness Thérésia Cabarrus, arrived in Bordeaux. I had met her once in Paris, four years before. Mme Charles de Lameth, who had been at the convent with her, had pointed her out to me one evening as we were leaving the theatre. She had seemed to me about fourteen or fifteen then, and I remembered her only as a child. It was said that she had divorced her husband in order to preserve her fortune, but it was more probably in order to be able to use—and abuse—her freedom. She had met Tallien at a spa in the Pyrenees and he had rendered her some service or other which she repaid with an unbounded devotion she made no effort to conceal. She had come to Bordeaux to join him and was staying in the Hôtel d'Angleterre.

Two days after her arrival, I wrote her the following note: 'A woman who met Mme de Fontenay in Paris and knows that she is as good as she is beautiful, asks her to accord a moment's interview.' She replied by word of mouth that the lady might come whenever she wished. Half an hour later, I was at her door. When I entered, she came towards me, staring and crying: 'Heavens, Madame de Gouvernet!' Then, having embraced me effusively, she put herself at my service—it was her own expression. I told her my position. She thought it even more perilous than I did myself and told me that I would have to flee and that she could see no other way of saving me. I replied that I could not leave without my husband and feared that if I abandoned my children's fortune, they would never see it again. She said to me: 'See Tallien, he will tell you what it would be best to do. You will be safe as soon as he knows that you are my main interest here.' I decided to ask him to remove the sequestration on Le Bouilh in the name of my children, and to give me permission to withdraw there with them. Then I left her, encouraged by the interest she had shown and wondering why she should have shown it.

Mme de Fontenay was not yet twenty. No more beautiful creature had ever come from the hands of the Creator and, in addition, she was highly accomplished. Every feature was perfect in its regularity. Her hair, which was ebony-black, was like the finest silk and nothing could dim the radiance of her wonderfully fair skin. An enchanting smile showed a glimpse of perfect teeth. Her height recalled that of Diana the Huntress. Her slightest movement had a matchless grace. As for her voice, its melody and very slightly foreign accent gave it a charm which it is quite impossible to describe. It was painful to remember that all this youth, beauty, grace and wit were abandoned to a man who every morning signed the death warrants of so many innocent people.

The following morning I received this short message from her: 'This evening at ten o'clock'. I passed the day in a state of agitation difficult to convey. Had I improved my position? Was everything lost? Should I prepare for death? Should I flee immediately? All these questions thronged my mind and I was greatly troubled. And my poor children? What would become of them without me and without their father? Finally, God took pity on me. I summoned all my courage and when nine o'clock came, took the arm of M. de Chambeau, who was even more alarmed than I, though he did not dare to let me know it. He took me to Mme de Fontenay's door, promising to walk on the boulevard until I came out.

I went up. Tallien had not yet arrived. The waiting was anguishing. Mme de Fontenay could not talk to me. There were many people there whom I did not know. Eventually, the carriage was heard—it was impossible to mistake it, for in those days it was the only one abroad on the streets of that great city.

Mme de Fontenay went out, and returning after a moment, took my hand and said: 'He is waiting for you.' If she had been announcing the executioner, my feelings would have been no different. She opened a door leading into a small passage at the end of which I could see a room with lights burning. It is no figure of speech to say that my feet were glued to the parquet. Involuntarily, I stopped. Mme de Fontenay gave me a push, saying: 'Go along, don't be so childish!' Then she turned away and shut the door of the room behind her. There was no alternative but to advance. I did not dare to raise my eyes. I walked, nevertheless, to the corner of the fireplace, on which two candles flickered. Without the marble support, I would have fallen. Tallien was leaning against the opposite corner. He asked me quite gently what I wanted and I stammered my request to go to our house at Le Bouilh and my petition for the raising of the sequestration put in error on the property of my father-in-law, with whom I lived. He replied brusquely that that was no concern of his. Then, breaking off: 'But it is you, then, who are the daughter-in-law of that man who was confronted with the Woman Capet? And you have a father? . . . What is his name? . . . Ah, Dillon. The General? . . . All these enemies of the Republic will have to go', he went on, at the same time making a beheading gesture with his hand. Indignation surged up within me and, with it, my courage. I boldly raised my eyes to the monster. Until then, I had not looked at him. I saw before me a man of twenty-five or twenty-six with a rather pretty face which he tried to make severe. A mass of fair curls escaped on all sides from beneath a large military hat covered in shiny cloth and surmounted by a tricolour plume. He wore a long, tightly-fitting redingote of coarse blue cloth, over which were slung a cross belt and sabre from one shoulder and a long silk tricolour scarf from the other.

'I have not come here, citizen,' I told him, 'to hear the death warrant of my relatives, and since you cannot grant my request, I will not importune you further.' As I said it, I slightly inclined my head in farewell. He smiled as if to say 'You are very bold to speak to me thus'. I went out by the door through which he had entered, and left without returning to the salon.

When I reached home, I thought my situation worsened rather than improved. If Tallien would not protect me, my death seemed inevitable. Mme de Fontenay had noticed, however, that I had made a good impression on him and was less easily discouraged. She accused him of not treating me kindly enough and told him I had decided not to return again to her house in case I should meet him there. He promised then that I would not be arrested, but at the same time told Mme de Fontenay that he knew that his colleague, Ysabeau, was denouncing him to the Committee of Public Safety in Paris for being too moderate and for protecting the aristocrats.

IV

Towards midwinter, the locksmith who was hiding my husband

arrived in Bordeaux to buy iron. He came to see me and I was able to tell him of my gratitude and trust in him. I took him to see my children so that he would be able to tell their father that he had found them well. He was a good peasant from the Saintonge region, very simple, very ignorant, understanding nothing of the state of the country, nor why, when he always got excellent white bread in Mirambeau, he had that morning seen people in Bordeaux buying bread so black that even his dog would have refused it. He was amazed when he paid for his iron that people should want mere pieces of paper and not the good golden louis he had in his hoard. Nor could he understand why foodstuffs were taxed. While he waited for the tide in order to return to Blaye, he walked about Bordeaux and unfortunately passed through the Place Dauphine where the executions were taking place. A lady was climbing the fatal ladder. He asked what she had done. 'She's an aristocrat,' he was told. This excellent reason, though he did not understand it, seemed to satisfy him. But then he saw a peasant like himself on the same ladder, about to meet the same fate. Tremblingly, he asked again: 'And what about him, what has he done?' It was explained that the man had given shelter to a nobleman and was therefore condemned to die with him.

In that poor man's fate, he saw his own. He forgot what had brought him to Bordeaux. He set out on foot and arrived home in the middle of the night to tell my husband that he could not shelter him an hour longer, that his own life and his wife's were at stake. He hurried off to waken his brother-in-law, the groom, who found it quite impossible to re-assure him. Seeing that he had completely lost his head, and having also heard during the day that the guillotine was about to make what was called a 'patriotic tour' and would pass through Mirambeau within a few days, this groom decided to harness a horse to a small cart. He heaped straw into it to hide my husband and set off by little-used roads for Tesson, which had been put under seals but where the concierge, Grégoire and his wife, had a secret entrance. One of the windows of the lodge where they lived opened on to the road. The groom knocked on the shutter. It was still dark. My husband climbed in by the window and these good people, who were most devoted to him, received him with joy. They put him in a room next to their own, and as the two rooms shared a chimney, my husband was able to have a fire all day without attracting the attention of people outside. My husband was particularly glad of this, for he suffered greatly from the cold.

Neither the fine library at Tesson nor the furniture had yet been inventoried. The seals had been put only on the outer doors, so that it was possible to walk about inside the house provided one did not open the shutters. M. de La Tour du Pin therefore had as many books as he wished. He also found means to remove certain papers and old letters of his father's which might have caused difficulties if they had become public. But he was not to enjoy this comparatively pleasant retreat for long without disturbance.

Seven or eight days after his arrival, instructions arrived at the municipality of Tesson that an inventory should be made of everything in the château, which was large and very well furnished. M. de La Tour du Pin's father had inherited it from his father-in-law, M. de Monconseil, who had lived there for forty years, bringing to it all the sumptuous elegance and noble magnificence which marked the reign of Louis XIV. This inventory would take two days to make, and from the attitude of the local people, it was certain that nothing would be spared and that no small corner would escape the search.

Grégoire did not hide his fears from the wretched fugitive. He told him he knew of nowhere where he could hide him, or of anyone in the village or the neighbourhood who would take him in. They both agreed that Grégoire would go to Saintes, to Boucher, the postmaster, a former groom of M. de Monconseil's and much attached to my husband, to ask him either to house the fugitive himself or to help him get through to the provinces that had risen in revolt.

Despite his age—he was over seventy—Grégoire set off very early in the morning, on foot, in most terrible weather. He could not find Boucher, who was in charge of the convoys of carts needed by the army which was gathering to crush the Vendeans, and who was still away from home. But his sister, equally devoted to our interests, agreed to take my husband and hide him in her brother's absence, though she made it clear that it would imperil their lives and fortunes. Grégoire returned immediately to Tesson without stopping to rest. At night he left again with my husband for Saintes, a town where there is no outer wall and which could therefore be entered by paths known to Grégoire.

I have not told you before that while my husband was still at Mirambeau, I had sent him a complete outfit of clothes such as were worn by better-class revolutionary peasants. With his slight figure thoroughly muffled up in it, he hardly recognised himself.

Mlle Boucher received him very well, but with such exaggerated precautions that he realised that the shorter he stayed there the better she would be pleased. Grégoire went back to Tesson. He has often told me since that never in his life had he been more weary, and that by the time he had completed his fourth trip, in the middle of winter, in terrible weather and along an almost impassable road, he had begun to fear he would die before reaching home.

The inventory at Tesson took three days to make and was as thorough as Grégoire had foreseen. But once it was complete, they were not disturbed again for a while. On the morning of the fourth day, Mlle Boucher came in great distress to the room where she had hidden my husband and told him that her brother was arriving that very evening with several generals and their staffs, that all the bedrooms of the house would be needed and that she could not keep him any longer there. She said she knew of no one in Saintes who would be willing to give him shelter, and only an immediate departure could save him. M. de La Tour du Pin saw that the woman was petrified with fear and wanted at any price to rid herself of such an awkward guest. To accept his unhappy fate without a struggle was all that could be done. And so, at nightfall, he set out alone. He knew the road perfectly well, but when he arrived at Tesson, intending to take a path which led to the park without passing through the village, he mistook the road in the darkness. Soon the barking of dogs warned him that he was in the village square, in front of the Church. To reach the gates of the château, he had to find a plank thrown across a ditch at the entrance to the drive and the noise he made in feeling for it drew all the dogs of the village to his heels. He could hear shutters opening and voices calling the dogs or asking who was there. At last, he found the plank and hurried on as fast as he could. Silence returned. Grégoire was delighted to see him and gave him the same room as before. He lived there for two months, often receiving news of me from letters I wrote to Grégoire. It was a strange fact for such times, but I never heard of the privacy of the post being interfered with, or at least, of letters failing to reach their destination. In Bordeaux, I often received letters from Mme de Valence who was in prison in Paris, and in them she told me all the gossip of the place where she was confined.

V

The terror in Bordeaux meantime reached its climax. Mme de Fontenay began to be anxious about her own safety and to fear that Ysabeau's denunciations would end in Tallien's recall. I shared her fears, for such a recall would have meant death for both of us. This happened shortly after the horrible procession which marked the destruction, at one sweep, of all the precious objects belonging to the churches of the city. All the loose women of the town and the criminals had been assembled and decked out in the most beautiful of the ornaments to be found in the sacristies of the Cathedral, of St Seurin, St Michael, churches as old as the city itself and endowed since the days of Gallien with the rarest and most precious treasures. These villains paraded along the quays and main streets, everything that could not be worn on their person being carried beside them in carts. In this manner, preceded by some horrible creature impersonating the Goddess of Reason, they reached the Place de la Comédie. There, on an enormous pyre, the burned all that magnificent treasure. And consider my terror that same evening when Mme de Fontenay said to me, as if it were a perfectly ordinary thing to say: 'Do you know what Tallien said this morning? That you would make a beautiful Goddess of Reason'. When I told her with horror that I would prefer to die, she was surprised and shrugged her shoulders.

Yet she was a truly good woman. I had many proofs of it. One evening, I found her alone, in great trouble and anxiety. She was walking up and down her room, and the least noise set her trembling. She explained that M. Martell, a Cognac dealer, to whose wife and children she was most attached, was at that very moment before the tribunal and that although Tallien had promised her on his own head that he would save him she feared Ysabeau, who wanted to have him executed. Eventually, after an hour of almost convulsive impatience, we heard someone running in our direction. She became terribly pale. The door opened, and a breathless man gasped 'He's acquitted'. It was Alexander, formerly M. de Narbonne's secretary, and at that time Tallien's. And then, seizing my arm, she drew me headlong down the stairs, stopping for neither hat nor shawl. We rushed along the street, without her ever telling me where we were going in such breathless haste. We reached a house unknown to me. She rushed in like a mad thing, crying: 'He's acquitted'. I followed her into a salon where a woman was lying prostrated on a sofa, surrounded by two or three young girls. Hearing the news, she revived, and threw herself to the floor at Mme de Fontenay's knees, kissing her feet. The girls kissed her dress. I have never seen such a pathetic scene.

When I went in the evenings to call on Mme de Fontenay, I was always accompanied by my negro, for he had a police card and after a certain hour—seven o'clock, I think—every patrol had the right to ask to see it. I only went out at night, in order to avoid the danger that my English looks and appearance might provoke.

Fortunately, in the very inconspicuous house where I lodged, there was no common table at meal times, otherwise we might have been caught up in a 'sweep', a frequent operation in those days. That is what happened to M. de Chambeau when he was visiting a friend. He arrived at the house where his friend lived just as twenty-seven people were gathering at table. Among them was someone the police wished to arrest. Since everyone denied all knowledge of this person, the police came in, closed all the doors, summoned several fiacres and made everyone climb in, six to a fiacre. They were all taken to the Fort du Hâ. M. de Chambeau was imprisoned there for twenty-eight days, in a state of boundless anxiety. Two of his cell companions, people unknown to him, were taken off one morning for questioning and when they did not return, he concluded that they had been sent to the guillotine. He himself expected death daily. Fortunately, no one recognised him. After twenty-eight days, someone came to his room and told him he could go if he wished. Needless to say, he did!

Then there was Ferrari, who carried a paper, well hidden and sewn into the lining of his coat, which accredited him as a secret agent of the Regent, later Louis XVIII. He had been clever enough to scrape acquaintance even among the Representatives of the People. There he often mentioned how necessary it was for him to return to Italy with his daughter. For among all the ways we had considered of leaving France, was a plan that he and I should take a passport to Toulouse, with my husband as our servant. I was to pass as his widowed daughter, taking her children back to Italy to her husband's family. In the main cities along our route, such as Toulouse and Marseilles, we would have given concerts. I sang sufficiently well to pass as a singer without my ability being questioned. Every day, we practised different pieces which we planned to offer. Among them, I particularly remember the duet of Paesiello: *Nei giorni tuoi felici* which we were convinced would be a great success.

Our accompanist during these rehearsals was M. de Morin, a young man of considerable talent. He had played a leading part in the Bordeaux Association of Young Men,[1] which had achieved so little, but on account of it, he was heavily compromised. He never slept two nights in the same place. He went out after dark, carefully avoiding patrols, for he had no identity card. I suspect, though I never asked him, that he sometimes slept in our house. When he had been hidden during the day in a house where there was little food, he arrived to see me in the evening half-dead from hunger. I used to give him the remainder of my dinner and my white bread from Saintongue, often eggs as well, for I was kept plentifully supplied by the peasants from Le Bouilh. They used to be turned into excellent omelettes, with truffles which my cook had abstracted from the stores of the Representatives of the People. In our hiding place, this was a source of much amusement and laughter.

[1] A group of royalist opponents of the Revolution. During the terror in Bordeaux they were all executed without trial, having been proclaimed, as a body, outside the law. (T)

One really had to be young and French to remain so gay when the blade of the guillotine was poised to strike. For we were all in danger from it and when we bade one another goodnight, did not dare to add 'Until tomorrow'.

CHAPTER FIFTEEN

———◦———

I

The situation became hourly more alarming and not a day passed without executions. I lodged near enough to the Place Dauphine to hear the roll of drums which marked the fall of each head. I could count the victims before seeing their names in the evening papers. The garden, which my room overlooked, lay next to the garden of a former church. It had been taken over by a club calling itself the 'Friends of the People' and when the evening gathering was noisy, I could hear, even in my room, the shouts, applause and clamour of the villains collected there.

The news I received from my husband described his position at Tesson as very precarious. Grégoire was continually being threatened with the occupation of the château by a body of troops, a military hospital or something of the kind, which would have forced my husband to move. I did not know where else to put him with any safety. To summon him back to join me in Bordeaux was not to be thought of, on account of the girl who looked after my child. From his hiding place, Dupouy had again had me warned to beware of her, but I did not dare dismiss her in case worse should befall.

A recent incident had proved to me that I was not so unknown in Bordeaux as I had hoped. The man who looked after my affairs had written to me from Paris that a law had just been passed establishing certificates of residence, signed by nine witnesses, to be renewed every three months under pain of confiscation of any property in communes where one did not normally live. As I had a house in Paris and certain state bonds, it was necessary to get this certificate. Bonie undertook to find the nine witnesses, none of whom had seen me before, but all of whom accepted his assurance concerning me. We went together one morning to the municipality and it was not without extreme distaste that I penetrated into a room where there were about a dozen clerks, all wearing the red bonnet. I sat down by the fire, while Bonie had the certificate made out and got the witnesses to sign it. He had asked that I should not be kept waiting as I was nursing my baby and this plea moved these cut-throats to compassion. One of them even rushed up to me and removed my sabots to warm them with hot cinders, a local courtesy in Bordeaux. Then, going to a cupboard, he took out a nice little white loaf and made me a present of it, calling me 'charmante nourrice' (charming wet-nurse). A look from Bonie warned me that I must not refuse it. But I took it with shame, for I had seen an old lady on the other side of the fire, wrapped in a pale blue satin pelisse edged with swansdown, who had been waiting for perhaps two hours without any breakfast. She was certainly cursing the young hussy with her gay madras kerchief knotted over one ear, her red waistcoat, her short skirt and her sabots. At last the moment came for me to sign, and the municipal official, with a respect which somewhat astonished me, gave me his chair so that I might sit down to write. Then, to my very great shame, the certificate was read aloud from beginning to end. At the name of Dillon, one of these monsters interrupted: 'Ah, so the citizenness would seem to be a sister or niece of all the émigrés of that name who are on our list?' I was just about to deny it when the chief clerk broke in: 'You don't know what you're talking about. She isn't even a relation.' I looked at him in some surprise and he said to me in a low voice as he passed me his pen to sign: 'You're the niece of the Archbishop of Narbonne. I come from Sorèze.' I thanked him with a slight inclination of the head, but thought as I went away that if I was so well known in Bordeaux, it would be necessary to move from there.

II

I was driven to the limit. I could see that Bonie was uneasy about me. Many ways of escape had had to be dismissed as impracticable. Every day there were executions of people who had thought themselves safe. The unfortunate young members of the Association had all, to the very last of their number, been arrested or denounced and then executed without trial, on a mere statement of identity, for they had all—in a body—been declared to be outside the law. I could no longer sleep at night and every time I heard a sound, thought they had come to arrest me. I hardly dared to go out. My milk dried up and I was afraid of falling ill just at the very moment when I needed my health more than ever before in order to be ready to act if need arose. It was then that, while paying a morning call on M. de Brouquens, who was still under house arrest, I happened to be standing by his table deep in thought when my eyes moved mechanically to the morning paper, which lay open. There, in the trading news I read that: 'The ship *Diana* of Boston, 150 tons, will leave in eight days' time, in ballast, by permission of the Minister of Marine.' Now, for over a year eighty American ships had lain mouldering in the port, unable to get permission to sail. Without a word, I rose immediately and was about to leave when M. de Brouquens looked up from what he was writing and asked me where I was off to in such a hurry. 'I am going to America,' I told him, and left.

I went straight to Mme de Fontenay and told her of my decision. She approved the more as she had received bad news from Paris. Tallien had been denounced there by his colleague and was liable to be recalled from one minute to the next. She thought this recall would be the signal for even greater cruelty in Bordeaux and did not want to stay on if Tallien left. We had not a minute to lose if we wished to be saved.

I went home and called for Bonie, telling him that he must find me a man he trusted who would go and fetch my husband. He said without any hesitation: 'The errand is dangerous. I know only one man to undertake it, and that is myself.' He assured me that he would succeed and I put my trust in his zeal and intelligence. He was risking his life, for if they were discovered, not only my husband's life, but his own would be forfeit. However, if that happened, my own would be in similar case, so I did not scruple to accept his offer.

I lost not a minute. I went to find an old ship owner, a friend

of my father's, who was also a ship-broker. He was very devoted
to me and undertook to reserve passages on the *Diana* for me, my
husband and our two children. I should have liked to take my
good Marguerite with me, but for six months she had been
suffering from a double tertian fever and no remedy had been
found for it. I feared that a sea journey in the bad season, for we
were then in the last days of February, would be fatal to her. In
any case, how would she manage in a country where she did not
understand the language, for she was already fairly advanced in
years and even more accustomed than I to all the comforts of
civilised living. I decided, therefore, to leave her behind. When
I returned to M. de Brouquens' house with everything already
arranged, he was amazed. He told me that an order had just
arrived from Paris setting him free and that he himself intended
leaving within a few days. He suggested that I should lunch the
following day at Canoles, which he had not visited since the day
of the search.

Returning home again, I confided my plans to my good
Zamore, for the greatest problem was to find a way of packing
our belongings without the maid being aware of it. She would
certainly have denounced us immediately to the 'section'. She
slept with my small daughter, then nearly six months old, in a
long room lined with cupboards in which I had stored all that
had been sent from Le Bouilh, as well as everything I had taken
with me when I went to live at Canoles. On one side was a door
leading into my room; on the other, a door leading into Marguerite's room and from there, still a third door opening on to a
small stair which led to the cellar. Bonie was a provident man
and had long ago arranged, without saying a word to me, that
if they came to arrest me, I would go down to this cellar and
hide there for a few hours. The cellar was full of old cases.
Luckily, being doubtful of the maid, I had always kept all the
cupboards locked. I arranged with Zamore that I would take the
maid and the children to Canoles with me the following morning
and that during our absence he would empty all the cupboards,
carry the contents down the small stair to the cellar and pack
them in the cases there. I warned him against dropping even the
smallest piece of thread, for it might betray that the cupboards

had been recently opened. He carried out the whole operation in his usual intelligent fashion.

III

The next day, therefore, I set out with M. de Chambeau to lunch with M. de Brouquens at Canoles. While we were all three at table, the garden gate opened and there stood Mme de Fontenay on Tallien's arm. I was greatly surprised, for she had not told me they were coming. Brouquens was dumbfounded, but quickly recovered. As for me, I was trying to master an emotion which had been much increased by the sight of a second man who had entered with Tallien, walking a little behind him. He had looked at me and put a finger to his mouth, so I immediately looked away. It was M. de Jumilhac, whom I had known very well and who was in hiding in Bordeaux under another name. Tallien, after courteously apologising to de Brouquens for the liberty he had taken in crossing his garden on the way to visit the Swedish Consul, came up to me with all the grace of manner which had characterised the great gentlemen of the former Court and said in the kindest possible way: 'I understand, Madame, that I can today make amends for the wrongs I have done you, and I wish to do so.' At that, I allowed myself to unbend and put aside the cold haughtiness I had at first assumed. In a more reasonably polite manner, I explained that I had certain financial interests in Martinique—it was almost true—and that, as I wished to travel there to deal with them, I was asking him for a passport for myself, my husband and my children. He asked: 'But where, then, is your husband?' To which I replied laughingly: 'You must forgive me, Citizen Representative, if I do not tell you.' 'As you wish,' he said gaily. The monster was attempting to please. His beautiful mistress had threatened not to see him again if he did not save me.

IV

Two hours after my return to Bordeaux, Alexander, Tallien's secretary, brought me the order enjoining the municipality of Bordeaux to issue a passport to Citizen Latour, his wife and their two small children for the purpose of visiting Martinique on board the ship *Diana*. Once in possession of that precious document, I was able to tell my husband to come to Bordeaux, for the American captain would not have agreed to take him on board if these papers had not been in order.

The journey from Tesson to Bordeaux was every bit as difficult as it was hazardous. As I have said, Bonie did not hesitate for a moment. He left for Blaye as soon as the tide was on the ebb. He had previously obtained a valid passport for himself, for without one it was impossible to leave the Department or to enter that of the Charente-Inférieure where Tesson lay, only ten leagues from the borders of the Gironde. Once in the Gironde, a simple identity card, without any details, was sufficient for travel anywhere. Bonie, indeed, had his own identity card, but he needed one for my husband as well. He therefore went to see one of his friends who was lying sick in bed and, on the pretext of having lost his own card, borrowed the friend's for a few days. The poor sick man, snug in bed, had no idea of the danger he was in, for one thing was certain: if my husband had been caught with the card on him, its real owner would have gone with him to the guillotine. Bonie's passport stated that he was going to fetch grain—the Charente-Inférieure was overflowing with it, but in Bordeaux there was none at all and the bakers were putting all kinds of flour into their bread, some of it made from oats, some from beans and so on.

It was evening when Bonie set out. If I had an enemy, I could not wish for him any worse punishment than to have to endure the mortal anxiety that I endured during the three days that followed. At a time when blood was flowing so freely day after day, when so many unfortunate victims had perished through the treason and cowardice of those they had once helped, I had put the life of the man I loved most in all the world into the hands of another man whom I had known for barely six months. He played the part of a revolutionary so very well. Was it really a part? Might it not rather be his kindnesses which were the pretence? I tried to push these terrible doubts away from me, but the more I reminded myself of the dangers Bonie was braving, the more difficult I found it to explain his devotion.

I had calculated every second of the time that dangerous

journey would take. Anxiously I counted the minutes and on the third day, towards nine o'clock in the evening, I thought I might begin to hope that the ferry boat which came daily to Blaye on the tide would bring the passenger for whom I so anxiously waited. Burning with impatience, I could not remain indoors. As soon as it was dark, I went with M. de Chambeau to the Quai des Chartrons, to the place where I knew the boat from Blaye arrived. It was so dark that it was impossible to see even the water in the river. I did not dare to ask for news, as I knew that all the points on the river where passengers landed were thickly posted with police spies. Eventually, after a long wait, we heard half past nine striking and M. de Chambeau, who had no identity card, remarked that we had only half an hour left if we were to return home in safety. At that moment, two sailors passed near us speaking together in English. I risked asking them, in their own tongue, the state of the tide. They told me without hesitation that it had been on the ebb for an hour. Hearing this, I lost all hope for that day and returned desolate to the house, where I spent the night imagining in anguish all the obstacles which might have delayed Bonie and his unfortunate companion. Seated on my bed, beside my two dear children, I listened for the slightest sound which might revive my hopes. Alas, never had the house been so still.

While I trembled thus with anxiety and impatience, haunted by terrible visions of my husband being recognised, arrested, taken before the tribunal and, from there, dragged to the scaffold, he was sleeping quietly on a comfortable bed which Bonie had prepared for him before he left in an unused room far from the other occupants of the house. In the morning, when the maid came to dress my small daughter, she said casually: 'By the way, Madame. M. Bonie is there and asks if you are up?' I made a prodigious effort not to cry out and you will understand that my toilette did not take me long. Bonie came in as soon as I was ready and told me that they had arrived at Blaye too late to take the usual boat, on which, in any case, my husband ran the risk of being recognised. Instead, he had hired a fishing boat and although the ebb still had three hours to run, the wind was favourable and very strong, so they had set sail and soon caught up and passed the regular boat. They had therefore already arrived when I was standing there on the bank, waiting so despairingly.

I was dying with impatience to go to the room which held the being I loved most in all the world. But Bonie advised me to dress as if I intended going out, so as to deceive the nurse, a very necessary precaution which was sheer torture to me. Finally, half an hour later, I went out on the pretext of doing some shopping and having rejoined Bonie, went with him by a secret stair to my husband's room. And so, at last, we found one another again after six months of most painful separation.

In every lifetime there are a few luminous memories that shine like stars in the darkness of night. The day of our reunion was one of them. We were not in safety. Indeed, the danger which now threatened was closer and clearer than any of the perils we had so far surmounted; yet we were happy, and death, which we felt so very close to us, no longer frightened us, for it was possible again to hope that if it struck it would strike us down together.

I wanted to know every detail of their dangerous journey and this is the story my husband told me:

When Bonie arrived at Tesson, his sans-culotte dress, his red bonnet and enormous sabre so terrified good Madame Grégoire that she firmly denied that my husband was there. In vain did Bonie beg and beseech her, and talk to her of me and my children: nothing would make her admit it. When all his arguments were exhausted, he ripped the lining of his jacket, took out a small piece of paper, put it on the table and went out into the courtyard. This small piece of paper bore only a few words in my handwriting: 'Trust the bearer. In three days we shall be in safety.' No sooner did Madame Grégoire see the brigand, as she called him, out of the room than she rushed off with the paper to the poor prisoner. When my husband saw it, he ordered Bonie to be admitted, but it was not without great trepidation that good Madame Grégoire allowed the man, that unknown man whom she could not bring herself to regard as a saviour, into the room which my husband had not left for two months.

At nightfall, M. de La Tour du Pin changed into some peasant clothes that I had previously sent him and set out with Bonie on foot, taking roads he knew. They reached the highway to Blaye at daybreak. After travelling a few leagues along this road which, like all French roads in those days, was in the last stages of disrepair, my husband said he could go no further and lay down by the roadside. Bonie, seeing how pale and weak he was, thought he was going to die and his despair was intense. Fortunately, a peasant passed by in a trap on his way to market at Blaye. Reassured by Bonie's patriotic dress, he agreed to let the two travellers climb up beside him so that they reached Blaye fairly rested and made their way to the port on foot. In those terrible days, everything represented a danger and two men, one of them looking like a beggar, could not have asked a boatman for the hire of a boat for their personal use without arousing suspicion. But Bonie thought of everything. He said he had been sent by a commune up river from Bordeaux to buy grain for the people. No one, therefore, was surprised that he should hire a boat for his own use, or that he should take along with him, out of charity, a poor ailing citizen who had escaped from the Departments in revolt. That last detail was necessary to avoid rousing any suspicion in the boatman's mind if he should happen to notice that M. de La Tour du Pin spoke with no trace of a Gascon accent.

Looking back, now, after many years, and calling to mind the depth of the mistrust, absurdity, unreasonableness and fear which held even intelligent minds in thrall during this period—so aptly known as the Terror—the whole situation seems inconceivable. The simplest of reasonings, even that of a ten-year old child, should have been sufficient to banish this confusion and fear. No one asked, for example, how it was that people were dying of hunger in Bordeaux, when just across the river the necessities of life abounded. No one could explain why, but the fact remains that no peasant from Blaye or Royan would have dared to bring two bags of flour to the great city. He would immediately have been denounced for hoarding. These facts have not been explained in any memoirs of the period. I leave the task to historians and return to my own story.

CHAPTER SIXTEEN

— ◆ —

I

Two months previously, I had obtained the certificate of residence in the name of Dillon Gouvernet, attested by nine witnesses. Now it was necessary to ask for a passport in the name of Latour, avoiding that of Dillon which was too well known in Bordeaux. I decided to drop the Dillon and adopt the name of Lee, which my uncle, Lord Dillon, had added to his own name after inheriting property from Lord Lichfield,[1] his great-uncle and my great-great-uncle. There could be no turning back.

The passport office shut at nine o'clock and it was half past eight when we went to the commune. It was quite dark. The date was the 8th of March 1794. My husband walked with Bonie and I followed with a friend of Bonie's, walking some distance behind them carrying my six-months' old daughter and holding the hand of my son, who was not yet four. Because of the English or American name I wished to use, I was dressed as a lady, but very shabbily, and was wearing an old straw hat. In the Hôtel de Ville we found ourselves in a room very full of people, and there we were given the permit which the passport office needed before it could issue a passport. I was terrified in case someone from Saint-André-en-Cubzac or Bordeaux should recognise us and, to reduce this danger, M. de La Tour du Pin and I were very careful to keep far apart and to avoid the lighted parts of the room.

Armed with this permit, we went up to the passport office, arriving just as the clerk was saying: 'That's more than enough for today; the rest can wait until tomorrow'. Any delay would have cost us our lives, as you will see. Bonie leapt over the counter saying: 'If you're tired, citizen, I'll do the writing for you.' The clerk agreed to this and Bonie drew up a collective passport for the Latour family. There were many people in the office so that when the Town Clerk, in his red bonnet, said: 'Citizen Latour,

[1] Robert Lee, 4th and last Earl of Lichfield.

take off your hat so that we can put down your description', my heart beat so violently that I almost fainted. Fortunately, I was sitting in a dark corner. At the same moment, my son, who had looked up, threw himself upon me, burying his face in his little hands. Thinking it was only from fear of those men in red bonnets, I said nothing.

When the passport was signed, we carried it off with a feeling of deep relief, though we were indeed still very far from being safe. To avoid being in the same house and having to cross Bordeaux together the following morning in broad daylight, we had arranged that M. de La Tour du Pin should sleep at the house of M. Meyer, the Dutch Consul, who lived in the last house on the Quai des Chartrons. He was most devoted to us. As for me, after taking my children home, I went to see Mme de Fontenay, thinking I would meet Tallien at her house and that he would visa our passport. I found her in tears. Tallien had been recalled and had left two hours earlier. She herself was to leave the next day and did not hide from me her fear that Tallien's colleague, the fierce Ysabeau, would refuse us a visa. But Alexander, Tallien's secretary, swore by his own head that Ysabeau would give us one. He said that since he always signed papers at ten o'clock, after leaving the theatre, he was in a hurry to get his supper, and did not look very closely at what was put before him. Providence in its goodness had ordained that Ysabeau should have asked Tallien to leave him his secretary, who was not only very useful to him, but had also been sufficiently clever to make himself indispensable.

As I entered Mme de Fontenay's house, Alexander was on his way out with papers for signature. He took the passport and put it among all the other papers. Ysabeau was that day very much occupied with the arrival of a new colleague who was due to reach Bordeaux the following day, and he signed without paying any attention. As soon as Alexander was free to leave, he rushed back to Mme de Fontenay's, where I was waiting for him, more dead than alive. I was not alone. A person of some distinction whom I did not know and who looked extremely worried, was also there. It was M. de Fontenay, who had ignored the most elementary notions of delicacy, and had come to ask his wife to save him. Alexander arrived with the passport unfolded in his hand. He was so out of breath that he fell into an armchair, unable to say more than: 'Here it is.' Mme de Fontenay embraced him most warmly, and so did I, for it was he who really saved us. I have never seen him since; he may have paid with his life for the services he rendered to so many people who have forgotten all about them.

The young emissary from the Convention who arrived the following day was Julien de Toulouse,[1] and the purpose of his mission was to revive the patriotism of the people of Bordeaux. He was nineteen years old, and his cruelty surpassed even the most atrocious crimes of those terrible years. By our flight, we had the honour of causing him the most burning regret. He tore his hair with rage when he heard that we had escaped him for, said he, we were mentioned in his notes.

Alexander was preparing to leave, for it was nearly midnight, and I rose to leave with him. But Mme de Fontenay kept me, saying she would send someone to accompany me home, and that first she wanted to show me something pretty. I followed her to her bedroom, where M. de Fontenay, still silent, accompanied us. From a drawer she took a handkerchief and spread it on a table. Then, opening a very beautiful box which served as a jewel case, she took out magnificent parures of diamonds of the finest quality and, after showing them to me, tumbled them pell mell into the handkerchief. When she had thus emptied all the compartments of the jewel case, leaving not even the smallest trinket behind, she tied the corners of the handkerchief and held it out to M. de Fontenay saying: 'Take them all.' And he did indeed take them, and left without a word. I made no attempt to hide my amazement, and seeing it, she answered my thought: 'He gave me some of them; the remainder came from my mother. He, too, is leaving tomorrow for America.'

I would not have mentioned this incident, for it does not

---

[1] Mme de La Tour du Pin is mistaken in saying that Julien de Toulouse of the National Convention—who at this time would have been 34 years old—succeeded Tallien in Bordeaux as the emissary of the Convention. Robespierre himself sent to this town, to replace Tallien and act as a check on Ysabeau, a young man of very advanced ideas, a member of the Jacobin club, aged only 18—Jullien de Paris, eldest son of Jullien de la Drôme, of the National Convention.

Marquise de La Tour du Pin,
1770-1853

Marquis de La Tour du Pin de Gouvernet,
1759-1837

Comte Arthur Dillon,
1750-1794

Comte de La Tour du Pin de Gouvernet,
1727-1794

Princesse d' Hénin,
1749-1826

Château de Versailles

Vista in the Royal Gardens at Versailles

Albany, New York, from van Rennselaer's Island

West Point, New York

Château du Bouilh, Gironde

*Coat of Arms of the Tour du Pin and
Dillon families*

Comte Humbert de La Tour du Pin
de Gouvernet, 1790-1816

Alix (Charlotte) de La Tour du
Pin de Gouvernet—Comtesse
Auguste de Liedekerke Beaufort,
1796-1822

Cécile de La Tour du Pin de
Gouvernet, 1800-1817

Comte Aymar de La Tour du Pin de
Gouvernet, 1806-1867

concern me, except for the fact that when I was in Madrid two years later, I heard that M. de Fontenay, when wishing to dispose of some of the diamonds there, had been suspected of complicity in a diamond theft from the Paris repositories. My story shows definitely that this suspicion was unjust. But M. de Fontenay, ashamed, it seemed, of his wife's marriage with Tallien, refused to admit that she had given him the diamonds or to say when it was that he accepted them, most willingly and without any false pride, in my presence.

I spent the last night packing some belongings and Zamore took them away very early the next morning. I had pretended to undress and was careful not to waken the maid. As soon as we were alone, my son, who slept in a bed beside mine, sat up and called me. I was terrified, fearing he might be ill, and went hurriedly over to him. Throwing his little arms about my neck and pressing his lips to my ear, he whispered: 'I saw Papa, you know, but I didn't say anything because of those wicked people!' The terror in the passport office had touched even a small child of less than four.

II

Our luggage had been aboard for three days and my spy was unaware that the cupboards and drawers were empty. I bade a tender farewell to my good Marguerite, who thought only of me and was glad to see me escaping from the threatening dangers. I left her under the protection of M. de Brouquens, who was well aware of my affection for her. At last, on the 10th of March, carrying my daughter Séraphine, and holding my son, Humbert, by the hand, I told the nurse that I was taking them to the Allées de Tourny, where the children were usually taken for their walk, and that I would be back in an hour or two.

I set off, instead, in the direction of the slopes of the Château-Trompette, where I joined M. de Chambeau whom I had appointed to meet me there. He also had obtained a passage in our boat. News had just reached him that his father, a good Gascon country gentleman living on his estate near Auch, had been denounced by a servant who had been thirty years in his service, and had been arrested and put into prison. They had learned from papers seized at the time of the arrest that his son, after being captured during the fighting of 1792, had later emigrated, but had since returned to France and was in hiding in Bordeaux.

So M. de Chambeau had to leave Bordeaux at once. But for where? During the morning of the day on which we were to go and fetch our passport, I happened to be at M. de Brouquens' house at the same time as M. de Chambeau. Hearing of his predicament, I said jokingly to him: 'If I were to give you a power of attorney to manage my house in Martinique, you could get a passport to leave on the *Diana*. The idea had more success than I foresaw. M. de Brouquens went to his lawyer. The power of attorney was drawn up. I signed it with my true name, and an hour later, M. de Chambeau was in possession of a good passport, visaed probably—in fact, certainly—by Representative Ysabeau. This passport did not reach him until eleven o'clock in the morning. By midday, he was ready to leave, his entire baggage consisting of a dozen shirts, and a purse with twenty-five louis which M. de Brouquens had given him. He was delighted to be escaping, and being only twenty-five, was in the highest spirits, turning his hand to whatever needed to be done. He was a charming and most pleasant companion in misfortune. His friendship for my husband grew into a devotion which never once wavered.

I found him, then, as we had planned, at the Château-Trompette, accompanied by a small boy carrying his portmanteau, which weighed very little. He took Humbert's hand and when we arrived at the end of the Quai des Chartrons and saw the dinghy from the *Diana* we each of us felt such joy as is not often experienced in a lifetime.

M. Meyer, at whose house my husband had spent the night, was waiting for us. We found, already at lunch, M. de Brouquens, Mme de Fontenay and three or four other people, including a Councillor of the Parlement de Paris whom Brouquens had hidden among the staff of his commissariat and whose real names I never knew. He was greatly teased because, charged with finding provisions for our journey, all he had been able to get in the space of three days was one lamb, which he had brought bleating along. The famine was indeed so bad that we ourselves had been unable to procure anything. A few jars of potted goose, a few sacks of potatoes or French beans, a small case of bottled jam and fifty bottles of Bordeaux wine contributed our entire store. It is true that Captain Pease had some barrels of biscuits, but they were a year and a half old and had already made the journey from Baltimore. M. Meyer gave me a small bag of fresh biscuits, which I saved to make soup for my small daughter. But what did it all matter in the face of what had been accomplished: my husband's life was saved!

Mme de Fontenay rejoiced in the result of her work. Her lovely face was wet with tears of joy as we climbed into the dinghy. She has since told me that, thanks to our expressions of gratitude, that moment counted as one of her dearest memories.

When the Captain seated himself at the tiller and shouted 'Off', an inexpressible happiness flowed through me. Seated opposite my husband, whose life I was saving, with my two children on my knee, nothing seemed impossible. Poverty, work, misery, nothing was difficult with him beside me. There is no doubt that the heave of the oar with which the sailor pushed us off from the shore was the happiest moment in my life.

The *Diana* had gone down on the preceding tide to the Bec d'Ambez, where we were to join her. We were compelled by the authorities to stop alongside a warship stationed on sentinel duty in the middle of the river, at the entrance to the port. The Captain prepared to show his papers and our passports. It was a bad moment. We did not dare to speak in French or to look up towards the warship's deck. The Captain went on board alone. He knew not a word of French, though his ship had been lying in embargo a whole year at Bordeaux. A voice shouted from the deck: 'Tell that woman to come up and interpret', and there followed some coarse words asking if she were young or old. I experienced a deadly fear. Our Captain leaned over the side and told me not to answer. I dared not even raise my eyes. At that moment, a French boat full of men in uniform drew near in a great hurry. The Captain took advantage of this to collect his papers, jumped into the dinghy and made off as fast as possible.

At last we reached our small boat, the *Diana*, and settled ourselves on board as best we could. The next ebb tide took us down

to Pauillac. There we had to submit to still another visit from two
more guardships. My husband, already seasick, was in bed. The
officers who came on board were very polite, but wanted to know
a great deal. They took a liking to my lamb which, unfortunately,
was still alive. They coolly asked me to give it to them and
promised to send a goat in exchange, which delighted me for my
children's sake. But they took away the lamb and we never saw
the goat, for shortly afterwards we weighed anchor to move in
towards Pauillac, where the sea was less rough.

III

Our small ship was a vessel of only 150 tons. Its solitary mast was
very tall, as in all American-built ships, and as there was no cargo
except for our twenty-five cases, the rolling was horrible. My
apprenticeship to the sea was of the very grimmest kind.

We had arranged that the Captain should get a supply of food
for us, but he had just as much difficulty as we in obtaining it and
had been able to get only such victuals as his consignees had
managed to procure for him from the naval stores.

As we left Bordeaux, one of the four sailors had a terrible fall
from the masthead to the hold. He was, naturally, out of commission, which meant that only three were left to man the ship.
The entire crew consisted of these three sailors, a cabin boy who
acted as steward, the Captain, a young man of no great ability,
his mate who came, like the Captain, from Nantucket and an old
sailor called Harper, well salted in experience who, though new to
the ship, was consulted by the Captain at every turn.

The cabin, used only by the Captain, was, as you may imagine,
very small. He had given one cabin to my husband and me, and
another to M. de Chambeau. He himself slept in his cabin on a
sort of chest which served as a bench during the daytime. For
thirty days my husband did not leave his bed. He suffered terribly
from seasickness and also from the bad food. The only nourish-
ment he could take was tea made with water, and a few pieces of
toasted biscuit soaked in sweet wine. As for me, when I look
back across the years, I cannot conceive how I was able to withstand the weariness and the hunger. I was feeding my baby at
the time and, being only twenty-four, had naturally a most

excellent appetite, but in this very strange life, I had not even time to eat.

Fortunately, the movement of the ship lulled my poor little daughter. She slept nearly all day. But for that very reason, she allowed me no peace when she felt me beside her at night and I could never sleep for more than half-an-hour at a time. I was so afraid of rolling over against her in my sleep and smothering her that I had a piece of cloth passed around the middle of my body and fastened to the wooden frame of the bed. I could neither turn nor change my position, but although at first it was torture I soon grew used to it.

In those days, the Americans were at war with the Algerians who had already seized a number of their ships. Our Captain's dread of these pirates was such that, when we were barely two leagues out from the Tour de Courdouan,[1] he headed due north declaring that nothing in the world would reassure him until he had reached the waters north of Ireland. He had little faith in the French Navy's power of protection against these marauders and put all his trust in the English Navy, considering that the Algerians would not dare risk provoking it.

In terrible equinoctial gales, we steered a course that kept us twenty leagues out from the coast of France, a course which, from our point of view, was not very reassuring. We had heard at Pauillac that a French frigate, the *Atalante*, I believe, had met an American boat carrying a number of French passengers at the entrance to the port of La Rochelle, had seized it and taken the French passengers to Brest, where they were all guillotined.

This encouraging story gave us something of a distaste for any course within reach of the French coast. However, though I pleaded hard with the Captain to set a direct course for his own country, he only repeated his fears of the Algerians and being cast into slavery and since M. de La Tour du Pin felt as he did, he encouraged him to hold to his northerly route.

One day, when the seas were so high that we had had to fasten the scuttles and were confined to the living quarters with the lights lit, even though it was midday, the hoarse voice of the sailor of the watch was suddenly heard to shout the news we so

[1] A light-house on a rock at the entrance to the Gironde estuary. (T)

dreaded: 'French man o' war ahead.' In one bound, the Captain was on deck, having first ordered us to remain out of sight. We heard a cannon shot, the opening round in a parley which meant life or death for us. The frigate declared her French nationality, running up the flag. We hastily declared ours in the same manner and after the customary questions, heard our Captain's reply: 'No passengers, no cargo.' To this, the *Atalante* replied, 'Come aboard.' The Captain said the seas were too high. It was indeed very rough and as we hove to, we were bounced around to such an extent that the only way to keep one's feet was to hold on to some support. The imposing challenger ended the exchange with one word: 'Follow,' and continued on her course. We unfurled our only sail and prepared to follow meekly in her wake.

The Captain came down from the deck saying gaily: 'In an hour it will be dark and a fog is coming up.' Never was a fog welcomed more joyfully. We soon lost sight of the frigate in the darkness and as we had put on as little sail as possible, despite a cannon shot intended to hurry us up, she drew slowly ahead of us. She had signalled to us that she was making for Brest and that we were to follow her there. As soon as it was dark, we set a directly opposite course and, the wind being high, and in a favourable direction, we made off to the north-west with all canvas spread, not worrying at all whether it was in the direction of Boston, the port for which we were bound.

This incident threw us right off our course and as the thick fogs made it impossible to take a bearing for twelve or fifteen days, the colour of the water was the only indication that we were off the coast of Newfoundland. Strong westerly winds drove us back continually. Food became short and water had to be rationed. At this point, we met an English boat coming from Ireland, and the Captain went on board and returned with a sack of potatoes and two small jars of butter for me and my children. Having compared his position with that taken by the English captain, he found we were fifty leagues north of the Azores. In fact, for several days, feeling himself out of reach of the Algerians, he had been steering south-west by a good north-east wind.

Learning this, my husband besought him to land us in the Azores, for we could have found our way from there to England, but the Captain refused to do this. Providence had decided otherwise for us, and how very grateful I have since been. However, at the time, in our human blindness, we grumbled. If we had gone to England, we would have arrived just as the expedition was preparing to set out for Quiberon Bay. It is certain that my husband would have gone with it, along with his two friends, M. d'Hervilly and M. de Kergaradec, and he would certainly have perished as they did. But God did not want to take from me all the years of domestic happiness with which I have since been blessed on this earth. If He has taken back to Himself the children I had then, and the later ones who made me such a happy, proud mother, I hope perhaps He will leave me, to close my eyes, the one I have loved most of all, the only son[1] remaining to me, and also my two grandchildren[2] whom I adore. Of these, one has been entrusted to me and I have had charge of her upbringing. I look on her as my own child, and at the same time as a very dear friend.

IV

My life on board, though hard, had one advantage: it put forcibly beyond my reach the small pleasures which we do not value when we have always had them. In fact, deprived of everything, without a minute of leisure, entirely occupied with caring for my children and my sick husband, not only had I not made what people call their 'toilette' since going on board, but I had not even had time to remove the Madras kerchief I wore on my head. Fashion still decreed quantities of powder and pomade. One day, after the encounter with the *Atalante*, I decided to dress my hair while my daughter was asleep. It was very long hair and I found it so

[1] Frédéric-Claude-Aymar.

[2] The children of Florent-Charles-Auguste, Comte de Liedekerke Beaufort and of Alix, known as Charlotte, de La Tour du Pin de Gouvernet:
  (a) Hadelin-Stanislas-Humbert, Comte de Liedekerke Beaufort, born in Brussels on the 11th March 1816, died in Brussels on the 3rd of January 1890;
  (b) Cécile-Claire-Séraphine de Liedekerke Beaufort, born at The Hague on the 24th of August 1818, died in Paris on the 19th of August 1893. Married in Brussels on the 28th of December 1841 to Ferdinand-Joseph-Ghislain, Baron de Beeckman.

tangled that, despairing of ever being able to restore it to order, I took the scissors and cut it quite short, anticipating, as it happened, the 'Titus' fashion. My husband was very angry. I dropped the hair overboard and with it went all the frivolous ideas which my pretty fair curls had encouraged.

My recreation during the journey was the time I spent in the galley. In shape it resembled a berline; there were no doors and it was secured to the mast. One sat right at the back and the pots boiled on a sort of furnace which had to be lit from outside. More than once, a wrong twist of the helm brought us a good wetting from some passing wave, but we were warm in there, or, to be more exact, our feet were warm. I say 'we' because I did not have this delightful kitchen to myself. A sailor known as the cook used to fetch me and instal me there beside him to spend an hour or two cooking those haricot beans which had already crossed the ocean from Baltimore and which had spent at least a year in store at Bordeaux. The cook's name was Boyd. He was twenty-six and it was obvious that under his mask of grime and grease he was very handsome. He was the son of a farmer on the outskirts of Boston and much better educated than a Frenchman of the same class would have been. He understood at once that I was a lady, who wanted information about country ways and customs in his homeland. It was indeed thanks to him that I acquired a knowledge of the tasks that were to fall to me when I became a farmer's wife. My husband used to say laughingly: 'The beans are boiled to a mash because my wife forgot herself with Boyd!'

When water became rationed, he promised to see that we did not go short. This was particularly useful to my husband, since tea was the only thing he could drink without a recurrence of the seasickness. Personally, I suffered greatly from the shortage of food. The biscuit had become so hard that I could not eat it without making my gums bleed. When I tried to soften it with liquid, the weevils came out, and I found this utterly disgusting. For my children, I crushed the biscuit into a kind of soup, and in making such mixtures had already used up the two small jars of butter given us by the English boat. The shortage of food caused my milk to dry and I could see my daughter shrinking visibly, while my son begged me, with tears, for one of our potatoes, though he had eaten the last several days before. Our plight was terrible and I could not rid myself of the fear that I would see my children die of hunger.

For ten days, we had been unable to take a bearing, and the fog was so thick that, even on our small ship, it was impossible to see the bowsprit. The Captain had no idea where he was. In vain did old Harper declare that he felt land breezes: we thought he was only trying to hearten us.

On the 12th of May 1794, at daybreak, the weather was warm and the sea calm, so we went on deck to sit with our children, to play with them and enjoy the fresh air. The fog was still just as thick and the Captain declared that, whatever land it was that we were approaching, it was still at least some fifty to sixty leagues away. I noticed, however, that the dog was excited. It was a black terrier bitch of which I was very fond and which had developed an affection for me, to the very great disgust of its owner, the Captain. The poor animal would rush forward, barking loudly, and then come back to me, licking my son's hands and face, and then rush off again. This odd behaviour had been going on for about an hour when a small decked-in boat, a pilot boat, passed near us and the man aboard her shouted in English that 'if we didn't change our course, we would founder on the point'. We immediately threw him a rope and he jumped aboard. It is quite impossible to describe the depth of our joy at seeing this Boston pilot.

Though we had been unaware of it, we were at the entrance to that magnificent roadstead which has no equal among even the most beautiful of the European lakes. Leaving a sea whose waves were breaking in fury against the rocks, we entered through a passage so narrow that two ships could not have passed abreast, into waters as smooth and peaceful as a mirror. A slight land breeze sprang up and, like the changing décor on a theatre stage, the friendly land appeared, waiting to welcome us.

My son's transports of joy defeated all description. For sixty days he had heard us talking of the dangers from which we had, thank God, escaped. With his four-year-old mind, he had grasped that, in order to avoid those men in red bonnets of whom he had been so frightened, and who had threatened to kill his father, he would have to live a life which lacked many of the good things to which he had been accustomed. He often remembered the fine white bread and the good milk of earlier days, and he found it very disagreeable to be without these things. Vague recollections such as these caused him sometimes to cry without apparent reason. But when, from the narrow creek through which we were sailing, he saw the green fields, the flowering trees and all the beauty of a most luxuriant vegetation, his joy was beyond words.

Ours, though less exuberant, was quite as deep.

CHAPTER SEVENTEEN

———————◆———————

At Lucca, 7th of February 1843.

I

It is probably very presumptuous to continue writing these memoirs when in ten days' time I shall enter on my seventy-fourth year. But today I finished copying out the part I had written on loose sheets of paper and I assure you, my dear son,[1] that you will have the remainder, God willing, either with or without crossings-out, so long as I retain a little strength, power of mind and the sight of my eyes to guide my pen. An undertaking of this kind needs memory above all and it seems to me that I have not entirely lost mine. You know that it is as good for the past as for the present, and the present holds memories perhaps as distressing as any in my earlier days, many as have been the misfortunes which have darkened my long life.

But let us set aside these preliminaries and return to the entrance to the Boston Roads, where I left your poor brother Humbert joyfully gazing once again on cows, fields, trees, flowers and all the other things that his youthful imagination had almost forgotten.

II

I admit with shame that the joy felt by the rest of us, the grownups, was entirely focused on the enormous fish which the pilot

[1] Aymar de La Tour du Pin.

had just caught and which, with a jar of milk, some fresh butter and white bread, was to provide what the Captain called 'a welcome breakfast'. While we were eating this meal and satisfying our famished appetites, the boat was drawing further into this magnificent bay, towed by our dinghy. At two cables' length from land, the Captain dropped anchor and then left us, promising to return in the evening after finding lodgings for us.

We had not a single letter of introduction and waited patiently for his return. Meantime, supplies of fresh food were arriving from all sides. So also were a number of Frenchmen, very impatient for news and besieging us with questions to which we could only give the scantiest of answers. One wanted to know what was happening in Lille, another in Grenoble, a third in Metz, and they were all amazed and indeed almost angry when we could only tell them about Paris or about France in general. For the most part, they were very ordinary people: tradesmen who had been ruined, workmen seeking jobs. They all seemed to us more or less in sympathy with the Revolution, and they, in their turn, looked on us as aristocrats fortunate to have escaped the death which, according to them, we fully merited for our past tyranny. They left us angrily, and we were rid of them for the remainder of our stay in Boston.

The rest of the day was spent in putting our belongings in order. In the evening, the Captain returned. He had found a small lodging for us on the Market Square and he brought offers of help from the owner of the ship. My husband resolved to call on him the following day when we landed. The Captain told us he was a rich man and greatly esteemed, and that we were very fortunate to be under his protection.

You will have no difficulty in believing that by dawn the next morning, I was already awake. I dressed my children and as soon as the dinghy was ready, said goodbye to all the crew, shaking hands warmly with each one, for these good fellows had been extremely kind and obliging. The cabin boy wept bitterly at being separated from what he called 'his boy'. Each had some personal regret to express and I myself was very sorry not to be able to take along with me 'Black' the dog, who had become so attached to me. I had asked my friend, Boyd, if the Captain would be willing to give her to me. But Boyd assured me he would refuse, so I did not dare to ask.

Someone who has never been exposed to the sufferings we had experienced for two months, the restrictions which I had had to endure before that, the anxiety for my husband's safety and also for my own, the anguish of mind caused by living for months in continual fear of imminent death, knowing that it would leave my two poor children entirely alone, without help or protection, will never be able to fully appreciate my joy when I set foot on that friendly shore. Our good Captain was as happy about it as we were ourselves. He took us first to one of the best inns, where he had previously ordered an excellent lunch with everything we had lacked for so long. Although it may seem trivial to people who have never been deprived of anything, I would ask them to indulge me for a moment while I say that when I saw that plentiful table, I felt a pleasure so vivid that it surpassed any pleasures I had known till then.

Afterwards, we set out for the small lodging chosen by our kind Captain, and my husband left me there while he went to call on the owner of the ship.

III

Mr Geyer was one of the richest men in Boston. Although he had returned after the peace treaty to enjoy his fortune in the country of his birth, he had been among those who supported England and he had taken no part in the revolt against the mother-country. Following the example of many other Boston merchants, he had even taken his family to England. My husband was received by him with a warm friendliness which quite charmed him.

I forgot to tell you that at Pauillac we had anchored alongside a ship which, like ours, was waiting for a favourable wind and which was headed for England. I therefore wrote a few hurried lines to Mme d'Hénin, who was living in London, asking her to write to us at Boston, in care of Mr Geyer, whose name the Captain had given me. Our crossing took so long that there had been time for a reply to arrive from my aunt and when we landed we found letters which settled for us the question of where in the United States, we were to live. I will come back to that in a minute.

The house in which our Captain had found us a lodging was inhabited by three generations of women: Mrs Pierce, her mother and her daughter. It stood on the Market Square, the busiest and most lively part of the town. Our apartment consisted of, on one side, a small drawing-room with two windows looking out over the Square, and on the other side, beyond a very small staircase, a good bedroom intended for my husband, my children and me. This room, being on the other side of the house, looked out over an isolated shipyard where the builders were busily engaged. Beyond, stretched the countryside. You will realise later why I give you these details.

We boarded with these good ladies, who fed us very well, in the English style. Sally, the young daughter, was passionately fond of children and she took my small daughter and wanted to look after her. The grandmother took charge of Humbert, already very tall for his age and most unusually intelligent. We could not have had a more fortunate start. By the evening of the first day, we felt as settled there as if no grief or anxiety had ever troubled our lives.

Towards the middle of the night, I was awakened by the barking of a dog and his whimpers as he scratched at the kitchen door, which opened on the shipyard side. The bark sounded familiar. I got up and opened the window and there, in the moonlight, saw Black. I went straight down to open the door for her and when I got her back to our room, found that the poor creature was so soaked that she must have spent a very long time in the water. I learned next day that she had been kept tied up on board all day but that at ten o'clock in the evening, the sailor had thought it safe to unfasten her. No sooner had he done so than she took a mighty leap over the side. Now, the *Diana* was anchored more than a mile from the quay, so the good animal had probably swum all that distance and having searched for us through that strange town, had eventually discovered the very door of the house which was closest to the room where we were sleeping. The Captain was almost superstitious in his determination not to cross such a well-proved attachment. Black never left us again and returned eventually with us to Europe.

During the morning of the following day, Mr Geyer came to call on me, bringing his wife and daughter. He himself spoke French fairly well but the ladies did not know a single word of the language. They were therefore delighted to find that their tongue was as familiar to me as to them. Their kindly hospitality did not need the formality of letters of introduction. The dangers through which we had passed in France evoked general sympathy and people were inclined to think our story had something of the miraculous about it. They insisted on believing that my hair had been cut short at the back as a preparation for execution. This belief still further intensified their interest in us and it was quite in vain that I explained that I had cut it for a very different reason. There seemed no means of persuading the good people of Boston that they were wrong.

Forty-five years ago, the town was still just like an English colony, yet it was there that the first movements of rebellion against the mother-country had begun to stir. We were shown with pride the column that had been erected on top of the hill where the people had gathered to pass the first resolutions against the unjust taxes with which England was crippling the colony; the part of the harbour where the two shiploads of tea were tipped into the sea rather than pay the exorbitant duty charged on that commodity; the fine lawn where the first armed troops had gathered and the site of the first battle: Bunker's Hill. But the richer and more distinguished inhabitants, although they submitted to the new government, regretted—though they did not disapprove—the separation from the mother-country. They were still linked to England by ties of affection and family. They preserved the customs of that country quite unchanged, and many of them who had taken refuge there, did not return until the peace had been signed. They were known as the Loyalists. Among them was Mr Jeffreys, brother of the famous editor of the *Edinburgh Review*, and a family named Russell who took care to make known their close relationship to the Duke of Bedford. All these people welcomed us with the greatest kindness and took an active interest in our welfare.

Mr Geyer suggested we should live on a farm of his about eighteen miles from Boston. Perhaps it would have been wiser to accept, but my husband wanted to be nearer to Canada, where he hoped to settle eventually. He spoke English with difficulty, though he understood it perfectly, and the knowledge that French was spoken in Montreal, as it still is today made him want to be close to that city.

We had just received letters from England. Our aunt, Mme d'Hénin, wrote that she was sorry we had not joined her there, but sent letters of introduction from an American friend of hers, a Mrs Church, to her family in Albany. Mrs Church was a daughter of General Schuyler, who so greatly distinguished himself during the War of Independence. He had captured General Burgoyne and the whole army corps he was bringing from Canada to reinforce the English army then besieged in New York. The capitulation of this Corps at Saratoga had won him great popularity.[1] Since the end of the war, General Schuyler, who was of Dutch descent, had been living on his estates with all his family. His eldest daughter had married the head of the Renslaer family, which lived in Albany and owned enormous wealth in the country.

And so, Mrs Church, seeing the deep and motherly interest taken in us by my aunt, who was a dear friend of hers, wrote to her parents and when we arrived in Boston, we received most pressing letters from General Schuyler telling us to come without delay to Albany, assuring us we would find it easy to settle there. He assured us of his full support in the matter. We therefore decided to accept his offer and shipped our belongings by sea to New York, and from there up the Hudson to Albany. We waited in Boston until we heard that they had arrived and then set out to follow them by the land route. We preferred to travel this way as the five hundred mile journey would give us an opportunity to see the country without involving us in any extra expense.

Before despatching our belongings, we had had to empty all the cases and re-pack them. In his haste, Zamore had piled things in pell-mell and quite indiscriminately. The cases held a multitude of things altogether useless to people like us, who were going to live very modestly in the country, in conditions comparable with those of peasants in Europe. There was nothing to indicate that

[1] According to historians of the American war, it was General Schuyler's successor, General Gates, who forced General Burgoyne to surrender at Saratoga. His forces were immensely superior to General Burgoyne's. (T)

the turmoil of the Revolution would permit us to return to Europe for many years to come, and I admit that I was glad my husband had been so well received in the United States that he had lost all wish to return to England, for I had a kind of presentiment that we might not be very well received by my family.

In Boston, I sold everything we had that would fetch money. As the *Diana* had made the crossing in ballast, no charge had been made for our luggage and we had brought a considerable amount. We now reduced it by more than half, clothing, materials, laces, a piano, music, porcelain, everything that would be superfluous in a small household was turned first into money and then into bills of exchange on reliable people in Albany.

IV

We stayed a month in Boston, going nearly every day to visit the kindly people who had showered attentions and kindnesses on us. I also received visits from many Créoles[1] from Martinique who had known my father. One of them, who had married in Boston, made us promise to spend a few days with him in the country, and we did so with great pleasure. He lived in Wrentham, a village half way between Boston and Providence. It was a delightful spot, cool, unspoilt and very fertile. There were lakes strewn with small forested islands which looked like gardens floating on the water; there were great trees, old as time itself, dipping their ancient trunks and their younger shoots into water clear as crystal. It was a place of enchantment. So that it should lack none of the material of a poet's dreams—if a poet there had been among us who were so taken up with clearing, ploughing and potatoes—there was also a love story. I will tell it to you.

It was during the last year of the war and Sally W . . . was to marry a young officer named William. Sally was young and pretty and had been very well educated in England. But the young man's regiment was suddenly ordered to embark and re-join the English army at Boston. The marriage was postponed. Sally's grief was so intense that her father, whose only daughter she was, consented to take her by boat to Providence, only eighteen miles away,

[1] French settlers in the West Indies were known as Créoles. (T)

where William's battalion was to disembark, and to arrange the wedding there.

Both father and daughter were happy as the boat carried them to Providence. But as they set foot ashore, they found themselves amid stretchers and carts filled with wounded. Suddenly afraid, Sally asked a soldier for news of William. He told her, without any attempt to soften the news, that he had been killed in the retreat, but that they had not found his body. On hearing this, the poor girl lost her reason and never recovered. An attempt was made to shut her away, but she became violent, throwing her head against the walls and refusing food. After several fruitless efforts, it was decided to allow her to go free. She immediately became quiet and gentle, and driven by her one fixed idea, started out on foot for Boston. Her family arranged that at different places along the road she would be taken in and cared for, given food and clothing, but always without letting her see that it had been planned. When I saw her, she was walking slowly along the road, a staff in her hand, still haunted by the idea that, under the leaves, in the tall grass, behind some bush, she would find William. When she reached Boston, she always went to the same point on the quayside and then, after watching the sea for a while in the hope that he would come ashore, she would set out again on her return to Providence.

For twenty years the poor woman had made this journey every week. When I saw her, she looked about forty. She was tall, beautiful and very pale, cleanly dressed, with a warm overcoat. In France, children would have mocked her, or teased her. In America, they respected her, offered her flowers and fruit and took her hand to lead her to shelter when it rained. But even in winter she refused to sleep indoors. She preferred a barn or a stable, provided the door was left open. I think I remember hearing that she was eventually found dead on the road. Poor Sally, she had rejoined her William at last!

V

We all three[1] left Boston during the early days of June, taking the children with us. A fortnight later, we arrived in Albany, having

[1] Mme de La Tour du Pin, her husband and M. de Chambeau.

travelled right across the State of Connecticut[1] and greatly admired its fertility and air of prosperity. But some very sad news made me so unhappy that I was unable to enjoy any of it: Before we left Boston, M. de La Tour du Pin had received news of my father's death.[2] He did not tell me until we had started out, hoping that the journey itself and the movement would be a distraction and help to dull my grief. It was at Northampton, where we spent a night, that he decided to tell me, fearing I might read it in some gazette. Indeed, all the news from France was printed in the American papers as soon as it arrived, no matter at which port of the Union it was received.

My father's death distressed me very deeply, despite the fact that I had been expecting it for a long time. For many years I had seen him only on rare occasions, but nonetheless I had a most tender affection for him. I wrote to my step-mother, who was living in Martinique, and to my twelve-year-old step-sister, Fanny. Long afterwards, I had a reply from Mme Dillon in which she told me that she was leaving for England with Fanny and Mlle de La Touche, her daughter by her first marriage. It was a very cold letter and my stepmother showed not the slightest concern for the condition in which I was living in America.

Despite my grief, I did find distraction in the beauty of the forests we crossed on our way to Lebanon, the last stage where we were to spend the night before arriving in Albany. Unbroken forest, fifty miles wide, separated the State of Connecticut[2] from that of, I think, New York, though doubtless by now it has disappeared. It offered a spectacle which I had never before seen: a forest in every stage of growth, from the tree which was a mere shoot, just showing above ground, to the tree which had fallen from age. The road through these magnificent forests was only wide enough for two carriages. It was no more than a cutting where the tree trunks had been felled at ground level, the mass of the tree falling to right and left to clear a path. But, what jolting we endured when those trunks had not been cut properly level with the ground! The remarkable fertility of this virgin land had

[1] It was, in fact, the State of Massachusetts.
[2] Arthur Dillon was executed on the 13th of April 1794.
[3] Read Massachusetts.

encouraged the growth of an enormous number of parasitic plants, wild vines and lianas which wound themselves from one tree to the next. In the more open areas, there were thickets of flowering rhododendrons, some of them purple, others pale lilac, and roses of every kind. The flowers made a vivid splash of colour against the grassland, which was itself studded with mosses and flowering plants, while in the low-lying parts which were furrowed, and watered by small streams or creeks, as they are called, every kind of water plant was in full flower. This unspoiled nature enchanted me to such an extent that I spent the entire day in ecstasy.

Towards midday, we stopped for lunch at an inn set up not long before in the midst of this immense forest. In America, when a house is built in a forest and close to a road, the owner's first expenditure is for a sign, even if only one traveller is likely to pass in the whole of the year, and his first task the planting of a pole on which to hang it. Then under the sign, a letter box is nailed to the pole. The road may be barely visible, but thenceforward the place is marked on the map as a town.

The wooden house at which we stopped had reached the second stage of civilisation for it was a frame house, that is to say, a house with glazed windows. But it is the incomparable beauty of the family who lived in it that particularly remains in my memory and which I still never forget. There were three generations: first, the husband and wife, aged about forty to forty-five, both remarkable for their strength and beauty and gifted with that exquisite perfection of form which is to be found only in the paintings of the greatest masters; about them were grouped eight or ten children, boys and girls, and in them you could admire everything, from the young girl so like one of Raphael's beautiful virgins, to the smaller children with the faces of angels whom Rubens would not have disowned; also in this house lived a grandfather, most venerable in appearance, his hair whitened by the years, but quite unhampered by infirmity.

After we had finished lunch, which we ate together, he arose, took off his cap, and in a most respectful manner, announced: 'We shall drink to the health of our beloved President.' In those days there was not a single cabin, even among those most deeply buried in the forests, where this demonstration of love for the great Washington was not renewed at the end of every meal. Sometimes the health of 'The Marquis' was added. M. de La Fayette had left a much-loved memory in the United States.

At Lebanon there was a sulphur bath establishment which was even then quite well known. The inn was very good, and above all, impeccably clean. But the luxury of white sheets was still unknown in that part of the United States. To ask for sheets that had not been used by others would have been considered a quite unreasonable caprice, and when the bed was fairly wide, you would even be asked, as if it were the most normal thing in the world, to allow someone to share it with you. This is what happened to M. de Chambeau that very evening at Lebanon. In the middle of the night, we suddenly heard a stream of French oaths, which could come only from him. In the morning we learned that towards midnight he had been awakened by a gentleman who was sliding, without so much as a 'by your leave' into the empty half of his double bed. Furious at this invasion, he promptly leaped out at the other side and spent the night in a chair listening to his companion's snores, for he had been in no way disturbed by M. de Chambeau's anger. This misadventure led to much teasing from everyone. When we arrived that evening at Albany, a small room was reserved for him alone, and that consoled him.

VI

Two years earlier, the town of Albany had been almost entirely burned down as the result of a negro plot. In the State of New York, slavery had been abolished for children born in the year 1794 and later. They were to be given their freedom when they reached their twentieth year, a very wise measure both for the negroes and the owners of slaves. It obliged the latter to support their slaves during childhood and it compelled the slaves, in their turn, to work sufficiently long for the masters to repay the cost of their upbringing. One negro, a very bad lot, who had hoped that the Government's measure would give him unconditional liberty, resolved to avenge his disappointment. He collected a few other malcontents and they arranged to set fire to the city on a certain day, where most of the buildings were still of wood. This horrible plot succeeded beyond their wildest imaginings. The fire caught hold in twenty places at once and despite the efforts of the inhabitants, led by old General Schuyler and his entire family, houses, shops and merchandise were reduced to ashes. A small twelve-year-old negress was caught in the act of setting fire to her master's hay store. She revealed the names of the plotters and the following day the Court assembled in the smoking débris of the building where it had been accustomed to hold its sessions and condemned the negro leader and six of his accomplices to be hanged. The sentence was carried out there and then.

The Renslaer[1] and Schuyler families accomplished wonders of intelligent generosity and the energy with which they set about repairing the effects of the disaster set an example to everyone. Convoys arrived from New York laden with merchandise, bricks and furnishings and a charming new town gradually rose on the ashes of the old. The new houses were of stone or brick, usually of the latter, and were roofed with sheets of zinc and tin plate. By the time we arrived in Albany, no trace of the fire remained.

The houses of General Schuyler and his son-in-law, Mr Renslaer, were both surrounded by gardens and had not been touched by the fire. There, we found a welcome that was as flattering as it was kind. When General Schuyler saw me, he exclaimed: 'And now I shall have a sixth daughter.' He entered into all our plans, our wishes and our interests. He spoke French perfectly, as did all his family. This is the place to tell you something about his family, or rather, about his son-in-law's family. It was very powerful in the county of Albany which was originally settled by the Dutch.

Before William III usurped the throne of England,[2] in the days when he was still only the Prince of Orange and Stadtholder of Holland, Dutch colonists sailed up the North River, or Hudson and settled on[3] the flats at the confluence of the Hudson and the Mohawk, a fine plain stretching from Albany to Half Moon Point.

---

[1] Mme de La Tour du Pin's spelling.
[2] He was, in fact, invited to the throne in 1688, his wife, Mary, being a daughter of King James II of England.
[3] This settlement was founded in 1625, before the birth of William III.

One of William's young pages, a member of a noble Guelder family named Renslaer, had been able to secure his master's good-will and one day, as he served the Prince at table, told him of a dream he had had. He had dreamed that he walked behind William carrying the train of the royal mantle at his coronation as King of England. Hearing this, the Prince of Orange replied that if ever the dream came true, the page might ask any favour and be sure that it would be granted.

Time and events made Renslaer's dream a reality. He reminded William III of his promise, presented him with a map of the county of Orange in the United States and asked for a concession of land in the Mohawk country. Taking a pencil, the King traced a rectangle forty-two miles long and eighteen miles wide, with the North River running through the middle.

Renslaer crossed over to America with his unchallengeably legal act of cession and settled in Albany, in those days only a very small settlement with few colonists. He drew others to the place by granting land on perpetual lease in return for annual payments in grain or silver, usually such very small payments that their only value lay in the recognition of the right of ownership. He also sold lands and farms, thus considerably increasing his fortune, which the Revolution still further enlarged.

When we landed in America, the Renslaer family was divided into numerous branches, all of them wealthy; the eldest member of the family, who was also its head, had married General Schuyler's eldest daughter. People had christened him 'The Patroon', a Dutch word meaning 'lord'. On the very day of our arrival in Albany, as we were walking in the evening down a long and lovely street, we came across some enclosed grounds sur-rounded by a plain white fence. It was a well-tended park, planted with beautiful trees and flowers, and in it stood a pretty house, simple in style and with no outward pretentions to art or beauty. Extensive outbuildings could be seen stretching away behind it and these gave to the whole establishment the air and appearance of a splendid farm, wealthy and carefully looked after. A boy opened a gate to allow us to go down to the river bank and I asked him who owned this large house. 'But,' he said in amazement, 'it's the Patroon's house.' I told him I did not know who the Patroon was, and he lifted his arms to heaven exclaiming: 'You don't know? You don't know who the Patroon is? Who can you be, then?' And he hurried off, horrified and slightly frightened at having spoken to people who had never heard of the Patroon.

Two days later, we were received in this same house with a kindness, an attentiveness and a friendliness which were never to change. Mrs Renslaer was a woman of thirty who spoke French well, for she had learned it when visiting the headquarters of the French and American armies with her father. She was blessed with a superior mind and a rare accuracy of judgement for both men and things. She had been unable to leave her house for many years, and for months at a time would be confined to her armchair, for her health was poor and she was already suffering from the illness from which she died a few years later. From the newspapers she had learned the state of the parties in France, the blunders which had caused the Revolution, the vices of the upper classes and the follies of the middle classes. With extraordinary insight, she had grasped the causes and effects of the disorders in our country better than we had ourselves. She was very anxious to meet M. de Talleyrand, who had just arrived in Philadelphia, having been forced to leave England at eight days' notice. With diabolical shrewdness, he realised that France had not yet completed all the phases of her revolution. He brought us important letters from Holland which Mme d'Hénin had entrusted to his care. She wrote, among other things, that M. de Talleyrand had come to the country of true liberty to await the end of the period of cruel madness through which France was passing. M. de Talleyrand asked where he could find me on his return from a journey into the interior which he was planning to make with M. de Beaumetz, a friend of his, and an English millionaire from India.

CHAPTER EIGHTEEN

I

As we did not want to stay in Albany itself, General Schuyler undertook to find a nearby farm for us to buy. Meantime, he advised us to board for three months with a farmer of his acquaintance who had a farm not far from that on which his brother, Colonel Schuyler, lived with his twelve children. We therefore spent only a few days in Albany, and then went to stay with this Mr van Buren to learn American ways, for we had made it a condition that we should live with the family and that they should not change the smallest detail of their ordinary routine. It was also agreed that Mrs van Buren would let me help her in the house as a daughter would have done. At the same time, M. de Chambeau apprenticed himself to a carpenter in the small new town of Troy, a quarter of a mile from the van Buren's farm. He travelled there on Monday mornings and returned on Saturday evenings to spend Sunday with us. The news of my father-in-law's tragic death[1] had just reached us, and at the same time M. de Chambeau learned of his own father's death. As I was a very good dressmaker, I made my own mourning clothes and my good hostess, seeing my skill with the needle, found it very convenient to have an unpaid sewing woman at her disposal. To engage one from Albany would have cost her a piastre[2] a day, as well as food, including two lots of tea.

My husband went to look at a number of farms, but we waited for the arrival of our money from Holland before deciding which to buy. General Schuyler and Mr Renslaer advised M. de La Tour du Pin to divide these funds into three equal parts: one third for the purchase of the farm itself, another third for its furnishings, the purchase of negroes, cows, agricultural implements and furniture, and the remaining third to be added to what was left

[1] He was executed on the 28th of April 1794.
[2] Probably the Spanish piastre, worth a little over 5 N. Francs today. (T)

to us of the 12,000 francs we had brought with us from Bordeaux, and put aside to cover our living expenses during the first year and to meet any unexpected demands, such as the loss of negroes or cattle.

I resolved to equip myself to run my house as well as any good farmer's wife. I began by accustoming myself to never remaining in bed after sunrise. In summer, I was up and dressed by three o'clock in the morning. My room opened on to a small lawn stretching down to the river. When I say 'opened', I am not speaking of a window, but of the door itself, which was level with the lawn. From my bed, I could have watched the boats passing.

The van Buren's farm was an old Dutch house occupying a delightful position at the water's edge. It had no approach from landward, but was easily reached across the river. Opposite, on the road to Canada, stood a large inn where all the news, gazettes and sales notices were to be found. Two or three stage coaches stopped there every day. Van Buren owned two canoes and the river was always so calm that it could be crossed at any time. The property was unbroken by any road and its boundaries were marked a few hundred fathoms[1] away by a mountain covered with fine trees which also belonged to the van Burens. We used to say sometimes that this farm would suit us very well, but it would have cost more than we could afford. It was indeed only that which prevented us from buying it, for in the America of those days, and I think it may not have changed, no matter how attached a man might be to his house, his farm, his horse or his negro, if he were offered a price one-third higher than the real value, he could be relied upon to sell. It was a country where everything had a reckoned value. A path led from the farm to the small new town of Troy. For a quarter of a mile, it passed between grasses which were cut each autumn to provide bedding for the cows. The speed at which plants grew in the soil near the stream was prodigious. Grasses which, when we arrived, had been only five or ten inches high had grown by the time we left, two months later— in September—to a height of eight or ten feet. You could walk in

[1] An old measure—a 'toise'—equalling the length of the arms outstretched, i.e., six feet. (T).

their shade. Later on, I rode on horseback through fields of Indian corn which stood much taller than both me and my horse.

A few days after our arrival at the van Burens, I needed to go to Troy to buy various things, I was told to follow the path and to be careful not to leave it. I came in this way to the point where a creek or stream, joined the Hudson River. It was filled with great logs on their way to a sawmill. They were tied together and could not separate. But not being, as yet, very hardened, I hesitated to trust myself to this moving bridge, especially as the tide was high. I noticed that the path ended at the water's edge, began again on the opposite bank and that the logs bore traces of footsteps. Obviously, it was a crossing. Black was with me and went backwards and forwards over the logs several times. But Black was very light and I . . . ? However, I was ashamed to return to the house and admit that I had not dared to cross. Everyone would laugh at me. It was a bad moment. And then, realising that if there had been any danger, I would have been warned, I put a foot on the first log. It dipped a little, but I realised that was the worst it would do and that the danger was not, after all, very frightening. I was careful not to tell anyone of my fears, and later on I crossed there every day without hesitation.

II

In September, my husband opened negotiations with a farmer whose land lay two miles inland on the other side of the river, on the road from Troy to Schenectady. It was on a hill overlooking a wide stretch of country, and we thought it a very pleasant situation. The house was new and pretty, and in good condition. Only a part of the land was in cultivation. There were 150 acres under crops, a similar area of woodland and pasture, a small kitchen garden of a quarter of an acre filled with vegetables, and a fine orchard sewn with red clover and planted with ten-year-old cider apple trees, all in fruit. We were told that the price was twelve thousand francs, which General Schuyler thought not excessive. The property was four miles from Albany, on the line of the road which it was planned to build between Albany and Schenectady, a town which was then expanding rapidly. In other words, it was 'in a thriving situation', an all-important phrase in that country.

The owner did not want to move until after the first snows. Since our agreement with the van Burens had been for only two months and since it was clear that they had had enough of us, this meant we had to find other lodgings from the 1st of September to the 1st of November. At Troy, for a modest rent, we found a little wooden house standing in a large yard enclosed by clapboard walls. We moved in and as it would eventually be necessary to buy certain furnishings for the farm, decided to buy them now. These furnishings, added to what we had brought from Europe, made it possible for us to move in without delay. I had engaged a very reliable white girl. She was to be married in two months' time and agreed to enter my service while waiting for her future husband to finish building the log house where they were to live after their marriage.

I must explain what is meant by a log house, though it is more easily drawn than described. A site fourteen to fifteen feet square is levelled off, and before any other work is begun, a brick chimney is built. This is the most important part of the house. When it has been completed, the walls are put up, built with large planks of wood still covered in bark and cut to fit very closely together. On top of these walls is set the roof, with a hole for the chimney. A door is then cut into the south wall. You can see many such buildings in Switzerland, in the pastures of the Upper Alps, where they are used only for sheltering the cattle and the herdsmen. In America they represent the first step in settlement—and often the last, for there are always the unlucky ones, and when a town has prospered, these log houses become the refuge of the poor.

Betsey, then, was waiting until her future husband, an odd-job man, had built a house for her to live in. He hired himself out by the day, working sometimes in the small gardens of the townsfolk who kept those shops where one found such an amazing assortment of goods: nails and ribbons, muslin and salted pork, needles and ploughshares. The rest of the time, he took on a variety of jobs. He earned up to a dollar or a piastre a day and by now is certainly a wealthy man and the owner of a property.

One day, towards the end of September, I was out in the yard, chopper in hand, busy cutting the bone of a leg of mutton which I was about to roast on the spit for our dinner. As Betsey did not cook, I had been left in charge of everything concerned with food and, with the help of the *Cuisine Bourgeoise,* acquitted myself as best I could. Suddenly from behind me, a deep voice remarked in French: 'Never was a leg of mutton spitted with greater majesty.' Turning quickly round, I saw M. de Talleyrand and M. de Beaumetz. They had arrived in Albany the previous day and had learned our whereabouts from General Schuyler. They had come to invite us, on his behalf, to dine and spend the next day with them at his house. These gentlemen were staying only two days in Albany as the English friend who was with them was extremely anxious to return to New York. However, as M. de Talleyrand was so much amused at the sight of my leg of mutton, I insisted that he should return the following day and share it with us. This he promised to do. Leaving the children in the care of M. de Chambeau and Betsey, we went off to Albany. And that is the whole story of my meeting with M. de Talleyrand, a meeting which Mme d'Abrantès and Mme de Genlis have invested with such stupid and ridiculously romantic circumstances.

III

We had a great deal to talk about on the way, and passed from one subject to another as people do when they meet after a long time. They had returned only the previous evening from their journey to Niagara and had therefore heard none of the latest news, which was worse than ever. Blood flowed everywhere in Paris. Mme Elisabeth[1] had perished. Each of us had relatives and friends among the victims of the terror. Nor could we see an end to it.

When we arrived at the good General's house, he was on the porch making signs to us from afar and shouting: 'Come along, come along. There's fine news from France!' We hurried into the drawing-room and each seized a gazette.

In them we found accounts of the revolt of 9 Thermidor, of

[1] Sister of King Louis XVI

the death of Robespierre and his supporters, the end of the murders and the just execution of the members of the Revolutionary Tribunal. We all rejoiced together, though the deep mourning worn by my husband and myself bore sad witness to the fact that, for us, this divine justice had arrived too late. We, personally, had less cause for rejoicing than M. de Talleyrand and M. de Beaumetz.

The former rejoiced especially that his sister-in-law Mme Archambauld de Périgord, had escaped death, but much later in the evening, taking up a gazette which he thought he had already read, he found the terrible list of victims executed on the morning of 9 Thermidor itself, during the actual session at which Robespierre was denounced,[1] and in that list he found her name. He was grievously stricken at the news. His brother, who never troubled about his wife, had left France as early as 1790 and as their fortune belonged to her, he had found it more fitting, and above all, more convenient, that it should be she who remained behind in France to ensure that the property was not confiscated. This virtuous woman had obeyed his wishes and when, after she had been condemned, it was suggested to her that she should declare herself pregnant, which would have ensured her safety within a few hours, she had refused to do so. She left three children: a daughter, Mme Juste de Noailles, now the Duchesse de Poix, and two sons—Louis, who died with the Army under Napoleon, and Edmond, who married the youngest daughter of the Duchesse de Courlande. If it had not been for this very sad piece of news, our evening with General Schuyler would have been extremely pleasant.

Mr Law, who was travelling with M. de Talleyrand and M. de

[1] Robespierre, lawyer, ardent disciple of Rousseau and a Jacobin. In July 1793 he gained control of the all-powerful Committee of Public Safety and became the most powerful man in France. He did not start the Terror, it was self-propagating, but he used it to further his ideal: a France depending on virtue, peace and religion. On the 7th of May, he had secured from the Convention a decree recognising Rousseau's 'Supreme Being' and on the 25th of July he made a long speech in the Convention aimed at establishing a more concentrated form of Government— perhaps even Rousseau's dictatorship. But the Convention mustered the courage to protest, and when he tried again the following day, 9 Thermidor, he was refused a hearing and arrested. After a night of fighting between the forces of the Convention and those controlled by Robespierre, he was captured and executed immediately. (T)

Beaumetz, might well be considered the most eccentric of Englishmen, though they are all eccentric in a greater or lesser degree. He was a tall, fair man, between forty and forty-five, with a handsome, melancholy face. When grappling with some idea, the entire house might fall about his ears without causing him to look up. In the evening, after they had returned to the inn, he suddenly said to M. de Talleyrand:

'Mon cher, we won't leave tomorrow.'

'Why not? You have booked your passage on the sloop sailing down to New York.'

'Oh, that doesn't matter. I don't want to go. These people from Troy whom you have been to see . . .'

'Well? What about them?'

'I wish to see them again, often. Will you be going to see them tomorrow?'

'Yes.'

'Then I'll come to fetch you in the evening. I want to see that woman in her own home.'

And he fell silent again. Nothing would persuade him to say anything more.

Next morning, M. de Talleyrand and my husband lunched with our fatherly General before returning to Troy. I had returned earlier in the morning, having to prepare dinner for our guest. A little negro boy driving a carriole, a carriage rather like the horse-drawn chairs—the 'baroccini'—which cover Tuscan roads at such a pace, and easily hired in Albany for a dollar, had carried me back to my duties as cook and steward.

M. de Talleyrand was amiable, as he unvaryingly was to me, and his conversation had a grace and ease which has never been surpassed. He had known me since my childhood and always talked to me with an almost paternal kindliness which was delightful. One might, in one's inmost mind, regret having so many reasons for not holding him in respect, but memories of his wrong-doing were always dispelled by an hour of his conversation. Worthless himself, he had, oddly enough, a horror of wrong-doing in others. Listening to him, and not knowing him, one thought him a virtuous man. Only his exquisite sense of propriety prevented him from saying things to me which would have displeased me, and if, as sometimes happened, they did escape him, he would recollect himself immediately, and say: 'Ah yes, but you don't like that.'

In the evening, Mr Law came with M. de Beaumetz to take tea with us. I already had a cow, and so was able to give them excellent cream. We went walking. Mr Law offered me his arm, and we talked for a long time together.

He was a brother of Lord Landaff, and when still very young had gone to India as Governor of Patna, or something of the kind. He was there fourteen years, and married a very rich Brahmin widow, by whom he had two sons, who were still children. His wife had died, leaving him a considerable fortune. He returned to England, but grew bored and decided to come to America and use part of the money he had brought from India to buy land. His intention was to discover whether this new nation merited the esteem he was ready to give it. I myself did not think it did, and made no attempt to hide this from him, but he did not agree with me. He had created for himself an imaginary America, and was unwilling to give it up. He was an idealist, but witty and cultivated, and both a poet and an historian. He had written a number of interesting pieces in English concerning the history of the Mogol,[1] and had translated a Hindu poem written by the last ruler,[2] whose eyes had been put out and who had been in prison for I do not know how many years. After promising to send me this translation the next day, he fell into a deep reverie and did not speak again till the end of our walk. Then, as he re-entered the house, he sighed deeply and murmured: 'Poor Mogol!'

Two days later, we went to spend the day at Mrs Renslaer's house with all the Schuylers. M. de Talleyrand had been extremely impressed by Mrs Renslaer's outstanding qualities of mind and found it impossible to believe, from her manner of judging men and events, that she had not spent many years in Europe. It was also very interesting to hear her talking about America, and the revolution that had taken place in that country, for she had a

[1] The Grand Mogol, ruler of the former empire of the Mogols, or Mongols, in Hindustan.
[2] Chah-Alem II, 1759–1806.

248 Memoirs of Madame de La Tour du Pin

wide and very profound knowledge of it, thanks to her brother-in-law Colonel Hamilton, the friend and most intimate confidant of Washington.

Colonel Hamilton was expected in Albany, where he intended to spend some time with his father-in-law, General Schuyler. He had just left the Ministry of Finance, of which he had been the head ever since the peace, and it was thanks to him that such excellent order had been established in that particular branch of the United States' Government. M. de Talleyrand knew him and had the highest regard for him. But he found it very strange that a man of his quality, blessed with such outstanding gifts, should resign a ministry in order to return to the practice of law, and give as his reason that as a Minister he did not earn enough to bring up his eight children. Such an excuse seemed most odd to M. de Talleyrand, and in fact, rather stupid.

After dinner, Mr Law took M. de Talleyrand by the arm and led him into the garden where they remained quite a long time. The departure of these gentlemen had been arranged for the following day, and it had been agreed that they would come to Troy in the morning to say goodbye to us. After talking with M. de Talleyrand, Mr Law said he had letters to write and returned to his inn. M. de Talleyrand, taking my husband and me into a corner of the drawing-room, told us that Mr Law had said to him, using these very words: 'My dear friend, I like those people (meaning us), very much and it is my intention to lend them a thousand louis. They have just bought a farm. They need cattle, horses, negroes and so forth. So long as they live in this country, they will not repay my loan . . . in any case, I would not allow them to do so . . . I feel that to be useful to them will procure my own happiness and if they refuse . . . my nerves are very bad . . . I shall fall ill. They will truly render me a service in accepting my offer.' Then he added: 'That woman, so well bred! Who does her own cooking . . . who milks the cow . . . who does her own washing. I find it unbearable . . . the thought of it kills me . . . two nights now, I have not been able to sleep on account of it.'

M. de Talleyrand was too sensitive to ridicule such a state of mind. He asked us very seriously what answer he was to give.

To tell the truth, we felt very deeply touched by this proposal, despite the odd manner in which it was made. We asked him to express to his friend all our very sincere gratitude and to assure him that for the moment we were able to meet all the needs of our establishment, but we promised that if, through unexpected circumstances, we should later find ourselves in difficulty, we would have recourse to him. This promise, of which he was informed that same evening, calmed Mr Law a little. The following morning, he came to say goodbye. The poor man was as embarrassed as if he had committed some error. I shook his hand warmly, and most sincerely, but made no mention of what had passed. He had brought me his translation of the Mogol poem in English verse. To my great surprise, I recognised it to be the story of Joseph and his love for Potiphar's wife, word for word as it is told in the Bible.

IV

We waited impatiently for the first snow to fall and for the moment when the river would freeze over for three or four months. The freeze-up happens suddenly, and if the ice is to be solid, it has to harden within twenty-four hours to a depth of two or three feet. This was a local peculiarity, unaffected by latitude, and due solely to the enormous stretches of forest which covered that huge continent to the west and north of the settlements in the United States. Since the lakes are today—that is to say, in 1843—almost entirely surrounded by cultivated land, it is very probable that the climate of the region where we lived has greatly changed. However that may be, at the time of which I am writing, things were as I shall describe them.

Between the 25th of October and the 1st of November, the sky would become covered by a mass of cloud so thick that the daylight faded. These clouds were driven violently before a horribly cold north-west wind and everyone began preparing to put under shelter everything that could not be left out and buried under the snow. Boats, canoes and ferries were hauled out of the water and those which were not decked in were turned keel upwards. It was a time of intense activity for everyone. Then the snow would begin to fall, so thickly that it was impossible to see a man at ten paces. Usually, the river would have frozen hard several days before. The first precaution was to mark out a wide path along one of the river banks with pine branches. Places where the bank was not steep and where it was safe to walk on the ice were similarly marked. It would have been dangerous to walk anywhere but between these markers for in many places the ice at the edge was not very solid.

We had bought moccasins, which are like shoes. They are made by the savages in buffalo-hide. Sometimes, as for instance, when they are embroidered with dyed bark or porcupine quills, they are quite costly.

It was when buying these shoes that I saw the savages for the first time, the last survivors of the Mohawk nation whose territory had been bought or seized by the Americans after the war. At about the same time, the Onondagas, who lived near Lake Champlain, had also sold their forests and dispersed, but now and again some of them were still to be seen. I was rather startled, I must admit, the first time I met a man and a woman, both stark naked, walking calmly along the road. But no one seemed to find it strange and I soon grew used to it. When I was living at the farm, I saw these people nearly every day during the summer time.

We took advantage of the days immediately after the marking out of the road and the hardening of the snow to begin our removal. The funds we had been waiting for from Holland had arrived and my grandmother, Lady Dillon, who was still alive but had never set eyes on me, had also sent me three hundred louis,[1] which we used to buy farm implements. We already owned four good horses and two work sledges. A third was kept for our personal use and was known as the 'pleasure sledge'. It held six people and was rather like a very shallow box. At the back was the main bench, a little wider than the remainder of the sledge, it was mounted over a cupboard which served to hold small packages. it had a back-piece higher than head level so that it sheltered us from the wind. The other benches, two in number, were just

---

[1] In fact, Lady Dillon, who died on the 19th of June, 1794, had left Mme de La Tour du Pin a legacy of three hundred guineas for the purpose, as her will states, of 'going into mourning for her'.

ordinary planks. Buffalo skins and sheepskins kept our feet warm. Two horses drew this sledge and it could travel very fast.

When this equipage was complete, we moved into the farm, although the people from whom we were buying it had not yet moved out. They showed little regard for our wishes or convenience and as they were in no hurry to leave, we found ourselves obliged literally to push them out.

During this time, we also bought a negro and this purchase, which seemed so very simple, gave me such a strange sensation that I shall always remember the smallest circumstance connected with it.

As I have said, the Government had decided that negroes born in 1794 would be set free on reaching the age of twenty. But there were some who had already been freed, either by their masters as a reward, or for some other reason. A custom had also been established which no master would have dared to disregard for fear of public displeasure: a negro who was dissatisfied with his situation could go to a Justice of the Peace and send his master an official request to be sold. By common usage, the owner was then compelled to allow him to seek another master willing to pay a certain sum for him. The master could enforce a delay of three months or six, but rarely did so, not usually wishing to keep a worker or servant known to be anxious to leave him. That is what happened to us. Betsey, who was very well thought of, had sung our praises and was very sad at leaving us. A few pieces of ribbon and some old gowns that I had given her had secured me, at very little expense, a surprising reputation for generosity, a reputation which had reached even the farmers in the old Dutch colony. There was a young negro there named Minck, who wished to leave the master on whose property he had been born. He was trying to escape from the severity of his father, a negro like himself, and of his mother. He brought us written permission to find another situation and when we made enquiries, we learned that he had indeed been treated with extreme harshness and as the boy's father himself asked us to buy his son, we agreed to do so.

We climbed into our red and yellow sledge, drawn by our two excellent black horses and drove about four miles to a part of the country where there were eight or ten neighbouring farms, all owned by people named Lansing. This arose probably from the fact that the first man to buy land in those parts would have had to pay only four or five sous an acre for it, since it was covered with forest. He would have begun the work of clearing, and his children would have continued it. The latter would, in due course, build on the land they had cleared, and each house would be exactly like the original one. And that is why it was not uncommon to spend an entire day going from farm to farm, finding in each someone of the same name, but never the person one was seeking.

However, since we knew the baptismal name of our negro— always supposing that he had been baptised—we reached the pretty house of Mr Henry Lansing, a brick house, a sign of prosperity that we ourselves had not yet aspired to. There we asked Mrs Lansing for Minck. True to her Dutch traditions, she was anxious to discover, in her rather halting English, if we had brought the money. My husband counted out on the table the thousand francs I had been holding under my cloak, and at that moment, Mr Lansing came in. He was a very tall man, dressed in a good coat of home-spun grey cloth. He called Minck in, and taking his hand, put it into my husband's saying: 'This is your master.' When that had been done, we told Minck that we were ready to leave. But Mrs Lansing having set out Madeira wine and cake for us, we had to stay a little longer, under pain of being thought unneighbourly. In the course of conversation, Mr Lansing learned that my husband had represented the King of France in Holland, his mother country, as he called it. His opinion of us rose prodigiously. We took our leave, and found Minck already installed in the sledge. He had gone up to his room to put on his best clothes. These belonged to him, for he took away nothing that had been bought with his master's money, not even his moccasins. All his other personal belongings, so few that they could have been carried in the crown of a hat, he put into the sledge locker and then turning to us and touching his hat like any well-trained coachman, he pointed to the horses and asked: 'Are they *my* horses?' Told that they were, he took up the reins and set off at a gallop for his new home, much less preoccupied than I, for it was the first time I had ever bought a man and I still felt quite overcome by the way in which it had been done.

V

A few days later, the people from whom we had bought the farm moved out, leaving it dirty and in bad condition, which considerably lowered their reputation. They were English colonists, that is to say, from the coast. They had lived several years on the farm and were leaving because it had become too small for them. They intended clearing fresh land on the far side of the river. These people had not been able to raise sufficient money to permit the different generations of the family to separate and have their own establishments. To continue living together was a sign of poverty, bad management or lack of intelligence. The Americans are like bees: swarms must leave the hive from time to time and settle elsewhere.

As soon as we had the house to ourselves, we used some of our money to set it in order. It consisted of only a ground floor, raised five feet above the ground. The builders had begun by sinking a wall six feet down, leaving only two feet above ground level. This formed the cellar and the dairy. Above this, the remainder of the house was of wood, of a type still frequently seen in the Emmenthal region of Switzerland. The gaps in the wooden frame were filled with sun-dried bricks so that the wall was compact and very warm. We had the inside walls covered with a layer of plaster into which some colour had been mixed, and the whole effect was very pretty.

M. de Chambeau had put his four months' apprenticeship to the master carpenter to good use and had become a very skilled workman. It would, in any case, have been impossible for him to dream of becoming careless, for my own activity allowed no slackening. My husband and M. de Chambeau could well have said of me as M. de Talleyrand said of Napoleon: 'Anyone who could teach a little idleness to that man would benefit the universe.' And indeed, during the whole time I lived on the farm, whether I were well or ill, the sun never caught me in bed.

Minck had thought that by taking a new situation he would escape not only from his master's severity, but from his father's.

He was therefore much disappointed when a few days later he saw his father arrive at our farm to settle the price of his purchase with us. He was a negro of forty-five to forty-eight years of age, with a considerable reputation for intelligence, experience and knowledge in agricultural matters. He had cleverly and rightly calculated that, with masters of good social standing but without experience, it would be easy for him to assume control of the house and to make himself indispensable. He really had a very superior mind, and had often thought of improvements, but old Lansing had never been willing to listen. He longed to be with new people who would not be ruled entirely by prejudice, as his Dutch master was; he refused to permit the slightest change in the ways of life that had been followed for a hundred years.

We went to consult General Schuyler and Mr Renslaer, both of whom knew this negro by reputation. They congratulated us on his wishing to belong to us and made us promise to take him. They even advised us to consult him on the details of the farm routine. We bought him very cheaply on account of his age, for it was against the law to sell a negro of more than fifty. Mr Lansing even invoked this law to prevent us buying him, but the negro produced his certificate of baptism which proved that he was only forty-eight.

We were very glad to see him settled on the farm. The only person who did not share our satisfaction was his son. The father's name was Prime, a nickname given him because of his all round superiority. To conclude this description of our settling-in, and of our negroes, I will tell you that we bought two more and in doing so made them very happy. One was a woman. She had been married for fifteen years and had lost all hope of being reunited to the husband she adored because her master, a brutal and wicked man, always refused to sell her. Prime persuaded us to buy the husband, an excellent man and a good worker, and I thought it would be a good idea to buy the woman as well. I needed a negress, for I had too much to do and a daily woman would have cost me too much.

I therefore went by sledge one morning, with a bag of money, and I fetched Judith from her master's house. He was a Mr Wilbeck, a brother of Mr Renslaer's agent. I told him that I had learned from the Patroon of his intention to sell Judith. He refused, saying she was very useful to him. I replied that he must know it was impossible to refuse to sell a negro who wished to be sold; and I added that I knew this woman had told him that this was her wish, whereupon he had beaten her almost to death and that she was still ill from the effects of it. He brutally replied that she could find another master when she was cured. 'Call her,' I told him, 'she has found one.' She came. Learning that I had bought her husband and wished to buy her also so that they might be reunited, the poor woman sank fainting on to a chair. Then Wilbeck, who knew of our friendship with Mr Renslaer, dropped his opposition. I counted out the money before him and told Judith that her husband would come to fetch her and her small daughter. This three-year-old child had, by law, to go with her mother. And that is how we collected our negro staff. We were indeed exceedingly fortunate. The woman, like her husband, was excellent, being active, hard-working and intelligent. They were passionately devoted to us, for a good negro does not give his affection by halves; their devotion can be counted on to death itself. Judith was thirty-four and very ugly, but that did not prevent her husband being madly attached to her. M. de Chambeau arranged so that they should have a room in the granary entirely to themselves, a comfort they had not dared to hope for even in their wildest dreams.

I remember these good people with pleasure. After serving me well, they gave me, as you will see later, what I have rightly called the finest day in my life.

CHAPTER NINETEEN

I

Two French families with whom we had become acquainted lived in Albany. They were quite different from one another. The first was the family of a small shopkeeper named Genetz, a very ordinary man, who had arrived in the district with a certain amount of money and a great variety of drapery goods. They were pleasant people, but Genetz himself was a thorough black-guard at heart and secretly supported the Revolution. However, his small lodging was rented from a French Créole who was a friend of ours, so we were careful to treat him as a compatriot.

This Créole friend was from San Domingo and had known my father well. I had met him myself at my father's house in Paris. His name was Bonamy and he had been completely ruined by the fire which destroyed the Cape.[1] All that remained to him was a small sum of money invested in France, where his wife, who came from Nantes, had taken refuge with her two daughters. She had since died and the daughters, still children, had gone to live with uncles who were bringing them up. Since M. Bonamy had been officially declared an émigré, he could return neither to San Domingo nor to France and was therefore looking for some way of earning his living when the ten or twelve thousand francs he had saved from the Cape were exhausted. He was a very well-bred man, knowledgeable, even learned, witty, charming and adaptable. He often came to our house. Prime fetched him in the sledge on his way back from market, where he went nearly every day to sell a load of wood, as well as butter and cream for breakfast.

My butter was much in demand. I cut it carefully into small pieces, stamped them with our monogram and arranged them daintily in a very clean basket on a fine cloth. We sold it to whoever was willing to buy. We had eight well-fed cows and our butter did not taste of winter feeding. My cream was always fresh. Every day, the butter and cream brought me in a not inconsiderable sum and the sledge-load of wood earned us at least two piastres.

Prime could neither read nor write, but he kept his accounts so accurately that there was never the smallest error. He often brought fresh meat back from Albany and on his return, my husband would write down receipts and expenditures according to what Prime told him.

---

[1] The town of Cap-Français, burnt down in 1793, and at that time the capital of the French colony of San Domingo. The town is today in the Republic of Haïti, and known as Cap-Haïtien.

M. Bonamy usually came on Saturday and stayed at the farm until Monday. Once, at the beginning of Spring, he made a longer stay; a fall from his horse kept him with us more than a fortnight.

The second of the two French families I mentioned was staying in Albany until it would be possible for them to settle in Black-river, near Lake Erie. The head of the family, M. Desjardin, represented a company that owned immense tracts of land, and it was his job to re-sell parcels of it to poor Irish, Scottish or even French colonists sent to him by agents in New York.

Let us follow one such group of colonists, people whom I knew, so that you can see how the system worked.

The household consisted of the husband, the wife, a son of fifteen or seventeen, and two daughters. I saw them set off on foot, across the snow, the first three carrying shoulder packs. The husband was leading a poor horse harnessed to a small sledge on which he had packed two casks, one containing flour and the other salted pork, several axes, gardening and other tools, some bundles and the two small girls.

Arriving in Kentucky, a State which is flourishing today but where there were then few settlers, they would seek out the person who had sold or rented them the land on which they intended to live. First, they cut down trees in order to build a log house. Meantime, neighbours would give them lodging. Then they would clear the ground of brushwood by burning it off inevitably scorching the lower branches of trees in the process. When the snows melted, they would rake off the charred pieces with a harrow and sow the corn. Nothing more was needed to ensure a good crop. They would use the big trees for building fences to divide the property into sections, and the best watered of these sections would be turned into a meadow or pasture. And here you had a family on the road to prosperity. Any passing traveller would see seven or eight children of all ages about the house, all fresh-looking and healthy, fed on maize flour and butter and trained from the age of four to some useful task.

Usually there would be a small rent to pay on the property, either in wheat or in money. Our farm paid Patroon Renslaer a rent of fifteen bushels of corn, or an equivalent in money, and a similar rent was payable on all the other farms on his immense property which was eighteen miles wide and forty-two miles long.

M. Desjardin had brought all his household of furniture from Europe, including a good library of 1,000 to 1,500 books. He used to lend them to us and my husband or M. de Chambeau would read to me in the evening while I worked.

We breakfasted at eight o'clock and dined at one. In the evening we had tea at nine o'clock, with slices of bread spread with our own excellent butter and the good Stilton cheese M. de Talleyrand had sent us. With this gift he had sent another which gave me the greatest pleasure: a beautiful and very handsome lady's saddle, complete with bridle, saddle-cloth and all the other accessories. Never had a gift been more timely, for when we bought the farm we had also bought two pretty mares with similar markings and of the same height, though vastly different in temperament.

One was lamb-like and although she had never before had a bit in her mouth, I was able to ride her the very first day she was saddled. It took only a few days to teach her manners that were every bit as good as those of a manège-trained horse. She had a very easy movement and followed me around like a dog whenever she could. The other mare was a little demon and not all the skill of M. de Chambeau, who had once been a cavalry officer, could tame her. We did not master her until the spring, and then we did it by making her work between two powerful horses, all three fastened by the nostrils to a wooden bar. The first few times, she was so furious at this treatment that she was in a lather after less than ten minutes. But gradually we were able to quieten her. She was a fine mare, worth at least twenty-five to thirty louis.

II

Speaking of the spring, it is interesting to note the suddenness of its arrival in those regions. The latitude—43°—then came into its own and took entire charge of the climate. During the first days of March the north-westerly wind which had been blowing throughout the winter, dropped suddenly and was succeeded by a southerly one. The snow melted so fast that for two days the roads were raging torrents. As our house stood on a hillside, our white blanket disappeared very quickly. The winter snow had been two or three feet deep, protecting the grass and plants from the ice, and as a result, in less than a week after it had melted, the meadows were green and carpeted with flowers and the woods were filled with countless varieties of plants unknown in Europe.

The savages, whom we had not seen during the winter, began to call again at the farms. At the beginning of the cold weather, one of them had asked me if he might cut branches from a kind of willow which has shoots five to six feet long and as thick as a finger, promising to weave baskets for me during the winter. I had put no trust in this promise, being very doubtful if savages were accustomed to keeping their word to such an extent, though I had been assured that they did. I was wrong to doubt, for scarcely a week after the snow had disappeared, the Indian was there with his load of baskets. He gave me six, all fitting into one another. The first, round and very large, was so closely woven that it held water as well as any earthenware bowl. I wanted to pay for them, but he firmly refused and would only accept a jar of buttermilk, which the Indians like very much indeed. I had been warned never to give them rum, for which they have an immoderate passion. I was therefore careful not to do so, but in an old box I had put away some old artificial flowers, feathers, ends of ribbon of all colours, balls of blown glass which once upon a time had been very fashionable and these I distributed among the women, who were delighted. One of these Indian women, who was very old and very repulsive looking, was called the 'Old Squaw', and whenever she appeared, my negress was terribly worried, for she had a reputation for being a witch and casting spells. If she appeared when chickens were about to hatch, cows about to calve, sows about to produce a litter, or when one was about to start some important household task, it was essential to make sure of her goodwill by offering her something for her personal adornment.

An old woman, even in a civilised setting, is always very ugly. Try to imagine this 'Old Squaw', a woman of seventy, with a black, leathery skin, who had spent her entire life with her body naked and exposed to all weathers, her head covered with grey hair that had never known a comb, whose only clothing was a sort of apron of coarse blue cloth and a small woollen covering thrown over her shoulders and fastened at the two corners under her chin with a wooden brooch, a nail or an acacia thorn—garments which were never renewed until they had fallen away in shreds. Well, this woman, who spoke English quite well, had a mad passion for adornment. She would like anything to this end: the tip of an old pink feather, a knot of ribbon, an old flower and any gift of this kind put her in a good humour. If, in addition, she were allowed to take a look at herself in the mirror, you could be certain that she would be favourable to your clutch of eggs and to your cows, that your cream would not turn and that your butter would be of the finest yellow.

But these savages, who knew only a word or two of English and spent all their time wandering from farm to farm, were as sensitive to good manners and a friendly reception as any Court gentleman. They soon realised that we did not belong to the same class as the other farmers living near us, and when they spoke of me, would say: 'Mrs Latour from the old country . . . great lady . . . very good to poor squaw.'

This word 'squaw' means savage. It is used for each and every creature or object from countries where European civilisation has not yet penetrated. Thus, birds of passage would be called 'squaw pigeons', 'squaw turkeys' and objects brought in by the savages would be 'squaw baskets' and so on.

III

One day we received a visit from a Frenchman who had been an officer in my husband's regiment, M. de Novion. Having come straight from Europe, he was very glad to learn that his former colonel had become a farmer. He had brought some funds with him and would have liked to use them to buy a small farm near us. But as he had no knowledge of agriculture, spoke not a single word of English, and had neither wife nor children, he lacked all the essential qualifications for running a reasonable establishment of that kind. M. de La Tour du Pin explained this to him. But he still wanted to see something of the country, so we went riding together. After a few miles, I realised that I had forgotten my whip. As M. de Novion had no knife with which to cut me a stick, he could not help. The undergrowth in the wood was fairly thick and at that moment, seeing one of my Indian friends sitting behind a bush, I called to him: 'Squaw John.'

It is impossible to describe the surprise, almost the horror, of M. de Novion at the apparition which emerged from the bush and came towards us with his hand held out to me: a very tall man wearing only a strip of blue cloth passed between his legs and fixed to a cord about his waist. His astonishment increased when he saw how well we knew one another and the calm way in which we engaged in a conversation of which he could not understand a single word. As we walked our horses on, and before I had had time to explain how I knew such an odd person in such extraordinary garments, Squaw John leaped lightly from the top of a hillock which dominated the road and politely offered me a stick which he had stripped of its bark with his tomahawk.

I am sure that in that moment M. de Novion resolved, deep in his heart, never to live in a country where one was exposed to such encounters. 'And if you had been alone, Madame?' he asked. 'I should have been just as little alarmed,' I told him, 'and, you know, if I had had to defend myself from you and had told him to throw his tomahawk at you, he would have done so without hesitation.' Such a manner of life did not seem to please him. On our return, he told my husband that I had odd friends and that he, for his part, had decided to go and live in New York, where civilisation seemed slightly more advanced.

Our ride was rather too long and tired me, with the result that I had a recurrence of the double tertian fever from which I had been suffering intermittently for two months. It had been brought on by a severe fright about which I will tell you.

One day that spring, I had had to go to Troy to fetch things that I needed for my work. The negroes were working in the fields with my husband and M. de Chambeau was busy in his carpenter's shop, so I went to the stable, saddled my mare, as I often did, and set out at a canter. On the way back, I crossed in the ferry, taking the mare with me, and went to call on a friend who lived in a mill about a mile from the town. She kept me to tea and as it was late I rode back to the ferry at a good pace, which made me very hot. As we were about to leave the bank, four large oxen and their driver insisted on coming too, despite the protests of Mat the boatman, who had noticed that the oxen were making my mare nervous. My first impulse was to get out, but it was late and I was afraid my husband would be worried, so I stayed. In midstream, these four enormous beasts, naturally unyoked, all leaned over the same side of the ferry to drink. It heeled over, and seemed likely to capsize. Mat told me to let go of my horse and hold on to his belt. I had not, until then, realised the imminence of the danger, but Mat's words made the blood freeze in my veins. Fortunately, just at that critical moment, one of the passengers drew his knife and plunged it into the rump of one of the oxen. The pain made the animal jump overboard. The other three followed and the ferry returned to an even keel, though not before it had shipped so much water that we were standing in it up to our ankles.

Mat urged me to drink a small glass of rum. I refused, which was a big mistake. Being in a hurry, I mounted and rode back to the farm at a fast gallop. As soon as I arrived, my negress forced me to take a hot drink, but in spite of it, I had a fever the next day. It returned daily after that, always at the same hour and for the same length of time. Nothing cured it, neither the excellent quinquina which M. de Talleyrand sent me from Philadelphia, nor the mixtures of a French surgeon, named Rousseau. He may have been no more a physician than I was myself but he was French and had rendered us several services, so that I had confidence in him.

These attacks of fever lasted between five and six hours, and hampered me greatly in my daily work. They weakened me, took away my appetite, and although I never remained in bed, set me shivering even when the temperature was at 30°.[1] In short, they rendered me quite incapable of work. When this happened, the daughter of some neighbours who lived in the woods not far from us used to come to my rescue. She was a good girl, a dressmaker by trade, and her work was perfect. She arrived at the farm in the morning and stayed all day, asking no wages, only her food.

My son, Humbert, was then five, but so tall that he looked at

[1] Centigrade.

least seven. He spoke English perfectly, much better than French. A lady living in Albany, a friend of the Renslaers and of the Anglican minister's wife, had become very attached to him. He spent many afternoons at her house and one day she suggested taking charge of him for the whole summer, promising to teach him to read and write. She pointed out that in the country I had not sufficient time to devote to him, that he might catch my fever and gave a number of other reasons in her endeavour to persuade me to agree to her request.

This lady was a Mrs Ellison. She was forty years of age and had never had any children, which was an inconsolable grief to her. I ended by agreeing to let her have Humbert, and he was very happy with her and very well cared for. This decision removed much of my anxiety. At the farm, I was always afraid of some accident befalling him, for he dearly loved to be among the horses. Also it was impossible to prevent him from going out into the fields with the negroes and, above all, from mixing with the savages, with whom he always wanted to wander off. I had been told that the Indians did sometimes carry off children, so that when I saw them sitting for hours motionless at my door, I used to imagine that they were watching for an opportunity to steal my son.

IV

A pretty cart laden with fine vegetables often passed our house. It belonged to the Quaker Shakers,[1] who had a settlement about six or seven miles from us. The driver always stopped at our house and I seized every opportunity of talking to him about their way of life, their customs and their beliefs. He invited us to visit their settlement, and one day we decided to go. They belonged to a reformed branch of the original Quakers who had come to America with Penn.

After the war of 1763, an Englishwoman proclaimed herself the apostle of reform. She made a number of converts in the States of Vermont and Massachussetts and many of these families pooled their belongings and bought land in the still uninhabited parts of the country. However, the clearing of neighbouring

[1] A sect of Quakers.

land continued and whenever it reached one of their settlements, they sold it and retreated still further inland. But they never moved until the land immediately next to theirs had been acquired by someone not of their sect.

The Quakers of whom I am writing were at that time protected by several miles of thick forest and had therefore nothing yet to fear from neighbours. Their settlement was bounded on one side by twenty thousand acres of forest belonging to the town of Albany and on the other by a river, the Mohawk. No doubt by now they have moved and withdrawn beyond the lakes. The settlement was an offshoot from their main settlement at Lebanon, in the great forest we crossed when travelling from Boston to Albany.

Our Negro, Prime, who knew all the roads in those parts, acted as guide. For the first three hours, we travelled through the forest, along a path which was nothing but a vague track. Then, after passing a barrier which marked the boundary of the Quakers' property, the path became clearer and even well kept. But we still had to cross a great stretch of forest interspersed here and there with meadows where cows and horses had been turned loose to graze. Finally, we came to a vast clearing surrounded on all sides by forest, with a fine stream running through it. In the middle of this clearing stood the settlement, consisting of a large number of fine wooden houses, a church, schools and the community house, the latter being built of brick.

The Quaker we knew gave us a kindly but reserved welcome. Prime was directed to a stable where he could put up the horses, for there was no inn. We had been warned that no one would offer us anything and that only our guide would speak to us. He took us first to a magnificent kitchen garden, perfectly cultivated; everything in it was as flourishing as was possible, yet the garden was entirely devoid of charm. Many men and women were busy tilling and weeding, for the sale of vegetables was the community's main source of income.

We visited the boys' school and the girls' school, the immense communal stables and the dairies where butter and cheese were made. Everywhere there was perfect order and total silence. All the children, both boys and girls, were dressed alike in clothes of the same shape and colour. The women, whatever their age, were dressed exactly alike in grey woollen cloth, very well cared for and very clean. Through the windows could be seen the cloth looms, the lengths of newly-dyed cloth and the workrooms of the tailors and dressmakers. But not one word, not one song broke the silence.

Eventually, a bell rang. Our guide told us it was for prayers and asked if we would like to attend. We gladly agreed and he took us to the largest of the houses. Outwardly, it looked just like all the others. At the door, I was separated from my husband and M. de Chambeau, and we were put at opposite ends of an immense room, separated from one another by a chimney in which burned a magnificent fire. It was early spring, and in those great forests, still very cold. This room might have been 150 to 200 feet long and about 50 feet wide, and it was entered by two lateral doors. It was a very light room, bare of decoration, its smooth walls painted light blue. At each end was a small platform on which stood a wooden armchair.

I was given a seat in the chimney corner and my guide asked me to remain silent, a request which was easy to obey, since I was alone. While sitting absolutely still, I had time to admire the floor, which was of pine, free from knots, of a remarkable whiteness and beautifully made. In it, running in various directions, were lines of copper nails, shining with polish, their heads so well buried in the wood that they were level with it. I was trying to guess what these lines might mean, for they seemed to have no connection with one another, when, at the last peal of the bell, the two doors opened and through the one on my side of the room there came fifty to sixty young girls and women, led by a woman of considerable age, who seated herself in one of the armchairs. There were no children.

The men came in in similar order through the door on the opposite side, where M. de La Tour du Pin and M. de Chambeau were waiting. I noticed then that the women stood on the lines of nails, taking care not to let even the tips of their toes pass beyond them. They remained motionless until the woman seated in the armchair gave a sort of groan or shout which was neither speech nor chant. Then they all changed places, so I concluded that that rather stifled cry must have been some form of command.

After several manoeuvres, they again stood still and the old woman muttered a fairly long passage in a language which was quite unintelligible to me, but in which I thought I caught a few English words. After this, they left in the same order in which they had entered. Having visited every corner of the settlement, we took leave of our kindly guide and climbed back into our waggon to return home, little impressed with Quaker hospitality.

Whenever the Quaker who took the community's vegetables and fruit to market passed our farm, I always bought something. He would never take money from my hand. If I said that the price was too high, he would say 'Just as you please', and I would put at the corner of the table the sum I thought sufficient. If this suited him, he took it, if not, he climbed back on to his waggon and went off without a word. He was a respectable looking man, always impeccably dressed in a coat, waistcoat, and trousers of grey homespun made at the settlement.

V

One action of mine had won me immediate popularity: on the day I moved into the farm, I adopted the dress worn by the women on the neighbouring farms—the blue and black striped woollen skirt, the little bodice of dark calico and a coloured handkerchief, and I parted my hair in the style fashionable today, piling it up and holding it in place with a comb. In summer, I wore cotton stockings and shoes. I only wore a gown or stays when I was going into town. Among the things I had brought to America were two or three riding habits. I used these to transform myself into a lady of fashion when I was going to visit the Schuylers or the Renslaers, for more often than not we dined and spent the entire evening with them, especially when there was a good moon and, above all, during the snow season. While the snow lasted, the road, once marked, formed a track a foot or two deep and the horses were in no danger of straying from it.

Many of our neighbours made a habit of passing through our yard on the way to Albany. As we knew them, we never objected. Besides, in talking to them, I always learned some fresh piece of news. As for them, they enjoyed talking of the old country. They also liked to admire our small improvements. What excited most

admiration was an elegant small pigsty made out of wood by
M. de Chambeau and my husband. It was a masterpiece of
carpentering, but the admiration was couched in such pompous
terms that it always amused us: 'Such a noble hog sty'.

At the beginning of the summer of 1795, we received a visit
from the Duc de Liancourt. He makes a very kind reference to it
in his book *Voyages en Amérique*. He was on his way from the new
settlements that had been formed on the banks of the Mohawk
after the War of Independence, in the territory ceded by the
Oneidas. M. de Talleyrand had given him letters to the Schuylers
and the Renslaers and after he had spent a day with us, I suggested
taking him into Albany to introduce him to these two families.
Had he really been seriously upset by my woollen skirt and calico
bodice? I do not know, but the fact remains that it was only when
he saw me appear in a pretty gown and a very well made hat,
though the milliner had had no hand in it, and when he saw my
negro, Minck, bringing round the smart waggon drawn by two
excellent horses in a harness which shone with polish that he
seemed to realise that we had not yet been reduced to beggary.
At that point, it was I who had to say that nothing would persuade
me to take him to call on Mrs Renslaer and Mrs Schuyler unless
he did something to improve his appearance. His clothes were
covered in mud and dust, and torn in a number of places. He
looked like some shipwrecked sailor who had just escaped from
pirates. No one would have guessed that such an odd collection
of garments clothed a First Gentleman of the Bedchamber!
We made a bargain: I agreed to take him to visit Mrs Renslaer
and Mrs Schuyler and he agreed to open his trunk, which he had
left at the inn at Albany, and dress more suitably. While he
changed, I went to pay a call in the town. The transformation
was not to be so complete as M. de Liancourt had led me to hope.
I reproached him bitterly, especially for the patch on the knee of a
pair of nankeen breeches, which must have come all the way from
Europe, so worn were they from laundering.

When we had paid our calls, he promised to visit the farm again
on the following day and I left him in Albany and took back with
me his travelling companion, M. Dupetit-Thouars.

The latter remained a number of days with us while M. de

Liancourt visited the neighbouring country. M. Dupetit-Thouars, a very amiable man, was on his way from Asilum, that French settlement in Carolina which had proved such a failure.[1] The settlers had disagreed among themselves and had not put their money to the best uses, so that at the end of a year everything had had to be sold at a loss and they had all gone their separate ways. M. Dupetit-Thouars, who was very witty and gay, gave us the most amusing descriptions of the breaking up of this settlement, and the three or four days he spent at the farm left us with very pleasant and agreeable memories. He died gloriously some years later at Aboukir.[2]

As for M. de Liancourt, I never saw him again. The double tertian fever from which I suffered continuously, made it impossible for me to ride or to go visiting. In any case, that philanthropic nobleman, always so ready to point out their shortcomings to the people of a country but never ready to learn from them, had displeased me greatly. The friends we visited together had liked him no better. Intelligent Mrs Renslaer had at first sight declared him to be a very mediocre man. I shall be thought ungrateful to speak so badly of him, for in his book[3] he has spoken of me most flatteringly, but I must admit, to my shame, that the only part of the book that I remember is the passage I inspired.

A few days after M. de Liancourt's visit, sometime about June, we received a letter from M. de Talleyrand telling us of something which might have had serious consequences for us, and of the very great service he had rendered us in that connection. The balance of the funds we had received from Holland, some twenty to twenty-five thousand francs, had been consigned to the firm of Morris in Philadelphia. M. de Talleyrand had undertaken to withdraw this sum and was waiting for the necessary authorisation from my husband. By a truly providential piece of luck, he

[1] Tradition has it that there were royalist plans to bring Queen Marie-Antoinette to this settlement. A house was prepared. After her execution, the plot centred around the Dauphin, and one of the legends is that he did actually come, but was almost immediately kidnapped by revolutionary agents and not heard of again. (T)
[2] M. Dupetit-Thouars, one of the leading settlers in Asilum, was by profession a naval officer. Nelson destroyed Napoleon's fleet in Aboukir Bay in 1802. (T)
[3] *Voyages dans les Etats Unis d'Amérique fait de 1795-1798*, by the Duc de la Rochefoucauld-Liancourt. Published in 8 vols. in 1800.

learned one evening from an indiscreet conversation, that Mr Morris was to be declared bankrupt the following day. Not losing a minute, he went round to see the banker, forced an entrance when admittance was denied him, and reached his office. He told Mr Morris that he knew of his position and obliged him to hand over certain Dutch bills of exchange which he held only in trust. Mr Morris allowed himself to be persuaded, for he greatly feared the dishonour into which he would have fallen if this breach of trust had become known—a course M. de Talleyrand would not have hesitated to take. He made only one condition, that M. de La Tour du Pin should sign a statement that the funds had been paid fully. M. de Talleyrand undertook that my husband would go to Philadelphia to settle the matter. He also advised me to accompany him for, he said, having consulted a number of doctors on the persistent nature of my fever, they had all said that, in their opinion, only a change of air would rid me of it.

Mr Law had a charming house in New York and had several times suggested that we should visit him there. The harvest would not be ready for a month at least. M. de Chambeau knew every detail of the farm routine. There was nothing to prevent such a journey. Susy, the neighbour whom I mentioned earlier, agreed to come and look after my small daughter. As for my son, Humbert, he was still with Mrs Ellison in Albany and would not even notice our absence.

CHAPTER TWENTY

I

Steamships had not yet been invented, but steam was already being used to provide motive power in a number of factories. We ourselves even had a steam jack[1] which worked perfectly and which we used every week for our Sunday roast: either a sirloin of beef or one of those very large brown and white turkeys which

[1] A contrivance for turning a spit.

are so infinitely superior to the European varieties. Since I am writing about steam, I will tell you here what first gave Fulton the idea of applying steam power to ships.

Between Long Island and New York there is a channel about a mile or so wide across which, when the weather permitted, small boats continually plied. As it is not a river, there is no current and the only movement is the rise and fall of the tide, which presents no difficulty to navigation.

There was a certain sailor who, poor man, had lost both legs in battle. Being still young, he enjoyed excellent health and had retained considerable strength in his arms. This man had the idea of fixing across his bark canoe a round bar fitted at each end with wings. These wings projected beyond the sides of the canoe and could be controlled from his seat in the stern. One day, when he was taking Fulton across to Brooklyn on Long Island, Fulton watched him operate this ingenious contrivance and realised for the first time that it might be possible to use steam power for ships.

The town of Albany did a considerable trade, the merchandise being carried in large sloops or brigs. Nearly all these boats were equipped to carry passengers and had good cabins and a pretty saloon. The journey down to New York took about twenty-six hours, but a part of that time, the period when the tide was rising, was spent at anchor. Boats always tried to leave Albany at daybreak, so we went on board the night before we were due to sail and before sunrise were already well on our way. The North River, or Hudson, is very beautiful. Along the banks are a number of houses and pretty little towns, and the river widens into a stretch of water several miles broad before narrowing to enter the gorge through that chain of very high, steeply rising mountains which run the whole length of the continent of North America and are called by different names in different regions: the Black Mountains, the Appalachians, the Alleghanies. The wide reach is very like that part of Lake Geneva known as 'le fond du lac', but with this difference: the mountains rise only at the very far end, and the point where the river flows between two sharp rocks into the gorge itself cannot be seen until one is almost upon it. The water in this wonderful gorge is so deep that a large frigate could tie up to the bank without any danger of running aground. We sailed through these beautiful mountains during all the morning of the following day and when the tide was against us, went ashore to visit West Point,[1] famous in history for the treason of General Arnold and the execution of Major André.

This incident is well known, but I will tell you about it briefly.

There had been no reason previously to doubt the loyalty of the American general, Arnold, to the cause of the independence of the United States, and it was with every confidence that he was entrusted with the defence of the Hudson at the point where it traversed the mountains. It was when trying to break through this same gorge that General Burgoyne had been defeated by General Schuyler at Saratoga.

The English general, Clinton, was cut off in New York, surrounded by the American Army commanded by General Gates. The capture and occupation of West Point was essential to the English in order to re-establish communications with Canada, which had belonged to them since the shameful peace of 1763.[2] Its capture meant salvation for the English Army, and there was apparently reason to think that Arnold's greed would prove stronger than his patriotism. Negotiations with him had already been started and were to be concluded by young André, a major in the English Army, who had visited Arnold several times at West Point. When General Gates discovered the plot, he sent an armed boat to the place on the bank where André would re-embark. The crew of André's small boat warned him of the presence of the American craft and persuaded him—not foreseeing the sad consequences of their advice—to put on a sailor's suit. Their small boat had not covered a quarter of a mile when it was seized by the Americans and Major André was taken prisoner. As he was in disguise, he was treated as a spy and, as such, condemned to be hanged.

[1] West Point is a strategic keypoint in the Hudson valley. In the War of Independence, General Washington established a headquarters there. It is famous today as the site of the U.S. Military Academy. (T)

[2] The Peace Treaty of Paris of the 10th of February 1763, which ended the Seven Years' War. At the time it was concluded, it was known in France as the 'shameful peace'. (T)

General Gates offered to exchange him for the traitor, Arnold, who escaped through the mountains. The English refused: their need of Arnold's help was too great for them to hand him back. Instead, they sacrificed André, whose execution became the subject of many laments in prose and in verse. This young man was only twenty, very distinguished in appearance and outstandingly well-bred. His death provided the motive, or the pretext, for cruel reprisals by the English.

Although I have travelled in many lands and seen many of the grandeurs of nature, I have never seen anything to compare with that stretch of river at West Point. Probably it has today lost much of its beauty, particularly if the fine trees leaning their centuries-old branches down to the river have been cut. However, since the steep mountain sides are not suitable for cultivation, my love of nature makes me hope that the soulless, frenzied clearing of land may have spared them.

II

We reached New York on the morning of the third day and found that M. de Talleyrand was staying with Mr Law. They gave us a most friendly welcome, but were shocked by my thinness and changed appearance. I had planned to travel by the stage coach to Philadelphia with my husband, spending two nights on the way, but this they absolutely refused to allow. My husband therefore went alone and I was given into the care of Mrs Foster, Mr Law's housekeeper. This excellent lady tried every restorative she knew in her effort to help me. Four or five times a day she would arrive with a small cup of broth and, curtseying in the English fashion, say 'Pray, ma'am, you had better take this'. I submitted very willingly to her care, so tired was I of listening to M. de Talleyrand's lamentations about my wasting away.

The three weeks that we spent in New York are among my happiest memories. My husband was away only four days, but had an opportunity to admire the fine city of Philadelphia and, what I envied still more, to see my hero, the great Washington. Even today, I still regret not having looked on the face of that great man of whom I had heard so much from his close friend, Mr Hamilton.

In New York, I met all the Hamilton family again. I had been in Albany when they arrived there in a waggon driven by Mr Hamilton himself. He had just retired from the Ministry of Finance to resume his legal practice, a profession more likely to enable him to leave some kind of fortune to his children. Mr Hamilton was then between thirty-six and forty years of age. Although he had never been in Europe, he spoke our language like a Frenchman and his distinguished mind and the clarity of his thought mingled very agreeably with the originality of M. de Talleyrand and the vivacity of M. de La Tour du Pin. Every evening, these three distinguished men, in company with Monsieur Emmery,[1] a member of the Constituent Assembly, Mr Law and two or three other persons of note, met after tea and sat on the verandah conversing together until midnight, or even later, under a beautiful starry sky and in a temperature of forty degrees. Whether it was Mr Hamilton telling of the beginnings of the War of Independence, the details of which have since been blurred by the insipid memoirs of that simpleton, La Fayette, or whether it was Mr Law talking to us of his years in India, of the administration of Patna where he had been governor, of his elephants and his palanquins, or whether it was my husband raising some argument over the absurd theories of the Constituent Assembly which M. de Talleyrand readily accepted, the talk never ran dry. Mr Law so enjoyed these evenings that when we spoke of leaving, he became deeply dejected and would say to his butler: 'Foster, if they leave me, I am a dead man.'

We also became acquainted with a very interesting French merchant family, M. and Mme Olive, who had eight charming children, of whom the eldest was less than ten years old. I went often to see them in the country where they had bought a pretty house in which to spend their summers.

After three weeks of all this, the rumour went around one evening that yellow fever had broken out in a street very close to Broadway, where we were staying. That very night, either because we had the first symptoms of the illness or because we had eaten too many bananas, pineapples and other fruit brought

[1] Emmery, Comte de Grozyeulx, President of the Constituent Assembly of the 4th of January 1790.

from the Caribbean in the same ship that had carried the fever, my husband and I were terribly ill. Fearing to be kept in New York by quarantine measures, I decided to leave immediately. We packed our trunk and went at daybrcak to reserve places on a sloop which was ready to sail. We then went to say goodbye to Mr Law. He decided to leave too, on the pretext of visiting certain properties he had bought in the new town of Washington, where building had just begun. He had invested the greater part of his fortune in these purchases. Our departure was so hurried that I did not even see M. de Talleyrand: by the time he had begun to think of getting up, we were already far from New York.

We saw again the fine scenery near West Point, this time from the opposite direction, but with quite as much appreciation.

We had crossed the wide part of the river beyond the mountains when our progress was suddenly halted by one of those accidents which are fairly frequent in summer when the water is low. The tide was almost at its highest point when the sloop went aground on a sandbank, and although it suffered no damage, it lay there in midstream unable to move. The Captain thought that the next tide might not be high enough to refloat it and that it would probably be necessary to wait for another boat travelling downstream to tow us off, re-float us, and set us back into the channel from which a false turn of the wheel had diverted us.

The prospect of lying for several days in the middle of that great river did not appeal to us. I remembered that some Créoles from San Domingo, friends of M. Bonamy, were living on the banks of a small river near by, not far from a town we had just passed. The Captain told us we were exactly opposite the point where this stream joined the main river and offered us his boat to take us to these French people, whom we knew as they had visited us. We accepted this offer and were soon in the boat, with the one trunk which constituted all our luggage. We entered the smaller river and rowed for three or four miles between steep, rocky banks, the channel being so narrow that climbing plants and wild vines threw their branches across the water in garlands. It was delightful. Our journey ended at a small farm where we were given a cart to take us to our destination. Our two compatriots, still fairly young men, were as delighted as they were surprised by our unexpected arrival. They understood nothing at all about the life they had adopted. They knew very little English and, being unable to use any of the agricultural methods they had employed in San Domingo, had almost died of cold and boredom during the winter. From the fire at the Cape they had been able to save a number of very fine trifles whose luxury contrasted strangely with the poverty and disorder of their establishment, where the only woman was an old negress. We slept at their house, but before going to bed talked for a long time with them about their farm and household arrangements. The following day, we were given our breakfast in wonderful, but unmatching porcelain cups, so chipped that I would have preferred an honest set of matching earthenware crockery like our own. Afterwards, we rode in their waggon to the highway, and from there regained our house. At our invitation, these two friends accompanied us to Albany and from there to the farm, where they were very astonished to find us able to sell them several bags of oats and a dozen bushels of potatoes.

III

I found my house in perfect order, although M. de Chambeau was not expecting us. My small daughter was in excellent health. We had been away a month, and it had seemed long to me, despite the amiability of the people among whom we had spent it. Yellow fever caused terrible ravages in New York that year so I was very glad I had decided to leave in such a hurry.

I returned to my country tasks with fresh ardour, for the change of air had cured my fever and I had recovered all my strength. I resumed my dairy work and the pretty patterns stamped on my butter told my customers that I was back. Our orchard promised a magnificent crop of apples and our loft held enough grain for the entire year. Our negroes, spurred on by our example, worked with a will. They were better clothed and better fed than any of those belonging to our neighbours.

I was very happy in this life when, suddenly, God dealt me the most unexpected and what seemed to me then the most cruel blow that any mortal could endure. Alas, I have since suffered others far more severe. My small Séraphine was taken from us by a short illness very common in that part of the continent: a sudden paralysis of the stomach and intestines without any accompanying fever or convulsions. She died within a few hours, and was conscious until the very end. The Albany doctor whom M. de Chambeau had ridden to fetch as soon as the illness began, told us immediately he saw her that there was no hope. He said that the illness was very widespread in the country just then and that there was no known remedy for it. The Schuyler's small son, who had played with my daughter throughout the afternoon of the previous day, also died a few hours later from the same illness and joined Séraphine in heaven. His mother adored him, and called him my dear child's little husband. This cruel loss threw us all into the deepest sadness and despondency. We brought Humbert home to live with us and I tried to find distraction from my grief in teaching him myself. He was then five and a half years old. His intelligence was very well developed and he spoke English perfectly and read it fluently.

There was no Catholic priest in Albany or anywhere else in the neighbourhood, and as my husband did not want a Protestant minister summoned, he himself performed the last rites for our child and buried her in a small enclosure intended as a cemetery for the people of the farm. It was in the middle of a wood. Nearly every day I went to prostrate myself on that earth which was the last home of a child I had so dearly cherished, and it was there, my beloved son,[1] that God bided His time to work a change of heart in me.

Until then, although far from irreligious, I had not been much concerned with religion. During my childhood, no one had ever talked to me about it. During my early youth, I had been constantly surrounded by the worst possible examples. In the highest circles of Paris society I had seen the same scandalous behaviour repeated so often that it had become familiar and no longer distressed me. It was as if all concern with morality had been stifled in my heart. But the hour had come when I was to be forced to recognise the hand that had stricken me.

I could not describe exactly the change which took place in me. It was as if a voice cried out to me to change my whole

[1] Aymar, only surviving son.

nature. Kneeling on my child's grave, I implored her to obtain forgiveness for me from God, Who had taken her back to be with Him, and to give me a little comfort in my distress. My prayer was heard. God granted me the grace of knowing Him and serving Him; He gave me the courage to bow very humbly beneath the blow I had received and to prepare myself to endure without complaint those future griefs, which in his justice, he was to send to try me. Since that day, the divine will has found me submissive and resigned.

IV

Although all the joy had gone from our home, we still had to go about our daily tasks and we encouraged one another, my husband and I, to seek distraction in the need in which we found ourselves to find employment for every single minute. It was almost apple-picking time. The crop promised to be plentiful, for the trees were heavily laden. There were almost as many apples as leaves. The previous autumn we had followed an old Bordeaux custom and hoed a patch four to five feet square around each tree. It was the first time this had been done to them. Indeed, Americans were ignorant of the benefit which this practice has on growth and when we told them that we had owned vines where this operation was repeated three times a year, they thought we were exaggerating. But when spring came and they saw our trees covered in blossom, they began to think it must be due to some kind of magic.

Another idea was also widely remarked upon. Instead of buying new barrels of very porous wood for our cider, we hunted in Albany for a number of Bordeaux casks and for some marked 'Cognac', of a type well known to us. Then we arranged our cellar with as much care as if it had been going to house the wines of Médoc.

We were lent a mill for pressing the apples and to it we harnessed an ancient, twenty-three-year-old horse which General Schuyler had given me. The mill was exceedingly primitive: there were two interlocking, grooved pieces of wood, like ratchets, and these were turned by the horse, which was harnessed to a wooden bar. The apples fell from a hopper into the interlocking pieces of wood and when there was enough juice to fill a large basket, it was taken to the cellar and poured into the casks.

The whole operation was exceedingly simple and as the weather was very fine, this harvesting became a delightful recreation for us. My son, who spent the whole of every day astride the horse, was convinced that his presence was vital to the task!

When the work was finished, we found that, after putting aside enough for our own use, we had eight or ten casks to sell. Our reputation for honest dealing was a guarantee that not a drop of water had been added to the cider, so that it fetched more than twice the customary price. It was all sold immediately. As for that which we kept for ourselves, we treated it just as we would have done our white wine at Le Bouilh.

The apple picking was followed by the harvesting of the maize. We had an abundance of it, for it is indigenous to the United States and grows there better than any other plant. As the corn must not be left in the husk for more than two days, the neighbours collect to help, and they work without stopping until it is all done. This is called a 'frolic'. First, the floor of the barn is swept with as much care as for a ball. Then, when darkness comes, candles are lit and the people assemble, about thirty of them, both black and white, and they set to work. All night long someone sings or tells stories and in the middle of the night everyone is given a bowl of boiling milk, previously turned with cider, to which have been added cloves, cinnamon, nutmeg and other spices, and five or six pounds of brown sugar, if one is being very grand, or a similar quantity of molasses if one feels less grand. We prepared a kitchen boiler full of this mixture and our workers paid us the compliment of drinking it all, eating toast which accompanied it. These good people left us at five o'clock in the morning, going out into the sharp cold, saying 'Famous good people, those from the old country!' Our negroes were often asked to similar frolics, but my negress never went.

When all the harvests had been gathered in and stored, we began the ploughing and all the other tasks which had to be finished before winter. The wood which we intended to sell was stacked under a shelter. The sledges were repaired and repainted. I bought a length of coarse blue and white checked flannel to make two shirts each for my negroes. A journeyman tailor installed himself at the farm to make good waistcoats and well-lined cloaks. Being white, this man took his meals with us. He would certainly have refused, had we suggested it, to eat with the 'slaves', though they were incomparably better dressed and far better mannered than he. But I was very careful to avoid even the slightest reference to this custom. My neighbours acted thus and I followed their example, never making in any of our dealings the slightest allusion to my former station. I was the owner of a 250-acre farm and I lived as did all owners of such farms, neither better nor worse. This simplicity and renunciation of the past earned me far more respect and consideration than I would have had if I had tried to 'play the lady'.

The work which tired me most was the laundering. Judith and I did it all between us. Every fortnight, Judith washed the negroes' clothes, her own and the kitchen linen. I washed my own clothes, my husband's and those of M. de Chambeau, and I did all the ironing. This latter task I greatly enjoyed: I excelled at it and could compete with the best. In my early girlhood, before my marriage, I often went to the linen-room at Montfermeil and there, as if by a presentiment, I learned to iron. Being naturally dexterous, I was soon as skilful at it as the girls who taught me.

I never wasted a minute. Every day, winter and summer, I was up at dawn and my toilet took very little time. Before the negroes went to their work, they helped the negress to milk the cows, of which we had at one time as many as eight. While they were doing that, I busied myself in the dairy, skimming the milk. On the days when there was butter to be made, which was twice a week, Minck stayed behind to turn the handle of the churn, a task too heavy for a woman. All the remainder of the butter-making, and much other tiring work which still remained to be done, fell to me. I had a remarkable collection of bowls, ladles and wooden spatulae, all made by my good friends the savages. My dairy was reputed the cleanest and even the most elegant in the country.

V

Winter came early that year. In the first days of November, the black clouds which heralded the snow began to gather in the west. Everything happened in the proper order: eight days of extreme cold, the river frozen within twenty-four hours to a depth of three feet, and then the first falls of snow. Once the snow started, it fell so fast that it was impossible to see a man at ten paces. Prudent folk took good care it was not they who harnessed up their sledges to mark out the road: that was left to the people in a hurry, to those compelled by business affairs to go into town or to the river. Before venturing on to the river, it was necessary to wait until the places where it was safe to cross the ice had been marked out with pine branches for, without this precaution, there was great danger. Every year there were accidents through lack of care. Indeed, since the tidal rise and fall at Albany, and as far up as the junction of the Mohawk, was some seven or eight feet, the ice was often unsupported by water.

It has therefore sometimes happened that careless people have driven their sledges down the bank at a trot or a gallop and been engulfed under the ice instead of gliding over it, and have perished thus as there was no possible means of rescuing them.

The winter passed in the same way as the previous one. We often went to dine with the Schuylers and Renslaers, whose friendship was very faithful. M. de Talleyrand, who was again living in Philadelphia, had managed under strange circumstances, to find certain objects belonging to me: a cameo of the Queen, the casket you[1] still have and a watch which had belonged to my mother. He knew from me that my banker at The Hague had told me he had entrusted these objects to a young American diplomat—fortunately for him, I have forgotten his name—asking him to deliver them to me. Despite numerous enquiries, M. de Talleyrand had never managed to discover this man. Eventually, one evening in Philadelphia, on a visit to a lady of his acquaintance, he was told by her of a portrait of the Queen which Mr X . . . had obtained in Paris, and which he had lent her to show to some of her friends. She asked M. de Talleyrand if the likeness was good. As soon as he saw it, he recognised it as mine. He took possession of it, telling the lady that it did not belong to the young diplomat. Then, going straight to see him, he demanded

[1] Aymar.

without any preamble the casket and the watch which the banker at The Hague had given him at the same time as the portrait. The young man was frightened and ended by returning everything. M. de Talleyrand sent these things to us at the farm.

CHAPTER TWENTY-ONE

———————◆———————

At Pisa, 14th of May 1843.

I

Towards the end of the winter of 1795–1796, I caught measles. It was a fairly severe attack, aggravated by the fact that I was in the first months of pregnancy. We were afraid Humbert would catch it, but he did not, although he slept in my room. I recovered quickly and was no sooner better than we received letters from Bonie in France telling us that he and M. de Brouquens had, by their combined efforts, succeeded in having the sequestration removed from Le Bouilh.

The property of those who had been condemned was being restored. My mother-in-law, with the assistance of her daughter's husband, the Marquis de Lameth, had acted on behalf of her children and again taken possession of the properties of Tesson and Ambleville, as well as of the house at Saintes which had been held by the Department of Charente-Inférieure. But when they asked for the removal of the seals on Le Bouilh, they were told that this could not be done in the owner's absence. They replied that he had gone to America *with a valid passport*, and that neither M. de La Tour du Pin nor I, who owned a house in Paris, had been on the list of émigrés. After much discussion, the authorities agreed to allow us one year's grace in which to present ourselves. If we did not do so within that period, Le Bouilh would be offered for sale as national property, unless M. de Lameth was able to prove his own children's rights as the grandchildren of the former owner. We were urged, therefore, to return as soon as possible. However, as the stability of the French government of the day inspired little confidence, we were also advised to take passage to a Spanish port instead of a French one, for the Republic had just signed a treaty of peace with Spain which seemed likely to last for a while.

The arrival of these letters at our peaceful farm had somewhat the effect of a firebrand, for in the hearts of all about me they suddenly set aflame thoughts of a return to our homeland, glimpses of a better life, hopes of achieving our ambitions, in short, they armed all those sentiments which animate the life of man. My own feelings were quite different. France had left me only memories of horror. It was there that I had lost my youth, crushed out of being by numberless, unforgettable terrors. Only two sentiments had remained alive in me, and to this day they are the only ones that remain with me: love of my husband and love of my children. However, religion, which from that time forward was my only guide in all my problems, prevented me from setting the slightest obstacle in the way of a departure which terrified me and filled me with dismay. I had a presentiment that I was embarking on a fresh series of troubles and anxieties. M. de La Tour du Pin never realised the intensity of my regret when I knew that the day on which we would leave the farm had been fixed. I set only one condition to our departure: that our negroes should be given their freedom. My husband agreed, and reserved the joy of telling them to me alone.

When these poor people saw the letters arriving from Europe, they feared there would be changes in our way of life. They were anxious and frightened, so that it was in trembling that they came, all four of them, to the drawing-room in answer to my summons. Judith was holding her small daughter, three-year-old Maria, in her arms: she was soon to give birth to her second child. They found me alone in the drawing-room and I said to them with much emotion: 'My friends, we are returning to Europe. What are we to do with you?' The poor things were stricken. Judith sank on to a chair, sobbing, and the three men hid their faces in their hands. All four remained motionless. I went on: 'We have been so pleased with you that it is right that you should be rewarded. My husband has charged me to tell you that he gives you your freedom.' Hearing this, our good servants were so amazed that they remained silent for some seconds. Then, falling at my feet, they cried: 'Is it possible? Do you mean that we are free?' I answered: 'Yes, upon my honour. From this moment you are as free as I am myself.'

The poignancy of such a scene cannot be described. Never in my life have I known a happier moment. These people whom I had just freed, surrounded me and wept. They kissed my hands, my feet, my gown; and then, suddenly, their joy vanished and they said: 'We would prefer to remain slaves all our lives and for you to stay here.'

The following day, my husband took them before the Justice in Albany, for the ceremony of manumission, which had to take place in public. All the negroes of the town gathered to watch. The Justice of the Peace, who was also the manager of Mr Renslaer's properties, was very displeased. He tried to object that since Prime was fifty years of age, he could not, under the law, be given his freedom unless he had an assured pension of one hundred dollars. But Prime had foreseen this difficulty, and produced his certificate of baptism, which showed that he was only forty-nine. They were told to kneel in front of my husband who laid his hand on the head of each in turn in token of liberation, exactly as used to be done in ancient Rome.

We leased our house and land to the man from whom we had bought it, and sold most of the furnishings and stock. The horses fetched quite good prices. I distributed many small pieces of porcelain that I had brought with me from Europe as souvenirs. To my poor Judith, I left some of my old silk gowns, which will doubtless have been handed down to her descendants.

II

About the middle of April, we boarded the boat at Albany for New York, having first taken affectionate and grateful leave of all those who, for two years, had surrounded us with care, friendship and attentions of every kind. Two years later, when we had to go once more into exile, I was often to regret my farm and those good neighbours.

In New York we stayed with Mr and Mrs Olive, at their pretty little country house. There we also found M. de Talleyrand who, like us, had decided to go back to Europe. Mme de Staël, who was back in Paris with Benjamin Constant, had urged him to return and serve the Government of the Directoire[1] which was anxious to make use of his ability. At one time we thought we would all be able to sail in the same ship, but when M. de Talleyrand learned of our intention to land at a Spanish port and travel from there to Bordeaux, he changed his plans. He had no wish to expose himself, even for such a short time, to the power of His Most Catholic Majesty who might, with some reason, consider he was not a sufficiently edifying Bishop. He decided, therefore, to take a ship sailing for Hamburg. We had hoped to find one leaving for Corunna or Bilbao, but there was none, only a superb English vessel of four hundred tons, which was sailing for Cadiz and due to raise anchor at any moment. For lack of anything else, and despite the long journey it would mean through Spain, we decided to book our passages in her. She was sailing under the Spanish flag, though she belonged, as did her cargo, to an Englishman. I believe the cargo was corn. The owner, a Mr Ensdel, was on board travelling as a passenger. He had formerly owned whaling vessels. He knew not one word of French, but the Captain, who came from Jamaica, spoke English. In any case, he immediately found a very intelligent interpreter in my son who, although only six, was of great service to him. We were able to stay a further three weeks with Mrs Olive, in company with M. de Talleyrand, and we spent this time making our arrangements and settling ourselves on board.

Anchored in the roadstead was a French sloop of war commanded by a Captain Barré. His father had been in the Household of the previous Duc d'Orléans[2] and my husband had known him there. He was a very pleasant man, though a true sea dog, and he came every day in his barge to take us out to various points of the roadstead. He took great care, however, not to go anywhere near Sandy Hook where Captain Cochrane, later Admiral Cochrane, had been lying in wait for two months to seize him if he should attempt to leave. We visited his sloop, which was armed

---

[1] A government of 5 Directors who governed France from 1795–1799 with the help of two Chambers: the Council of the Elders (Conseil des Anciens) and the Council of the Five Hundred (Conseil des Cinq-Cents). See Translator's Note in Appendix, p. 443. (T)

[2] Louis-Philippe, duc d'Orléans, 1725–1785, father of Philippe Egalité.

with fifteen guns. It was a gem of order, cleanliness and care. I would have dearly liked to return to Europe in that lovely ship.

But the *Maria-Josepha* was waiting for us. We all four[1] went on board on the 6th of May 1796, and set sail the same day. There were a number of other passengers, including a French merchant, M. Tisserandot, whose wife, like me, was expecting a baby.

I did not suffer from seasickness and, as the weather was excellent, was busy all day long. This meant that I had soon exhausted the work I had brought for my husband and myself, so I set up as wardrobe mistress to all on board and sent out an appeal for work. Everyone brought me something. There were shirts to be made, cravats to be hemmed, linen to be marked. The crossing lasted forty days because the Captain, refusing to accept Mr Ensdel's advice, had sailed southwards with the currents. As a result, I had time to put the crew's entire wardrobe in order.

Eventually, towards the 10th of June, we saw Cape St Vincent and the next day entered the Cadiz roads. The Captain's ignorance and lack of skill had lengthened our crossing by at least fifteen days, for he had allowed himself to drift towards the coast of Africa and from there it was very difficult to strike northwards. He thought himself so far from land that he had not even bothered to post a watch in the crow's nest and when Cape St Vincent was sighted at dawn, he was much disconcerted.

III

We dropped anchor alongside a French three-decker, the *Jupiter*, part of a French fleet which was unable to leave owing to an even larger force of English warships which sailed past every day, almost within sight of the port.

A quarantine boat visited us and told us we would have to spend eight days on board in quarantine. We preferred this to going to the quarantine station to be devoured by the many varieties of insect life with which Spain abounds. If there had been a boat sailing even to Bilbao or Barcelona, we would have taken passages in it, for the journey would have been much

[1] M. and Mme de La Tour du Pin, Humbert and M. de Chambeau.

shorter, as well as less tiring and less expensive than by road.

M. de Chambeau had not been crossed off the list of émigrés and therefore could not return to France. He wanted to go to Madrid, where he knew several people, but would nonetheless have been only too willing to accompany us to Barcelona, for it would have taken him so much nearer to the town of Auch, where he owned several properties.

The uncertainty of our plans formed the topic of all our conversations during the period of quarantine, which in fact lasted ten days. It might have been much longer still, because one of our sailors deserted, and it was naturally impossible, therefore, to produce him. This man, who was French, had been captured after a fight on a war sloop. He had recognised a sailor on board the *Jupiter*, which was lying very close to us, and had spoken to him through the hailer. That same night he swam over to the *Jupiter* and when the Health officials called the roll the following morning, all that was left of him was his shirt and trousers. They were his only possessions. This somewhat prolonged our quarantine as we were not allowed to leave until he was found. He was eventually discovered in the French ship.

This quarantine nearly proved fatal to me. Fruit sellers came alongside all day long and Mme Tisserandot and I spent our time lowering a basket on a string to have it filled with figs, oranges and strawberries. This surfeit of fruit gave me violent dysentery and I was very ill.

At last, we were declared out of quarantine. The Captain set us ashore and never in my life have I been so embarrassed as then. When we landed, Mme Tisserandot and I were taken to a small room opening on to the street, and we had to wait there while our luggage was examined with the most exaggerated thoroughness. Our coloured gowns and straw hats soon drew a huge crowd of people of all ages and all kinds: sailors and monks, dockers and gentlemen, all curious to see what they doubtless regarded as two strange animals. As for our husbands, they had to stay in the room where our luggage was being searched. Mme Tisserandot and I were therefore alone, with only my son for company. He was not at all frightened, but asked me a thousand questions, especially about the monks, the first he had ever seen. At one moment, when a young, beardless monk was passing, he shouted: 'Oh, I see now, that one is a woman!'

This indiscreet curiosity made my companion and me decide to dress like the Spanish women. And so even before going to the inn, we bought a black skirt each and a mantilla so that we would be able to go out without shocking the inhabitants. We lodged at an hotel which was said to be the best in Cadiz, but I had become so accustomed to the exquisite cleanliness of America that it seemed to me disgustingly dirty and I would willingly have returned on board.

I remembered that one of the sisters of poor Theobald Dillon, who had been massacred in Lille in 1792, had married an English merchant living in Cadiz, a Mr Langton. I wrote him a civil note and he came immediately to see us, and was all courteous solicitude. Mrs Langton was in Madrid, staying with her daughter, the Baronne d'Andilla, and had with her their youngest daughter, Miss Carmen Langton. Mr Langton invited us nonetheless to dine with him and even wanted to carry us off to stay, but this invitation we could not accept as I was too unwell for the strain of visiting. It was agreed that the dinner would be postponed until the first day I was feeling better.

On the day after our arrival, my husband took our passport to be visaed by the French Consul-General, a certain M. de Roquesante, a ci-devant Comte or Marquis turned ardent republican, possibly even terrorist. He asked my husband innumerable questions and noted down all his answers. It was, in fact, remarkably like an interrogation. Then, doubtless in order to see what effect it would have, he said to my husband 'Today we have received a piece of excellent news from France, Citizen'—such being still the form of address—'that wretched Charette[1] has at last been captured and shot.' 'That is a pity,' replied M. de La Tour du Pin, 'it means one brave man the less.' The Consul said no more, signed the passport and reminded us that it would have to be presented again at the French Embassy in Madrid. Later, we were to hear what he reported to Bayonne about us.

At that time, after concluding a peace treaty with the French

[1] François-Athanase Charette (1763–1796), a royalist leader in the Vendean war. He was defeated in 1796 at Prélinière by Hoche, captured and executed. (T)

Republic, Spain had disbanded the greater part of her army, probably without pay. The highroads were therefore infested with brigands, especially the mountains of the Sierra Morena which we had to cross, and people would only travel in convoys of several carriages at a time. They did not hire a military escort for fear it might be in league with the brigands, all of whom were ex-soldiers, but any travellers on horseback who accompanied the convoys took the precaution of arming themselves to the teeth. A convoy usually consisted of fifteen to eighteen covered waggons drawn by mules.

It was in such a convoy that we left Cadiz. My husband, my son and I occupied one of these waggons, lying at full length on the mattress we had used aboard ship. Under it, on the floor of the waggon, was our luggage. It was covered with straw and straw had also been stuffed into the spaces between the trunks. A wicker hood artistically fashioned and covered with tarred cloth sheltered us from the sun during the daytime and from the damp at night, for we preferred sleeping in the waggon to staying at the inn.

But I am going too fast, for we spent still another eight days in Cadiz, walking beside the sea in the evening along the fine Boulevard de l'Alameda, enjoying the cooler air after a daytime temperature of 35°. My small Humbert came with me and one day we met a young gentleman of seven summers wearing a silk dress coat, richly embroidered, a sword at his side, his hair powdered white and his hat under his arm. My son looked at him in astonishment and then, thinking it might be one of the performing monkeys I had taken him to see in New York, asked: 'But is it a real boy, or is it a monkey?'

A spectacle he never forgot, and which I myself still remember was a magnificent bull fight on the Feast of St John. This national feast has been so often described that I will not try to do so here. The amphitheatre was enormous and there were at least five thousand people on the steps, sheltered from the sun by a cloth stretched over them, in the manner of the awnings of a Roman amphitheatre. Fine sprays kept this cloth damp on the inside and even when the fight began after midday Mass and did not end until sunset, I do not remember ever having suffered from the heat.

They killed ten bulls of a magnificent strain, each of which would have made the fortune of any American farmer. The matador was the leading one of the day, a fine young man of twenty-five. Despite the terrible dangers he courted, he was so agile that one could not feel the slightest anxiety for him. But there is no doubt that, at the moment when the two adversaries were there alone, face to face, in the second before the bull hurled himself at the matador, the spectators were held in the grip of a most exquisite emotion, and not a sound broke the stillness. The matador does not drive the sword home, he holds the point so that the bull impales itself upon it. This spectacle was epoch-making in my life: none other has left such a deep impression. I remember even the tiniest details as clearly as if I had watched the bull fight only yesterday.

IV

On the day fixed for our departure, we let the convoy start out without us, my husband, my son and I remaining behind to dine with Mr Langton. We had arranged for a boat to take us to the other side of the bay, to rejoin the convoy at Port-Sainte-Marie, where it was to spend the night, for it travelled at no more than a walking pace during the whole of that long journey.

I was so ill from the terrible attack of dysentery, complicated by fever, that my husband hesitated to let me start on our travels. But it was impossible to postpone it. Our luggage was already loaded and we had paid half the cost of the journey as far as Madrid. Our passport had been visaed and M. de Roquesante, the Republican Consul, would have taken umbrage if there had been any delay. He would have thought it merely a pretext, though I cannot imagine for what. Since I have always believed that it is possible to overcome any handicap, no matter what it may be— except, perhaps, something like a broken leg—it did not even enter my head to remain in Cadiz. We dined, therefore, with Mr Langton after assisting at the departure of our travelling companions for Port-Sainte-Marie.

Nothing could have been more charming than Mr Langton's house, which, in English fashion, was impeccably clean and well cared for. The only Spanish customs that Mr Langton had adopted were those which eased the difficulties of living in a torrid climate. The house was built around a square courtyard filled with flowers. On the ground floor was a cloister-like loggia, and on the first floor, an open gallery. Stretched over the whole courtyard, at roof level, was a sheltering cloth sprayed by a fountain in the middle of the courtyard. This gave a delicious coolness to the whole house. I admit it was very distressing to think that, despite a pregnancy already six months advanced, I had to set out on a long journey in a temperature of 35° instead of remaining in such an agreeable place. But the die was cast: departure was essential. After this farewell dinner we went on board the boat towards evening and ninety minutes later, the wind being favourable, we were at Port-Sainte-Marie. There we found our convoy, which consisted of fourteen coaches and six or seven gentlemen armed from head to foot.

The second day's stage was to Xérès, only five leagues further on. As I needed rest, we decided once again to let the caravan leave without us and to rejoin it there in the evening. We therefore dined early in the pretty town of Port-Sainte-Marie and then climbed into a 'calesa' or cabriolet similar to those I see here in Pisa where I am writing these memoirs. Our carriage was drawn by an enormous mule. It had no bridle, which seemed very odd to me, but on its head waved tall plumes hung with small bells. A young boy armed with a whip leapt lightly on to the shaft, uttered a few cabalistic sounds and the mule set off at a trot as rapid as any hunting gallop. The road was superb, we went like the wind and the mule, docile to the voice of its small driver, avoided all the obstacles and wound through village streets with a wisdom that savoured of the miraculous. At first I was frightened, then, thinking that it must be the local custom to travel like that, I resigned myself.

When I arrived at Xérès, I was curious to know what such a mule might be worth. I was told sixty to seventy louis, which seemed to me expensive.

The next day, the real journey began. I was still ill, but lying at full length on a good mattress, and the road being excellent, I suffered no more than if I had remained quietly at home. We always stopped two hours for dinner at appalling inns and two or three times we preferred to spend the night in our waggon rather than to sleep in such revoltingly dirty beds.

We were approaching Cordova when poor Mme Tisserandot was seized with the pains of labour. We were still four leagues from the town, in a great plain where there was no sign of a house. She safely gave birth to a small daughter, whom the muleteer washed in wine from his flask. We had no coverings for her, for the mother happened to be lying on the trunks which held the baby linen, and we could not wait to unpack them for the remainder of the convoy had continued on its way and was already far enough ahead to make it dangerous for us to delay longer. The muleteer handed me the unclothed baby, and I wrapped it as well as I could in scarves belonging to our companions. We continued on our way at a trot, trying to catch up with the caravan. Poor Mme Tisserandot suffered terribly from the speed, but it had to be endured.

It was night by the time we reached Cordova. As we had been travelling some distance behind the others, they were already settled by the time the inn servants reached our carriage. Seeing someone sick lying there, they thought she had been the victim of an attack. It is a well known fact that whenever there has been a crime, or if it seems likely that it will become necessary to bear witness in a court of law, country people inevitably disappear. Then they can say, with truth, that they haven't seen anything. These inn servants, true to tradition, set their lamps down on the ground and disappeared. The muleteer guessed why they had gone, but although he called them back, they did not re-appear. I spent part of the night unpacking the sick woman's cases to find the things she needed for herself and for the baby. But first we had to eat, and in that inn there was only sleeping accommodation. We were therefore forced to go and look for a tavern and, with enormous difficulty, because it was so late, did eventually manage to get some bread and a few slices of fried bacon.

V

Next morning, the departure of the convoy was delayed an hour so that I could have the poor baby baptised. The infant was healthy despite its adventures. It was thanks to this ceremony that

I saw the magnificent cathedral of Cordova. As you will easily understand, travelling in such discomfort, sick and six months' pregnant, oppressed by the dry heat of an Andalusian summer, where everything came to a standstill between midday and three o'clock, I was not as a rule inclined to visit monuments. But after this ceremony, which was by immersion, for the baby's head was dipped into the water of the font, we spent an hour wandering through that forest of pillars. The muleteers came to urge us to hurry. That day, we carried provisions for the two meals we would have to eat in the open, as there was no house at all in the country we were about to cross.

For about an hour after leaving Cordova, the road runs through well-watered gardens of lemon trees and Moorish olive trees, before it reaches the walls of the old city. Parts of the wall can still be seen, and like the boundaries of ancient Rome, it gives some idea of the immense area which this great Moorish city once covered.

We dined, as we had been told we would, near a well, in the middle of a pasture full of grazing sheep. The plain stretched further than the eye could see, for it was several leagues long and covered in places with fine grass and in others with dwarf myrtle. About the well stood a few pomegranate trees covered in blossom. This halt had about it something very oriental which appealed to me in a strangely powerful way. I infinitely preferred it to those three-hour stops in horrible, dirty inns where the heat was even worse than in the open.

The next day, and for several days afterwards, we crossed the Sierra Morena. We saw the two pretty little towns there of La Carlota and La Carolina built for the German colonists invited to Spain by M. de Florida Blanca,[1] the great minister of Charles III, and we noticed that certain German characteristics still remained. We met children with fair hair whose sun-tanned Spanish skins contrasted oddly with their blue eyes. These small towns are very

---

[1] The foreign agricultural colonies which gave rise to the two small towns of La Carlota and La Carolina, were actually founded in about 1768 by M. Olavides, a Spanish statesman, at that time Administrator of Seville. The Comte d'Aranda was then Prime Minister to Charles III and the Comte de Florida Bianca did not succeed to this post until 1777.

lovely, built as they are to a regular pattern and in beautiful sur-
roundings. On all the slopes, the road is edged with a marble
parapet and very picturesque. At that time, this was the only road
linking Castille with southern Spain.

To my great regret, we did not pass through Toledo. We arrived
at Aranjuez in time for dinner on, I think, the fifteenth day of our
journey, and spent the remainder of the day there, admiring the
cool shade, the beautiful weeping willows and the green fields
which, to any traveller coming from burned-up Andalusia,
exhausted by the July sun, seemed like a green oasis in the midst
of a desert. It is the Tagus, still a small stream wandering prettily
through this charming valley, which keeps this place so deliciously
cool. The Court was not at Aranjuez, but for some reason that I
have now forgotten, we did not visit the castle.

The following day we arrived in Madrid, after a two-hour halt
at the Puerta del Sol where the luggage and all the occupants of
the fourteen waggons of our convoy were examined, searched and
inspected. Even those who had already been passed were not
allowed to leave. Nothing can hasten the deliberateness of a
Castilian. It would have been useless to show impatience; the
customs officials would not even have recognised it for what it
was. The signal to depart was eventually given and we were taken
to the Hotel Saint-Sebastien, a mediocre inn in a small street,
where we had a fairly good room.

My husband immediately despatched the letters and packages
which Mr. Langton had given us for his wife and two daughters.
Then I made a more careful toilette than I had been accustomed to
do in the waggon, intending to call on these ladies after dinner.
But they were before us. Barely half-an-hour had passed when we
saw two of the most beautiful women in the world arriving at our
hotel: the Baronne d'Andilla and Mlle Carmen Langton. Their
mother was indisposed and unable to come with them, but they
were accompanied by a brother-in-law, the widower of a third
Miss Langton who had been considered even more beautiful
than her sisters. They proved to be of unequalled kindness and
attentiveness, and their brother-in-law suggested that we should
take a small furnished lodging in the quarter of the city where
these ladies were living. He undertook to make all the necessary

arrangements and put himself at our disposal for the whole of our stay in Madrid. We were to remain there for a month or six weeks at least, as we had to wait for letters and replies from Bordeaux to the letters we had written from Cadiz.

But my pregnancy was advancing and I wanted to be at Le Bouilh before the 10th of November so that my child could be born there. My husband went the next day to call on the Ambassador of the Government of the Directorate, to have his passport put in order. Remembering vividly the reception accorded him by Citizen, çi-devant Comte or Marquis, de Roquesante, he was most agreeably surprised at the Ambassador's amiability. He was Général Pérignon, later a Marshal of France. He had served under my father, who had greatly assisted him in his career. He had not forgotten this and was full of attentions for my husband. His gratitude, however, did not stretch so far as calling on me: the former aristocracy had not yet attained the vogue it was to enjoy later.

We stayed six weeks in Madrid, surrounded by the care, attentions and kindnesses of the Langton and Andilla families. M. Broun, Mrs Langton's son-in-law, whose wife had died the previous year, took us to visit all the most interesting parts of the city and every evening Mme d'Andilla took us to the Corso and afterwards to eat ices in a fashionable café at the bottom of the Rue d'Alcala.

CHAPTER TWENTY-TWO

I

At last a letter arrived from Bonie appointing a day when he would be at Bayonne to meet us. This time we engaged a returning 'collieras' to transport us and our baggage. M. de Chambeau was forced to remain in Madrid. The deep friendship he bore us, which had shown itself in so many different ways, made this separation very painful to him, and to us as well. For nearly three years he had shared all our vicissitudes, our interests and our griefs. My husband loved him like a brother. During the long years of exile, we had shared our very thoughts. He had no money. No one had thought to send him any. Luckily, we were able to leave him fifty louis, and by very good fortune, he was able to go and stay in the house of the Comtesse de Galvez, where he remained until 1800.

We left Madrid at two o'clock in the afternoon in order to reach the Escurial for the night. The 'collieras' was a berline, old, but solid, drawn by seven mules, and driven—or let us rather say, persuaded and exhorted—by a coachman who sat on the box and a postilion armed with a long whip who leaped from one mule to another in turn. They had no bridles and obeyed his voice. I think the mules next to the cross-beam must have had reins, but the other five certainly did not. One of them, the seventh, walked in front, alone. She was called the 'generala', and her job was to guide the others.

Fifteen minutes after leaving Madrid, the coachman noticed that he had forgotten his coat. Despite the stifling heat, he refused to go one step further until the postilion had been despatched on one of the mules to fetch it. This delayed us considerably and we did not arrive at the Escurial until well on into the night.

We spent nearly all the following day visiting the remarkable monastery of St Laurence of the Escurial—the Escurial, as it is usually called. There have been many descriptions of it, but not one of all those I have read since our visit has seemed to me to give a true impression. None conveyed the melancholy, devout calm with which the soul is filled by this masterpiece of all the arts, set in the midst of desert. The collection of so many treasures in such a solitary place seems to have no other purpose than to make us aware of the futility and vanity of the works of man.

Each year since the discovery of America and the gold and silver mines of Peru, the Kings of Spain have presented a magnificent gift made in these two precious metals to the Church of the Escurial.

In consequence, its collection of treasure has become the richest in the whole of Europe. All these splendid gifts are arranged chronologically, so that a sensitive eye can follow the steady decline in taste since the first gifts, which bear the signature of Benvenuto Cellini.

The reredos of the high altar was a bas-relief in silver representing the apotheosis of St Laurence, patron saint of the Escurial. In magnificence, it was unequalled, but as a work of art it was unsatisfactory. I use the past tense for there is reason to believe that the misfortunes of Spain have resulted in the destruction of all these masterpieces. The various articles used in the ceremonies of the Church were arranged in glass-fronted cupboards made from the most beautiful of East Indian woods. I remember very clearly a ciborium in the form of a globe, surmounted by a cross with an enormous diamond mounted in the middle and a large pearl at the end of each of the four branches. There were monstrances glittering with precious stones. We were shown the Easter vestments of red velvet embroidered all over with fine pearls graduated in size to form the design. Many people might not perhaps, have appreciated the magnificence of these vestments, for the most ordinary material ornamented with silver would have been far more striking to the eye. Yet that plain velvet was sewn with millions of pearls.

We climbed up to the rood loft where there was a wonderful collection of Church books. Their pages were of vellum and their margins ornamented with paintings by the pupils of Raphael, using their master's designs. These large folio volumes, silver-cornered and bound in soft brown leather, were kept in a kind of open cupboard, separated from one another by thin wooden partitions. It would normally have been difficult to take the books from their compartments on account of their great weight, but the problem had been solved by fitting the bottom of each compartment with small ivory rollers turning on iron rods. In this way, the books could be taken out with very little effort. I have not seen this system in any other library.

Benvenuto Cellini's fine, life-sized Christ in silver is in the upper gallery of the Escurial. When we had finished exploring this magnificent Church and had admired all it contained, my husband and M. de Lavaur left me there alone while they went off to visit the monastery and the library, which contained Raphael's fine painting known as 'The Pearl':[1] They had not warned me in Madrid that a woman needed special permission to visit this library, which is inside the monastery. I greatly regretted not being able to see it.

I had to wait quite a long time for my travelling companions and had leisure to meditate on many things. I thought of the beauty of this building, and then of the Battle of Saint-Quentin[2] for the Escurial had been built by the fierce father[3] of Don Carlos,[4] to commemorate that victory over the French. And so it was that when my husband returned and touched my shoulder saying: 'Let us go and see the Prince's House', I felt almost annoyed at having my thoughts interrupted. My son had been able to accompany his father to the library, and proudly told me of all he had seen.

We directed our steps towards this Prince's House, built by Charles IV when still Prince of the Asturias, and used by him as a retreat when the Court was at the Escurial and he wanted to escape from the rigid etiquette. It was no more than a very elegant villa, and today would barely satisfy a modest stockbroker. Its elegant furniture, nondescript paintings, the doubtful taste of the ornaments and a quantity of exceedingly ugly hangings, all combined to make it resemble the lodging of some favourite. What a contrast with the fine Church we had just left. I disliked it exceedingly.

We returned to the inn and soon set out for La Granja,[5] where we were to spend the night. The Court was in residence and there we were to collect certain packets from the American Minister, Mr Rutledge, for his consul in Bayonne. He invited us to supper and next day we set out for Segovia, a very picturesque small town with a castle. All we saw of this castle was its courtyard, which was surrounded by arcades, in the Moorish style.

The remainder of our journey was almost uneventful. We spent one day in Vittoria to rest 'la generala', without whom we would have been unable to proceed, and another in Burgos,

[1] Or The Virgin of the Pearl.
[2] On the 10th of August 1557, the Feast of St Laurence.
[3] Philip II, King of Spain, 1527–1598.
[4] Son of Philip II and Mary of Portugal, 1545–1568.
[5] The royal castle of La Granja is in the town of San Ildefonso.

where I visited the Cathedral. Finally, we reached San Sebastian where Bonie was waiting for us.

II

I felt no pleasure at returning to France. In fact, the sufferings I had endured there during the six months before our departure had left me with feelings of horror and terror which I could not overcome. My husband had lost his fortune, he was faced with the disagreeable task of tackling difficult problems of every kind, and we would be forced to live in a vast, empty château since everything in Le Bouilh had been pillaged and sold. My mother-in-law was still alive and she had again taken possession of Tesson and Ambleville. She was not an intelligent woman, and being by nature very suspicious and exceedingly obstinate, she trusted no one in business matters. How deeply I longed for my farm and the peace we had enjoyed there. It was with an aching heart that I crossed the bridge over the Bidassoa and realised that I was back on the territory of the 'one and indivisible' Republic.

We arrived at Bayonne in the evening and had scarcely entered the inn when two Gardes Nationaux came to fetch M. de La Tour du Pin and take him to the local authority, represented at the time, so far as I remember, by the President of the Department. Such a beginning revived all my fears. My husband, accompanied by Bonie, was brought by the two Gardes before the assembled members of the tribunal who questioned him about his views, his plans, his actions, the causes and purposes of his recent absence, and of his return. He realised immediately that M. de Roquesante had denounced him and told the tribunal so, remarking at the same time how favourably impressed he had been by the Ambassador in Madrid. After at least two hours of questioning—to me, waiting anxiously at the inn, it seemed a century—my husband returned. He was authorised to continue his journey as far as Bordeaux, but was given a sort of official route map with every stage marked, and this had to be counter-signed at each halt. In fact, if I had felt tired or indisposed, as might easily have happened for my pregnancy was far advanced, it would have been necessary to ask the local authority to provide an official declaration to that effect.

Bonie left us and returned to Bordeaux by mail coach. We our-selves engaged a bad coachman who took us by short stages. Our journey was marked by one incident: at Mont de Marsan I sent for a hairdresser to dress my hair and to my amazement he offered me two hundred francs for it! Fair wigs were so much the fashion in Paris, he said, that he would certainly make a profit of at least one hundred francs if I would agree to sell it to him. I naturally refused, but from then on have held my hair in great respect. Modesty aside, it was very beautiful in those days.

At Bordeaux we met the excellent Brouquens again. He had prospered during the war with Spain and had been re-engaged in the company which supplied food to the armies in Italy. He welcomed us with the affectionate friendliness that we have always unfailingly received from him but I was impatient to reach home and made all the necessary arrangements with good Dr Dupouy, who was to look after me. Then, the matter of raising the sequestra-tion being settled, we arrived at Le Bouilh to have the seals removed.

I must admit that the first moments strained my courage to the uttermost. I had left this house well furnished, not perhaps in a particularly stylish or elegant manner, but with everything in it comfortable and plentiful. I returned to find it absolutely empty. Not a single chair was left to sit on, not a table nor a bed. I almost gave way to discouragement but to complain would not have helped. We set about opening the cases we had brought with us from the farm, for they had reached Bordeaux long before us, and the sight of the simple furniture in that vast house gave us much food for reflection.

The next day, many of the inhabitants of Saint-André, who now felt shame at having attended the auction of our furniture, came to see us and suggested that we should buy it back at the prices they had given for it. This enabled us to recover for a reasonable sum the articles we needed most and we were very careful to limit our dealings to those who had most probably bought our belongings only from cowardice. As for the good republicans, they had no intention of showing such unpatriotic readiness to help. One of the most valuable possessions of the house had been a very fine collection of kitchen utensils. It had been removed to the district of Bourg, with the intention of sending it to the Mint. It was returned to us, however, as was the library, which had also been put into the official store. We spent many days in the agreeable occupation of putting the books back on the shelves and before Dr Dupouy arrived, had finished arranging the interior of the house, so that it looked as if we had been back for at least a year.

It was then that a very great happiness befell me: my dear Marguerite arrived. When Mme de Valence had been released from prison in Paris, she had sent for her to come and look after her two daughters. But as soon as Marguerite heard of my return, nothing could dissuade her from rejoining me. It gave me the greatest pleasure to see that excellent woman again. Despite her aristocratic white apron, she had escaped the dangers of the Terror. A month after my departure for America, she arrived in Paris where a friend had taken her in. Some days later, she went out, dressed as usual in the clothes normally worn by a maid in a good household, her apron snow-white. She had gone only a few steps when a cook, her basket on her arm, drew her into one of those dark passages known in Paris as alleys and said to her: 'Don't you know, you unfortunate woman, that you will be arrested and guillotined if you are seen wearing an apron like that?' My poor maid was astounded to find that she was in danger of death for wearing a garment to which she had been accustomed all her life. She thanked the woman for warning her, hid her anti-republican apron and hurried off to buy several lengths of coarse cloth to disguise herself, as she put it.

Shortly afterwards, passing through the Place Vendôme, she saw two children of six or seven playing in front of a carriage entrance, and finding them pretty, she stopped and spoke to them. She learned that they were living with their grandfather, who was an invalid, that there were sentries in the house, that their father and mother were in prison, that all the servants had left and they were therefore alone with their grandfather. Kind-hearted Marguerite did not hesitate a minute. She asked the children to take her to their grandfather, who confirmed their story. She suggested that she should remain in his service to look after him and the children. He was delighted, and two hours later she had settled in. She lived there until the death of Robespierre, when Mme de Valence took her into her house. As soon as I returned, she came to find me at Le Bouilh and was in time to receive my dear daughter Charlotte, who was born on the 4th of November 1796. I called her Charlotte because her godfather was M. de Chambeau. On the register of the Commune, however, she was named Alix, the only name, therefore, that she could use in legal documents.

III

In December, when I had recovered, my husband went to visit Tesson, Ambleville and La Roche Chalais. As a result of the abolition of feudal rights and leaseholds, all income from these properties had ceased and we were left with only a few old, tumble-down towers. I remained alone in the great house at Le Bouilh with Marguerite, two maidservants and old Biquet, who got drunk every evening. The farm workers were some distance away. The unfinished part of the ground floor was secured by only a few dilapidated planks, and this was the time when gangs of brigands known as 'chauffeurs'[1] were spreading terror throughout the south of France. Every day fresh horrors were told of them. Only two leagues away from Le Bouilh, they had burned the feet of a certain M. Chicous, a Bordeaux shop-keeper, to force him to tell them where he kept his money. Many years later, I saw this unfortunate man, still using crutches. I am ashamed to admit it but these gangs filled me with a paralysing terror. I often spent half the night sitting on my bed, listening to the barking watch-dogs, thinking that at any moment the brigands would break through the flimsy planks covering the ground-floor windows. I do not remember ever in my life having been more anxious! How I longed for my farm, my good negroes and the peace of those months. My days were no happier than my nights. It was mid-winter, and all my thoughts were with my husband, travelling about the countryside on a poor horse, over the terrible roads of the southern provinces, which in those days were especially bad.

Our financial position was another constant worry. I will not

[1] Robbers who tortured their victims with fire. (T)

go into details of our ruin—most of them I have by now forgotten, and in any case, I never knew them very exactly. I only know that when I married, my father-in-law was understood to have an income of eighty thousand francs. Since the Revolution, our losses amounted to at least fifty-eight thousand francs a year. To this might be added the loss on the house at Saintes, which had been a fine residence in perfect repair, and would have been worth three thousand francs in rent. The Departmental authorities had requisitioned it and when they returned it to us several years later, it was in such a state of dilapidation that it had lost all its value.

We also lost the furnishings of the Château de Tesson. M. de Monconseil had left this house to my father-in-law and as it stood in his command, which included Poitou, Saintonge and the region of Aunis, he had not only kept it in good condition but had also considerably enlarged it. He carried out all his public duties from there and entertained on a large scale. The furnishings were sold at the same time as those of Le Bouilh, that is to say, during the months between his condemnation and death and the passing of the decree which restored the goods of those who had been condemned to their descendants. It is safe to say that it was during those few months[1] that nearly all the contents of the large mansions of France were sold. The only exceptions were the libraries, which were first transferred to the chief town of the district and later returned to their owners. These sales were fatal to the continuity of family tradition and sentiment. No one would see again the room in which he had been born, or the bed in which his father had died, and there can be no doubt that the sudden dispersal of all these family possessions, with all the memories attached to them, contributed very considerably to the decadence of the young nobles.

IV

We lived at Le Bouilh right through the winter and for a part of the Spring. Towards July 1797, my husband realised it would be necessary to go to Paris to see M. de Lameth and finish putting his affairs in order. As if driven by presentiment, I asked to go

[1] Between April 1794 and April 1795. (T)

with him. Mme de Montesson, who had always shown me great kindness, suggested to me, through Mme de Valence, that I should stay in her house in Paris. She herself intended spending the summer in the country, in a house she had recently bought near Saint-Denis. The six weeks we intended to spend in Paris before returning to Le Bouilh for the gathering of the grapes and the vintage did not call for a great quantity of luggage, so we took with us only what was strictly necessary for ourselves and the children.

Many émigrés had come back under borrowed names. Mme d'Hénin had taken that of a milliner in Geneva, a Mlle Vauthier, and had gone to stay with Mme de Poix at Saint-Ouen. Mme de Staël, under the protection of Barras, one of the five Directors, and many others were in Paris.

M. de Talleyrand wanted us to come to Paris, particularly my husband. There was beginning to be talk of a counter-revolution and everyone believed in it. There were many royalists in the Government itself. Barras was one of the most influential of the Directors, and his salon, presided over by the Duchesse de Brancas, was always filled with royalists. Although it seemed unlikely that the other four would follow his example, there is no doubt that the Bourbon cause had never had such good hopes of success as at that time.

We set out in a hired carriage, my husband, myself, my good Marguerite and our two children: Humbert being then seven and a half and Charlotte, whom I was feeding, eight months old.

We spent several days at Tesson. The house was in an appalling state of dilapidation. Not only had the furniture been carried off, but the paper had been torn from the walls, the locks from many of the doors, the shutters from many of the windows, the iron pots and pans from the kitchen and the gratings from the ovens. The house had been veritably pillaged. Fortunately, Grégoire had piled as many mattresses as he could on his own bed and on those of his wife and daughter, and it was on these that we slept during our stay at Tesson.

It was with considerable emotion that I saw that good couple again for they had hidden my husband with so much care and devotion. On our way through Mirambeau, I had already seen the locksmith, Potier, and his wife, with whom M. de La Tour du Pin had remained shut away for three months in a space too dark even for reading. I thanked God again for having permitted him to escape from all the dangers of that dreadful Terror. The memory of it remained so deeply impressed on my mind, that I still had frequent nightmares in which I thought my husband was being hunted, followed from room to room. Then I would suddenly wake up, covered in a cold sweat, my heart beating heavily and painfully.

At last, we reached the end of our journey. Mme de Valence welcomed me with joy and Mme de Montesson, who had not yet left for the country, greeted me with the greatest kindness. In Paris, to be a little different always attracts attention, so that I immediately caused something of a sensation.

Shortly after our arrival, my husband and I were at supper with Mme de Valence when M. de Talleyrand was announced. He was very happy to see us and was soon asking: 'Well, Gouvernet, what are your plans?' Taken by surprise, my husband replied that he had come to settle some personal affairs. 'Ah,' said Talleyrand, 'I thought . . .' and changed the conversation to unimportant, trifling matters. A few minutes later, he began to say to Mme de Valence with that nonchalance which must be seen, for it cannot be described: 'By the way, you know the Ministry has been changed. New Ministers have been appointed.' When she asked who they were, he hesitated a little as if he had forgotten their names and was trying to recall them, and then continued: 'Ah, yes. Let me see. So-and-so at the Admiralty and somebody else at the Treasury.' 'And who,' I asked, 'is at the Foreign Office?' 'Ah, at the Foreign Office? Well, I expect I am!' And, taking his hat, he left.

My husband and I looked at one another, but without surprise, for it was impossible to feel surprise at anything M. de Talleyrand did, unless, perhaps, it should be something lacking in taste. Although he served a government drawn from the dregs of the gutter, he himself remained a very great gentleman. By the following day, he was already as much at home in the Foreign Office as if he had spent the last ten years there. The influence of Mme de Staël, all-powerful at that time through Benjamin

Constant, had made him a Minister. He had arrived at her house one day, and flinging on the table his purse, which held only a few louis, had said: 'There is what remains of my fortune. I must have a Ministry by tomorrow or I shall blow my brains out.' None of all this was true, but it was dramatic and Mme de Staël loved drama. In any case, the appointment was not difficult to secure. The Directory, especially Barras, were only too honoured to have such a Minister.

I will not tell again the story of 18 Fructidor.[1] You can read it in all the memoirs of the period. The royalists were full of hope, and intrigues and counter-intrigues were legion. Many of the émigrés had returned. They wore badges so that they would know one another, and all these badges were well known to the police: the black velvet coat collars, some form of a knot in a corner of the handkerchief, and so on. It was by such absurdities that they thought they could save France. Mme de Montesson used to come back purposely from the country to give dinners for deputies favourably disposed to the royalist cause. M. Brouquens, our very good friend, also gave such dinners and the talk was most incredibly unguarded. Every day, my husband and I met people we had once known and the strangeness of the life I had led in America and my wish to return there made me quite the rage for at least a month.

As I have told you, Mme d'Hénin had returned under an assumed name and with a Genevan passport and she was living with Mme de Poix who was staying for the summer in a house that had been lent to her in Saint-Ouen. We spent several days there, to the delight of Humbert who was very bored in Paris, where he could not go out.

I was struck by the extreme lack of prudence in the talk at table and before the servants. People loudly discussed the royalist plans and hopes, and talked by name of émigrés they had met during the morning who had come back with false papers. Nor were they

---

[1] The coup d'état of September 1797. The elections in March had gone in favour of the moderates and anti-Jacobins. There was fear of reaction. The three Jacobin Directors appealed to Napoleon for help. He sent troops commanded by Général Augereau. There was no military action, but the extreme Jacobins were re-established and revolutionary rigours re-imposed. A royalist coup was indeed preparing, but the deputies were arrested. (T)

any more careful in the presence of deputies on whom they thought they could count. I was thought ridiculous and pedantic when I said that M. de Talleyrand was aware of every single plot that was being discussed and that he was laughing at them. Yet I knew that it was so.

I saw Mme de Staël nearly every day. Despite her more than intimate friendship with Benjamin Constant, she was working for the royalists, or rather, for some form of compromise. One day when I was dining with her and the guests included eight or ten of the most distinguished deputies: MM. Barbé-Marbois, Portalis, Villaret de Joyeuse, Dupont de Nemours and Tronson du Coudray, the Queen's champion, the latter said to Benjamin: 'You who visit Barras every day, you know well that the way lies clear for us.' To which Benjamin replied with a quotation from one of M. de Lally's poems:

'Ils n'arracheront pas un cheveu de ta tête'[1]

'I'm quite sure they won't,' flashed Tronson du Coudray, 'I wear a wig'. And that is how those unfortunate people talked among themselves, happily unaware that only a fortnight later they would all be on their way to Cayenne.

V

While all this was going on, a Turkish embassy arrived in Paris and M. de Talleyrand gave a magnificent luncheon in honour of the Ambassador and his suite. Instead of having the luncheon at a table, a buffet was arranged along one side of a large salon. It rose in tiers half way up the windows and was laden with exquisite dishes of every kind and decorated with vases of the rarest flowers. Around the other three sides of the room were sofas for the guests, and small tables, already laid, were carried in and set before them. M. de Talleyrand led the Ambassador to a divan, seated himself in Eastern fashion and invited his guest, through an interpreter, to choose the lady whose company he would like at luncheon. The Ambassador did not hesitate and indicated me. I did not feel unduly flattered, for of all the ladies present, none could stand the brilliant light of a mid-August noon, whereas my own complexion and fair hair had nothing to fear from it. I

[1] 'They shall not touch a hair of thy head'. (T)

was, nonetheless, extremely embarrassed when M. de Talleyrand came to lead me to this Moslem, who offered me his hand in a most graceful manner. He was a handsome man of between fifty and sixty, well dressed in the Turkish style of that day and wearing an enormous turban of white muslin. During the luncheon he was very attentive and I completed my conquest by refusing a glass of Malaga wine. Through his Greek interpreter, M. Angelo, who was well known in Parisian circles, he paid me a thousand amiable compliments. He asked me, among other things, if I liked perfumes. As I replied that I liked what we in France called aromatic pastilles, he took my handkerchief, spread it on his knees, and then, from an enormous pocket in his pelisse, filled both hands with small pastilles no larger than peas, of a kind which the Turks were in the habit of putting in their pipes. Pouring the pastilles into my handkerchief he presented them to me.

The following day, he sent me, by M. de Talleyrand, a large flask of attar of roses and a very fine piece of green and gold cloth woven in Turkey. And that was the whole extent of my triumph, which created such a stir. None of the ladies usually referred to as being of the Directory—the Duchesse de Brancas, Mme Tallien, Mme Bonaparte, for instance—had been invited to this luncheon.

You may well imagine, my son, that my first care on arriving in Paris was to call on Mme Tallien, to whom we owed our lives. I found her living in a small house called 'La Chaumière' at the end of the Cours de la Reine. She received me most affectionately and wanted straight away to explain why she had found herself obliged to marry Tallien, by whom she had had a child. She was already finding life with this new husband unbearable. His readiness to take offence and his suspicious mind were, it seems, unequalled. She told me that one evening, when she returned home at one o'clock in the morning, he had been in such a fury of jealousy that he had been ready to kill her. Seeing him load a pistol, she had fled for shelter and protection to M. Martell, whose life she had saved at Bordeaux. But he had refused to let her into his house. She wept bitterly as she told me of this ingratitude. The expression of my own gratitude, into which I put all the warmth that I so sincerely felt, was very sweet to her. Tallien

came into his wife's room for a moment. I thanked him fairly
coolly and he told me that I could always count on him. You will
scc later that he kept that promise.

CHAPTER TWENTY-THREE

———————•———————

I

We were still in Paris, my husband being much occupied with his
affairs and deeply engaged in negotiations to buy back a part of
the Hautefontaine property which had recently been sold, when,
at daybreak on 18 Fructidor,[1] as I sat on the bed feeding my
daughter, I heard a noise like gun carriages on the boulevard. My
room opened on to the courtyard, so I told Marguerite to go and
see from the dining-room window what was happening. She
returned to tell me that large numbers of generals, troops and
guns were pouring into the boulevard. I rose hastily and sent to
awaken my husband, who slept in the room above mine. We both
went to the window and were soon joined by Mme de Valence.
Augereau was shouting orders in the street below. Both the Rue
des Capucins and the Rue Neuve-du-Luxembourg had been
closed. M. de La Tour du Pin soon left us and went to see M.
Villaret de Joyeuse who lived in one of the first houses in the
Rue Neuve-du-Luxembourg. He was with him when he was
arrested.

Towards midday, as no one had brought us any news, Mme de
Valence and I had become so curious that we set out, modestly
dressed in order not to attract attention, to call on Mme de Staël.
We had intended taking the Rue Neuve-du-Luxembourg, but it
was barred by a gun. So also was the Rue des Capucines. The
Rue de la Paix did not exist in those days, so we had to go as far
as the Rue de Richelieu to find a street that was still open. All
the shops were shut and the streets full of people, silent people.
When we reached the archway passages, we found our way
blocked by a mass of men and women who were being refused

[1] See note on p. 305.

access to the Quais.[1] By pushing and threading our way between them, we finally managed to reach the front of the crowd, which was being held back by a solid hedge of soldiers. They were keeping a way clear for five or six very strongly escorted carriages which were advancing at a foot's pace towards the Pont Royal. In the last of these carriages we recognised M. Portalis and M. Barbé-Marbois. They saw us and made friendly signs which seemed to mean: 'We don't know what they're going to do with us.' Seeing these gestures, a number of those horrible women who appear only during revolutions or disorders, began insulting us, shouting 'Down with the royalists'. I admit that I was terrified. Fortunately, as we were standing immediately behind the line of soldiers, we were able to slip between them and cross the road to Mme de Staël's house.

She was with Benjamin Constant and very angry with him because he maintained that by arresting the Deputies, the Directory had made a coup d'état inevitable. When she expressed a fear that the Deputies might be tried before a Government commission, he did not deny the probability, saying with his usual hypocritical air: 'It would be unfortunate, but perhaps necessary!' Then he informed us that all émigrés who had returned would be ordered to leave France again, under pain of trial by military tribunal. Much dismayed, I hurried home to tell my husband. Alas, the Decree was already being cried in the streets. When I reached home, I found my husband wondering anxiously how he could warn his aunt, for she was living at Saint-Ouen and all the gates of Paris had been closed. No one could pass the barricades without special permission.

By an extraordinary piece of good fortune, I met Mme de Pontecoulant whom I knew through having often seen her at the house of Mme de Valence. I will explain later who she was. She was on her way to Saint-Denis, where she had a country house, and she held a pass from the Section for herself and her maid. I begged her to let me take the place of the maid and, with her usual kindness, she agreed. I could not abandon my small Charlotte, as I was still feeding her, so I asked her to take me not as a maid, but as a nursemaid. She was very amused at the idea that

[1] Carriage roads beside the Seine. (T)

at her age—she was between forty-five and fifty—the guards at
the barricades should think her the mother of an eight-month-old
baby. We set out together. The poor woman was very quickly
disillusioned. Indeed, when we arrived at the gate of the city,
the toll collectors and soldiers, instead of congratulating the
mistress, directed all their flatteries at the nurse. Mme de Pontecoulant was very annoyed, and instead of taking me to Saint-
Ouen, a detour which would have added only ten minutes to her
journey, she just deposited me in the road, at the end of a very
long avenue, which my plump small daughter's weight made
seem all the longer.

You will easily picture the exclamations with which I was
received by Mme de Poix and my aunt. The latter decided to
return immediately to England. With these two ladies were a
number of former émigrés who were in despair at being forced to
leave France again. It put an abrupt and irrevocable end to all
negotiations with those who had bought so-called national[1]
property and who were at that time often willing to consider
selling it back to its former owners. It would be true to say that
the happenings of 18 Fructidor were as fatal to private fortunes as
the revolution itself.

The Decree ordered all émigrés who had returned to French
soil to leave Paris within twenty-four hours and France within a
week. My own opinion was that we should set out at once for
Le Bouilh. As we had left France with a valid passport and
returned on the same document, duly visaed by the French and
Spanish authorities, I thought the Decree might not apply to us.
There had been nothing clandestine about our return. But to make
sure that this would be the view taken by the authorities, my
husband went to see M. de Talleyrand. He, however, was greatly
worried about his own future and had no time to spare for that
of others. He replied without hesitation that it was no concern of
his and told us to submit the case to Sottin, Minister of Police.
I went, then, to see Tallien, who welcomed me warmly. He drew
up a statement of our circumstances, omitting our names: 'A
private person, who left in 1794, with a passport . . .' and so on,

[1] Private property confiscated by the State during the Revolution and often put up
for sale.

setting out our circumstances most favourably. Tallien promised to go straight away to see Sottin to ask him to add his recommendation. Without it, it would be impossible to get a visa for the passport given us by the municipality of Saint-André-de-Cubzac for our journey to Paris, and which had to be produced in order to pass the barricades on leaving the city.

I returned home in some anxiety and began to pack. A police order had just been posted up in Paris calling on all householders to report anyone living in their houses without the proper papers. We did not want to create difficulties for Mme de Montesson, who had provided us with a lodging. She was already sufficiently anxious on her own account, for she had been receiving the deported Deputies at her house for several months past, welcoming them with the greatest kindness and feared that she might, as a result, be heavily compromised.

Eventually, after many hours of extremely anxious waiting, Tallien sent back the request he had submitted to Sottin. The Minister had added a signed note in his own hand: 'This person is within the law.' Tallien also sent a short letter, written in the third person, apologising very civilly for not having been able to obtain anything, but the end of the letter might have been construed to mean: 'I wish you a good journey'.

II

Two courses were open to us. We could ask for a passport to Spain and travel by way of Le Bouilh, where I would remain for a time while my husband went on to San Sebastian. It would have been the wiser course. The alternative was to go to England and from there, according to circumstances, return to America. My aunt, Mme d'Hénin, had great influence over my husband and she persuaded him to adopt the second course. We had very little money, but knowing that in London we would find my stepmother, Mme Dillon, and many other very close relatives who would doubtless come to our aid, we decided to go to England.

As it had been our intention to spend only five or six weeks in Paris, we had brought very little with us. I had had a few gowns made for me in Paris, but two very small trunks were all we

needed for our meagre baggage, including that of my good
Marguerite, who this time was fully determined to come with us.
This departure was to have the most unfortunate consequences
for us. We were in the midst of our negotiations with the buyers
of Hautefontaine, intending merely to become the buyers of the
estate in their stead, for my grandmother[1] was not dead. However,
it had been laid down in my marriage contract that I was her sole
heir, so that I thought it not unreasonable to consider that I
could, with a clear conscience, acquire property that was hers.
This new emigration ruined all these arrangements. Providence
had decreed that my husband and I were to finish our lives in the
most complete ruin. It also condemned us, unfortunately, to
many other very cruel griefs. But I must not anticipate the sorrows
that have befallen me: that tale will sadden the last pages of this
account.

We spent the two or three days before our departure in a state
of gloom and uncertainty. Perhaps we should have returned to
Le Bouilh. There was a rumour that Barras, although giving
way for the moment to the demands of his colleagues, would soon
regain all his power and that, when that moment came, he would
resume his favourable attitude towards the émigrés.

Everywhere one met people distraught by this fresh emigration.
We booked three places in a carriage which would take us to
Calais in three days. Two other places were taken by M. de
Beauvau and by a cousin of Mme de Valence, young César
Ducrest, a pleasant young man who was to die very miserably a
few years later.

The French are by nature gay, so that although we were all
desolate, ruined and furious, we nonetheless succeeded in pre-
serving our good humour and our laughter. Our cousin, M. de
Beauvau was on his way to join his wife, Mlle de Mortemart,
and his three or four children. She lived in a country house at
Staines, near Windsor, with her grandfather, the Duc d'Harcourt,
once tutor to the first Dauphin who died at Meudon in 1789.

We reported to each municipality along our route, including that
of Calais, where we embarked on a packet at eleven o'clock in the
evening.

[1] Comtesse Edward de Rothe.

I sat on a hatch cover on the deck, with my daughter, Alix, in my arms. Marguerite put my son, Humbert, to bed and my husband felt sea sick the very moment he stepped on board, though there was very little wind and the night was superb. Beside me was a gentleman who, seeing me burdened with a child, suggested in a very English voice that I should lean against him. I turned to thank him, and as I did so, the moonlight shone on my face and he cried 'Good God, can it be possible!' It was young Jeffreys, son of the editor of the *Edinburgh Review*, whom I had met daily at his uncle's house in Boston during our visit to that hospitable city three years before. We spoke for a long time of America, and of my regret at having left it, a regret which these new threats of emigration had made even more vivid. I explained to him that despite the presence of all my family in England, I was going there with only one idea and purpose: to return to my farm, if all hope of returning to France should die or be postponed indefinitely.

While I talked to my companion, the night was passing and the first gleams of daylight revealed the white cliffs of Albion, towards which we were being driven by a strong south-easterly wind. When we dropped anchor on British shores, the sad faces of the passengers could be seen emerging from the hatches, all in various stages of pallor and dishevelment. My poor maid, whose longest sea journey had been from Le Bouilh to Bordeaux, was enchanted to see dry land again. We disembarked and found ourselves at the mercy of the rough English excisemen, who seemed to me far worse than their Spanish counterparts. When they saw my passport, which I presented at the office charged with examining them—the Aliens' Office—I was asked if I was a subject of the King of England. When I said that I was, I was told I would have to find someone of standing in England to vouch for me. When, without hesitation, I named my three uncles—Lord Dillon, Lord Kenmare and Sir William Jerningham—the tone and attitude of the officers changed at once. These formalities occupied the whole morning. After an English lunch, or, more exactly, dinner, we left Dover for London and put up at one of the inns in Piccadilly. From Dover, I had sent news of our arrival to my aunt, Lady Jerningham, and she had sent her dear and amiable Edward[1] to

[1] Lady Jerningham's third son.

meet us and take us to her house in Bolton Row. Her welcome was a very motherly one. She told us that she was leaving for the country, for Cossey, where she would be staying at least six months, and made us promise to come and spend them with her, saying that this would give us plenty of time in which to settle our future plans. My good aunt was especially kind to my husband and since she dearly loved children, immediately conceived a passion for Humbert. It is true to say that, at the age of seven and a half, he was a most extraordinarily intelligent child, speaking and writing fluently both English and French, and already writing dictations in both languages.

We established ourselves, therefore, in Bolton Row as if we had been children of the house. There I found my good old friend, the Chevalier Jerningham, brother of my aunt's husband, Sir William. The faithful friendship he had shown me ever since my childhood was as heart-warming as it was useful during my stay in England.

I was preparing to call on my stepmother, Mme Dillon, who had been living in England for nearly two years, when she arrived at my aunt's house. She was very moved to see me again and to hear about the last months of my poor father's life, for I had spent the winter of 1792–1793 with him.

III

My arrival in London was an event in the family. I found Betsy de La Touche, my stepmother's daughter, who had been entrusted to my care in 1789 and 1790 when she was at the Convent of the Assumption. I had often gone to visit her there and was the only person permitted to occasionally take her out. Betsy had recently married Edward de Fitz-James and was expecting her first child. She was a gentle, sweet girl and deserved a better fate. She was deeply in love with her husband, who did not return her devotion and whose cruel and flagrant infidelities broke her heart.

Her brother, Alexandre de La Touche, was three years younger than she. He was a handsome young man, very carefree and gay, with little intelligence and even less learning; he had all the faults of young people of his kind, who had had idleness forced upon them as a consequence of emigrating. In addition, Alexandre was completely lacking in talent. He loved horses, fashion and small intrigues, but he never opened a book. My stepmother who, to my knowledge, had never had a book on her table, would certainly have been incapable of giving him a taste for such things. She herself was not without a certain natural wit and she was well bred and knew the ways of society. But I often wondered why my father, gifted as he was with a superior mind and great learning, had married this woman older than himself. It is true that she was wealthy, but she was by no means an heiress. He longed above all for a son, and from his marriage with her had only three daughters. Two died in very early childhood and only the eldest, Fanny,[1] survived.

My uncle, the Archbishop, and my grandmother, Mme de Rothe, were also living in London. I had not seen them since leaving their house in 1788, nine years before. My aunt, Lady Jerningham, thought I should show them some mark of respect and the good Chevalier undertook to ask them if they would receive me. Seeing that the Archbishop wished to see me, my grandmother did not dare to refuse, but she set the condition that M. de La Tour du Pin should not accompany me. I could have used this as a pretext for not visiting them, but pretended not to know of it. In any case, my husband was delighted to be dispensed from the visit, for he already knew, he admitted to me later, that my grandmother had spread very malicious stories about him since coming to London. If I had known it at the time, I would certainly not have called on her.

One morning, then, I set out for Thayer Street with my small Humbert. It was not without emotion and conflicting feelings that I knocked on the door of that modest five-windowed house where my uncle and my grandmother were living. For me, there had been no intermediate stages between that house and the beautiful hôtel on the Faubourg-St-Germain where I had spent my childhood in all the luxury and splendour that an income of 400,000 francs could provide, for such was the income the Archbishop of Narbonne then enjoyed. But let it be said here, in passing, that this princely income did not prevent him leaving debts amounting to 1,800,000 francs when he left France.

The door was opened by an old servant, who burst into tears

[1] Frances, or Fanny, Dillon who later married Général Bertrand.

when he saw me. He was from Hautefontaine and had been at my wedding. He preceded me and I heard him announce in a voice shaken by emotion: 'Here is Mme de Gouvernet.' My grandmother rose and came to meet me. I kissed her hand. Her welcome was very cold and she addressed me as 'Madame'. At the same moment the Archbishop entered the room and throwing his arms about me, kissed me tenderly. Then, seeing my son, he embraced him too, over and over again. He asked him a number of questions in both English and French and the child replied with an intelligence and shrewdness that charmed my uncle. When he asked me if Humbert might accompany him to a nearby house where he went every morning to have electric treatment for his deafness, I was a little afraid that Humbert would not wish to go. But I need not have worried: the child replied without hesitation that he would like very much to go 'with the old gentleman'.

I was extremely uneasy at being thus left to spend half-an-hour alone with my grandmother. I was afraid she would begin her long list of accusations and trembled also at the thought that she might turn the conversation to my poor father or my husband. She detested them both in an equal degree and I never felt sufficiently mistress of myself to endure unmoved the attacks her inveterate hatred was capable of inspiring. Fortunately, she was able to restrain herself until the Archbishop returned, delighted with Humbert who had not been in the least frightened by the electrical apparatus and who had even received several shocks without flinching.

My uncle invited me to dine the following day with six aged bishops of Languedoc whom he boarded at his table. They were all old acquaintances of mine. As for my husband, there was no question of his coming. I announced my plan to stay at Cossey with my aunt for the whole of her stay there. The Archbishop was pleased to hear of this arrangement, but I could hear my grandmother muttering wordlessly to herself, a sign I remembered as heralding some disagreeable remark which she would not be able to keep back. I therefore rose to leave, kissed my grandmother's hand and was again embraced by the Archbishop who complimented me on my looks.

Lady Jerningham had been very anxious about this visit and

was pleased that it had passed off well. The following day I was taken to call on two other uncles.

One was Lord Dillon, my father's eldest brother. He received me pleasantly, but with a cool courtesy which made it only too clear that he felt not the slightest interest in us. He offered us his box at the Opera for that very evening, and we accepted it. It was the only service he was ever to render me. He gave a pension of £1,000 a year to my eighty-four-year-old uncle, the Archbishop, but so far as I myself was concerned, the fact that I was his brother's daughter availed me nothing.

The second uncle I visited, this time with Lady Jerningham, was Lord Kenmare. He received me quite differently, although I was only his niece by his first wife, my father's sister. She had been dead for many years, and he had re-married. By his first marriage, he had had a daughter, the Lady Charlotte Browne my cousin, who later, by her marriage became Lady Charlotte Goold.

Lord Kenmare, his daughter and all his family welcomed me with a kindness and a readiness to help that were unequalled. The friendship of Lady Charlotte, in particular, never failed me. She was then eighteen and much sought-after in marriage, as her dowry was a goodly £20,000.

IV

I went to see our aunt, Mme d'Hénin, at Richmond. She was very offended by our plan to stay at Cossey with Lady Jerningham.

Mme d'Hénin was an extremely dominating woman, in fact, a tyrant, and the slightest infringement of her authority or her influence roused her to fury. Most of her tyranny was exercised on M. de Lally, but it must be admitted that her decision and firmness were really of the greatest help to him. She would brook no rival, and the fact that M. de Lally had been so unwise as to stay at Cossey during the three or four months that Mme d'Hénin had been in France, as happy there as a schoolboy on holiday, had given my aunt the greatest dislike for Lady Jerningham. When she heard that her nephew and I were planning to stay there for six months, she made no attempt to hide her anger. But despite her choleric, authoritative nature, Mme d'Hénin did not lack a sense of justice. This forced her to admit that it was only natural for us, arriving in England without a penny, to be overjoyed at being adopted by a relative so close and so well esteemed in the world as my aunt Jerningham.

Mme d'Hénin and M. de Lally shared an establishment. Their ages should have guaranteed them from scandal, but they were none the less the butt of considerable ridicule. Despite her really great qualities, Mme d'Hénin was not generally liked. Some of her friends remained faithful, but her quick temper and dominating nature created enemies for her, sometimes without her being aware of it.

After three days in London, I realised that it would give me no pleasure at all to stay there longer. Emigré society, with its gossip, petty intrigue and scandal-mongering, was odious. I went one evening to visit Mme d'Hénnery, whose daughter, the young and pretentious Duchesse de Lévis, was one of the pale constellations about which fluttered all émigrés aspiring to fashion. I met there Mme and Mlle de Kersaint, and learned that that inveterate aristocrat, Amédée de Duras, so haughty and so intolerant, was by no means disdainful of Mlle de Kersaint's income of 25,000 francs. Mme de Kersaint had been able to save her Martinique properties. I was six years older than Mlle de Kersaint, and she has told me since that she stood much in awe of me then.

To my great joy, the departure for Cossey was finally arranged. Lady Jerningham was to leave first and it was therefore decided that I would stay for a few days with my stepmother, Mme Dillon. There, I heard with pleasure that Edward de Fitz-James was taking some saddle horses and that, since I was known to be an excellent rider, he had included a lady's saddle for me. My stepmother gave me a charming habit and we looked forward to some good riding.

We left London in a convoy: in the first berline were my stepmother, myself, my daughter, my son, Marguerite and Flore, Mme Dillon's mulatto maid; in the second were Mme de Fitz-James, Alexandre de La Touche and my husband. Then there was Betsy's old governess, and last of all, M. de Fitz-James, with his horses, grooms and so on.

We spent the night at Newmarket, where the famous races are held, and which I was curious to see. We stayed there all the following day, which was the last of the racing season and therefore the day of the King's Cup race. We spent the whole day on the course and by a piece of good fortune very rare in England, the weather was heavenly. I still remember it as one of the most enjoyable and interesting days in my life. The next day we left for Cossey. It was, I think, the beginning of October 1797.

My aunt loved children and took charge of Humbert. She would take him to her room immediately after breakfast, and keep him there the whole morning, giving him lessons and making him write and read in English and French. She even took charge of his wardrobe and I saw coats arriving, and overcoats, linen and so on, a whole wardrobe for my children. She also showed me the very greatest kindness. She noticed that I made my own dresses, and on the pretext of encouraging my cousin, Fanny Dillon,[1] who was also at Cossey, to do likewise, brought to my room and put at my disposal lengths of muslin and materials of every kind. I particularly appreciated this attention as I had arrived from France very lightly clad for the English climate.

Vaccine (against smallpox) had recently been discovered, and when my aunt learned that my children had not yet been inoculated with it, she undertook to have it done and sent to Norwich for her own surgeon to perform the operation. In short, she surrounded us with attentions of every kind and the time I spent at Cossey was as agreeable as we could have wished.

We were a large party, nineteen, including the chaplain; most of us very closely related. The French cook was excellent and the food plentiful and not too elaborate. Sir William had an income of about £18,000 sterling, which was not considered a great fortune in England, but which was sufficient to permit him to live liberally. The house was old but comfortable. The Chapel was in the attics, as was customary in Catholic houses before Emancipation.

V

The winter passed very pleasantly. Towards March, Mme Dillon, my sister Fanny and M. and Mme de Fitz-James returned to London for the birth of Mme de Fitz-James's baby, but we stayed

[1] Daughter of Lord Dillon.

on at Cossey until May. My aunt was to spend the summer in London, so Sir William suggested that while they were away, we should live in a pretty cottage he had had built in the park. As I was four months' pregnant and in consequence fairly ill, I preferred not to be so far away from everyone, fearing that something might go wrong and prevent my pregnancy reaching its full term. Mme d'Hénin, too, was breathing fire and brimstone at the idea that we might prolong our stay in the country and insisted that we should go to stay with her at Richmond, where there would be room for all of us in her house. We accepted her invitation, though much against my inclination. However, my husband did not want to offend his aunt and there were also certain business matters to be attended to in London, as you shall hear.

I did not re-read the earlier parts of these memoirs, and so am not sure if I told you that when we reached Boston, I wrote to my good tutor, M. Combes, who was with my stepmother in Martinique. My father had made him Registrar of the Island, a post he had previously held in St Kitts and Tobago. Living, as he did, in my father's house, he had been able to lay aside all his earnings and had eventually accumulated 60,000 francs. Mme Dillon had borrowed this capital against payment of interest. When M. Combes heard that we intended buying a property near Boston, that excellent man, who loved me like a daughter, decided to add his savings to the funds we already had, so that we could buy a larger property, and then he would come to live with us.

He asked Mme Dillon for the capital he had loaned her. She not only refused to repay it as a whole, but even in instalments. Desperate at seeing his plans come to nothing, he begged and threatened: all in vain. Each boat from Martinique brought me a letter from him. He wrote that he did not dare to leave Mme Dillon, hoping by his presence to force her to repay at least something. Before Mme Dillon went to England, he had managed to extract a statement from her acknowledging her indebtedness for the 60,000 francs of capital and for the interest, which amounted by then to nearly 10,000 francs.

While we were at Richmond, I heard the sad news of my old friend's death. He had told me in a letter written not long before that the climate, and above all, the grief of knowing me to be in a foreign country and without funds, were killing him.

In his will, he left me this 70,000 francs, which Mme Dillon owed him, together with the current interest, which amounted to 1,500 or 1,800 francs. From the day Mme Dillon heard of this bequest, her attitude towards us changed completely. She herself maintained a good house in London and spent lavishly on dinners, evening parties and private theatricals. But whenever we stood in need of money, she referred us to a Créole émigré who looked after her affairs. To all our requests that she should pay the interest owing to us, she returned evasive answers: sometimes the sugar crop was bad, sometimes funds had not arrived, in fact, each day there was a fresh excuse. I spoke to her personally about it, and was very badly received. We spoke to her son, Alexandre de La Touche, and my husband spoke to her man of business. But we met with no success.

We were given as alms what was really our own property. But nonetheless, we had to pay Mme d'Hénin our share in her household expenses and this was causing us increasing embarrassment. There was also the need to make a new layette for the baby, all the baby clothes having been left behind in France. Oh, I very often regretted leaving Cossey.

I found sharing a house with Mme d'Hénin intolerable. She gave us such poor accommodation that we could not receive visitors—we had only two small bedrooms on the ground floor and it is not customary in England to receive visitors in the room where one sleeps. I shared one of these rooms with my daughter and M. de La Tour du Pin shared the other with our son. It was only in the evenings that we joined my aunt in her pretty salon on the first floor. It was certainly very uncomfortable, but if life had been pleasant, this would not have worried me. I was fully aware of the outstanding and really great qualities of Mme d'Hénin and was never lacking in respect towards her; but I had to admit that our characters were not compatible. Perhaps it was my fault; perhaps I should have remained unmoved by the shower of pin-pricks I received from her. M. de Lally, that most timorous gentleman, never dared to risk the slightest jest which might have given me some amusement. And I was still young and laughter-loving. It would surely have been unnatural for me, at twenty-eight, to have acquired the serious mien proper to my aunt's fifty years? She was entirely wrapped up in politics and her sole interest was the future constitution of France. It bored me to death. And then, there were the writings of M. de Lally, which had to be read and re-read, word by word, sentence by sentence...!

In short, I longed for a house of my own, however small, but since I could see no means of fulfilling this longing, I had to resign myself.

CHAPTER TWENTY-FOUR

I

The Princesse de Bouillon, of whom I wrote in the first part of these memoirs, had come to England in the early summer of 1798 to settle certain matters connected with a legacy left to her by her friend, the Duchesse de Biron. Although Mme de Bouillon had always lived in France and had married there the 'cul de jatte' who had never been her husband except in name, she was by birth a German, a Princess of Hesse-Rothenbourg. There had been a long and faithful attachment between her and Prince Emmanuel de Salm, by whom she had had a daughter who was known as Thérésia. . . . While an émigrée, Mme de Bouillon had married this daughter to M. de Vitrolles.

My aunt had taken a small apartment for Mme de Bouillon and her son-in-law not far from the house where we were living. Mme de Bouillon's visit to Richmond brought us a number of very enjoyable invitations. The Duchess of Devonshire gave a great lunch party for the émigrés in her delicious country house at Chiswick; her sister, Lady Bessborough, gave a fine dinner at Roehampton, where she was spending the summer in a very lovely house. We were invited on both of these occasions and I went with the greatest pleasure despite the fact that I was more than seven months' pregnant.

People who had not seen Mme de Bouillon for some years hardly recognised her. As I have told you, she had never been pretty, but at the time of which I am writing, when she was fifty-four or fifty-five years old, she stooped and looked literally dried up. Her yellow, dried skin clung to her bones, and through her cheeks you could count her black and broken teeth. Her face was truly frightening to see and her health, which had been very bad for a number of years, showed no sign of improving. But I must quickly add that her wit, her grace and her kindness had lost nothing of their charm. I often used to go to visit her in the morning, and she received me with the kindness she had always shown me.

One day, Mme d'Hénin came in and announced that she and Mme de Bouillon had arranged everything for me: 'M. de Vitrolles is leaving and Mme de Bouillon does not want to stay alone in her lodging. But the lease has still three months to run, so she will exchange apartments with you. You will be much more comfortable there for your lying-in.' My husband signed to me to accept this offer.

II

So I went to stay in Mme de Bouillon's lodgings and there gave birth to a son whom we called Edward, his godparents being Lady Jerningham and her son, Edward.

The good Chevalier Jerningham came to see me and I learned from him that Lady Jerningham considered that when I left my present lodging, it would be impossible for me, with three children, to return to the two small bedrooms of the modest apartment I had formerly occupied in Mme d'Hénin's house. Also, no matter how short of funds we might be, and, in fact, on that very account, she thought we would prefer to be by ourselves and independent. For this reason, she had charged him to find us a small house in Richmond and his search had been successful beyond anything we could have wished. Some rather difficult negotiation was involved, but the Chevalier conducted it with all the zeal that his friendship for me inspired.

The house belonged to a former Drury Lane actress who had been very beautiful and much in fashion. She never lived there, but it was so clean and so beautifully kept that she was not anxious to let it.

However, the Chevalier's eloquence and a gift of £45 from Lady Jerningham persuaded her to do so. This small place was a real gem, with a frontage that could not have been more than fifteen feet wide. Downstairs was a corridor, a pretty drawing-room with two windows and a concealed staircase. On the first floor were two charming bedrooms; above them two servants' rooms. At the end of the corridor on the ground floor, a pleasant kitchen opened on to a minute garden with a path and two flower borders. There were carpets everywhere and good English oil-cloth in the passages and on the stairs. Nowhere would you have found a daintier, cleaner or more elegantly furnished house, so small that it could have been set in its entirety in any room of medium size.

Yet, on the day we moved in, I was profoundly distressed. On that very day, my poor baby son, a strong and beautiful child only three months old, died suddenly from a pleurisy for which I blame the carelessness of the English nurse who looked after him. It was late autumn, which comes early in England. I had been feeding the dear angel myself and the grief I felt at his death curdled my milk. I became very ill and was myself near to death when we arrived at the house with my two remaining children, Humbert who was nine and a half and Charlotte who was just over two. Having only two children left to care for, we dismissed the English servant. While I had been in the United States, Marguerite had learned something of cookery and willingly turned her talents, and above all, her devotion, to feeding us.

England, a country, where there are immense fortunes and people who live in sumptuous elegance, is also the country where the poor can live most comfortably. For instance, there is no need to go to market. The butcher never forgets to call regularly at the same hour every day, coming to the door and shouting 'Butcher' to announce his presence. You open and tell him what you want. A leg of lamb, perhaps? He will bring it to you all prepared and ready to be put on the spit. Cutlets? They are laid neatly on a little wooden tray, which he collects the following day. A small wooden skewer fastens a paper to the meat showing the weight and price of whatever you have bought. There are no useless pieces or so-called 'make-weights'. The same system is followed by all the other tradesmen. There are no arguments or complications.

My son, who spoke English like an Englishman, called at the shops in the morning on his way to school, and on Saturday he paid our accounts for the week. Never a mistake or a muddle.

Humbert went to school every day after our lunch, stayed there to dinner and returned home again at six o'clock. Then came the great pleasure of his day: a visit to an excellent French family, Monsieur and Madame de Thuisy and their four sons, who lived quite near us at Richmond. M. de Thuisy was educating the boys himself. Humbert went alone to their house every day after dinner and stayed from seven to nine o'clock. On the rare occasions when he did not return until after nine, the Chevalier de Thuisy accompanied him home. This excellent man, a Knight of Malta, was Providence itself to all the émigrés living in Richmond. Once a week, and sometimes oftener, he walked to London and it is unbelievable how inconsiderate people were in the number of commissions with which they charged him.

I saw him every day. Once a week, I did the ironing. On those days, he sat by the fire and handed me the irons, first cleaning them on brick and sandpaper, as has to be done when they are heated on coal. Sometimes when we met in the evening at the house of Mme d'Ennery, who always had a lot of company, or at that of Mrs Blount, an English lady, the Chevalier would come up to me in his best social manner and then ask quietly: 'Is it tomorrow that we iron?'

Many ladies among the émigrés of his acquaintance never went out into society: they had to earn a living. The Chevalier knew of my skill with the needle and when they were particularly rushed, often brought me some of their work, especially linen for marking, because it was at that kind of work that I excelled.

III

After a while, we found ourselves very short of money because Mme Dillon was creating difficulties about payments. Our entire wealth consisted of five or six hundred francs, and we said to

one another that when that was spent, we would literally not
know where to turn—not for shelter, since our little house cost
us nothing, but for food. My friend, the Chevalier Jerningham,
had told me that our uncle, Lord Dillon, had most hard-heartedly
refused to help us. And all communication with France was cut.

It was just then that we received a despairing letter from M. de
Chambeau, who was still living in Spain. He had had no news
from France and no one had sent him a penny. His uncle, a
former 'fermier général', whose sole heir he was, had died not
long before leaving a will in his favour, but the Government had
confiscated the legacy, claiming that it was émigré property. On
the day he wrote, he had only one louis left and could no longer
count on the Spaniards of his acquaintance, for he had already
exhausted their charity. When M. de La Tour du Pin received this
letter, he did not hesitate for a moment to share with his friend
the few francs left in the bottom of his purse. He hurried to a
reliable banker and took out a bill of exchange for £10 sterling,
payable on sight in Madrid. It was sent off that very same day.
It represented nearly half our fortune, for we were left with only
£12 in the exchequer and no means of meeting our needs when
that money was spent. Out of consideration for my family and,
above all because of Lady Jerningham, we did not want to claim
the help which the English Government offered to émigrés. So far
as Lord Dillon was concerned, I felt under no obligation at all.
But the other reason for not accepting this help was that respect
for my father's memory made me unwilling to let it be publicly
known that his widow, Mme Dillon, who was also my stepmother,
and who owned a house in London where she gave dinners and
evening parties with theatricals, refused to come to my assistance.

One last £5 note remained to us when my good and very kind
cousin, Edward Jerningham, rode out one morning to see me.
He was a charming young man and had just celebrated his
twenty-first birthday. Everything about him justified his mother's
adoring love. He was intelligent, thoughtful, well read and
combined all the qualities of maturer years with the charm and
gaiety of youth. The kindness of his nature equalled the loftiness
of his sentiments and the distinction of his mind. He showed me
great friendship and I, in return, loved him like a younger

brother. He was about to leave for Cossey and told me that his father had just given him some sum or other from a legacy bequeathed to him in childhood. 'I wager that a good part of it will go to providing winter clothing for the good Fathers of Juilly', I told him. These Fathers were the Oratorians with whom he had spent many years of his childhood. 'Not all,' he replied, blushing to the very roots of his hair and turning the conversation to other things.

When he prepared to leave, I went to the door to see him mount. He remained behind a moment and I saw him slide something into my workbasket. I pretended not to notice, so great was his embarrassment. After he had gone, I found in the basket a sealed letter addressed to me. It contained the words 'Given to my dear cousin by her friend, Ned' and a note for £100.

M. de La Tour du Pin returned a minute later and I told him it was a reward for what he had done for M. de Chambeau. As you may imagine, he went the very next morning to London to thank Edward, but found that he had already left for Cossey.

A few days later, I too went to London with two English ladies of my acquaintance whom I often saw in Richmond. They were sisters; the elder of the two, Miss Lydia White, was a well-known blue-stocking. My adventures in America had led her into a sort of romantic attachment for me. One of these ladies sang well and we made music together. They put their books at my disposal. When I visited them in the morning, they would keep me at their house for the whole day and when evening came, I would not be allowed to leave until I had promised to return during the week. When they decided to spend a week in London, they begged M. de La Tour du Pin to allow me to accompany them.

This little journey with Miss Lydia White and her sister brought me once more into slightly closer touch with society. We went to the Opera, where they were playing *Elfrida*. The singer was Mme Banti, whom I had already heard with Lady Bedingfield. I was also taken to a large gathering in the house of a lady whom I scarcely saw. People overflowed on to the stairs and no one even dreamed of trying to sit down. By chance, I was crowded into a corner of the salon where someone was playing the piano, though no one was paying the slightest attention to the music. The pianist was a man and I listened in some surprise, for I could not recall ever having heard anything so agreeable, in such excellent taste and expressing so much feeling and delicacy. After a quarter of an hour, the pianist realised that no one was listening, so he got up and left. I asked his name . . . it was Cramer! There were so many guests that we had some difficulty in detaching ourselves from the throng, but the doorman's cry: 'Miss White's carriage stops the way' forced us to hasten. It is a summons that has to be obeyed under pain of losing one's turn in the line and being condemned to wait a further hour.

The week seemed long and wearisome and by the end of it I was glad to return to Richmond.

During this time, on the 19th of August, Mme de Duras[1] gave birth to my dear Félicie, a very good friend who will perhaps read these memoirs when I am no longer here. I had come to know Claire quite well during a short visit she made to Richmond and although our characters were never particularly compatible, we grew to like one another very well. In those days, she was madly in love with her husband, whose infidelities, when she knew of them, roused her to storms of fury and despair which were scarcely likely to bring him back to her. Shortly after Félicie's birth, they took a house at Teddington, a village two miles from Richmond. Amédée de Duras was the oldest of my friends. When we were very young, we made music together. We resumed the habit at Teddington, and I often spent the day there. M. de Poix, who was living in Richmond, had a very good horse and a tilbury. I often walked over to Teddington and drove back to Richmond with M. de Poix. It was in this manner, that we passed the summer of 1798.

We made an excursion which lasted a week of which I have the happiest memories. My children were in such safe hands with my good Marguerite that this short absence gave me no anxiety at all. M. de La Tour du Pin rode and I travelled with M. de Poix in his tilbury. We went through Windsor and spent the night at Maidenhead, where we stayed the following day, visiting Park Place, and taking a boat on the river.

[1] Mlle Claire de Kersaint, who had married Amédée de Duras.

'Where beauteous Isis and her husband Tame
With mingled waves, for ever flow the same.' (Prior)

From there, we went to Oxford, to Blenheim, to Stowe and so on, returning by way of Aylesbury and Uxbridge. I was charmed with the beautiful country houses we were fortunate enough to visit. Only in such settings do English gentlemen really become 'grands seigneurs'. We had very fine weather during the whole week we were away on this journey, the expenses of which we shared. I must say that the English climate away from London is much maligned. I found it no worse than that of Holland and incomparably better and less uncertain than that of Belgium. In my long life there have been a few, a very few shining moments —rather like the paintings of Gherardo delle Notti[1]—and this short excursion is one of them.

IV

When we returned to Richmond, I resumed my household occupations. The news from France seemed less black. My husband was even planning to send me over for a few days, armed with an English passport, which would not have been entirely false, as I would have signed it with my own name: Lucy Dillon. But just at that moment, we heard that two émigrés who had returned secretly, M. d'Oilliamson and M. d'Amnécourt, had been caught and shot. They had been given no form of trial and I do not think the incident has been mentioned in any of the numerous memoirs that have been written since then. I had met M. d'Oilliamson at balls in the old days and had even danced with him, so that his death made a much greater impression on me than that of his companion in misfortune, M. d'Amnécourt.

This tragic news reached us on the very day I was intending to leave for France and we decided to renounce all thought of such a journey. Personally, I was delighted, not because I feared the dangers, but because I so greatly minded leaving my husband and children. I firmly resolved never again to try to return without them.

My life in Richmond was very monotonous. After some very

[1] Gérard Honthorst.

forthright correspondence between M. de La Tour du Pin and Mme Dillon's man of business, we had finally managed to extract some money from Mme Dillon, and as a result, I no longer saw her. M. de Fitz-James and M. de La Touche no longer came to Richmond to visit us and when I went to London, which was but once or twice, I saw only Lady Jerningham and Lord Kenmare who, for the past year, had been making me an allowance of six louis a month.

After the birth of her second daughter, Clara, Mme de Duras and her husband went to Hamburg on their way to Mittau. King Louis XVIII was still living in Mittau and officers of the Crown and members of his Household joined him there when it was their tour of duty. The First Gentlemen of the Bedchamber lived with the King when on duty.

It was the turn of M. de Duras, and he wanted his wife to accompany him. The children were left in the care of Mme de Thuisy. But M. de Kersaint,[1] Mme de Duras' father, had been a member of the Convention at the time of the King's trial. Fearing that this offence, for which her father's death might not have been accepted as sufficient atonement, would prevent her being received at Mittau, Mme de Duras gave as the reason for her departure the need to look after certain business affairs on behalf of her mother, who had herself gone to Martinique to sell her house there. However that may be, I have reason to think that when M. de Duras arrived in Hamburg, he found the Duc de Fleury waiting to tell him, on behalf of the King, that his wife would not be received. So there ended Mme de Duras' journey, but I have forgotten whether M. de Duras himself went to Mittau. In any case, they returned to Teddington shortly afterwards.

Their marriage was unhappier than ever. M. de Duras' attitude towards his wife became increasingly difficult, and she wept day and night, unfortunately putting on deplorable airs which bored her husband to death. With a wounding lack of dissimulation for which I often reproached him he let her see it, and said that love could not be commanded and that he hated scenes.

Having lectured the husband, I consoled the wife. I tried to

[1] The Comte de Kersaint, member of the Convention for the Department of Seine et Oise.

instil a little independence into her, to convince her that her
jealousy and her reproaches, by making their home unbearable,
were alienating her husband. The days passed, one way and
another. Their house was never free from guests and there was
never an evening when they were alone. An old officer of the
Bodyguard, M. de La Sipière, almost invariably interrupted any
tête-à-tête. Often Amédée de Duras took advantage of this to go
off to London. And then would follow endless tears and re-
criminations from his wife. Poor Claire wanted romance and her
husband was the least romantic of men. There is no doubt he
would have enjoyed his home if it had been made pleasanter for
him. But Mme de Duras' character barely concealed, under an
outward show of passion, an arrogance and a tyranny which have
since become even more intense. Intelligent as she was, she
brought great unhappiness on her family and on herself.

V

Towards the end of the winter, Miss White left Richmond. This
was a grief to me, not because we had formed a lasting friendship,
but because she had been so kind that I found it very pleasant to
have her near.

For some time, my health had not been as good as it should
have been. I felt extremely listless, but did not know why. It was
out of the question for me to have a carriage, and our house was
on the Green, near the edge of the town. I had therefore stopped
going out after supper and spent my evenings reading the books
which Miss White sent me in large numbers from her well-
stocked library. Subscriptions were costly in England and I
could not myself have afforded such a luxury. So you may
imagine my joy when one day a box arrived addressed to me, and
I was handed the key by the messenger. On opening it, I found
ten volumes from Hookham's Library in London—Hookham's
Circulating Library. There was also a catalogue of the twenty
thousand volumes of every kind, in English and French, which
the library possessed. A receipt in my name for a year's subscrip-
tion was attached to the parcel, together with instructions that,
if the box were fastened and put on the stage-coach by seven
o'clock in the morning, it would be returned by the evening stage

with the new books that had been requested. No attention ever gave me greater pleasure. I decided it must have been the work of Miss White, and when I had no reply to my letter of thanks, concluded that she did not wish it to be known.

My health improved a little during the summer of 1799. Our house on the Green was semi-detached, and the adjoining house belonged to a rich London alderman. In accordance with English custom, there was a small railing about eight or ten feet in front of the ground floor windows to prevent people coming too close. The alderman's house had a pretty lawn surrounded, as was our own, with railings which marked the boundary. My son had arranged this very small space in flower beds, and he called it his garden. He reached it through the drawing-room window, a very low one where I always sat to sew. His sister, Charlotte, was often out there with him. As we lived in a rather out-of-the-way place, there were no passers-by.

One day I heard my son talking to the alderman, who had arrived a short time before to spend the summer in his pretty house. A few minutes later, Humbert came to ask my permission to accept the gentleman's invitation to visit him. I said he might do so and off he went to the house of this neighbour whose name I did not even know. He questioned the child about us, about my solitude, my tastes and so on, accompanying the conversation with generous helpings of cake and fruit. From then on, the kindly alderman—whom I myself never saw—sent us a constant flow of baskets filled with the finest fruit from his hothouses. Sometimes they were addressed to 'The young gentleman' and sometimes to 'The young lady'. Then, in his front garden, as close as possible to the boundary railings, he put a stand of shelves with pots of every variety of the most sweetly smelling flowers. This anonymous and mysterious compliment continued through the whole summer.

CHAPTER TWENTY-FIVE

I

The summer of 1799 was unremarkable. Lady Jerningham went to Cossey and again invited me to join her for the six months she was to spend in the country. Since the rent of our house at Richmond was about to fall due, and since it was she who paid it, it would have been tactless in the extreme to ask her to renew it. So we were preparing to set out to join her at Cossey when news arrived of General Bonaparte's unexpected return from Egypt. He had landed at Fréjus.

We hoped that we might be able before long to return to the Continent, perhaps even to France. While we were at Cossey, we learned the good news of the fall of the Directorate and the revolution of 18 Brumaire (9th and 10th of November 1799). Shortly afterwards, M. de Brouquens and our brother-in-law, the Marquis de Lameth, wrote telling us to return to France with German passports, travelling by way of Holland.

Lady Jerningham suggested that my husband should go alone. It would perhaps have been the wiser plan, for I was more than six months' pregnant and could have remained at Cossey until my baby was born. But nothing would persuade me to be separated indefinitely from my husband. While the war lasted, there was always danger that communications between England and France would be completely cut. As it was, the news we received through Hamburg was already taking a month to reach us. In short, I rejected Lady Jerningham's advice. One of the principal reasons which strengthened my determination to go with my husband was an unfortunate remark made one day by my aunt. She said that when the baby was born, it would be hers and she would keep it. I would never have consented to this. On the other hand, I had little confidence in this return to France. I reasoned this way: 'My husband may be banished yet again. If it should be while he is at Le Bouilh, he will go to Spain. How if it were impossible to travel through France could I ever rejoin him there on my own, with three children? Also, I have a house in Paris and it cannot be sold if I am not there.' In short, I did not want to leave my husband and refused to listen to reason.

A Danish passport for my husband, myself and my children was sent to us from London and we left for Yarmouth to board a packet belonging to the Royal Navy.[1] In those days, there were no steamships. Our wait at Yarmouth dragged on through the whole of December. We did not dare return to Cossey, though it was only eighteen miles away, for the Captain had said that as soon as the wind veered to a favourable direction, in other words, to the south-west, he would set sail within the hour. He was so anxious to leave the very minute it became possible that he was scarcely willing for us to live ashore. Every post brought dispatches from the Government.

Never have days seemed drearier than those that passed during that month at Yarmouth. We were badly housed in two small rooms, where our meals were brought to us, and which we could not leave because of the terrible weather. Contrary winds blew at gale strength and every day we heard of ships that had run aground or foundered. You cannot imagine how such stories depress people who may be called on to set sail at any minute. I was terrified as time slipped by and the date of my baby's birth drew nearer. The fear that it might be born on the journey was always with me, and that is just what did eventually happen. Ten times a day my son, Humbert, would go down to the harbour and look at the weather-vane. But the wind continued to blow from the north-west—quite the wrong direction for us. Eventually, one fine morning, we were summoned on board. Our luggage had been there for some time already, and scarcely had we set foot on the deck when anchor was weighed.

I straight away took refuge in a bed. As the passengers were numerous, it would have been unwise to delay finding and staking a sure claim to some place of shelter. In any case, in my state, the rolling of the boat, which was only a cockleshell, might have been fatal to me. I lay down fully dressed. My bunk was in a dormitory

---

[1] At the period, it was customary to use warships for commercial purposes when they were not otherwise employed. (T)

which served all the passengers. They numbered fourteen and
included people of every nationality and every degree of social
standing: Frenchmen, Russians, Germans, messengers and so on,
some stricken with seasickness and all it entails, others drinking
punch, brandy or wine. Everyone was huddled in that small room,
where the only fresh air was that which managed to penetrate by
the door. The seas were so high that the port-hole had been
battened down. By day or night, our only light came from a foul-
smelling lamp which only added to the horrors of every kind which
surrounded us in that dreadful hole. I do not think I have ever
suffered so greatly as during the forty-eight hours of that crossing.

My husband and the maid were both overcome by seasickness
and lay on their bunks like dead things. My daughter, Alix, lay
beside me, terrified by the sight of the men about us. My son,
by virtue of his ten years, remained up and looked after everything. He had scraped acquaintance with the passengers, spoke
English to the crew and was known to the Captain as 'My brave
little fellow'. Towards the middle of the second night, we had,
during a few hours, the additional cruel anxiety of knowing that
if the river were not free from ice, it might be necessary to set us
ashore on Heligoland, a small island in the estuary of the Elbe,
and besides that the Captain said that if the wind should veer the
slightest degree to the north, the heavy weather would force
him to return to England without trying to land anyone, as the
danger of running aground would be too great. Fortunately,
neither possibility came to pass. We sailed past the island of
Heligoland without stopping, entered the Elbe and anchored off
the small port of Cuxhaven.

The Captain was anxious to be rid of his passengers. Our
baggage was bundled out into a long-boat. My husband and the
maid took my son with them. Out of regard for my state, the
Captain sent me and my daughter off in a private boat and ordered
the two sailors manning it to put me ashore as close as possible to
the town. This order nearly proved fatal to me. As the tide was
low when we came alongside the jetty, I had great difficulty in
climbing up on to it. The two sailors therefore caught hold of my
wrists and, despite the rocking of the boat, did not let me go:
fortunately, for I should certainly have fallen into the sea. They

hauled me up on to the jetty in such a way that for a moment or two I was suspended by the arms. Then they left me there with my small Charlotte. I felt as if I had hurt myself badly, but we had to start off to find my husband whom I could see in the distance on a waggon with the maid and all our belongings. With great difficulty, I reached them. There was a violent pain in my right side and I am convinced now that I had received some internal injury in the region of my liver. The doctors have never been willing to admit this damage, but it is none the less true that since that day, I have never ceased to suffer from it and today, at seventy-three, I still feel it.

We knocked at two or three inns without being able to find a lodging, for there were so many émigrés travelling to and from England. Finally, when the people at one of the inns saw that I was distressed, they took pity on me and brought a straw mattress and blankets and made me up a bed on the floor. Marguerite undressed me and, for the first time in three days, I was able to lie down. A few minutes later, I was seized with a violent fever and delirium which lasted all through the night. M. de La Tour du Pin feared a miscarriage or some serious illness and was so worried that he sent for a doctor. After a long search, one was found, but he could not speak a word of French. With the help of an interpreter, I managed to make him understand that I thought the pain in my side was due to having been suspended by the arms when the sailors were lifting me from the boat to the jetty. He applied a great plaster of barley boiled in red wine to the place which hurt and prescribed a drug so soporific that I slept for twenty-four hours. When I woke up, I was quite well again.

II

While I was resting, my husband bought an old barouche for two hundred francs. It was small, but with room enough for us all. After a second day's rest, we set out in this open carriage: it was January, and we were in northern Germany. Fortunately, the weather was good during the first days of the journey. On the fourth day, rain fell in torrents without stopping. Marguerite and I were more or less protected in the depths of the carriage, but M. de La Tour du Pin and Humbert were soaked to the skin,

despite their umbrella. We stayed two days at Bremen to dry their
suits and overcoats in the warmth of those wonderful great stoves
which one finds in German houses, and also to rest ourselves.
Then, the weather having cleared, we set out again. Much snow
had fallen and on the heaths over which we were travelling it was
difficult to distinguish the road. Although we never went at more
than a foot's pace, we overturned no less than three times that
day. However, none of us was hurt, at least, we were not aware
of anything at the time.

Towards evening, we arrived in a small town called Wildeshausen where we were to spend the night. It was in the Electorate
of Hanover, and had, therefore, a Hanoverian garrison. The
officers were giving a great ball that night for a regiment passing
through the town and every room in the one and only inn was
taken. We took refuge in the hall beside the stove and were feeling
very low at the thought of spending the night on wooden benches
when a dapper little officer, elegantly dressed for the ball, came
up to us and gallantly told me in English that he expected to
dance all night and his room was therefore at my disposal. We
accepted this offer and asked for our supper to be served there.
My husband noticed during the meal that I was not eating anything and asked if I felt ill. I could no longer hide from him that I
felt quite unable to go any further and that the time of the baby's
birth was very near. It is impossible to describe his despair when
he realised this. It was my turn then to comfort him, telling him
that babies could be born anywhere, and that everything would
be all right. However, we could not stay in the Captain's room.

By signs, we managed to convey the difficulty to the host of the
inn and he sent to the other end of the town to fetch an old French
barber who had deserted during the Seven Years' War and lived
in Wildeshausen ever since. The barber came immediately, for he
had been so busy getting people ready for the ball that he had not
yet gone to bed. His first care was to find the local doctor, who
turned out to be an elegant young man in white gloves, straight
from the ball, and still out of breath from a waltz. His knowledge
of French was limited to a few grammar book phrases concerned
with medicine. As I was lying on the bed wrapped in a cloak, he
could not see my figure, and began by asking me what was the

matter: 'Fever?'—'No'—'Then what?' Luckily, Denis, the barber, returned just then and was able to explain. He asked if I could be taken to two rooms on the edge of the town which he knew were to let. The doctor said this would be quite all right, and went back to his ball. Denis hurried off to rouse the owner of the two rooms, and before dawn I was settled in them.

The house, like all those belonging to substantial farmers in that part of Germany, had a large carriage entrance opening into a roomy coach-house running the whole depth of the house. In front, to the left and right of this coach-house, on the ground floor, were two good bedrooms, very clean and passably well furnished. Marguerite and my two children took possession of one of them, the larger one was given to me and my husband was put in a small room adjoining it.

Fortunately, we had with us all the linen and everything necessary for the new baby. As I was not yet in much pain, I had time to attend to all our small arrangements and it was not until the following morning, the 13th of February, 1800, that I gave birth to a small and very frail baby girl,[1] who had completed only a seven and a half months' term. She was so thin and delicate that I hardly dared to hope that she would live. But I had her with me for seventeen years, only to see her die at the very moment when she was able to enjoy to the full all the gifts of beauty, character, intelligence and charm with which she was blessed. God took her from me—may His blessed will be done.

We named her Cécile, a dear name borne later by one who took her place and who will perhaps glance through these pages.[2] May she also read in them my gratitude for all the happiness with which she has comforted my old age.

On the day after my daughter's birth, the local magistrate, who had already sent once for our passports, sent one of his town guards to bring M. de La Tour du Pin before him. In good French, he said to my husband: 'Monsieur, your Danish passport is in a

[1] Cécile-Elisabeth-Charlotte de La Tour du Pin de Gouvernet, betrothed in September 1816 to Charles, Comte de Mercy-Argenteau, died in Nice on March the 20th, 1817, before her marriage.
[2] Cécile de Liedekerke Beaufort, daughter of Charlotte de La Tour du Pin and Auguste de Liedekerke Beaufort. Lived from 1818 to 1893 and married Baron Ferdinand-Joseph-Ghislain de Beeckman.

false name. You are French and an émigré, and in the Electorate of Hanover where you now are, such persons are forbidden to remain longer than forty-eight hours.' M. de La Tour du Pin was horrified to hear this. He said I could not be moved, as I had given birth to a baby only a few hours before. But the magistrate was adamant so far as my husband was concerned, telling him that he must leave Hanover by the end of the day or return to Bremen, whichever he preferred. Then he added: 'Monsieur, since you admit your French nationality, tell me your true name.' My husband did so, and the Magistrate exclaimed: 'Good Heavens. Were you once French Minister at The Hague?' My husband said that he had been. 'Well, Monsieur, since that is so, stay as long as you wish. My nephew, M. Hinuber, a very young man, was Hanoverian Minister at The Hague. He visited you often and you were very kind to him . . .' and that good man went on to produce a long list of the suppers, cups of tea and glasses of punch which his nephew had enjoyed at our house, as well as the quadrilles he had danced in our salons. He put himself at our service with an enthusiasm that never flagged. Truly I would not have been surprised to learn that he had issued a decree that all the inhabitants should place themselves at our disposal! Never has there been a more generous hospitality, or a more thoughtful care than that which surrounded us from then on.

After a fortnight, I was well again and on the twenty-first day after our arrival, we set out, though not before we had taken tea at the houses of the Magistrate, the Burgomaster, the Parish Priest and a number of other local notables. Wildeshausen had a Catholic Church and my very small daughter was baptised there. Her sponsors were Denis, the old barber, and his wife who, during forty years of marriage, had never learned a single word of French. I was also churched there.

III

We took the Lingen road to Holland. A number of young men accompanied us on the first leagues of our journey, staying with us until we reached the inn where we had to stop to give the children their lunch. Before leaving, they insisted that I should drink a cup of some German brew which they had mixed themselves. I expected it to taste horrid, but found it, on the contrary, excellent. It was warm Bordeaux wine, into which had been mixed spices and the yokes of eggs. The doctor was among those who accompanied us and it was by his advice that I took this drink, which made me slightly light-headed.

Our kind escort left us with fervent good wishes for our journey. Their wishes must have been effective, for nothing untoward happened and my small daughter bore the journey amazingly well for a child of less than a month. It is true that she did not leave my arms by day or by night and that I took the greatest care that she should not breathe, not even once, the icy air of those northern plains. If it had not been for the infinite care with which Marguerite and I surrounded her, she would hardly have survived such a long, difficult journey in the month of March.

We eventually arrived at Utrecht, and my husband went immediately to The Hague to get a proper passport from M. de Sémonville, the Ambassador of the Republic of France to the Batavian Republic. M. de Sémonville was a man who trimmed his sails to every wind and he had found means to ingratiate himself with the new government headed by Bonaparte. M. de La Tour du Pin had known him intimately for many years, so that he was received with open arms, and a magnificent passport was drawn up showing that he had not left Utrecht since 18 Fructidor.

During M. de La Tour du Pin's short absence, Mme d'Hénin happened to arrive in Utrecht and my husband was greatly astonished to find her there when he returned from The Hague. So far as I remember, she was on her way to visit M. de La Fayette who had been living at Vianen, near Utrecht, ever since he had been freed after the Treaty of Campo-Formio. I cannot remember if Mme d'Hénin was coming from France or England, she always had two or three different passports and was for ever adopting a different name.

We stayed two days with her and then left for Paris, taking advantage of a carriage that was being sent back, and which we undertook to see safely returned.

On arriving in Paris, we went to the Hôtel Grange-Batelière. My husband was awakened in the middle of the night by a curious incident. An inn servant had heard us using my son's name—Humbert—a number of times during supper. It so happened that the police were searching for a certain Général Humbert who was to be arrested for some reason that I have now forgotten. The servant reported to the police that we had often mentioned 'Humbert', and, when the police arrived, took them to my husband's room. The misunderstanding was soon explained. The police were very annoyed with the servant for misleading them and complained to the master of the house, an ex-tailor named Pujol, who had already made a fortune and whose pretty daughter was later to marry Horace Vernet, the famous painter.

My brother-in-law, the Marquis de Lameth, and our friend Brouquens were already both in Paris. M. de Lameth had found lodgings for us in a charming and well-furnished small house in the Rue de Miromesnil; until then it had been occupied by two of his friends who had recently left to spend the entire summer in the country. We were fated to live in houses belonging to favourites! Our house at Richmond had belonged to an actress, and this one had been furnished for Mlle Michelot, a former mistress of the Duc de Bourbon. The walls were covered with mirrors, so many of them that I was obliged to drape muslin over most of them for I found it exceedingly irritating to see a full-length reflection of myself every time I moved.

In Paris, I found that many of my acquaintance had already returned from abroad. All the young men were beginning to turn to the rising sun—Mme Bonaparte—who was living at the Tuileries in apartments that had been entirely re-decorated, as if by the wave of a wand. She already bore herself like a Queen, but a very gracious, amiable and kindly one. Although not outstandingly intelligent, she well understood her husband's plan: he was counting on her to win the allegiance of the upper ranks of society. Josephine had, in fact, given him to understand that she herself had belonged in those circles; this was not quite true. I do not know if she had been presented at Court or had had the *entrée* at Versailles—though the rank of her first husband, M. de Beauharnais, would certainly have made this possible. However, even if she had been presented, she would have belonged to that class of lady who, after their first presentation, returned to Court only on New Year's Day.

Between 1787 and 1791, I used to see M. de Beauharnais daily in fashionable society. As he had also seen a great deal of M. de La Tour du Pin while my husband was aide-de-camp to M. de Bouillé during the American War, M. de Beauharnais asked him to call so that he might meet his wife. M. de La Tour du Pin did call on them once, but not again. They moved in different circles from ours. M. de Beauharnais, however, was accepted everywhere for during the war he had become acquainted with many of the highest in the land. He was a handsomely-built man and in those days, when dancing was considered an art, he was thought —and with some reason—to be the finest dancer in Paris. I had often danced with him myself, so that when I heard of his death on the scaffold, I was much affected. I could not imagine him elsewhere than in a quadrille . . . a bitter contrast!

IV

I saw M. de Talleyrand again and found him unchanged towards me: amiable, but not really helpful. During the two previous years, he had steered his fortunes with such skill that I found him established in a fine house of his own in the Rue d'Anjou, laughing quietly to himself at the readiness of all those who returned to France to secure a post under Government. He asked me what my husband was doing and if he needed anything. I told him that he did not and that we intended settling at Le Bouilh. 'So much the worse for you,' he replied, 'it's folly.' I told him we were not in a position to remain in Paris, but he merely answered that there was always money to be found when one needed it. Such was his philosophy.

As soon as Madame Bonaparte learned from Mme de Valence and Mme de Montesson that I was back in Paris, she asked me to go and see her. She longed to be able to boast to the First Consul that she had secured the allegiance of a woman who was still young and very fashionable, and a former member of the royal Household. It would have been a victory indeed, if I may be forgiven for saying so. But I determined to increase the value of my condescension by keeping her waiting a little. Then, one morning, I went with Mme de Valence to call on her. In the salon I found a group of women and young men, all of whom I knew. Mme Bonaparte came towards me exclaiming: 'Ah, here she is,' seated me beside her and paid me a thousand pretty compliments, repeating more than once: 'How English she looks,' a remark which was soon to imply the very opposite of praise. She studied me from head to foot and was particularly intrigued by the thick braid of fair hair which circled my head and from which she did not take her eyes. When we rose to leave, she could not help asking Mme de Valence in a whisper if the braid were really of my own hair.

Mme de Bonaparte spoke to me of Mme Dillon, my step-mother, with much kindness, expressed a keen desire to meet my sister, Fanny, who was also her niece, Mme Dillon's mother and Josephine's mother having been sisters. She went on to say that all the émigrés would return, that this delighted her, that there had been enough suffering, that General Bonaparte wanted, above all, to set a term to the ills of the Revolution, and so on. A whole series of reassurances. She also enquired after M. de La Tour du Pin and said she would like to see him. She was leaving for Malmaison and invited me to visit her there. All in all, she was extremely pleasant and I saw clearly that the First Consul had left her to deal with the feminine side of the Court, trusting her to win it to his cause whenever opportunity arose. It was not a difficult task, for everyone was hastening to gather about the rising star and I know of no one besides myself who refused to become a Lady-in-waiting to the Empress Josephine.

In Paris, I met my cousin, General Sheldon, again. He had had many misfortunes since his triumphant return from Grenada with the captured standards. Eventually he accepted the invitation of the famous Colonel St Leger, a close friend of the Prince of Wales, and went to live in England. There he stayed with the Prince, who was very kind to him, and it was he who, as an English Catholic, acted as a witness at the marriage of the Prince of Wales with Mrs FitzHerbert. This marriage has been widely denied. But as Mrs FitzHerbert was a Catholic, and it was a Catholic priest who blessed the marriage, it is very probable that the necessary dispensations had been granted. This explains why even the strictest of the Catholic ladies, including my aunt, Lady Jerningham, continued to visit her, despite the publicity of her marriage with the Prince of Wales.[1]

M. de La Tour du Pin and I had never been put on the list of émigrés, though I cannot understand why. We therefore had to obtain a certificate of residence in France signed by nine witnesses, a necessary formality which deceived no one. For this purpose, I presented myself at the municipal offices of the district with my cloud of witnesses. When the certificate was signed and inscribed with all the necessary lies, the Mayor politely handed me a copy, whispering: 'But that doesn't alter the fact that every stitch of your clothing comes from London!' and roared with laughter. Such a farce!

During that summer of 1800, the best company in Paris was to be found at a house in the Place Vendôme. Looking towards the Rue St Honoré, it is on the right, at the corner of the Place Vendôme and the Rue St Honoré. It was there that the *Commission des Emigrés* held its sessions.[2] This Commission could be conciliated fairly easily if one took care not to arrive empty-handed. The crowd collected there included everyone, from the highest in the land to tradesmen of every kind. Two phrases dominated all conversations, no matter what the topic: 'Have you been struck off?' and 'Are you going to be struck off?' A man who could produce the most respectable and complete series of certificates of residence in France as proof of how unjust it had been to include his name on the fatal list, would be heard talking openly on the very threshold of the building of what he had done and said in Coblentz, or Hamburg, or London.

The French find enjoyment in anything. The *Commission des Emigrés* became a meeting place. People arranged to meet there, went there to find old friends, to talk over their plans, their

[1] The existence of this marriage was for a long time questioned. It took place on the 15th of December 1785 and is now accepted, for King Edward VII of England authorised publication of relevant documents which had until then been kept secret. But the details of the marriage ceremony are not quite as Mme de La Tour du Pin describes them. The marriage was canonically valid, but not legally valid, since it contravened the Royal Marriage Act, the King's permission not having been obtained.

[2] The Board charged with carrying out Napoleon's order of 18 Brumaire (November 1799) that many persons should be deleted from the famous list of émigrés. (T)

choice of a residence and so forth. Many of those who had come back from abroad looked on it as an employment agency. Fathers began to wonder whether their sons might enter the Army. People began to talk of 'the country', that country which had bothered them so little a few years ago. In the entrance to this establishment, the bearers of the greatest names in France could be seen rubbing shoulders with nobles from the provinces. What a pity that there was not some kind of scale at that door, or a weigh-bridge like those used to weigh carriages on the railway! If there had been, many a good and loyal gentleman from the provinces, returned from exile to find nothing but the four bare walls of his home, often without even a roof to shelter him and his family, would have weighed far heavier than some duke with high-sounding titles!

We ourselves had no dealings with the *Commission* as we had not been on the list, but it was necessary to have my mother-in-law's name removed from it. Despite the fact that she had lived for thirty years in the Convent of the Dames Anglaises in the Rue des Fossés-Saint-Victor, without once leaving it, her name had been put on the list. The consequence of this error was the sale of all the furnishings of her château at Tesson and on two of her farms.[1]

V

Before his departure for the famous crossing of the Great St Bernard, Bonaparte had had the idea of creating a regiment of hussars manned by young volunteers. Soon all the youngest scions of great families were enrolled in this corps, among them our eighteen-year-old nephew, Alfred de Lameth. Their uniform was light yellow, so the people of Paris inevitably nicknamed them the 'Canaries'. The excuse to buy fine horses and make a splash would have quickly attracted young men, but when they saw that people were making fun of the corps, they gradually merged themselves into the rest of the Army.

I went one morning to Malmaison. It was after the Battle of Marengo. Mme Bonaparte received me extraordinarily well and

[1] Inclusion in the list of émigrés meant the confiscation of all property and death if captured.

after luncheon, which was set in a charming dining room, she took me to visit her gallery. We were alone and she took advantage of this to give me the most boring accounts of the origins of the masterpieces and also of the collection of very fine small pictures standing on easels: it was the Pope who had insisted that she should accept that fine painting of the Albanian woman; Canova had given her 'La Danseuse' and 'Hebe'; the City of Milan had presented her with this and that. I was careful not to take these tales literally, but as I had a great admiration for the victor of Marengo, I should have preferred Mme Bonaparte to tell me the truth—that they had all been taken at the point of the sword. The good woman was an inveterate liar. Even when the plain truth would have been more interesting, or more striking than an invention, she preferred to invent.

Poor Adrien de Mun, then a brilliant young man, accompanied me on that visit. At Malmaison I found the families of de L'Aigle and La Grange, Juste de Noailles and everyone else, all dreaming of the chamberlains' uniforms I have since seen them wearing.

One thing struck my husband and me very forcibly: the apathy with which the usually enthusiastic people of Paris heard the news of the Battle of Marengo. On the anniversary of the 14th of July, we went with M. de Poix to walk on the Champ de Mars. After the review of the Garde Nationale and the garrison, a small formation of one hundred men marched into the enclosure, all in dirty, torn uniforms, some with an arm in a sling, others with their head bandaged, but carrying the standards and Austrian flags captured at Marengo. I expected wild and very justifiable cheering. But there was not a single shout, and scarcely a sign of rejoicing. We were surprised and indignant, and afterwards, thinking it over at leisure, could find no explanation for this apathy. Those brave soldiers had travelled post, we were told, in order to take part in the public review held that day.

Mme de Staël had left my house. Her husband had died, I think,[1] or gone back to Sweden. She moved first to a small apartment, and then began preparing to go to her father's at Coppet. Bonaparte could not bear her, although she had made every effort to win his liking. I do not think she visited Mme

[1] He did not die until 1802.

Bonaparte either. But one day, I did meet Joseph Bonaparte in her salon. She received people of all shades of opinion. You would find at her house large numbers of former émigrés side by side with former supporters of the Directorate.

CHAPTER TWENTY-SIX

1

Towards September, we decided to leave for Le Bouilh. We had sold our house in Paris,[1] but for very little as it stood in a shabby quarter—the Rue du Bac. I can no longer remember what my husband did with the money from this sale. On his return, he had found his father's affairs and his own in such great disorder and so much ill luck had dogged everything he undertook that, despite his intelligence and ability, everything turned out badly for him. You may be quite sure that everything he did was animated by one sole purpose: to improve his children's fortunes. He is therefore to be remembered with love and respect.

We took with us from Paris a tutor for my son. He was a M. de Calonne, a priest who had emigrated to Italy and made a thorough study of that country's language. As a companion, he was a mixed blessing, but although he was in very difficult circumstances, we had received excellent reports concerning him and his conduct. That decided us to engage him. My husband went off alone by way of Tesson, and I hired a coachman to take us by easy stages in a great carriage which held not only myself, but M. de Calonne, my son Humbert, my two daughters, my maid Marguerite, and a daughter of Humbert's nurse whom we had engaged as a maidservant. Humbert sat beside the coachman. At Tours, we met a woman driving to Bordeaux in a small cart laden with Cholet cloth and handkerchiefs.[2] She was alone, and delighted to travel with us, for the roads were far from safe.

---

[1] It was sold in 1797.
[2] Cholet, a small town near Angers, was famous for its fine cloth and handkerchiefs. The town was almost completely destroyed in the fighting in the Vendée. (T)

Humbert struck up a conversation with her and ended by travelling in her cart all the way to Le Bouilh.

This woman came from the Vendée. She had fought in the war and taken part in all that went on, crossing and re-crossing the Loire time and again. She told Humbert of her exploits and all that she had seen. He listened to her happily for hours at a time and afterwards came and repeated it all to me. And that is how I learned the story of that interesting and very brave war. During our five months in Paris, I had scarcely heard it mentioned, for the Government took the greatest pains to prevent the details becoming known. Later, I knew for certain that Bonaparte himself did not know much about this heroic struggle until he read the memoirs of Mme de La Rochejacquelein in manuscript.[1]

We eventually arrived at Le Bouilh, and I was very happy to be back again. I greatly needed to rest. An excellent woman whom I had left in charge had taken care of everything, despite the nominal sequestration which had been re-imposed on the château. My husband arrived a few days later and we were at last all united in our home.

M. de La Tour du Pin devoted himself to farming and the education of his son. To the latter task, I also contributed my share, making sure that he did not forget his knowledge of English. Humbert was then ten and a half, Charlotte nearly four and Cécile six months old. My good Marguerite devoted herself to the dear children with even greater care and tenderness than I did myself.

I was delighted to meet again our good and amusing neighbour, Mme de Bar. Her daughter, then in her twentieth year, became a great friend of mine. There was also a son, a boy of seventeen, and I exercised a considerable influence on his life, though he may not perhaps have realised it. But the knowledge has made his memory very dear to me and very painful, too.

Mme de Bar was a remarkably intelligent woman, the widow of a very distinguished officer of engineers who had been one of my

---

[1] The Marquise de La Rochejaquelein, neé de Donnissan, widow of the Marquis de Lescure.

father-in-law's closest friends. He died at the beginning of the Revolution and his wife had retired to the country without any means of support except some vineyards. By her efforts, she had made these a profitable concern. Despite her intelligence, her kindliness and her excellent breeding and despite a passionate attachment to her son who, at the time of his father's death, was only ten years old, she had completely neglected the boy's education. M. de La Tour du Pin reproached her bluntly for it, but she replied that he did not want to work, that he hated books and showed no taste for any career. She admitted, however, that he was naturally intelligent. I was not very convinced by her reasoning, which arose from misguided motherly love. She asked me to speak to her son. I willingly agreed and one morning when I was alone in the library arranging books, he came to see me. I asked him to help me, and he did so with an enthusiasm and an intelligence which surprised me. It seemed a propitious moment to shame him a little for his ignorance and afterwards I made him promise to remedy his laziness, and to study and to read. I gave him books to take home, asking him to write short accounts of them for me to correct and I promised to speak of it to no one, not even his mother. He was extremely grateful. A fortnight later, Mme de Bar told me I had accomplished a miracle; her son now spent his days and nights writing. He brought me his first attempts and I corrected them. By the end of two months, his very superior mind had developed to such an extent that I had to admit I was no longer competent to teach him. He decided he would like to enter the Navy, and as I knew M. Bergevin, the Naval Commissioner in Bordeaux, very well, I was able to obtain his admission into the Ecole de la Marine as a cadet. At the moment of departure, the poor child was terribly wrought up. He asked me if he might write to tell me how he got on and I promised to reply regularly. His ardent nature and warm heart had led him into an affection for me of which he himself was unaware. But it betrayed itself in the need to believe that I would be interested in his progress. However, I must not allow myself to be diverted from his sad story, which I will finish here.

Young de Bar went to Bordeaux, where he studied with such

unusual distinction that, at the end of a year, after the examinations of the celebrated Monge,[1] he was sent to Brest with the rank of Junior Midshipman. On his way to join the famous school which he would leave as an officer, he came to call on me. He was in uniform, and it is impossible to convey the depth of happiness, pride and triumph which filled him. When he came into the salon, I did not at first recognise him. He had grown taller and more manly. I talked to him with interest of his successful studies, and he replied with tears in his eyes: 'I owe it all to you.' Poor child! At Brest he was just as successful as in the first examination. He was included among the candidates for promotion to Senior Midshipman and posted to a warship. But there was still much studying to be done, and he did it at night. To spare his mother as much expense as possible, he economised on food. He became ill and his blood, already thinned by work and late hours, grew fevered. Within a few days he was dead and it was I who had the cruel task of telling his mother. Of all his belongings, only a small case of mathematical instruments ever found its way back to her: his father had given it to my father-in-law, and I had given it to the boy.

Except for family sorrows, the death of this charming young man is the saddest of my memories. The feeling I had aroused in him had been the torch which lit his path, but in the end it consumed him. When he died, I felt almost responsible, for if I had not intervened, he would have lived on peacefully—ignorant, it is true, but he would nevertheless have lived. His mother, though she grieved deeply for him, did not reproach me for having developed qualities in him which she herself had left undisturbed. What would have become of him if I had not been there? Would his life have fulfilled the promise it had shown as a result of my influence?

II

Shortly after our return to Le Bouilh, Mme de Maurville, a cousin of my husband, came to live with us. She had been

[1] Gaspard Monge, Comte de Péluse (1746–1818). A very famous French mathematician and the author of a number of works on this subject. A revolutionary and at one time Minister for Marine. (T)

dispossessed of everything she had owned in France and her principal income was a pension of £40 paid to her by the English government. This was a widow's pension, granted to her because her husband, a French Admiral, had ended in the service of England—not a very honourable thing to have done. All that remained to her in France was an income of 500 to 600 francs. We offered her a roof and she accepted it with the simplicity that is characteristic of the true nobility. She was four years older than M. de La Tour du Pin, to whom she was devoted. She had one son, Alexandre, who had been educated at the school founded by the famous Burke for the children of émigrés. When he returned to France, he was eighteen, and having no fortune whatsoever, enlisted as a trooper in the light cavalry.

Mme d'Hénin came to Le Bouilh several times during the eight years we lived there. On her first visit, she brought with her M. de Lally's daughter, who had just left Mme Campan, and asked me to complete her education. Mlle de Lally was nearly fifteen. I welcomed her gladly. She was a gentle, biddable child, fairly proficient in spelling, music and dancing. The education of her mind, however, had been completely neglected. I looked on the task entrusted to me as a very important and rather heavy responsibility. My husband made me promise to undertake it nonetheless, and his wishes were law for me. I would not have even considered questioning them. As we were too poor to undertake extra expense without inconvenience, my aunt wanted M. de Lally to pay for his daughter's keep, sending us the same sum that he had formerly been paying to Mme Campan. To accept such an arrangement seemed to me to lower us a little socially, but we ended by agreeing to it. M. de Lally also remained responsible for his daughter's personal expenses. She had no reason for complaint in these arrangements and I, on my side, can say that we never found reason to regret them. What I did for Mlle de Lally was a preparation for the education I was later to give my own daughters. My husband undertook to teach her history and geography; it was agreed that I would teach her English, of which she already had a slight knowledge, and that my son's tutor would give her lessons in Italian. She was also to benefit from our custom of reading aloud to one another. She was much attached to my children, especially to Cécile, and it was she who gave Cécile her first lessons. She was a good-natured, dependable child and got on very well with Mme de Maurville. They were both about equally lacking in intelligence and I suspect that their feelings towards me were closer to respect and awe than to affection. But despite whatever may have been said about me, I am not a dominating woman. I have never asked of those with whom I have lived more than they were capable of.

My husband and I were much preoccupied with our children's future: this was the foremost of all the anxieties caused us by the low state of our fortunes. The Le Bouilh estate, so far as the value of the land was concerned, was worth very little. The war with England had brought the price of wines down to rock bottom, especially white wines which had never been very profitable in that area. They could be bought for four to five francs a cask. My husband installed a brandy distillery and spent considerable sums of money to ensure that it worked properly, but the profit from this innovation was only just enough to cover our current living expenses, and it would soon be necessary to think about my son's future. This problem occupied our minds to such a degree that other anxieties paled before it.

My aunt and M. de Lally wrote us from Paris that all the people we had formerly known were rallying to the Government. The Concordat had just been signed and the re-establishment of religion had had a tremendous effect in our provinces.[1] Until then, Mass had had to be celebrated in private rooms, not perhaps in total secrecy, but certainly quietly enough not to compromise the priest, who was nearly always a returned émigré.[1] Therefore, when M. d'Aviau de Sanzai, a regularly-consecrated Archbishop, was known to have arrived in Bordeaux, and when the irregularly appointed usurper disappeared—I have never known where— there was a joy that bordered on ecstasy. We had the honour of

---

[1] The treaty of peace of 1802 between France and the Papacy. The people of France had never accepted the revolutionary attempt of 1791 to separate the Catholic Church in France from Rome and attach it to the State, still less the later extravagances of deism, rationalism, etc. Under this Concordat, the Church in France entered again into communion with Rome, was accepted as the established religion of France. Napoleon, like the Kings of France before him, reserved the right to nominate the highest Church dignitaries. (T)

having M. de Sanzai at Le Bouilh for the first two days after his return to the diocese and we invited all the good parish priests of the nineteen parishes on what had once been on our property to welcome him. Most of them were back from abroad and had only recently been appointed. Some had lived nearby, either hidden by their parishioners, or in private houses. Our saintly Archbishop was soon revered by everyone and his entry into Bordeaux was a triumphal progress.

The gratitude of the people went out to the great man who held the reins of government and when he declared himself Consul for life, this gratitude found expression in the almost unanimous approval of those who had to vote on the matter.

Not long afterwards, lists were posted up in the communes and people were summoned to enter their name and reply 'yes' or 'no' to the question whether the Consul for life should proclaim himself Emperor.

M. de La Tour du Pin was extraordinarily exercised over the problem before finally deciding to put 'yes' on the Saint-André-de-Cubzac list. I used to see him pacing alone up and down the paths of the garden, but would not permit myself to intrude upon his uncertainties. Eventually, I learned with pleasure when he returned to the house one evening, that the result of his deliberations had been 'yes'.

You will have noticed that I am inclined to confuse the order of events. I have certainly not kept in their proper sequence the happenings which filled the eight years we spent at Le Bouilh. There were six particularly happy months when Mme de Duras and her children stayed with us.

My aunt was away at the time, which caused us no grief at all. Despite her intelligence, her kindness and her devotion to her nephew—me, she had never loved, except as a reflection of him— life with her was very fatiguing. Her excitable nature banished all ease from daily life. We did not dare to disagree with her on any subject. But though we submitted to all her wishes and caprices, even that did not always ensure peace.

III

Mme de Duras arrived at Le Bouilh to await her husband. He was to meet her there and travel with her to Duras, his family seat, which lay between Bordeaux and Agen. They had just bought Ussé[1] and Mme de Kersaint, mother of Mme de Duras, had put into this purchase all the money she had received from the sale of her house in Martinique. The Duchesse de Duras, Amédée's mother, had added 400,000 francs from her personal fortune. This fine house cost them altogether 800,000 francs and was an excellent bargain.

I had last seen Claire Duras at Teddington, at a time when she was enduring all the wretchedness of knowing that her love for her husband was not returned. I found her quite changed. She had become one of the leaders of the anti-Bonapartist circles of the Faubourg Saint-Honoré. Realising that she could never hope to be outstanding in looks, she had been sensible enough to renounce all pretentions in that field and to aim instead at dazzling by her wit. It was not difficult, for wit was a quality she possessed in abundance and besides earlier it was combined with ability, an indispensable attribute in anyone who aspired to the first place in the circles in which she moved. In Paris it is essential to be definite in one's views, otherwise one is eclipsed: to use a naval term, one must mount a heavier broadside than one's neighbour.

In 1805, I went with Elisa—Mlle de Lally—to spend some time in Bordeaux. At Mass one day, Elisa attracted the notice of M. Henri d'Aux who, by birth, appearance and fortune, was the most distinguished young man in the town. Elisa was very small, with masses of fine black hair, a dazzling complexion, the bloom of a rose and the loveliest eyes in the world. Our friend Brouquens had returned to Bordeaux indefinitely, his fortune disastrously reduced by the collapse of the army's food supply company. He learned from friends that M. Henri d'Aux had spoken in glowing terms of the young person staying with Mme de La Tour du Pin. None of the young ladies of Bordeaux, he had declared, could equal her in propriety and modesty of bearing. He had made enquiries about us, our way of life, our habits and so on.

My husband had been appointed President of the Canton,[2] an

[1] One of the finest châteaux in the valley of the Loire. (T)
[2] An area, usually comprising several communes, which forms the administrative region of a Justice of the Peace. (T)

office he had done nothing to seek, and had gone to Paris for the Coronation. I wrote to tell him what I had heard and he talked it over with M. de Lally. The latter was at the time busy trying to get payment from the State of a fairly large sum which he had been promised would be reimbursed. It had been owing to him ever since his father's honour had been posthumously restored and his death sentence annulled—that is to say, since three months before the Revolution began.

The Council of State (Conseil d'Etat)[1] had recognised the validity of the debt, but since, like all State funds, it had been reduced to one-third of its original value, it amounted by then to only one hundred thousand francs. Napoleon was trying to persuade M. de Lally to join his Government and therefore wanted the claim met in full. When my husband told M. de Lally what I had written, he declared at once that if he obtained payment of the debt, he would give the money to his daughter on the day she married. He kept his word. We arranged to spend the days of the Carnival in Bordeaux so that M. d'Aux might have occasion to meet Elisa at the balls given in the salons of the former Intendance.

About this time, I suffered a very cruel loss: my dear maid Marguerite died. I had loved her as a daughter and my grief was deep. She remained conscious until the end, and bade me the tenderest of farewells. Humbert and Charlotte also felt deeply sad, and their sensibility touched me. They had always had every possible care from that excellent woman.

IV

In Paris, my husband saw many of his former acquaintances, all of them attached to the Government. Among them was M. Maret, who was later created Duc de Bassano.[2] They urged my husband

---

[1] One of the four legislative bodies. Its members were appointed by Napoleon himself and were responsible for drafting bills and legislation. (T)

[2] Hughes-Bernard Maret, 1763-1839. He started as a lawyer in the Parlement of Burgundy, came to Paris early in the Revolution, and published summaries of Constituent Assembly debates. Bonaparte appointed him his Secretary-General and in 1809 created him Duc de Bassano. In 1811 he became Foreign Minister and after a period of exile between 1814 and 1820, he returned to public service under the Orléanists. (T)

to take steps to obtain an appointment. He did not exactly refuse, but said that if the Emperor desired his services, he knew where to find him, that the rôle of petitioner was distasteful to him, and so on. M. de Talleyrand could not understand any form of reluctance, but he did nevertheless perceive, with his mind rather than his heart, that there was a certain distinction in standing a little apart from the mob of petitioners. He contented himself with saying, with a shrug of the shoulders, 'You will come to it' and then thought no more about it.

M. de La Tour du Pin returned to Le Bouilh. He had seen M. Malouet, who had just been appointed Préfet Maritime[1] at Antwerp, charged with establishing there the great shipbuilding yard to which he was to give such tremendous impetus. They arranged between them that when Humbert was seventeen, he should enter the offices of M. Malouet. There were no Auditeurs[2] at the Conseil d'Etat in those days, but there was talk of recruiting them and we thought it would be useful for a young man destined for the public service to work for a while under the aegis of a man as enlightened and as able as M. Malouet. Since he was a good friend, we could entrust our son to him without anxiety. But the thought of the separation weighed heavily on my heart.

My husband returned from Paris and shortly afterwards I realised that I was to have another child. It was to be you, my dear son. I had had a miscarriage the previous year and to avoid any fresh accident, resolved not to take any violent exercise during my pregnancy. But I was unwell nearly all the time. Mme de Maurville, Elisa, my aunt and M. de Lally all went to Tesson and I remained at Le Bouilh with my daughters.

On the morning of the 18th of October, 1806, as I was dressing, I saw my good Doctor Dupouy, who had been staying at Le Bouilh for several days, passing along the terrace. I asked him laughingly where he was coming from at that early hour. He replied that he had been called out to sign a death certificate for one of our neighbours who had died suddenly as she got out of

[1] An admiral in charge of the administration of a coastal area. (T)
[2] Very highly qualified professional civil servants—Auditors—just starting their career. The first rank in the hierarchy of the Conseil d'Etat and the Cour des Comptes (Audit Office). (T)

bed. I knew the person well and had had a long talk with her the evening before. I was so upset that I was seized there and then with the pains which brought you into the world to be the happiness of my later years.

I recovered but slowly from the after-effects of your birth, for I developed a double tertian fever. It did not, however, prevent me from continuing to feed you myself.

We did not lose sight of the important matter of Elisa's marriage. On the excuse of having the baby vaccinated, we went to Bordeaux for six weeks during the Christmas season, staying with our good friend, Brouquens. This incomparable man had managed to enlist the support of M. Marbotin de Couteneuil, a former Councillor to the Parlement and an uncle of M. d'Aux. M. de Couteneuil wanted to return to the magistracy and the fact that M. de Lally was thought to have some influence was an additional help in securing his support for his nephew's marriage. In any case, and I say it without conceit, we were of sufficient standing in Bordeaux to ensure esteem for anyone who had been allowed to share our family life for five years.

The young people met at a number of balls. In those days, people did not waltz and dancing was an art: Elisa danced enchantingly and was at her best on these occasions. They met again when out walking and at Church, where one was certain to see M. d'Aux. Eventually, Mme de Couteneuil called on me one day formally to request the hand of my protégée for her nephew. I replied like a good and experienced diplomat that I did not know what plans M. de Lally had for his daughter, but that M. de La Tour du Pin would go to Le Bouilh, where M. de Lally was staying, to tell him of the proposal she had just made me.

He did indeed go and returned the next day with M. de Lally himself. Everything was soon arranged and then came the congratulations, the dinners and the parties. We received a visit from the father of M. d'Aux, a gentleman of the old school, without a vestige of intelligence or learning. It used to be said of him that he had, quite literally, bored his wife to death. Nonetheless, he enjoyed an income of sixty-thousand francs or more a year.

When the marriage contract was signed, M. de Lally kept his word and counted out to M. d'Aux the dowry he had promised his daughter—one hundred bags, each containing a thousand francs. It is the only time in my life that I have seen so much money at one time.

The wedding took place at Le Bouilh on the 1st of April 1807. The only flowers in season were small red and white double daisies, so Mme de Maurville, Charlotte and I had to use them for the centre-piece at dinner. We contrived a charming effect: the flowers formed the names of Henri and Elisa against a background of moss.

All these preliminaries and the marriage itself had put me to a great deal of trouble, and had disturbed the tranquility and order of my days. I was very happy to return to my usual ways and to be able to enjoy my son's last months with us.

CHAPTER TWENTY-SEVEN

I

Towards the end of the summer or, as a countryman would put it, immediately after the vintage, I had to part for the first time from my dear son, Humbert. I felt the separation most cruelly and needed all my commonsense and submission to the will of God to enable me to bear it. His father went with him as far as Paris. It was heartbreaking to embrace him when he left, not knowing how long it would be before we saw him again. His eldest sister also felt the separation very deeply. Charlotte was then eleven, and so forward for her years and so sensible that her brother no longer thought of her as a child: to her, it meant the loss of a companion in her studies and her games, a real comrade. The gaiety of our home went with him and when M. de La Tour du Pin returned a month later, all our grief revived.

Le Bouilh was much plagued with demands for military billets. All the troops sent to Spain had to pass through Saint-André-de-Cubzac and we often had to give lodging to the officers. This was exceedingly tiresome, especially when I was alone, for they had to be received at dinner and in the drawing-room. During one of my husband's absences, this gave rise to a small incident which I was able to turn to account. It gave me an excuse to ask that in future I should be asked to lodge twice as many soldiers or troopers, but no officers.

Two officers had been sent to Le Bouilh, one of them fairly elderly. When he saw our fine house and the pretty room set aside for him, he launched into a demagogic tirade worthy of the Convention at its worst. He was so carried away that when he met me in a corridor, he let fly torrents of abuse, saying that he knew they had cut off the head of the previous owner of the house, but that he wished they would do the same to all nobles who owned such fine houses and that it would give him the greatest pleasure to see the house set on fire. He looked as if he might be accustomed to carrying out his threats, so I said calmly: 'Sir, I warn you that I shall lodge a complaint.'

I immediately wrote a very civil letter to the Colonel, who was staying in Saint-André, telling him of the threats made by this Captain, whose name I had enquired. Half an hour later, the Colonel ordered the firebrand to return and place himself under arrest.

After this incident, no more officers were sent to us. It is true that we still had to receive a number of uncouth characters, but their noisy gatherings were confined to the butler's pantry. One evening, when a dozen of these roughs were billeted in the stables, we suddenly heard a terrible noise in the hall. We were at dinner and it so happened that the Colonel, Philippe de Ségur, was dining with us. We went to see what was happening, but when the trouble-makers saw their Colonel in our midst, they were petrified. Never had I seen such consternation as on their faces. They disappeared into the hayloft and by the time a search was made for them after dinner, they had become invisible.

On one of the great feasts, I was at Mass in Bordeaux when I suddenly noticed that the attention of the whole congregation was fixed on something at the back of the chapel where I was. Rising to leave, I saw a magnificent officer, wrapped elegantly in a great white cloak which, being thrown back to leave his sabre arm free, allowed glimpses of deep purple baggy trousers. He left the Church with everyone else and went off along the road leading to M. de Brouquens' house. He went in, and when I followed him into the courtyard, turned around. Seeing me, he cried: 'Ah, so it is my aunt!' and embraced me warmly.

It was indeed my nephew, Alfred de Lameth. How fine he was! An Apollo of Belvedere in the uniform of an aide-de-camp to Murat! The poor boy then took his last leave of me. He had a foreboding that all would not go well with him, and after talking to me for two hours about his youthful follies, of which he was beginning to weary, and of the war in which he had not yet, he said, received a single scratch, he said he would like to leave me something by which to remember him. So saying, he opened his escritoire and gave me this knife with a mother-of-pearl handle which you have always seen on my table. Then he embraced me affectionately many times and, as my eyes filled with tears, said 'Yes, dear Aunt, it is for the last time.' The poor boy was wickedly murdered while crossing a small Spanish village on his way to lunch with Maréchal Soult, right in the midst of the Marshal's headquarters. The murderer was never discovered but, in reprisal, the village was left to the fury of the soldiers, who left it a bloody and burning hecatomb.

II

There was much concern in Bordeaux over the events in Spain. A few Spanish refugees had already arrived in the town. My aunt wrote from Paris that the Emperor was to go to Spain, accompanied, perhaps, by the Empress Josephine, and that M. Maret[1] would be in their suite. She advised her nephew to pay his homage to the Emperor and to call on M. Maret who took an interest in him. M. de La Tour du Pin received this letter just as he was setting out to ride to Tesson, where a matter concerning some bill of exchange urgently required his presence. He was to be away only two days so was sure he would be back before the Emperor arrived. But the very next day, orders reached the posting house for horses to be ready for the Emperor. I was very much upset that my husband should be away, but quite determined not to let it prevent me seeing this remarkable man.

So Mme de Maurville, my daughter Charlotte and I went to

[1] Secretary General to Napoleon (see footnote p. 355). (T)

Cubzac, determined to remain there until we had seen Napoleon. We knew the Chief Transport Commissioner and asked him to take us in. We settled ourselves in a room overlooking the port. The brigantine which was to carry them across the Dordogne lay ready, with the crew at their posts. The entire population of the region stood along the route. The peasants might curse the man who had taken their children and sent them off to the war, but they were nonetheless eager to see him. A madness, a kind of delirium descended on everyone. The first courier arrived and people tried to question him. General Drouot d'Erlon, the Commander of the Department, asked him when the Emperor would arrive. The man was too weary to reply, and could only repeat over and over again: 'Let us cross.' He led his horse, still saddled, into the boat and then fell on the deck like one dead. When they reached the opposite bank, he was dragged ashore and set back on his horse.

After seeing the courier, our impatience reached fever point. As for me, I could think of nothing but the ill chance which had taken my husband so far from the place where he should have been carrying out his official duties. The municipal authorities of Cubzac were all there and he, the President of the Canton, whose place was among them, was absent. An opportunity had been lost which would not occur again. I was exceedingly annoyed. We waited all day and towards evening the first carriage appeared. It was soon followed by a berline drawn by eight horses and escorted by a detachment of Chasseurs.[1] It drew up under the window where we were and the Emperor got out. He was wearing the uniform of a Chasseur of the Guard and was accompanied by two chamberlains, one of them being M. de Barral, and an aide-de-camp. The Mayor read an address of welcome, to which the Emperor listened with an air of great boredom and as soon as it was over, he went on board the brigantine, which cast off immediately.

And that was all we saw of the great man. We returned to Le Bouilh, all three of us tired and very out of temper.

My husband returned the next day. I allowed him only enough time to eat lunch and then sent him off to Bordeaux, where the

[1] Lightly-armed troops, both infantry and cavalry. (T)

Empress was expected the following day. As soon as he arrived in town, he called on M. Maret, who professed much friendship and good will for him. My husband found him amiable and obliging, but was exceedingly astonished when M. Maret said to him: 'You must indeed have been very upset at having to go to Tesson just when the Emperor was to pass through, and have certainly hurried back.'

'Have you seen Brouquens, then?' asked M. de La Tour du Pin.

'No.'

'Then, how do you know?'

'The Emperor told me.'

You can imagine my husband's amazement. 'Mme de La Tour du Pin is to come to Bordeaux,' added M. Maret 'and she will remain here while the Empress is in residence. There will be a Drawing Room tomorrow and the Emperor wishes her to attend.'

My husband immediately sent a carriage for me, hesitation being unthinkable. I had a few gowns in Bordeaux, made when I was accompanying Elisa to the balls and parties given in honour of her marriage. But not one of them was black, and the Court was in mourning. The Drawing Room was at eight o'clock and it was already five. Fortunately, I found a pretty gown of grey satin. I added a few black ornaments and a good coiffeur arranged black ribbons in my hair, a fashion which seemed to me admirably becoming to a woman of thirty-eight who, I say it without vanity, looked less than thirty. We collected in the great dining room of the Palace. I knew hardly anyone in Bordeaux except Mme de Couteneuil and Mme de Saluces, the very two people who were not there. Between sixty and eighty ladies were present, placed according to a list read aloud by a chamberlain, M. de Béarn. He told us that on no account must any of us move, otherwise he would never be able to match people to their names. He also told us to straighten our lines, and hardly had we completed this almost military maneouvre when a loud voice announced the Emperor. My heart beat fast with excitement. He began at the end of the line and spoke to every lady. As he drew nearer to where I was standing, the Chamberlain said something in his ear. He looked at me and smiled most graciously, and when my turn came, said laughingly to me, in a friendly fashion, but looking me up and down: 'I see you are not at all affected by the death of the King of Denmark.' To which I replied: 'Not sufficiently, Sire, to renounce the happiness of being presented to Your Majesty. I had no black gown.' 'Ah, that is an excellent reason,' he replied, 'and then, you were in the country!' He spoke next to the lady beside me: 'Your name, Madame?' She stammered something, and as he did not catch what she said, I told him that her name was Montesquieu. 'Indeed,' he remarked, 'that is a fine name to bear. I went to La Brède this morning to see Montesquieu's study'.[1] The poor woman, thinking to please him, went on 'He was a good citizen.' At the word 'citizen', the Emperor winced. He threw Mme de Montesquieu a glance from his eagle eye that would have terrified her had she realised its meaning, and said brusquely: 'No, he was a great man.' Then, shrugging his shoulders, he looked at me as if to say 'What a stupid woman!'

The Empress followed a little behind the Emperor, and all the ladies were named to her in the same order. But before she reached me, a footman came to ask me to go to the salon to await her Majesty there. The poor Chamberlain, finding Mme de La Tour du Pin no longer in her appointed place, got into a muddle which became the source of many jokes for the remainder of the evening.

When the Empress came into the salon, she was extremely amiable, both to me and to my husband, whom she had also had summoned. She expressed a wish to see me every evening during her stay in Bordeaux and began a game of backgammon with M. de La Tour du Pin. Tea and ices were served. I still hoped to see the Emperor again and was cruelly disappointed to hear that a courier had arrived from Bayonne and that he had left immediately for that city.

The Empress was accompanied by two Ladies-in-Waiting, Mme Maret and another whose name I cannot remember, by her charming reader who has since become the lovely Mme Sourdeau with whom the Emperor Alexander (of Russia) fell in love, and also by old General Ordener, M. de Béarn and others.

Although the Emperor had, to use a common expression, all

[1] The Château de La Brède, near Bordeaux, belonged to the Montesquieu family and it was there, in retirement, that the great Montesquieu did most of his writing. (T)

Spain and Europe on his hands, he found time to dictate orders of the day for the Empress in most meticulous detail, even indicating the gowns she was to wear. Unless she were ill in bed, she would not have dreamed of changing the smallest detail, nor would it have been possible to do so. I learned from Mme Maret that the Emperor had commanded that my husband and I should spend every evening with her, and this we did.

But the poor Empress was beginning to be cruelly anxious about the rumours of divorce which were already being discussed. She spoke of it to M. de La Tour du Pin, who reassured her as best he could. But, having done that, he tried to silence the confidences which the imprudent, irresponsible Josephine seemed disposed to make to him, thinking it would be wiser not to hear them. She was very bitter against M. de Talleyrand, whom she accused of urging the Emperor towards divorce. No one was more convinced than my husband that her accusations were well founded, for M. de Talleyrand had often spoken to him about it during his last journey to Paris, but this he was very careful not to mention to Josephine. Accustomed as she was to the adulation of some and the treachery of others, she found it very comforting to talk to M. de La Tour du Pin and to open her heart to him on a subject she did not dare to discuss with any member of her entourage. She longed desperately to leave for Bayonne, and every day asked Ordener when they were to set out. Each time he replied in his heavy German accent: 'Truly, I do not know yet.'

One evening, when I was sitting beside the Empress near the tea table, she received a note from the Emperor. It was only a few lines, and leaning towards me, she said in a low voice: 'His writing is impossible. I can't read this last sentence.' And she held out the note to me, putting a furtive finger to her lips to enjoin secrecy. I had only time to see that he used the familiar 'thou' and to read the last sentence, which ran thus: 'I have here the father and the son;[1] it is causing me much embarrassment.' Since that day, this note has been quoted in a document, but much lengthened. The original was only five or six lines long and was

[1] Charles IV, King of Spain (1788–1808) and his son Ferdinand. After a series of humiliating treaties imposed by France, and to appease Spanish rioters, Charles IV abdicated in 1807 in favour of Ferdinand. (T)

written across a sheet of paper torn and folded into two. I would recognise it if I saw it again.

After tea, General Ordener came up to the Empress and said: 'Your Majesty leaves tomorrow at midday.' The oracle had spoken at last and everyone was delighted. The visit to Bordeaux had involved me in considerable expense, because for ten days I had had to attend in full Court dress every evening. I longed to see my children again. Elisa was feeding her son herself and therefore, to her very great regret, had not been in attendance on the Empress. She had come only to a Drawing Room, where she had been made most flatteringly welcome. Her husband had worn the uniform of the mounted Garde d'Honneur to which all the young men of good family in Bordeaux belonged.

III

We returned to Le Bouilh and despite the warmth with which we had been received by the exalted personages in Bordeaux, we had little or no hope of future preferment. Indeed, how could one expect the eagle eye of the man who controlled the destinies of France to single out someone so entirely aloof from all intrigue, a man, so to speak, unknown to those in power, who had had no connection with the events of the last few years and who, due to an almost complete lack of fortune, had been living in retirement in his country house.

M. de La Tour du Pin remained in Bordeaux to complete some business matters and I was sitting beside the lamp one evening at about nine o'clock with Mme Joseph de La Tour du Pin, a poor cousin who lived with us, when a peasant arrived in haste from Bordeaux with a note from my husband. It said only: 'I am Prefect of Brussels . . . of Brussels, which is only ten leagues from Antwerp!' I admit that my heart filled with a tremendous joy, most of all at the thought of seeing my son again.

M. Maret had not known that this Prefecture was vacant. Working papers arrived in Bayonne from the Minister of the Interior just as they would have arrived at the Tuileries, or Saint-Cloud, for nothing was allowed to change the Emperor's routine. He might be overturning the Spanish monarchy, banishing two Spanish Kings—father and son—to prison and exile, and all this might be causing him 'much embarrassment'—as I have seen it described in his own hand—but despite it all, when working papers arrived from a Minister, he read them, corrected them and changed the appointments. 'Préfecture de la Dyle':[1] beside it a suggested name for the post. The Emperor took his pen, crossed that name out and wrote instead 'de La Tour du Pin'. We learned this later from M. Maret, a man who never raised objections, but who, by the same token, never made suggestions. He was a very honest machine.

My son was in Antwerp, in the office he occupied as secretary to M. Malouet, when he saw the latter running across the court-yard. Now, M. Malouet was the most dignified of men and never had he been known to hasten his step for anything whatsoever. He hurried in, calling as he came 'Your father is Prefect of Brussels'. Dear Humbert, how happy he was.

I have omitted one incident about which I will tell you now. I find it somewhat remarkable, my dear son, that although six months beyond my seventy-fourth year, I still remember so clearly all that has befallen us. However, this particular incident did slip my mind until now.

A few days before M. de La Tour du Pin left Le Bouilh for Brussels, I received an express courier from our friend Brouquens. He told me that a carriage had been sent to Cubzac because King Charles IV of Spain and his worthless Queen were arriving at the Palace of Bordeaux, and the Emperor had commanded that I should serve as Lady-in-Waiting to the Queen during her stay there, a matter of some three or four days. Fortunately, all that I needed for ceremonial occasions was still at Brouquens' house. The other things I needed were soon packed and my husband and I set out together. As soon as we reached Bordeaux, I dressed quickly and went to the Palace, where their Majesties of Spain had just arrived. In the Household salon I found people I knew and their greeting—'Come along, dinner is ready and we were waiting for you'—was welcome indeed, for I had taken only a cup of tea before leaving Le Bouilh.

[1] The Department of the Dyle was an administrative area comprising Brussels, Louvain and Nivelle, and named after the River Dyle. The Department existed only from 1794 to 1814. The Prefecture was in Brussels. (T)

The King and Queen had gone to their private apartments, with the Prince de La Paix.[1] In the Household salon, I found M. d'Audenarde and M. Dumanoir, the first an equerry and the second a chamberlain to the Emperor; also Général Reille, M. Iyequerdo, a chaplain and two or three other Spaniards whose names I did not know and who spoke no French. We sat down to dinner. These gentlemen told me that two other Ladies-in-Waiting had been appointed—Mme d'Aux (Elisa) and Mme de Piis—and I was charged with telling them that they were to be at the Palace at noon the following day. I was also told that Their Majesties would receive official visitors in the morning and the ladies in the evening. M. Dumanoir added that I myself was to be at the Palace at eleven o'clock in order to be presented to the Queen, and that I, in my turn, would have to present the two other Ladies-in-Waiting appointed to serve her.

During the meal, these gentlemen were most attentive to their new companion. They said over and over again that they would take me with them, even to Fontainebleau. I was very much afraid they meant it and when I protested, they invariably replied: 'But when the Emperor wishes something, it has to be done.' After dinner, we tried to think of some form of entertainment for the King during the two evenings he was to spend in Bordeaux. The problem was complicated by the fact that he either could not or would not go to the theatre, fearing the reception which might await him. I remembered hearing it said in Spain that he was passionately fond of music and that every evening he formed a quartet in which he played, or thought he played, the alto violin. We therefore decided to organise a small concert and the Prefect, M. Fauchet, was put in charge of the arrangements. It should be mentioned in passing that the Prefect was very annoyed because his wife had not been appointed to the Queen's service. There was nothing I could do about it. My own appointment had, in fact, caused me great inconvenience.

After returning home, I remembered that it was also said in Madrid that when the King played, there was always a musician beside him who was familiar with the King's part, It was, in fact,

---

[1] Charles IV was completely dominated by his wife, Marie-Louise of Parma, and by her favourite, Godoy, whom he created Prince de La Paix. (T)

the musician who played, but so discreetly that the King thought he was doing it all himself. I determined to employ the same ruse, but without telling anyone, out of respect for such a sorely tried royal majesty.

I was at the Palace at eleven o'clock the next morning and M. Dumanoir begged admittance to the Queen's apartments in order to present me. Before opening the door, he turned to me saying: 'You mustn't laugh.' Naturally, I immediately wanted to, and with some excuse for I beheld the most amazing and unexpected sight.

The Queen of Spain stood in the middle of the room before a great cheval mirror. She was being laced. Her only garment was a little cambric skirt, very narrow and very short, and across her bosom—the driest, leanest and darkest bosom you can imagine—lay a muslin handkerchief. Her grey hair was dressed with a garland of red and yellow roses. She came towards me, the maid still lacing her, making those movements which a woman uses to try and draw herself out of her corset. Beside her was the King, accompanied by several gentlemen whom I did not know. The Queen asked M. Dumanoir who I was, and on being told, enquired my name. He told her that too, and the Queen said something to the King in Spanish to which he replied that I, or rather, my name was very noble. Then she finished her toilette, telling while she did so how the Empress had given her several of her own gowns as she had brought nothing from Madrid. I found such humiliation very distressing. I did indeed remember having seen the Empress in the gown of yellow crepe lined with satin of the same colour which was at that moment being passed to the Queen. At the sight, I suddenly lost every desire to laugh and felt far more inclined to weep.

When the Queen was dressed, she dismissed me. I went to the salon, where I found Elisa and Mme de Piis and we waited together for the arrival of the official visitors whom I was to present to Her Majesty. It was during that time that a large man with a black plaster on his forehead crossed the room. I recognised him as the famous Prince de La Paix. He walked rudely in front of us and we all agreed that neither his face nor his figure justified the favours credited to him by the gossip of the day.

By then, the salons were full and the Queen was informed. I presented to her, one by one, the heads of the various municipal bodies and of the administration, beginning with the Archbishop, the only person to whom she spoke. M. Dumanoir performed the same office for the King, who was far more gracious. When the presentations had been completed, we went back to the small salon where the Queen spoke to me in carrying tones of her anxiety at being without news of the arrival of La Tudo, the mistress of the Prince de La Paix. She went on to say, equally loudly, that she knew her two sons[1] were prisoners, that she was very glad of it, that their sufferings would never match their true deserts, that they were both monsters and the cause of all her misfortunes. The King, poor man, made no attempt to silence her. It made me shudder. Finally, she dismissed us with the words 'A ce soir'.

My companions at this improvised Court wanted me to remain to dinner, but I refused their invitations and returned home to tell my husband of this wicked mother's remarks.

In the evening, there was a Drawing Room and many ladies to present whom I did not know. Mme de Piis told me their names and I repeated them to the Queen. Afterwards, we went to the small salon where the musicians were waiting, the King shouting at the top of his voice for 'Manuelito'—the Prince de La Paix. The King was handed his violin; he tuned it himself and the quartet began. But he was continually losing his notes and his part was really played by someone else, as I had secretly arranged. Later, ices and chocolate were served and then we went to bed.

The following day, there was a visit lasting a quarter of an hour in the morning and the same music in the evening. The next day, I heard to my great joy that the members of the Spanish Royal Family were shortly to continue their journey. The Prefect and the Archbishop came to take leave of them. We climbed into the carriages which were to take us to the river crossing, for in those days there was no bridge. We found the brigantine lying ready and when we reached the opposite bank, I bade farewell to these

[1] Ferdinand, Prince of the Asturias, later King Ferdinand VII of Spain, and Don Carlos, who later took the title Charles V, refusing to recognise the accession of his niece, Isabella, to the throne of Spain.

unhappy sovereigns. The unfortunate King never, for a single moment, seemed to realise the wretchedness of his position. He was totally without dignity, or even propriety. He spent the entire river crossing talking to my servant who was on deck, a good German who refused to believe that it had really been the King. He said to me afterwards: 'But, Madame, has he no grief for what has happened?'

And that is the tale of my short time at the Court of King Charles IV, in attendance on the Queen, his dreadful wife.

CHAPTER TWENTY-EIGHT

I

And now began a new life. It was, as I have said, about nine o'clock in the evening when the messenger brought me the note from M. de La Tour du Pin announcing that he had been appointed Prefect of Brussels. It meant a lot of planning and the chatter of my cousin, Mme Joseph de La Tour du Pin, was so distracting that I suggested we should go to bed.

But I could not go without writing to Mme de Maurville to tell her that my husband's new appointment would change nothing, and that I hoped she would come with us to Brussels. She was staying with friends about two leagues away and I gave instructions for my note to be given to her at break of day so that she would not have time to ask herself the sad question: 'What is to become of me?' I could have left her at Le Bouilh, which would not have meant any extra expense for us. But why should she not share our good fortune, since she had shared the bad? Also her devotion would help us in many ways. She was without learning, and had little natural intelligence, but she did have the gift of observation and a very penetrating understanding of people. I have, thank God, never had to have a governess for my children, but I knew that I could leave them with Mme de Maurville without any anxiety whenever social duties—which I tried to limit as much as possible—took me away from them for a while. I thought more in those few hours than I would normally have done in half a year. In the important moments of life, any thought which has not occurred in the first twenty-four hours is either pointless, or idle repetition.

By the time my husband arrived next morning for lunch, I was ready to discuss this change in our lives and to tell him the plans and arrangements which seemed to me necessary.

Charlotte was then eleven and a half years old. She was very forward for her age and longed to know all about everything. She pored over every available gazetteer and map of Belgium so that when her father returned and, knowing her well, questioned her concerning the Department of the Dyle, she was able to tell him about it in considerable detail. As for little Cécile, at eight years of age she was already a good musician and proficient in Italian, so that her first question was to know whether she would have a singing master in Brussels.

My husband immediately made all the necessary arrangements at Le Bouilh, and unfortunately he put everything into the hands of a man on whom he thought he could rely as on himself. I was to deal with all the household arrangements and the packing.

M. de La Tour du Pin had been instructed to travel to Paris without delay, his predecessor—M. de Chaban—having already left to organise the departments in Tuscany, which had just been annexed to the Empire. Our friend Brouquens came for him a few days later and they left together for Brussels. His pleasure in our good fortune was almost greater than my husband's.

The news of this appointment astounded all those who had for a long time been seeking favours in vain. No one would believe that M. de La Tour du Pin, like Cincinnatus, had been summoned from his plough and given the finest Prefecture in France.

But the choice was one of the wisest that the prodigious foresight of Napoleon could have made, and for this reason: Brussels was a conquered capital and until then no effort had been made to create any ties which would bind her to her new motherland. It was a city with a Court and an aristocracy, yet it had always been governed by people of obscure and even doubtful origin.

M. de Pontecoulant, the first Prefect, was admittedly a man of good family and aristocratic courtesy. He had been an officer in the Gardes Françaises and had spent his youth at Versailles and in Paris, so that he might, perhaps, have been a success in Brussels if it had not been for his wife. She was said to have saved his life during the Terror. She had once been the mistress of Mirabeau, the man to whom she was married at the time—Lejai—being Mirabeau's librarian. They said she had been beautiful, but no trace of it remained. After becoming Mme de Pontecoulant, she was seen in the salons of Barras, which was scarcely in her favour. When her husband brought her to Brussels, her origins held little attraction for the nobles and aristocrats at the Court of the Archduchess.

M. de Pontecoulant, surrounded by scheming compatriots who had fallen upon Belgium as upon a prey, had never concerned himself with administrative matters. The Emperor recalled him, nominating him to the Senate, and sent M. de Chaban in his stead.

M. de Chaban was worthy, enlightened, firm and an excellent administrator. He abolished many abuses and punished those who had misappropriated property, confiscating it. All his measures had been just and enlightened and to govern the country well one only had to follow the path he had marked out. But he had made no attempt to overcome the aloofness of the upper classes towards the French domination, and it was this task which fell to us, to my husband and, I dare to claim, to me as well. For the source of any influence of this kind must perforce be in the salons.

It is true that M. de Chaban was married, but his wife was ailing and of an obscure family from, so far as I could gather, a very modest level of society. She did not receive and, as a result, no one ever saw her.

A sort of romantic legend had preceded me to Brussels. It was based on my adventures in America, which had become known owing to a note to Delille's poem 'La Pitié'.[1] This lady from the Court of Marie-Antoinette, the Queen whose sister was so well beloved throughout Belgium, this lady who, in those distant lands, had milked cows and lived in forests, was sufficiently intriguing to arouse curiosity.

[1] Jacques Delille (1738–1813) was one of the first poets of the romantic school. He was very highly considered in his day and had a great influence on later romantic poets. (T)

II

After I had made all my arrangements at Le Bouilh and sent off by waggon everything I thought might be useful in Brussels and lessen the very great expense of equipping a large house, I set off with Mme de Maurville, my daughters and my small Aymar. M. Meyer of Bordeaux had lent me a carriage, which I sold for him in Brussels, and we travelled post. We stayed two or three days at Ussé to see Mme de Duras, to the great joy of her daughters and mine, and then went on to Paris where I stayed for three or four weeks with my aunt. She was living then with M. de Lally in a pretty house in the Rue de Miromesnil.

Mme Dillon had returned from England long before, and I called on her for she had given M. de La Tour du Pin a warm welcome the previous year when he had passed through Paris with Humbert. My half-sister, Fanny, had grown up. She was then twenty-three, and although not pretty, was most distinguished. She had many suitors, but the one she preferred and would have married was Prince Alphonse Pignatelli, a pleasant young man who died of a chest illness. He wanted to marry Fanny before he died, in order to leave her his fortune, but despite his insistence, she refused. The unfortunate young man's days were numbered and she thought it would have shown a lack of delicacy towards his family to have married him then, though she loved him dearly and would have been happy, even in her grief, to bear his name. I myself was very disappointed at her decision, for I would have much preferred my sister's name to be Pignatelli rather than Bertrand.

Since this very ordinary name has now been mentioned, I will tell you what had happened during my husband's previous visit to Paris.

The Emperor had repeatedly made it known to the Empress and to Fanny herself that he very much wished her to marry Général Bertrand,[1] who had long been in love with her. My sister would not consent and the Emperor was annoyed. When he knew of her feelings for Alphonse Pignatelli, he ceased to plague her, but

---

[1] Napoleon's favourite aide-de-camp, later Grand Marshal of the Household.

after the Prince's death, he re-opened his campaign. M. de La Tour du Pin happened to arrive in Paris just at the time when Mme Dillon had to send a final answer and she asked him to see the Empress on her behalf and tell her of my sister's definite refusal to marry Général Bertrand. It was a difficult commission, but my husband agreed to undertake it. The Empress received him in her bedroom, where the deep alcove was curtained off during the day by thick, heavy material, almost a wall of embroidered damask, its folds held in place by an edging of heavy gold fringe. She told him to sit beside her on a sofa placed against this curtain. As they were alone, M. de La Tour du Pin went straight to the point, delivered his message and apologised for bringing a decision contrary to the Emperor's wishes. The Empress was most persistent. In the course of a long conversation, M. de La Tour du Pin expressed certain very aristocratic sentiments which did not displease her. Finally, after talking to him about himself, about me, our children, his fortune and his plans, the Empress dismissed him. My husband went immediately to Mme Dillon to give her an account of the interview. That same evening, he called on M. de Talleyrand who took him by the arm, as was his custom when he wanted to talk privately in a corner: 'What on earth have you been doing, refusing Général Bertrand's offer for your sister-in-law? Is it any concern of yours?' 'But that is what Fanny wished' replied M. de La Tour du Pin, 'and my age puts me in a position to act for her in the place of her father.' 'Well,' continued the wily old fox, 'fortunately your aristocratic airs have not ruined your chances. They happen to be the fashion at the Tuileries just now.' 'Who told you all this,' asked my husband, 'have you seen the Empress?' 'No,' replied the other, 'but I have seen the Emperor, who was listening.' So it was perhaps to this conversation, overheard from behind a curtain, that M. de La Tour du Pin owed his appointment as Prefect of Brussels.

III

I was received in Brussels with the greatest kindness. It is a city which appreciates good society and people were delighted to know that the salons of the Prefecture were to be presided over at last by an aristocrat. The behaviour of the wives of various officials sent to the town had not made a good impression, for they had mistakenly thought to please the Government by making no attempt to receive the Belgian ladies. Two of these French-women were senior to me by reason of their husband's position. One was the wife of the General commanding the division stationed in Brussels, and the other was married to the First President of the Imperial Court, which also had its headquarters in Brussels.

The former was Mme de Chambarlhac, a good-looking Savoyarde and a member of the de Coucy family. It was said that she had once been a nun or a novice and that her husband had carried her off during one of the Italian campaigns and married her. She was forty, but still quite beautiful. Living so long among military men of all kinds had ruined her manners, though a few remnants of her original breeding remained. Naturally, I could not consider any connection with such a person, nor did I wish to do so. The life she had led disgusted me. I always thought of her in the hussar's uniform she was said to have worn in order to follow her husband on his campaigns. As for Général de Chambarlhac, he was a fool, jealous of my husband from the very beginning and therefore hostile.

The second was the wife of the First President, M. Betz, a learned German who was both intelligent and able. Her origins were at the very bottom of the social ladder. She was fifty when I knew her, and fairly ugly, though it was not impossible to believe that she had once been beautiful. Her jewels, low-cut dresses and the style in which she dressed her hair were all far more suitable for a young girl than for someone of her age. I received her on important occasions, but do not remember ever having entered her house, though I did not omit to call on her from time to time, at long intervals.

The bitter jealousy of these two ladies was due to the fact that they were not invited to the Dowager's suppers. These marked the dividing line in Brussels society and an invitation was a coveted honour.

The Dowager, as the Dowager Duchesse d'Arenberg was always known, was by birth the Comtesse de la Marck and the last descendant of the Sanglier des Ardennes.[1] She was, as the Abbé de Pradt, Archbishop of Malines, remarked, the perfect Queen Mother. She had retired to the house set aside for the widows of the House of Arenberg and there lived simply, but in a manner befitting her rank, every day inviting to supper a company of people of all ages, both men and women. She always dined alone, used an open carriage no matter what the weather, and saw her children every day, especially her blind son, whom she loved most tenderly. Whenever a slight attack of gout prevented this son from going out, she never omitted to visit him at his home. She received from seven o'clock until nine. Anyone who called after that was asked by the footman if he had been invited to supper. If he had not, he was not admitted. The supper guests arrived at nine and so great was the respect in which the Duchesse was held that there was no one in Brussels who would have dreamed of arriving at half past. At ten o'clock, if someone should ever have kept her waiting until then, she would ring and say without the slightest trace of impatience: 'You may serve now.'

After supper, the guests played lotto until midnight. When her son was there, he would organise a game of whist or backgammon with M. de La Tour du Pin, if he happened to be among the guests. There were never more than fifteen or eighteen people present, all chosen from among the most distinguished people of the town, or visitors of note. But foreigners were rare, for France was at war with the whole of Europe and people could not visit from abroad as they have done since.

In the days before the Revolution, I had often met Mme la Duchesse d'Arenberg in Paris at the Hôtel de Beauvau, where I had always been received with the greatest kindness. Also, Mme de Poix and Mme la Maréchale de Beauvau had, I knew, both written to the Duchesse to tell her that I would be arriving. On the day after we reached Brussels, I therefore went with my husband to call on this venerable lady. We were particularly kindly received and invited to supper on the following day. The Duchesse also wanted to see my son Humbert, who had come to Brussels to meet us. Her kindness set the standard for the

[1] Guillaume de la Marck (1446–1485) who ravaged Brabant and Liège and was eventually defeated and executed by Maximilian of Austria .(T)

attentions we were to receive. The whole town signed our book. They came in person to do so and I took the greatest care to return each visit. I forgot none of them. I made lists of all the people who had called, putting after their names a summary of any family details I had been able to gather in the course of conversation or from the peerage books which I borrowed from the Bibliothèque de Bourgogne which was, and still is, very rich in works of this kind. In my task, I had two helpers: for contemporary matters, M. de Verseyden de Wareck, Secretary-General of the Prefecture, and for the past, Commandeur de Nieuport, a former Commander of the Order of Malta, who visited me every evening. After a month, I was as familiar with Brussels society as if I had known it all my life. I knew about all the different liaisons, the animosities, the bickerings and so on. It involved really hard work, and I applied myself to it with all the ardour that I have always put into whatever lay at hand to be done.

Our establishment cost us a great deal of money. I seem to remember that my husband received an allowance for this purpose, but am not sure. The staff included two liveried servants, and a liveried office boy, a porter, a butler-valet, an office footman who helped the house staff when we entertained, and two stable boys. We lived in the palace where the King of Holland[1] was later to live. My private apartment consisted of a pretty salon and a billiard room. I let it be known immediately that I never, for any reason whatsoever, received visitors in the morning. I devoted all my mornings to the education of my daughters, being present at their lessons or going out with them either for a walk or a drive.

Before long, we could count many close friends, among them M. and Mme de Trazegnies, Prince Auguste d'Arenberg, Commandeur de Nieuport and others. My husband was delighted to meet again the Comte de Liedekerke,[2] for in the days before the Revolution they had been companions in arms in the Régiment de Royal-Comtois when M. de La Tour du Pin was second-in-command. The Comte de Liedekerke had married Mlle Désandrouin, who would eventually inherit an immense fortune, much of which was already in her possession. They had only one son

[1] King William I of the Netherlands.
[2] Marie-Ferdinand-Hilarion, Comte de Liedekerke Beaufort, 1762–1841.

and two daughters. The young man was then twenty-two and an Auditeur (Probationer) at the Conseil d'Etat. There was talk of attaching one of these young men to the personal staff of each Prefect, to act as his secratary and to gain experience in administration. M. de Liedekerke therefore asked M. de La Tour du Pin, his former Colonel, to request that his son be appointed to his staff in that capacity.

Our own son, Humbert, left Antwerp, where M. Malouet had been a second father to him and returned to Brussels to study for the entrance examination to the Conseil d'Etat which was to be held a few months later.

IV

In September 1808, I received a letter from my stepmother, Mme Dillon, telling me that my sister had at last decided, after many hesitations and much uncertainty, to marry Général Bertrand. She had yielded in part to his constancy and in part to the renewed persuasions of the Emperor to whom one could refuse nothing, so gracefully and so winningly did he set about obtaining what he wanted. My sister was in those days extremely frivolous, a Créole quality she shared with her mother. Napoleon had wanted her to accompany the Empress Josephine on a journey to Fontainebleau and so that she might appear there to her best advantage, had sent her 30,000 francs to buy a wardrobe for the eight days of her stay. It was during that period that he obtained her consent to the General's proposal which, until then, she had so obstinately refused.

The Emperor decided that the marriage was to take place immediately, despite my sister's protests that her mother had recently lost her other daughter, poor Mme de Fitz-James. Faced with a long delay and certain that the two women would never be free from one impediment or another, the Emperor said to Fanny: 'Tell your sister to come; she will arrange everything. . . . I am leaving for Erfurt in eight days' time. You must be married by then.'

I learned of all this in a letter from the Duc de Bassano,[1] for neither Mme Dillon nor Fanny had thought to write to me.

[1] M. Maret had recently been created Duc de Bassano.

Although the letter was a very friendly one, it was so clearly a command that I did not even consider refusing. Two hours after receiving it, I left for Paris. I reached Mme d'Hénin's house at dawn; she was astonished to find me beside her bed when she awoke. She still kept a room at our disposal in her pretty house in the Rue de la Miromesnil, where she was living at the time. I remained with her only long enough to change my dress and send for a livery carriage. Then, after drinking a cup of tea, I was driven to Mme Dillon's house in the Rue Joubert. There I learned that she had left some days before for the country, not far from Saint-Cloud, and that she was staying with Mme de Boigne. She had left no messages for me, so I asked the name of the house and how to reach it, and as soon as I had written a note to the Duc de Bassano to tell him of my arrival, set out for the country.

It took me an hour and a half to reach Mme de Boigne's house, Beauregard, a little above Malmaison. It was striking half-past eleven as I arrived and Mme Dillon was still in bed. Fanny cried 'Ah, we're saved. Here is my sister!' Her mother, on the other hand, was alarmed at the thought of the bustle which my energy was about to force upon her. She had made no preparations. I began by advising her to get up, dress, eat luncheon and return to Paris with my sister and me. Just at that moment, Général Bertrand arrived. I had never met him before and he probably knew that it was my husband whom Mme Dillon had charged with refusing his proposal of marriage two years before. Being by nature extremely shy he was much embarrassed. To put him at ease, I suggested a walk in the park until Mme Dillon was dressed. We walked for more than an hour and came to understand one another so well that by the time we returned to the house, we had settled everything.

In the salon, we found Mme de Boigne, whom I had not seen since she was a child, and her mother, Mme d'Osmond, a sister of Edward Dillon and of all the Dillons of Bordeaux.[1] Neither of these ladies could abide me but when luncheon was announced, they could hardly do otherwise than suggest that I should share

---

[1] See p. 47. The Comtesse de Boigne, 1781–1866, was a lady of liberal thinking and Orléanist sympathies. Her 'Mémoires' were published in 1907 and show a very sharp pen. A translation (abridged) was published in London in 1956. (T)

it with them. I was very happy to do so because I had eaten
nothing since taking that cup of tea with Mme d'Hénin at seven
o'clock. The poor General, delighted to find that someone was
at last going to put a term to the dilatoriness of his future mother-
in-law, looked on contentedly as we climbed into the carriage
to return to Paris and promised to re-join us there during the
evening.

I will not go into detail, but the following morning everything
was ready and the signing of the contract had been arranged for
the evening of the next day. A notice was posted up at the Mairie.
By special order, the tribunal met in extraordinary session. Grand-
Juge Régnier[1] was awakened at five o'clock in the morning to
send a certificate which was to serve as my sister's certificate of
baptism, for Mme Dillon had lost the original, or perhaps had
never had one. My sister had been born at Avesnes in Flanders
and no courier, however fast, could have ridden there and back
before the day the Emperor had set for the marriage.

Napoleon had also decided that the ceremony should take place
at Saint-Leu, at the house of Queen Hortense.[2] He said he might
be present, so the Queen paid great attention to the instructions
he had given for the ceremony and saw that every single detail
was carried out. At a moment when all the sovereigns he had
conquered were about to meet, this great man had found time to
arrange the smallest details of his favourite aide-de-camp's
marriage.

V

I was presented to the Emperor at Saint-Cloud by Mme de
Bassano. I had to be at her house at eight o'clock in the morning,
wearing Court dress and plumes. The Emperor greeted me most
graciously, questioned me about Brussels and Brussels society—
'high society', he added with a smile, as if to say 'the only kind
that interests you'. Then he laughed at having made me rise so
early and teased Mme de Bassano a little about the same thing,

[1] Claude-Ambroise Régnier (1746–1814). A lawyer. In 1802 Napoleon appointed
him to the Conseil d'Etat, made him a Grand-Juge, and shortly afterwards, Minister
of Justice. (T)
[2] Hortense-Eugénie de Beauharnais, daughter of the Empress Josephine, who
married Louis Bonaparte, King of Holland.

a teasing which she accepted with a slight air of sulkiness which became her exceedingly well. She has since told me that he was most attentive to her at that time.

I can see you smile, my son, as you read that when I was arranging the salon for the signing of the contract and wanted to set an escritoire with paper and pens on the table, I could find no such objects anywhere in the apartments of either my stepmother or her daughter. It was fortunate that I had thought of it, and as d'Expilly, the best stationer of the day, lived quite near, I was able to send my servant to fetch everything necessary for the occasion. My stepmother was agreeably surprised at my forethought.

The great of the earth arrived with the bridegroom. The evening before the wedding was spent in a rather insipid way, listening to music. Luncheon the following day was little better. The wedding ceremony was to take place at half-past three. All the mighty arrived; marshals, generals and the like, and we walked in procession to the Chapel. The nuptial blessing was given by the Abbé d'Osmond, Bishop of Nancy, who later became Archbishop of Florence. After the ceremony there was dinner, followed by dancing. A number of young people had come from Paris. But Queen Hortense, who loved dancing and excelled at it, was rather out of temper on account of a most amusing incident. The Emperor had not come, but he had made it known to Queen Hortense that he had seen the parure of emeralds set in diamonds which the Empress had given Fanny and did not consider it sufficient. He knew she had a similar set, he said, and asked her to add it to that which her mother had given in order to complete it. Queen Hortense had not expected any request of this kind and was extremely angry. But she had to do as she was told.

CHAPTER TWENTY-NINE

———◆———

I

Before returning to Brussels, I attended some of the dinners held in honour of the marriage, including those given by the four witnesses, M. de Talleyrand, the Duc de Basano, M. Lebrun and a fourth person whose name I cannot remember. They were all very tedious and I was delighted when I was able to leave to re-join my husband and my children. We spent a very pleasant autumn and winter in Brussels. I gave two or three fine balls and Mme de Duras came to spend a fortnight with us, bringing her daughters. I arranged dances for them and took them to the theatre, where we sat in an excellent box reserved for the Prefecture. They thoroughly enjoyed themselves.

Queen Hortense also passed through Brussels. It was the last time she made the journey to join her husband and spend a few days with him in Amsterdam. I saw her while she was in the city. She pretended to be unutterably bored with having to fulfil her duties as Queen.

It is not a history that I am writing, so I shall say nothing of the marriage of the Emperor Napoleon to the Archduchess Marie-Louise.[1] I will only give you my sister's account of the arrival of this Princess at Compiègne. Not only was she herself there, but she also heard from her husband, Bertrand, details which were not general knowledge.

The Emperor was at Compiègne with the new Ladies-in-Waiting appointed to serve the Empress, and vastly impatient to see his new wife. In the courtyard of the Château, a small calèche stood ready, the horses put to, waiting to take him to meet her. When the first courier arrived, Napoleon leaped into the calèche and set off to meet the berline bringing this wife whom he so ardently desired. The carriages drew up. The door of the berline was opened and Marie-Louise prepared to get out. But her husband did not give her time. He climbed into the carriage, embraced her and, having unceremoniously bundled out his sister, the Queen of Naples, telling her to ride in front, he seated himself beside Marie-Louise. When they arrived at the Château, he left the carriage first, offered his arm to his bride and led her into the Household Salon where all the people who had been

[1] There were no children of the marriage between the Emperor Napoleon and the Empress Josephine. In 1808 he divorced her, not for personal reasons, but for political and international considerations. He wanted an heir, and after the battle of Wagram he asked the defeated Emperor of Austria for his daughter, Marie-Louise, in marriage. (T)

invited were assembled. It was already dark. The Emperor presented all the Ladies of the Household in turn, and then the Gentlemen. When the presentations were over, he took the Empress by the hand and led her to her apartment. Everyone expected her to make a change of toilette and then re-appear. They waited for an hour and were beginning to think longingly of supper when the Grand Chamberlain came to announce that Their Majesties had retired. Bertrand whispered in his wife's ear: 'They've gone to bed.' Everyone was greatly surprised, but no one allowed it to appear and they all went in to supper.

The following day, my sister learned from her husband that Marie-Louise had given the Emperor a statement signed by the Archbishop of Vienna declaring that 'the marriage could be consummated without any further ceremony, the proxy marriage being sufficient'. As my brother-in-law was a most truthful man, I have no doubt at all that this detail is true.

II

In Brussels, this marriage with an Archduchess caused great rejoicing, for memories of Austrian rule were far from forgotten. Until now, the nobility of Brussels had remained aloof from the new government, but attracted by the courteous manner of a Prefect of aristocratic origin, they felt the time had come to renounce their old prejudices, which were becoming rather irksome.

When M. de La Tour du Pin learned that the Emperor intended to bring his young Empress to the city which had once been the capital of her father's[1] Belgian possessions, he formed a Garde d'Honneur for duty at the Château de Laeken. This Garde was formed exclusively of Belgians and did not include anyone engaged in the service of France. The Marquis de Trazegnies was in command, and the Marquis d'Assche was appointed second-in-command. Many members of the leading families of Brussels were enrolled and young men who intended to prepare for a career either in the administration or in the army, took the occasion to come forward. Among them was young Auguste de Liedekerke and our own poor son, Humbert. The uniform was

[1] The Emperor Francis I of Austria.

very plain: a green coat and maroon-coloured trousers. It was a mounted corps, and very well mounted too. My sister came to Brussels and stayed with us at the Prefecture. She was present at a big dinner we gave in honour of the Garde, all the ladies wearing favours of the same colours as the uniform.

The Emperor reached Laeken just before dinner time. The next day, he received the Garde d'Honneur and all the officials of the administration. The Mayor, the Duc d'Ursel, presented the town officials. In the evening, there was a Drawing Room and I presented the ladies, nearly all of whom were known to me. Marie-Louise spoke to none of them personally. Even the most illustrious names—that of the Duchesse d'Arenberg, for instance, or the Comtesse de Mérode who was a Princesse de Grimberghe— made no more impression on her than that of Mme P., the wife of the Receveur-Général.[1]

After the Drawing Room, I had the honour of being summoned to play cards with Her Majesty. I think we played whist. The Duc d'Ursel let me know which cards I was to put down when it was my turn to play. This comedy lasted half an hour. Afterwards, the Emperor having gone to his study, we separated and, to my great delight, I was able to go home.

The following day there was to be a ball at the Hôtel de Ville. I was therefore rather annoyed to receive an invitation to dine at Laeken, not seeing how it would be possible to change my toilette, or at least my gown, between dinner and the ball. However, the pleasure of seeing and listening to the Emperor for two whole hours was too great for me not to appreciate such an invitation to the full. The Duc d'Ursel escorted me and as he had to be at the Hôtel de Ville in time to receive the Emperor, I told my maid to be waiting there for me with another toilette all ready.

That dinner is one of the events I remember with the most pleasure. We were eight, sitting in this order: the Emperor, with the Queen of Westphalia on his right, then Maréchal Berthier, the King of Westphalia, the Empress, the Duc d'Ursel, Mme de Bouillé and, finally, myself, on the Emperor's left. He spoke to

[1] Officials appointed to receive domaine produce and taxes in a certain area on behalf of the Treasury. They were, in effect, the Government's bankers. (T)

me nearly all the time of materials, laces, wages, the lives of lace-makers, and then of monuments, antiquities, charitable organisations, the convents of the Béguines,[1] and the customs of the people. Fortunately, I knew something about each. 'How much does a lace-maker earn?' he asked the Duc d'Ursel. The poor man hesitated, embarrassed and trying to work out the amount in centimes. The Emperor saw his hesitation, and turning to me, asked what the local currency was called. I told him that it was the 'escalin', worth 63 centimes, to which he remarked 'Ah, yes'.

We were at table for less than three-quarters of an hour, and when we returned to the salon, the Emperor took a large cup of coffee and continued the conversation. He talked first of the toilette the Empress was wearing, which he liked, and then, breaking off, he asked me if I was comfortably housed. 'Not too badly,' I told him, 'we are in Your Majesty's apartment.' 'Ah, indeed,' he said, 'it certainly cost enough. It was that rascally . . .' —his name escapes me—'M. de Pontecoulant's secretary, who saw to its furnishing. But half the money found its way into his own pockets, if my brother,' he added, turning towards the King of Westphalia, 'will forgive me for saying so. He has taken him into his service, for he likes rascals,' and he shrugged his shoulders. Jerome was about to reply when he realised that the Emperor was already launched on a quite different subject. He had gone back to the Duke of Burgundy[2] and Louis XI and from them he suddenly passed to Louis XIV, saying that he had been truly great only during his last years. Noticing how interested I was in what he was saying and, above all, that I showed some understanding of his remarks, he returned to Louis XI, saying 'I have my own ideas on that fellow and know well they are not shared by everyone.' After mentioning the shameful events of the reign of Louis XI, he mentioned the name of Louis XVI, and there stopped, saying sadly and with respect: 'An unfortunate Prince!'

He went on to speak of other things, teased his brother, who

[1] Women living in communities, principally in Belgium, and vowed to poverty, chastity and obedience. Their vows are not permanent. After six years in a large convent, they move to a small house attached to it and occupy themselves with prayer, good works, lace-making and embroidery. (T)
[2] Charles the Bold, 1433–1477.

had gathered into Westphalia the dregs of France, and Heaven knows how many barbed jests Jerome might not have had to endure if someone had not remarked that it was time to leave for the ball.

I fled with M. d'Ursel to his carriage and we were driven at full gallop to the Hôtel de Ville. I rushed up the stairs as fast as I could. A fresh toilette lay ready for me and I was able to make a complete change and reach the ballroom before the Emperor arrived.

He complimented me on my speed and asked if I intended to dance. I told him that I did not, being a woman of forty. He laughed and said there were many indeed of that age who danced and did not reveal their years so frankly. The ball was very beautiful. It continued after supper, at which we drank to the health of the Empress and hoped, though we did not say so, that she might have a very good reason for not dancing.

The Emperor and his young wife left the following morning. A very richly decorated yacht took them to the end of the Brussels Canal, where carriages were waiting to take them on to Antwerp. As M. de La Tour du Pin went on board the yacht, he saw the Marquis de Trazegnies, who was commanding the Garde. Fearing that the Emperor might not invite the Marquis to accompany him in the yacht, for there was not a great deal of space, M. de La Tour du Pin mentioned his name to the Emperor and added that one of his ancestors had been Constable of France during the reign of St Louis. This piece of information worked like magic; the Emperor immediately summoned the Marquis de Trazegnies and talked with him for a long time. Shortly afterwards, his wife was appointed a Lady-in-Waiting. She pretended to be rather bored at this appointment, but secretly she was delighted.

III

After the Emperor's visit, our life in Brussels returned to its normal routine. The summer passed in a series of visits to different country houses, where we were invited to dine. We went to Antwerp for the launching of a large seventy-four,[1] one of the new ones on the stocks at that time.

[1] A ship of the line, armed with 74 guns. (T)

Humbert went to Paris for his examination. It is, under any circumstances, an ordeal for a young man of twenty to have to answer a long list of questions, but it became infinitely worse when it meant standing before the Emperor while he, from his armchair, took over the examination and asked the most unexpected things. Humbert heard the examiner, who was pointing towards him at the time, whisper to Napoleon: 'That is one of the most outstanding . . .' and was a little comforted. The Emperor asked him if he knew any foreign languages, and he replied that he spoke English and Italian as well as he spoke French. It was his fluency in Italian which decided his appointment to the sub-Prefecture of Florence. To increase the number of vacancies for 'probationers', some were sent as sub-Prefects to the chief towns of Departments where all the duties had, until then, fallen upon the Prefect.

Although many years have passed since the events I am about to describe, and time has slightly clouded my memories, it seems to me that it was in this summer of 1809 that the English made their ridiculous attack on Flushing and Antwerp.

Shortly before, M. de La Tour du Pin had undergone a painful operation for the removal of a tumour below his ankle. For many years he had felt a sharp pain whenever he knocked the small growth, which was no larger than a pea. But for some months it had been gradually growing bigger and more easily hurt if rubbed against hard surfaces. In Brussels, he consulted a bad surgeon who told him to apply a caustic to the affected part in order to destroy the skin and make it easier to remove the growth. Unfortunately, my husband did as he was advised. A few hours afterwards, he was seized with terrible pains and his entire foot became greatly inflamed. I was so worried that I sent to my aunt in Paris a diagnosis written by my good Dr Brandner. My aunt took it herself to M. Boyer, who studied it carefully and then wrote underneath with cruel bluntness: 'If M. de La Tour du Pin is not operated on within four days, within eight it will be necessary to amputate his leg.'

Mme d'Hénin was terrified and decided to send M. Boyer's leading pupil, M. Dupuytren, to Brussels. He arrived at five o'clock in the morning and went to take a bath before coming to the Prefecture. A few minutes before his arrival, I received a letter from my aunt telling me that he was coming and what M. Boyer thought should be done.

M. Dupuytren arrived, examined the wound and when my husband asked him when he intended to operate, replied 'Immediately.' After talking for a moment to his assistant, he asked me to withdraw, saying it would not take long. I went into the next room and the twenty minutes that the operation lasted seemed to me twenty hours. When M. Dupuytren came out, he told me he had never performed a more difficult operation. The sweat poured down his brow. He retired to the room prepared for him and went to bed. I found my husband very pale and our son, Humbert, who had stayed with him, paler still. But the patient's sufferings were over, and he was soon sleeping peacefully for the first time in ten days.

That evening, I gave M. Dupuytren one hundred louis, as well as the expenses of his journey by postchaise. I also gave ten louis to his assistant. In addition, I gave M. Dupuytren a pretty lace veil for Mlle Boyer, whom he said he was to marry a few days later. But the wedding never took place. M. Dupuytren quarrelled with M. Boyer, his teacher and benefactor, and did not marry his daughter—though he did keep my veil.

IV

M. de La Tour du Pin had barely recovered from this operation, and was still unable to walk when, one morning—or more exactly, one evening—an express arrived from M. Malouet with news that the English fleet had entered the Escaut. It consisted of several large warships and a great number of transport vessels. The news was telegraphed to Paris, where it arrived at dawn, but Napoleon was away. Arch-Chancellor Cambacérès busily set about collecting troops. Every detachment was sent post, which meant tremendous activity and movement. The English, instead of taking Antwerp and destroying our arsenals and dockyards, as they could easily have done, spent their time laying siege to Flushing. This gave Bernadotte time to assemble an army of Gardes Nationales and troops from several garrisons. The details of this ridiculous English attack may be read in all the memoirs of the day. Although M. de La Tour du Pin had no responsibility in military matters, he assembled the entire Garde Nationale of the Department of the Dyle. But this did not prevent him being accused later of having been slow in doing so.

I will tell you here a small personal incident which was rather strange.

Interest in this expedition ran so high that we drove to Antwerp nearly every day. There were no railways, so we stabled three carriage horses at intervals along the route and used them in relays. One was at Malines. We used to leave Brussels at five o'clock in the morning, and would be in Antwerp by eight o'clock. There, we would breakfast with M. Malouet and by midday would be back in Brussels in time for the arrival of the courier. On one of these journeys we stopped to drink a cup of coffee at the house of Monseigneur de Pradt, Archbishop of Malines. The conversation was entirely about this famous English expedition and during the course of it, the Archbishop said to us: 'This Lord Chatham is a fool. Instead of entering the Escaut, from which he is now unable to withdraw, he should have gone to Breskens and landed his troops there where we would not have had a single man to oppose them. It would have enabled him to impose levies on a considerable part of Belgium—on Bruges, Ghent, Brussels and so on.' M. de Pradt had worked out every detail. He traced the route they should have followed, calculated the money and silver that might have been seized, as well as the booty that could have been pillaged from churches and strong-rooms, and ended by saying: 'And what could he not have done over there, in the depths of Germany!' All this was said with a cold calculation very out of keeping with his cloth, and so amused me that when we returned to Brussels, I included an account of it in a letter to my aunt who was staying at Mouchy with Mme de Poix. My letter never reached her, and I will tell you later what became of it.

The Gardes Nationales from the Vosges and the Departments in the east travelled post from their mountains and were sent to the Island of Walcheren, where they were soon suffering far more severely from the ravages of fever than from the attacks of the English. Within a week, all the hospitals of Antwerp, Malines

and Brussels were overflowing. M. de La Tour du Pin improvised
an extra one in the workhouse which had recently been opened in
the Abbaye de La Cambre, near Brussels. The generous response
to his appeal for gifts to equip this hospital showed clearly the
esteem in which he was held by all classes. In the first twenty-
four hours, three hundred mattresses, four hundred pairs of
sheets and a large number of other things had been handed in at
the Prefecture and sent on from there to La Cambre. I visited this
improvised hospital a few days later. All the patients were young
conscripts. In a ward of a hundred beds, not a single face had seen
more than twenty summers. It was a distressing sight.

When the Emperor returned, my husband's enemies, led by
Général Chambarlhac, did everything in their power to discredit
him, declaring that it was the fault of the Prefect that the Garde
Nationale of Brussels had not marched on Antwerp. M. Malouet
had just been appointed a Conseiller d'Etat and he warned my
husband of the intrigues being fomented against him. Among those
seeking his removal was the Duc de Rovigo. He was doing so for
purely personal reasons: some time before, he had sent to Brussels
a certain Mme Hamelin, well known as a scheming woman of
easy virtue, to persuade M. de La Tour du Pin to arrange the
marriage of his brother-in-law, M. Faudoas, to Mlle de Spangen,
who later became Mme Werner de Mérode. My husband flatly
refused and so saved the girl from marrying a most undesirable
person. She has remained deeply grateful to him.

The Emperor made a tour of Belgium, but spent only a few
hours at Laeken. My husband went to the Palace and asked for a
private audience, but before it could take place, the town authorities and staff officers of the Garde Nationale were announced.
Acting on reports he had already received, Napoleon dealt with
them severely. The Commander of the Garde Nationale tried to
justify himself by attacking the Prefect. At this, a young sub-
lieutenant stepped forward and declared courageously: 'With your
Majesty's permission I deny all that this gentleman has just said.'
He went on to explain in detail what had passed. The Emperor was
delighted with his self-confident manner and clear account. He
heard him to the end without interrupting and when he finished,
clapped him on the shoulder, saying: 'You're a courageous young

man. Who are you?' 'I am in charge of the Garde Nationale office at the Prefecture,' replied the young man.

'Your name?'

'Loiseau.'

The Emperor turned then towards the accusers and told them: 'All that he has told me is true.' Returning to his study, he summoned M. de La Tour du Pin, and listened quietly to what he had to say, his earlier irritability quite gone.

That same evening, Loiseau was commissioned as a sub-lieutenant in a regiment and the following day set out to join his new unit. The poor boy fought in all the campaigns and towards the end received a wound which shattered his face and from which I believe he eventually died.

V

Towards the end of the winter of 1810 or 1811, M. de La Tour du Pin and I went to Paris for two months to accompany our son Humbert, who was leaving for Florence. My sister, Fanny, was in Paris with her two children, the youngest of whom was only three months old. The baby, whose name was Hortense, had been born immediately after my sister's return from a long journey in Germany with her husband, Général Bertrand, a journey during which her coach had been several times overturned. Shortly before the baby's birth, she spent a few days in Paris with me, while Général Bertrand accompanied the Emperor on a visit to the Antwerp area. At one point, he rolled with his horse to the bottom of a dyke. The Emperor shouted from the bank to know if he had broken a leg. Learning that he had not, he told him to come to me in Brussels and to re-join him later in Paris. They both stayed with us until Fanny, already in the ninth month of her pregnancy, decided to leave for Paris so that her baby might be born there.

We left Mme d'Hénin, my daughters and M. de Lally in Brussels. The latter was generally understood to be an English prisoner, a misunderstanding he was extremely anxious to preserve, as it meant a pension of £300 from the English Government, though I have never understood why.

In Paris, I found Mme de Bérenger, who was staying in the same house as we were. I saw her daily in Brussels when she was there with her father, the Comte de Lannoy. He was a Senator, and when he had to come to Paris for a session, his daughter came with him. Mme de Bérenger, Mme de Lévis and Mme de Duras were the three priestesses of the temple devoted to the worship of Chateaubriand. He allowed himself to be flattered, loved and admired to such an exaggerated extent by these three women that, to me, it was ludicrous. They were all jealous of one another, and under the mask of close friendship, lost no opportunity of belittling one another in the eyes of their god—who accepted the incense of their praise with remarkable complacency.

One morning, Mme de Duras found me reading a book lent to me by M. de Narbonne. It was the first work M. de Chateaubriand had ever published.[1] He had written it on his return from America and it was full of ideas that were both revolutionary and irreligious. He had had it published in England but only a few copies were printed and he later tried to trace them all and have them burned. The work was not known in Paris and the copy I was reading was probably the only one ever to reach the city. Seeing it, Mme de Duras threw herself upon me like a tigress, trying to snatch it away. But I sat on it, and finding she could not get it by force, she went on her knees and begged me, with tears, to give it to her. She was furious when I still refused. The scene was one of rare melodrama.

I also read another strange and interesting book, the Memoirs of Mme de Rochejaquelein. She had lent the manuscript to M. de Talleyrand so that he could give it to Napoleon who wanted to read it. Mistrusting the Duc de Rovigo, Minister of police, M. de Talleyrand refused to part with the original manuscript and himself dictated the text to a secretary. It was that copy which he gave the Emperor, and which the Emperor lent to me. He had pencilled remarks and underlined passages.[2]

---

[1] *Essai historique, politique et moral sur les révolutions anciennes et modenres, considérées dans leurs rapports avec la Révolution française* (London, 1797).

[2] When the Comtesse Auguste de La Rochejacquelein read the manuscript of the *Journal d'une Femme de 50 Ans*, she commented beside this paragraph: 'What Mme de La Tour du Pin says of my sister-in-law's "Mémoires" is not quite correct. It was M. de Barante to whom the "Mémoires" were entrusted, and he lent them to M. de Talleyrand. The latter unscrupulously had a copy made, which forced Mme de La Rochejacquelein to have them published'.

My dear Humbert left for Florence. This departure was the beginning of a long separation and was exceedingly painful to me. You, my dear Aymar, have the three hundred and fifty letters he wrote to me during the course of his very short life. I was his friend as well as his mother and his absence caused me an anguish which each of his letters renewed. I was anxious, therefore, to return immediately to Brussels, but my husband thought it proper to remain in Paris until the birth of the Empress's baby, which was expected hourly.

One evening, I was invited to a play given at the Tuileries in a small gallery which had been turned into a theatre. We met in the Empress's salon. The Emperor came straight up to me and spoke with the greatest kindness of my son, Humbert, and then admired the simplicity of my gown, my good taste, my very distinguished appearance—all this to the great astonishment of certain ladies covered in diamonds who wondered who the new-comer could possibly be. When we entered the gallery, I was given a place not far from the Emperor. The actors were excellent and the play—*L'Avocat Patelin*[1]—very funny. Napoleon was extraordinarily amused and roared with laughter. The great man's presence did not prevent me from doing likewise, and that pleased him, he said afterwards, scoffing a little at those ladies who thought it proper to keep a solemn face. It was considered a great favour to be invited to the play, and there were not more than fifty ladies present.

VI

The Empress was finally brought to bed on the evening of the 19th of March. Mme de Trazegnies, who was in Paris just then, went to the Tuileries and spent the night there with all the other members of the Household, the principal officers of state and many others. The next morning, at about eight or nine o'clock, I hurried to her house in the Rue de Grenelle, only four doors away. As M. de La Tour du Pin and I were talking to M. de Trazegnies, who had been to the Tuileries for the latest news, his wife returned. We immediately bombarded her with questions. She was herself pregnant, and utterly exhausted. She told us that

[1] An early 18th-century play by Brueys and Palaprat.

the Emperor had come to the Household Salon, where she was waiting with her companions, and had told them: 'Ladies, you may go home for two or three hours. There is a pause in the labour. The Empress is asleep and Dubois[1] says the baby will not be born until about midday.' So everyone went away. Mme de Trazegnies had already removed her mantle, for they had all been in full dress, when we heard the first maroon fired from the Invalides. She hurried downstairs as fast as she could and climbed back into her carriage. We went out into the street. Carriages had stopped, merchants stood in the doorways of their shops and people came to their windows; everyone was counting the salute. On every side could be heard a murmur '. . . three . . . four . . . five . . .' There was nearly a minute between each round. After the twentieth, there was a hushed silence. But at the twenty-first, there were spontaneous, excited shouts of 'Vive l'Empereur!' A few moments later, we saw Victor Sambuy's horse fall as he turned into the Rue Hillérin-Bertin. He was First Page, and it was therefore his duty to carry the news of the King of Rome's birth to the Senate—a duty which would bring him a pension of 10,000 francs. As he crossed the Pont Royal, he saw that the Rue du Bac was blocked and thought it wiser to take the longer route. He was very badly shaken by his fall, but did not lose consciousness and was able to mutter: 'Set me back on my horse.' Then, having drunk a glass of brandy, he set off again at a gallop to earn his ten thousand francs.

That evening, I dined at my sister's and people came to tell us that the newly-born baby[2] would be given provisional baptism at nine o'clock that evening and that ladies who had been presented might attend the ceremony.

We all went—Mme Dillon, my sister and I. We had to enter by the Pavillon de Flore and walk right through the apartments to the Salle des Maréchaux. The salons were filled with the men and women who made up Empire society. People crowded together, all trying to be close to the passage which the ushers were keeping free for the procession down to the Chapel. We manoeuvred very cleverly so that we stood at the head of the staircase and were able

[1] The surgeon, Antoine Dubois.
[2] François-Charles-Joseph-Napoléon, King of Rome, Napoleon II.

to follow the new-born baby. From our point of vantage, we had a wonderful view of the veterans of the 'Vieille Garde' (the Old Guard),[1] posted one on each step, their chests covered in medals. They were not allowed to make the slightest movement, but deep emotion was plainly visible on their rugged faces and I saw tears of joy on their cheeks. The Emperor appeared, walking beside Mme de Montesquieu, who was carrying the baby, its face uncovered, on a cushion of white satin covered with lace. I had time to look well at the baby and to this day I remain convinced that the child had not been born that morning. It would be pointless now to try to throw light on the mystery, for the child it concerns had such a short career. But at the time I was worried and troubled, although I naturally told no one of my doubts, except possibly my husband.

CHAPTER THIRTY

I

A few days later, we returned to Brussels, which the Emperor had announced his intention of visiting in the spring. His brother, Louis, had abandoned the throne of Holland, frustrated by Napoleon's interference from afar, which was preventing him from carrying out the reforms he wanted. King William[2] has told me himself that Louis is remembered by the Dutch with great respect. Quite other was the administration of M. de Celles, a son-in-law of Mme de Valence, who is remembered in Holland with horror even to this day. The Emperor appointed him Prefect of Amsterdam, and there he perpetrated all the evil that is possible when an unprincipled man combines intelligence with his wickedness.

It was, so far as I can remember, towards the spring of that year—1811—that we endured the official visit of inspection of a Conseiller d'Etat. In other words, the visit of a superior kind of

---

[1] The original members of the Imperial Guard formed in 1804. (T)
[2] William I, King of the Netherlands.

spy determined to find fault even in those he cannot but esteem, and for that very reason always dreaded by Prefects. M. Réal fell to the lot of M. de La Tour du Pin, and on his very first visit, my husband realised that this man would try to do him all the harm he could. While he was staying with us, we gave a dinner in his honour, followed by a reception. I had told the ladies I knew to be well-disposed towards me that I hoped they would spend the evening with us. When we returned to the big salon after dinner, we found a gathering that included some of the most distinguished men and women in Brussels society. M. Réal was astounded at the illustrious names, the nobility of their bearing and their elegance. He was quite unable to keep his feelings to himself and told M. de La Tour du Pin that he was horrified to see such a salon. My husband replied that he regretted it, but that fortunately, it did not have the same effect on the Emperor.

Napoleon came to Belgium towards the end of Summer, accompanied by the Empress. He did not stop in Brussels, but as Marie-Louise was still in very poor health after her son's birth, he left her at the Château de Laeken.[1] We were invited there every day to spend the evening and play lotto. This went on for about a week and was very tedious. The Empress continued to be as dull as she had seemed at first. Every day, as she gave me her pulse to count, she asked the same question: 'Do you think I have a temperature?' and every day I would reply that I was not competent to tell. A few gentlemen, including the Maréchal Mortier and M. de Béarn, would be there to converse during tea. As Mayor, the Duc d'Ursel was responsible for suggesting morning outings suited to the weather. One day, Marie-Louise visited the museum and as she seemed to be paying particular attention to a fine portrait of her illustrious grandmother, Maria-Theresa, the Duc d'Ursel offered to have it hung in her salon at Laeken. But she replied, 'Ah that, no. The frame is too old-fashioned.' On another occasion, he suggested to her that it would be interesting to visit part of the Forest of Soignes known as the Archduchess

[1] This is not quite exact. The Emperor left on the 19th of September, 1811, to visit the camp at Boulogne, the French fleet and the northern part of the Empire. After his departure the Empress went to Laeken, near Brussels, driving during the night of the 21st–22nd of September and awaited the Emperor's instructions. She rejoined him at Antwerp on the 30th of September.

Isabella's pilgrimage. The holiness and goodness of that Archduchess were still warmly remembered. But Marie-Louise replied
that she did not like forests. In short, this insignificant woman,
so utterly unworthy of the man whose destiny she shared, seemed
to make a point of being discourteous in every possible way to the
people of Belgium, who were so ready to give her their affection.
I did not see her again until after she had lost her throne; she was
still just as stupid.

In the summer of 1811, Talleyrand came to preside over the
election of a senator and two deputies to the Legislative Assembly
—at least, I think that is what it was, for I get the different constitutions very muddled. He arrived with a great train of servants
and gave several dinners in the fine apartment which the Duc
d'Arenberg (the blind one), had put at his disposal in the Hôtel
d'Arenberg. Once again, he had reverted to his grandest and
most charming manner. It made a very comic contrast with
that of the Archbishop of Malines, who looked like Scapin in a
purple cassock.

On his previous journey through Malines, the Emperor had
pointedly questioned the Archbishop, in front of everyone,
about the plan of campaign he would have followed had he been
Lord Chatham. This confirmed his suspicion that it was I who
had betrayed the conversation at his house in Malines after my
husband and I had lunched with him one morning during the
English attack on the Island of Walcheren, for it was then that he
had developed this plan in some detail.

The Emperor liked people to keep to their own professions
and his comments on the archiepiscopal invasion plan were
therefore ruthlessly scathing. They roused in M. de Pradt a
strong dislike for me. He spoke of it to M. de Talleyrand, who
laughed both at him and at his suspicion that I was a spy. The joke
lasted the four days of the official visit of the Prince Vice-Grand-
Elector, for such, I believe, was the title of M. de Talleyrand's
office. That angered the Archbishop still further and embittered
him not only against me, which I could have borne with equa-
nimity, but also against my husband. He became relentless in his
efforts to undermine my husband and I do not think I am mistaken
in attributing M. de La Tour du Pin's eventual dismissal to him

and to Commissioner-General of Police Bellemare. However that may be, there is no doubt that they would have been capable of it. Bellemare had an excellent understanding with the Archbishop concerning the arrest of priests who showed no particular attachment to the Government or who refused to recognise the Concordat. Many had already been sent to the prisons of the Château de Ham. It was said that one day, when Bellemare was demanding that the Archbishop should hand over to him a number of priests who had taken refuge in his diocese, M. de Pradt replied: 'You want eight? Well, I will give you forty-five.' The leader of these priests, one named Steevens, was in hiding in the Department of the Dyle, and it must be admitted that M. de La Tour du Pin was not particularly active in searching for him. He would have been if he had thought it his duty, but these persecutions seemed to him to harm the Government rather than to serve it.

II

Towards the middle of the spring of 1812, we began to see troops moving towards Germany. Several regiments of the 'Jeune Garde'[1] (Young Guard) came to Brussels and remained there a while. Others posted straight through. Instructions came for the requisitioning of farm waggons drawn by four horses. Sometimes an order would arrive in the morning for eighty to a hundred carts to be ready by evening, each provided with two days' forage. Police would gallop out in every direction to warn the farmers. The latter, obliged to leave their ploughing and other farm work, were very cross about it. But who dared resist? From Bayonne to Hamburg, no one even thought of doing so. We gave many large meals to groups of officers who arrived at ten o'clock in the evening and had to be off again by midnight. It is certain that very few of those fine men ever returned from that ill-starred campaign.

It was difficult to accustom oneself to the idea that French

[1] Part of the Imperial Guard. When it was formed in 1804, the Imperial Guard numbered 10,000 men and included all arms. As its numbers increased, a 'Jeune Garde' was formed, the original corps becoming known as the 'Vieille Garde'. By 1814, the Imperial Guard numbered 120,000 men. (T)

armies should go as far as Moscow. Therefore, when M. de La Tour du Pin returned from a short visit to Paris with a fine map of Germany, Poland and Russia, we were astonished that Lapie should have added at the edge a small square of paper showing Moscow. The map itself did not stretch as far as that city, and when it was hung on the wall of the salon, people never failed to comment that the geographer seemed to have taken a very unnecessary precaution. It was an omen!

During the last months of that year, young de Liedekerke[1] paid assiduous court to my elder daughter, Charlotte. She was sixteen and very tall. She was not pretty, but most distinguished: a noble 'demoiselle' in the full meaning of the word. She was quick-witted and sensible, and her understanding and memory were all that my motherly concern with her education could desire. Although she was already very well informed, her passion for learning was such that her books had to be taken from her, and at night every form of lighting had to be removed to prevent her reading or writing until dawn. But she could not have been accused of pedantry or pretention. She was gay, and independent in her thinking, but never intolerant of others. Her qualities of heart surpassed even those of her mind. Charity was a matter of conscience with her and in her willingness to be of service to others, she neglected no opportunity of helping people. Her amiability and charm of manner were such that her outstanding qualities evoked no envy.

Young de Liedekerke, carried away by his feelings, but by no means unaware of the material advantages, realised that Mlle de La Tour du Pin, with her personal charm, her name and her connections would, despite her lack of fortune, be more helpful to his advancement than some good Belgian girl of wealth but undistinguished birth. He told his parents that he would have no other wife than my daughter. His father raised several objections but his mother, hoping that her son's political career would be furthered by a marriage which would take him outside his own country, managed to obtain her husband's consent. On New Year's Day, 1813, at ten o'clock in the morning, Mme de Liedekerke called on me to ask my daughter's hand in marriage

[1] Comte Auguste de Liedekerke Beaufort.

to her son. I was prepared for this request, which I received and agreed to with pleasure. Mme de Liedekerke wished to see my daughter, whom she embraced, and it was agreed that the marriage should take place six weeks later. We settled an income of only 2,000 francs on Charlotte and my aunt, Mme d'Hénin, gave her her trousseau.

My other daughter, Cécile, had been for six months at the Convent of the Ladies of Berlaimont, preparing for her First Communion. I promised her that she should come home on the day her sister was married. At the same time, we heard that Humbert had been transferred from Florence and appointed Sub-Prefect of Sens, in the Department of the Yonne. The news set the seal on our content. We were far from suspecting the catastrophe which hovered so close.

III

M. de La Tour du Pin had gone to Nivelles to be present at the conscription ballot or, more exactly, the new levy of men made necessary by the continuation of the Emperor's war. One day I was at home alone when, before lunch, I saw the Secretary-General of the Prefecture arrive, looking very distressed. He told me that the courier from Paris had just brought the news that my husband had been dismissed and that M. d'Houdetot, Prefect of Ghent, had been appointed in his stead.

This news hit me with the force of a thunderbolt, for in that first moment I saw it as a possible excuse for the breaking off of my daughter's marriage. However, I decided not to give in without a struggle and, without waiting for the return of M. de La Tour du Pin, to whom I sent a special messenger, I left in advance for Paris. In justice to M. de Liedekerke, I must say that he came to see me with a speed and a warmth which would surprise him today, if he remembers the occasion, and he begged me not to change our plans.

I left my aunt and Mme de Maurville to pack everything in the Prefecture that belonged to us and by four o'clock was on my way to Paris. In the two hours before I left, there had been so many things to do and decide that I was already tired before I set out. A night spent in an uncomfortable postchaise and anxiety about our new circumstances resulted in a fairly high fever which I still had when I arrived in Paris at ten o'clock the next evening. I went to Mme de Duras' house, but she was out. Her daughters had just gone to bed. They got up and sent someone to fetch their mother. When she came in, she found me lying on her sofa, prostrated with fatigue. There was no room in the house to put me up, but she had the keys to the apartment of the Chevalier de Thuisy. My maid and the servant who had followed me, went to prepare a bed for me there. I took refuge in it as soon as I could, but was unable to find the rest I so greatly needed. Mme de Duras came early the next day with Dr Auvity, for whom she had sent. He found me still very feverish. But I told him that he must, at any cost, put me on my feet, because I had to be in a fit state to present myself at Versailles before evening. He gave me a calming potion which made me sleep until five o'clock. I do not remember whether I felt recovered or not. In any case, that was the least of my worries.

I ordered a livery carriage and, wearing a very elegant toilette, went to call for Mme de Duras. We left together for Versailles. But the Emperor was at Trianon. We went to an inn in the Rue de l'Orangerie and engaged a suite for the two of us. I immediately got out my escritoire. All I had told Mme de Duras was that I wished for an audience with His Majesty, and when she saw me take out a large sheet of fine paper and copy out a draft which I had taken from my letter case, she asked me to whom I was writing. 'To whom?' I replied, 'to the Emperor of course. I do not like half-measures.'

When the letter was written and sealed, we climbed back into our carriage to take it to Trianon. There, I asked for the Chamberlain on duty. I had taken the precaution of preparing a short note for him. By good fortune, it was Adrien de Mun, a very good friend of mine. He came over to the carriage and promised me that at ten o'clock, when the Emperor came to see the Empress at tea-time, he would hand him my letter. He kept his word, and was as pleased as he was surprised when Napoleon, looking at the direction, said to himself: 'Mme de La Tour du Pin writes an excellent hand. It is not the first time I have seen her writing.' These words confirmed my suspicion that the letter to Mme d'Hénin which never reached her, in which I had given a rather humorous account of the plan of campaign which the Archbishop of Malines would have followed had he been Lord Chatham, had been seized before reaching its destination.

After the drive to Trianon, we returned to our hotel. At about ten o'clock that evening, as Claire and I were discussing my chances of being granted the audience I had asked for, an inn servant who, until then, had considered us ordinary mortals, opened the door and announced in an awe-stricken voice: 'From the Emperor.'

As he spoke, a man came in. He was wearing quantities of gold lace and informed me: 'His Majesty will see Mme de La Tour du Pin tomorrow morning at ten o'clock.'

This good news did not trouble my sleep and the following morning, after drinking a large bowl of coffee made by Claire herself—to make sure, she explained, that I should be properly awake—I left for Trianon. I had to wait ten minutes in the salon immediately next to that in which Napoleon was receiving. There was no one there, for which I was very glad, as I needed that moment of solitude to arrange my thoughts. A tête-à-tête conversation with that extraordinary man was certainly one of the most important occasions of a lifetime, yet I can assure you, in all truth and perhaps with a certain pride, that I felt not the slightest embarrassment.

The door opened, the footman signed to me to enter, and closed both halves of the door behind me. I was in the presence of Napoleon. He came forward to meet me, saying quite amiably, 'Madame, I fear you are very displeased with me.'

I bowed in assent, and the conversation began. I have lost the account I wrote of this long audience, which lasted fifty-nine minutes by the clock, and now, after so many years, I cannot remember all the details. The sum of it was that the Emperor tried to prove to me that he had been compelled to act as he had done. I then briefly described to him the general attitude of Brussels society, the esteem which my husband, unlike all his predecessors, had succeeded in acquiring, the visit of Réal, the stupidity of Général Chambarlhac and his wife, an ex-nun, and so on. I told him all this very rapidly and, encouraged by signs of approval, ended by telling him that my daughter was about to marry a member of one of the noblest families in Brussels. At this he interrupted, placed his beautifully-shaped hand on my arm and said: 'I hope that this will not prevent the marriage, but if it should, then you would have no reason to regret it.'

Then, as he walked to and fro in that great salon, with me trying to keep pace beside him, he spoke these amazing words: 'I was wrong. But what can be done about it?' It was, perhaps, the only time in his life that he made such an admission, and it was I who was privileged to hear it.

I replied that it lay in his power to set matters right, and, passing a hand across his brow, he said: 'Yes, there is a report on the Prefectures. The Minister of the Interior is coming this evening,' He went on to name four or five Departments and added: 'There is Amiens. Would that suit you?'

'Perfectly, Sir,' I replied without hesitation.

'In that case, it is settled. You may go and tell Montalivet.' And, with that charming smile which has so often been spoken of, he added: 'And now, am I forgiven?' I replied politely that I also needed forgiveness for having been so outspoken. 'Oh, you were quite right to be so,' was the answer. I curtsied, and he walked to the door to open it for me himself.

On my way out, I met Adrien de Mun and Juste de Noailles, who asked me if I had managed to set things right. I told them only that the Emperor had been very amiable. Without wasting a moment, I returned to Paris, taking with me Mme de Duras who, in her impatience, had come to wait for me in the Allée de Trianon.

After taking Mme de Duras home, I went to see M. de Montalivet, arriving at his house at about half-past two. He gave me a friendly, but rueful welcome, saying: 'I could not prevent any of it. The Emperor has been told a thousand tales against your husband and is very annoyed with him. It is said that people go to your house as if to Court.' To amuse myself a little at his expense, I asked: 'But would it not be possible to re-instate my husband?' 'Oh,' he replied, 'I would never dare to suggest it to the Emperor. When he is angry with someone, whether justly or unjustly, it is difficult to bring him round.' 'Well,' I went on, with a slightly sanctimonious air, 'we must bow to his will. But when you go this evening to ask him to sign the four Prefectoral appointments . . .'—'How do you know about that?' he asked sharply. Pretending not to hear, I went calmly on '. . . you will propose M. de La Tour du Pin for the Prefecture of Amiens.' He looked at me in amazement, and I added simply: 'The Emperor told me to tell you.' M. de Montalivet exclaimed, took my hands in warm friendship and good will and, at the same time looking me up and down, said that he might have guessed that such a charming toilette at that early hour was not intended for him.

The appointment of M. de La Tour du Pin appeared that same evening in the *Moniteur* and I was congratulated by people of my acquaintance who had been concerned at the news of his fall from favour. As you will see, it turned out that this transfer was a piece of good fortune for my husband.

I stayed in Paris for several days, awaiting the arrival of the Comte de Liedekerke and M. de La Tour du Pin, who came to join me for the signing of our children's marriage contract. During this time, there was a Drawing Room at Court and I attended with Mme de Mun. I was very simply dressed, without a single jewel, unlike the ladies of the Empire who were always laden with them, and I found myself placed in the last row in the Throne Room, standing a head above two small women who, without so much as a by-your-leave, had stationed themselves in front of me. The Emperor came in and took in the three rows of ladies at a glance. He made a few rather absent-minded remarks to some of them and then, seeing me, smiled that smile which all historians have tried to describe and which was truly remarkable because it contrasted so strikingly with his usually serious and even hard expression. But the surprise of the ladies near me was very great when Napoleon, smiling broadly, asked me: 'Are you pleased with me, Madame?' Hearing this, the people about me withdrew to right and left, and without knowing how it happened, I found myself in the front row. I thanked the Emperor most sincerely. After a few amiable words, he continued on his way. It was the last time I was to see that great man.

IV

I left again for Brussels, where I could rejoin my children and where a thousand and one things awaited my attention. M. de La Tour du Pin travelled by way of Amiens to prepare accommodation for us there. He then joined me in Brussels, accompanied by my dear Humbert, who had returned from Florence and who, while he was in Paris, had received his appointment to the Sub-Prefecture of Sens. Who could have foreseen then that only ten months later he would be driven from that city by the Wurtemburgers?[1]

When M. de La Tour du Pin arrived in Brussels at the end of March, he found me and my children living in the house of the Marquis de Trazegnies who, with great generosity, had offered us warm and liberal hospitality. With a total lack of delicacy, M. d'Houdetot had announced that he would take over the Prefecture on the second day after my return to Brussels. I did not want him to find any trace of our five years' residence there, so everything that belonged to us was packed and sent away. As to the furnishings, each article was put back in the place assigned to it in the inventory. Nothing was missing. M. d'Houdetot was annoyed by this scrupulousness, but even more so by the regret openly expressed by all classes at the transfer of M. de La Tour du Pin. He found a pretext for returning to Ghent and stayed there until our departure, which was fixed for the 2nd of April. My daughter's marriage was to be on the 1st of April.[2]

My husband could say with Guzman: 'J'étais maître dans ces lieux, seul j'y commande encore.'[3]

He therefore summoned M. Malaise, the Chief of Police, and asked him to prevent any too open expression of popular feeling during our daughter's marriage. For the same reason, the Mayor, the Duc d'Ursel, arranged to conduct the civil marriage at a very

---

[1] The King of Wurtemburg's army fought in Napoleon's campaigns from 1802 until 1813. After the battle of Leipzig, he deserted to the Allies and his troops marched with them into France. (T)

[2] An error of memory by the author: the civil marriage took place on the 20th of April, 1813.

[3] Literally: 'I have been master in these places and I alone command here still'. Guzman was a character in Voltaire's tragedy *Alzire ou les Américains*. (T)

late hour—at ten o'clock in the evening. That did not prevent people from crowding into all the streets through which we had to pass and also around the Town Hall, which was brilliantly lit. On all sides one heard expressions of regret and goodwill towards M. de La Tour du Pin. When, after the ceremony in the Town Hall, we returned to Mme de Trazegnies' house, we found all the ground floor reception rooms brilliantly lit and in the street, beneath the windows, all the musicians of the city were waiting. They had come to serenade us. My husband was naturally very touched by these proofs of the people's goodwill.

The following day, my daughter was married in the Duc d'Ursel's private chapel. After a fine luncheon for relatives and friends, she and her husband left for Noisy,[1] whither her father-in-law had preceded them by a few hours. I went with them as far as Tirlemont. It was a cruel separation, but I had to look happy none the less. Not long before, my son-in-law had been appointed Sub-Prefect at Amiens. Charlotte and I were therefore, thank God, not to be separated for very long from one another.

But I must tell you more about M. de Chambeau. He had entered into possession of a part of the fortune which belonged to him and spent as much time as possible in Brussels. But his affairs forced him to spend long periods in the south of France. For the past year he had held a post in Antwerp, a temporary one it is true, but it gave promise of advancement. When he heard of the catastrophe which was causing us to leave Brussels so suddenly, knowing the perilous state of our finances, he came to us immediately, and said to M. de La Tour du Pin: 'You are marrying your daughter and you are losing your post. I have 60,000 francs in bonds and will bring them to you. Use them as if they were your own.'

As I write these lines in Pisa in 1844, I am without news of this excellent man. I saw him ten years ago in Paris. Then, he was living in a small country house at Epinay, ruled by two young serving-maids who had won a dangerous influence over him in his old age. They were careful to prevent him moving nearer to us. It is likely that our poor old friend is no longer alive.

[1] The Château de Noisy, near Dinant in the Ardennes, belonging to the de Liedekerke·Beaufort family.

CHAPTER THIRTY-ONE

I

It was in April 1813 that we arrived in Amiens, where we were to witness events we were far from foreseeing. Our brother-in-law, the Marquis de Lameth, was there when we arrived and his friendly offices had already ensured us a favourable reception from the nobility and leading citizens of the town who, until then, had been most dissatisfied with their Prefects.

The officials were ill-assorted. The Receveur-Général (Collector of Taxes), one of the most important officials in any departmental town, had been a regicide and had committed suicide not long before. His post had been given to his son-in-law, M. d'Haubersaert. One of the magistrates, M. de la Mardelle, the Procureur-Général (Attorney-General) was an ex-officer of a hussar regiment and behaved as if he were still in the army. The Presidents were all utterly vulgar. Their wives were remarkable for their grotesque appearance and ridiculous behaviour. They addressed their husbands in public as 'ma poule' or 'mon rat'.[1] The General commanding the division was M. d'Aigremont, whose wife was pretty and good natured. Such society was quite unacceptable to Charlotte and me and I was careful to ensure at the very outset that my circle of acquaintance should include only the more important local families. The Régiment des Chasseurs de La Garde was garrisoned at Amiens, under the command of a major, M. Le Termelier, a very agreeable, well-bred man. The de Bray family, who were very highly esteemed merchants of Amiens, were also among those we knew, together with many others whose names I have unfortunately forgotten.

The house used as the Prefecture was charming. It had just been re-furnished and everything was new, elegant and very comfortable. One apartment was on the ground floor, and it was there that my husband and I lived. Next to it, was the Prefect's

[1] Roughly equivalent to 'ducks' and 'my pet'. (T)

office, which communicated directly with the other offices. All the rooms opened on to a magnificent and well-stocked garden of seven or eight acres. It was almost as pleasant as living in the country.

The first part of the summer passed very agreeably. We often dined at country houses where our neighbours were spending the summer: Mme d'Hauberville, the Rougé family, M. de Vismes, the Marquis de Lameth. My daughter Cécile, then about thirteen, was already a very talented musician and had a charming voice with a good range. During our five years in Brussels, I had had an excellent Italian master for her. He came from Rome, and since he spoke no French, my daughter had become accustomed to speaking to him in the fine Roman dialect, and by now spoke it fluently. Charlotte and she not only read in Italian, but also in English. We were living very comfortably there when the first rumbles of the approaching storm were heard. Public confidence in Napoleon's fortunes was so great that no one would ever have admitted that he had any enemy to fear except the frost and snow which had been so fatal to his Russian campaign.

Yet, after the Battle of Leipzig,[1] there had been the first requisitionings and levies, the compulsory conscription of men and the formation of the Gardes d'Honneur.[2] This last measure spread consternation in many a family.

To face such problems, M. de La Tour du Pin needed all the firmness of which he was capable. He served the Government loyally. The possibility of a restoration had not then occurred to him. He neither looked for it nor desired it. All the errors and vices which had been at the root of the first revolution were still too vivid in his memory for him to consider a return of the exiled royal family with anything but misgiving. Their weakness would bring in its train abuses of every kind. The remark which

[1] Sometimes known as the Battle of the Nations. It lasted for three days in October 1813 and resulted in the defeat of Napoleon and the destruction of what remained of the Grande Armée. His opponents were Russia, Prussia, Sweden and Austria. It should have been possible for Napoleon to win, but he was overtaken by one of the curious fits of lassitude which were beginning to afflict him, lost vital time and the French were driven back. (T)

[2] A Corps of Napoleon's Imperial Guard. The corps, consisting of four regiments, was created in 1813, after the defeat of Leipzig. It was recruited among the upper classes, and disbanded in 1814. (T)

has since been so well justified: 'They have forgotten nothing and learned nothing' was often in his mind. But he did try, so far as it lay in his power, to soften the hardship involved in forming the Gardes d'Honneur. It was among the wealthy that resistance to some of the new measures was strongest and I have often heard him say: 'They give their children more readily than they give their money.' In a wool manufacturing town like Amiens, the levies were very heavy and my husband dreaded most of all the greed and dishonesty of those charged with collecting them.

It was not until we heard the booming of the cannon at Laon that we realised there was a possibility of our part of the country being invaded. A few days later, M. d'Houdetot, Prefect of Brussels, fleeing before the invasion, entered our salon at the very moment when the Receveur-Général, optimistic M. d'Haubersaert, was telling us that he had just received a letter from Brussels and that Belgium was secure against any sudden attack.

Soon afterwards came the news that a Cossack formation commanded by General Geismar had appeared in the plains surrounding Amiens. It was at this point that Général Dupont[1] passed through Amiens under police escort. He had already been transferred from the Château de Joux—where Napoleon had had him shut up after the capitulation of Baylen—to the fortress of Doullens. He was then being taken to Tours so that he could not be set free by the allies. He got no further than Paris, and it was the rigorous severity of his treatment that saved him.

They came so close that we could watch them from the bell tower of the Cathedral. The squadron of Chasseurs stationed in the town under the command of our amiable Major, rode out to meet them, and frightened them so thoroughly that they disappeared and were not seen again.

My daughter, Charlotte, was awaiting the birth of her baby. We did not dare to leave her at the Prefecture, for if the town were captured, it would be among the first houses to be pillaged. An apartment was most generously put at our disposal and we

[1] Général Comte Pierre-Antoine Dupont de l'Etang, 1765–1840. In 1791, he became aide-de-camp to Général Theobald Dillon. He was one of Napoleon's most brilliant generals, victorious everywhere until 1808, when he had to surrender at Baylen, in Spain. Napoleon was unforgiving and imprisoned him at Joux. After the Restoration he was successively Minister of War, and a member of the Privy Council. (T)

settled her there with her sister Cécile, and yourself, my dear son. We also transferred to it most of our personal belongings; my husband and I remained at the Prefecture.

One evening, a man we had never met before, Merlin de Thionville, arrived from Paris saying that he had been instructed to form a 'corps franc'.[1] He carried an order from the Minister of Police, Rovigo, empowering him to enrol any prisoner except those held for capital crimes. He marched off all his ne'er-do-wells and none of them was ever heard of again.

II

My aunt, Mme d'Hénin, was spending the autumn with the Princesse de Poix at the Château de Mouchy, near Beauvais. Mme de Duras and her daughters were also there and I was invited to join them for a few days. M. de La Tour du Pin told me to accept and asked me to return by way of Paris in order to see M. de Talleyrand and hear the latest news. M. de Talleyrand had sent him a note by M. de Thionville, but it was such nonsense, and the reputation of the bearer was so bad that my husband, far removed from intrigues, strongly suspected that he was being involved despite himself in some scheme of M. de Talleyrand's, for he would stop at nothing and had no scruple whatsoever in leading people into danger and then abandoning them in order to save himself.

I left for Mouchy, and spent three days there. I arrived two hours before dinner and after paying my respects to the good Princesse de Poix and to my aunt, went up to see Mme de Duras. I found her in a very bad humour indeed. She had already quarrelled with her son-in-law, Léopold de Talmond,[2] after a series of ridiculous scenes and they had reached the point of writing their arguments to each other in letters four pages long, headed 'From my own apartment'—just like the *Spectator*. She poured out her woes to me and then showed me a letter from Léopold. It had been written that very morning, and its contents convinced me that he was in the right from beginning to end. I said so, with the frankness of affectionate and sincere friendship.

[1] Any volunteer unit raised in time of war. (T)
[2] Prince Léopold de Talmond, who had married Mlle Felicie de Duras.

Her anger was diverted to me and I spent the next two days trying to persuade her to listen to reason, but without success. Mme de Poix was very weary of the scenes which Mme de Duras made in the salon, at table and before the servants, but she lost all hope of their ceasing when I admitted that my influence, too, had failed.

I left in the morning after breakfast, to return to Amiens by way of Paris. Since I did not intend staying overnight, I went to the apartment of M. de Lally, who was at Mouchy.

Stopping only long enough to make a slight change of dress, I went straight to the house of M. de Talleyrand. He was alone and received me, as always, with the amiable courtesy of long friendship. Much ill has been spoken of him—less, perhaps than he deserved, though many of the criticisms were, in fact, ill-founded—and it might have been said of him, as Montesquieu wrote of Caesar: 'This man without a fault, but with many vices.' And yet, despite it all, he possessed greater charm than I have known in any other man. Attempts to arm oneself against his immorality, his conduct, his way of life, against all the faults attributed to him were vain. His charm always penetrated the armour and left one like a bird fascinated by a serpent's gaze.

There was nothing particularly remarkable in our conversation that day. I noticed merely that he repeated rather pointedly that M. de La Tour du Pin was 'well placed' in Amiens. I told him that I intended to leave the following morning and he told me not to do so. He said the Emperor was expected the very next day, that he would be seeing him and would come to fetch me on his way back and let me know for what hour I should order my post horses. It would certainly not be before ten o'clock in the evening.

I went home feeling very annoyed at being kept a further twenty-four hours in Paris. After writing to my husband to warn him of the delay, I tried next day to occupy my time by lunching with my good friend, Mme de Maurville, and by making various calls. Paris seemed very dull, but before nightfall I heard salvos announcing the Emperor's arrival. The great man was returning to his capital, but with the enemy close behind.

At ten o'clock, my horses were put to and waiting at the door. The postilion was growing impatient, and so was I, when at eleven o'clock, M. de Talleyrand arrived.

'What madness to set out in this cold, and in a barouche, too! Whose house is this?'

I told him it belonged to Lally. Taking a candle from the table, he began to study the engravings hanging in fine frames around the walls of the room: 'Ah, Charles II, James II, just so.' And he put the candlestick back on the table.

'Heavens,' I cried, 'what is all this talk of Charles II and James II? You have seen the Emperor. How is he? What is he doing? What does he say after a defeat?'

'Oh, don't talk to me about your Emperor. He's finished.'

I asked him what he meant and was told: 'He is a man who will go to ground.' At the time this description did not shock me so greatly as it did after the events which followed. I was, indeed, aware of M. de Talleyrand's hatred of and rancour against Napoleon, but had never heard him express it so bitterly. I asked him many questions, but he only replied: 'He has lost all his stores and equipment. He has shot his bolt. It's all over.' Then he felt in his pocket and drew out a paper printed in English. Throwing two logs on the fire, he added: 'Let's burn a little more of poor Lally's wood. Here, since you understand English, read this passage,' and he pointed to a fairly long article marked in pencil in the margin. I took the paper and read: 'Dinner given by the Prince Regent for Mme la Duchesse d'Angoulême.'

I stopped and looked up at him. But his face was inscrutable, and he only said: 'Well, go on. Your postilion is getting impatient.' I went on reading. The article described the dining-room hung with sky-blue satin decorated with bunches of lilies, the centre-piece on the table decorated with the same royal flower, the Sèvres service with its views of Paris and so on. When I came to the end, I stopped and stared at him in amazement. He took the paper, folded it slowly and put it back into his enormous pocket, saying with that shrewd, malicious smile that was so characteristic of him: 'Ah, how stupid you are. And now, away with you, but don't catch cold.' And ringing the bell, he told my servant to call my carriage to the door. He left me then, calling out as he put on his coat: 'Give Gouvernet my good wishes. I am sending him this news for lunch. You will arrive in time.'

I reached Amiens so early that M. de La Tour du Pin was still in bed. Without losing a minute, I told him about the conversation I have just described. It had been puzzling me all through the night and I had been unable to sleep. My husband saw in it an explanation of certain embarrassed remarks made by Merlin de Thionville and told me not to say a word about it, for, he said, if it was by such means that the Bourbons meant to regain the throne, they would not remain on it long.

III

A few days earlier, a special envoy had arrived in Amiens to speed up, so he said, the recruitment for the Gardes d'Honneur. He was a young 'auditeur' of the Conseil d'Etat, a young man of charming appearance and very elegant manners. His name was M. de Beaumont. Gradually, his excessive pretensions became apparent. There was nothing in his behaviour to justify reproach or open censure, but M. de La Tour du Pin had him very closely watched and soon learned that he was in touch with all the riff-raff of the town. Our son, Humbert, had brought with him from Florence a young Italian whom my husband had appointed to a post in the Prefecture and who also gave Italian lessons to my daughters. He was exceedingly intelligent and the task of keeping track of the activities and movements of M. de Beaumont was entrusted to him. It did not take him long to discover M. de Beaumont's intrigues against my husband, his connection with all the former terrorists of the town, as well as his dealings with André Dumont, Sub-Prefect of Abbeville.

M. de La Tour du Pin decided to get rid of M. de Beaumont. He called him to his office and told him without preamble that his conduct was known and that it endangered the peace of the town, for which the Prefect was responsible. He therefore required M. de Beaumont to leave Amiens within an hour and the Department within two hours. My husband added that if he did not comply willingly with this order, two policemen waiting in the ante-room would take him into custody. The man was so surprised by this ultimatum that he did not dare to resist.

At the same time, my husband sent Humbert to Paris to discover what was going on there. My son had been driven from his Sub-Prefecture by the Wurtembergers and had been in Amiens for the past fortnight. He had taken refuge with us as he was in poor health and needed care. He had been taken ill in Sens with a pleurisy, and this illness was at its height just when the enemy advanced on the town. He wanted, at all costs, to avoid being taken prisoner, and left Sens at the last minute, in the middle of the night, taking with him two sick soldiers he had been sheltering at the Prefecture. He had himself set on a horse, with one of the soldiers riding postilion to hold him in the saddle. In that fashion, they set out for Melun, and by the time they arrived, he was half-dead. However, the two soldiers looked after him so well that two days later they were able to put him into a carriage and bring him to Paris, to the house of Mme d'Hénin, where he completed his recovery. From there, he came to Amiens to join us. To reward the two men who saved him, he had them enrolled in the Garde. He was to meet them again at Ghent.

When Humbert arrived at M. de Talleyrand's house in Paris, he found the Emperor Alexander[1] staying there. Humbert spent the night on a bench, M. de Talleyrand having charged him on no account to move from it as he wanted to be able to lay hands on him the minute he judged it time for him to set out for Amiens. At six o'clock in the morning, M. de Talleyrand tapped him on the shoulder. Humbert saw that he was fully dressed and wearing his wig. 'Go now,' M. de Talleyrand told him, 'wear a white cockade and shout "Long Live the King".'

Humbert was not entirely sure that he was awake. But rousing himself, he set out for Amiens where the news of these events had already begun to filter through and where M. de La Tour du Pin was wondering whether to confirm or deny the rumours. But public opinion soon made itself heard. All classes had been exasperated by the requisitions, the 'Gardes d'Honneur' and so forth. Fear of foreign countries was the spark which set off the smouldering unrest. In less than a minute, as if touched off by electricity, there arose on all sides shouts of 'Long Live the

[1] The Emperor Alexander I of Russia, 1777–1825. A mixture of autocrat, Jacobin and mystic. Openly admired French institutions, and admired and mistrusted Napoleon. After the latter set fire to Moscow he hated him bitterly and felt he had received a divine mission to become the peacemaker of Europe. He was the most powerful monarch in Europe after the fall of Napoleon and worked hard to organise its re-settlement.

King'. People rushed into the Prefecture courtyard, clamouring for the white cockades which Humbert had stowed away in the luggage space of the barouche before leaving Paris. His stock was soon exhausted, but I managed to save enough for the officers who came to receive them from me, led by good Major Le Termelier. But the expression on their faces belied the sincerity of their action: it was clearly against their inclination. Only one among them, an elderly man with white moustaches, said to me quietly: 'I wear it again with pleasure.' The younger ones looked gloomy and sad. It seemed to them that glory was withdrawing beyond their reach.

During the day, as rumours of the arrival of Louis XVIII became increasingly general, people began to pay their court to M. de La Tour du Pin and to me. A few days later, when it was learned that the Prefect was going to Boulogne to meet the King and that His Majesty would stop at Amiens and spend the night at the Prefecture, many people came to offer me articles of all kinds with which to decorate the house: clocks, vases paintings, flowers, orange shrubs and so on.

M. de Duras, who was due to begin his year of attendance upon the King, had passed through the town on his way to meet him at Boulogne. Despite the upheavals, he retained all the prejudice, hatred, pettiness and bitterness of an age that was over. It was as if there had never been a revolution and, though he has denied it, there is no doubt that in his heart he was still as convinced as in his youth that 'the mob must sweat'—a conviction we ourselves had heard him voice.

M. de Poix also set out for Boulogne, but went no further than Amiens. He was very anxious about the reception he would get from the King, for his son, Juste de Noailles, was an Imperial Chamberlain and his daughter, a Lady-in-Waiting to the Empress. In vain did I tell him that, like so many other families, he had paid a terrible toll to the Revolution, for both his father and his mother had perished. He was not reassured. However, I had no time to spend reasoning with him, trying to bolster his courage. I entrusted this task to my daughter and busied myself with the arrangement of a table for twenty-five persons, to be presided over by the King. While I was in the dining-room, a gentleman came in and spoke to my servant in a manner which displeased me. I went over to him and asked him straightly what concern it was of his. He thought to awe me by saying he was a member of the King's suite, and was greatly surprised when he realised that I was fully determined to remain mistress in my own house and little disposed to allow him to give orders there. He went off grumbling—it was M. de Blacas.[1]

M. de La Tour du Pin had sent me word that the King had received him with much kindness and that he and Mme la Duchesse d'Angoulême[2] would sleep at the Prefecture. Everything was ready by the agreed time. Twelve young ladies of the town, led by my daughter, Cécile, whose fourteen-year-old charm was delightful, were ready to present bouquets to Madame.

The carriage containing the King and Madame was drawn by the company of millers of Amiens, who claimed their ancient privilege. These men, fifty to sixty strong, all wearing new suits of light grey cloth and wide hats of white felt bought at their own expense, drew the royal carriage first to the Cathedral, where the Bishop sang a *Te Deum*. The doors of the Cathedral had been kept shut and not until the King was seated in his chair at the altar steps were they flung open. Then came a roar as of a flood breaking its banks, and in less than a minute that enormous church was so closely packed with people that not even a grain of dust could have fallen to the floor.

When I think now of the multitude of stupidities which cost his brother, Charles X, his throne, I feel almost ashamed of the emotion I felt then, at the sight of that old man[3] thanking God for restoring him to the throne of his fathers. Madame, who was in tears, prostrated herself at the foot of the altar and I shared with all my heart the feelings she was experiencing. Alas! My illusions were to last less than twenty-four hours.

[1] Favourite of Louis XVIII. A rigid reactionary who had to be dismissed in 1814. (T)
[2] Daughter of King Louis XVI, married to the Duc d'Angoulême, elder son of the Comte d'Artois. Later referred to as 'Madame'.
[3] When Louis XVIII returned to France in May 1814, he was nearly sixty, gouty and obese. He was plagued, as during his exile, by ultras like the Comte d'Artois, the Duchesse d'Angoulême and his favourite, the Comte de Blacas. But he was, as always, clear sighted and a good diplomat. He had led the royalist movement inside and outside France since 1791, for he left at the same time as his brother, Louis XVI, but by a different route. He spent the last seven years of his exile in England.

Next, the millers drew the King's carriage to the Prefecture. Before dinner, the King received the municipality and the entire city, both men and women. He received them with the courtesy and ready interest, as well as the wit and charm with which he had been so generously blessed. At seven o'clock, we sat down to dinner. It was excellent and the wines were perfect, a fact which the King particularly appreciated and which brought me many kind compliments. It was only then that M. de Blacas realised that this Prefect's wife whom he, a plain gentleman from Provence, had thought he could address in such a cavalier fashion, was in fact a lady of the former Court. He was overcome with confusion at his blunder and tried—unsuccessfully—to cajole me into forgetting the incident.

IV

My cousin, Edward Jerningham, and his charming wife, Emily Middleton, had accompanied the King from England to France. The King very graciously declared that Edward had served his cause by the articles he had written in the English papers. They had had a great success. Both Edward and his wife were afraid that Madame's thoroughly English manner of dressing would be far from pleasing to the members of Napoleon's Court who had gathered at Compiègne to await their new sovereign. Both of them realised that it was essential for the first impression not to arouse antagonism. At their urging, I spoke of this to Mlle de Choisy, later Mme d'Agoult, Lady-in-Waiting to Madame, and also to M. de Blacas, who mentioned it to the King. But the obstinacy of the Princess was immovable.

Alas, it was not to be the only reproach she earned during her short stay in Amiens.

On the morning of her departure, I presented several ladies to her. One was Mme de Maussion, née de Fougerai, wife of the Rector of Amiens University, a woman of noble virtue and conduct and worthy of the greatest respect. Respect is indeed not too strong a word, as you will see from the following incident, which I related to Mlle de Choisy: Mme de Maussion was a prisoner in the Conciergerie at the same time as the Queen. She was given an opportunity to escape, and found means to suggest to that unfortunate princess that they should exchange clothes, and that she should lie in the Queen's bed, while the Queen left the prison. Mme de Maussion was only eighteen at the time and such devotion on the part of such a very young woman surely deserved at least a courteous acknowledgement. This it did not receive. Madame did not even speak to her. I do not know which was stronger in me, amazement or indignation. I have never forgotten the incident, and looking back over the past thirty years, feel that what has happened since has, after all, been just.

My son-in-law, no longer French, but a subject of the new King of the Netherlands[1]—that same Prince of Orange whom I had met in England when his fortunes were so precariously low—returned to Brussels with my daughter in order to re-join his family. I missed them terribly. I returned to Paris, and my husband and I established ourselves in a pretty apartment at No. 6 Rue de Varenne. Our son, Humbert, came to live with us.

On the very evening of my arrival, I went with Mme de Duras to a fête given by Prince Schwarzenberg, Generalissimo of the Austrian forces. There I saw all the victors and also all the petty meannesses which surrounded and, indeed, almost overwhelmed them.

It was the oddest spectacle, to anyone given to reflection. Everything recalled Napoleon: the furnishings, the supper, the people. I could not help thinking that not one of all the people there—some of whom had trembled in defeat before him, others who had courted his favour, even so small a favour as a smile—was worthy to be his conqueror. Despite its profound sadness, it was an undeniably fascinating situation. Mme de Duras was aware of nothing beyond her own good fortune in being the wife of the First Gentleman of the Bedchamber for that year. The downfall of such a great man as the Emperor, the invasion of the country, the humiliation of being a guest of the victor did not seem to trouble her. I myself felt a shame which was probably shared by no one else in the whole gathering.

M. de La Tour du Pin foresaw that a career in the administration, though greatly to his taste, would place him in a lower social category than that to which he had been born. He therefore

[1] King William I of the Netherlands.

thought it best to resume his diplomatic career at the point where the Revolution had interrupted it. M. de Talleyrand, Minister for Foreign Affairs, offered him The Hague. The new King of Holland favoured his appointment and M. de La Tour du Pin accepted it willingly, though it would not have been unreasonable for him to have expected a more senior post. But a remark of M. de Talleyrand: 'Take that post for the time being,' led him to think it was intended to employ him in some other capacity.

My son, Humbert, unfortunately succumbed to the attraction of becoming a member of the King's military Household. Général Dupont, now Minister for War, had once been aide-de-camp to my father and was therefore very well disposed towards me. Humbert wished to marry and so preferred to remain in Paris rather than to be sent as Prefect to some small town in a distant part of France. His charming appearance, his wit, his manners and breeding gave him the entrée to all the best houses in Paris, at every level. He was appointed a Lieutenant in the Mousquetaires Noirs (Black Musketeers), so called on account of their black horses, and this gave him the rank of major in the army.

CHAPTER THIRTY-TWO

I

At the time when it was decided to hold a Congress in Vienna, I happened one morning to be in M. de Talleyrand's office. M. de La Tour du Pin had gone to Brussels to attend the coronation of the new King, William I, and to present his letters of credence. He was to return within a few days.

I was just leaving and already had my hand on the door when, looking at M. de Talleyrand, I saw an expression on his face which I knew meant that he wanted to play one of his trump cards. He asked me when my husband would be back. I said I expected him the following day.

'Well, hurry his return, as he must leave for Vienna.'

'For Vienna?' I asked. 'Why?'

'So you have not understood. He is to go to Vienna as our Minister and when the Congress meets, he will be one of our ambassadors.'

I exclaimed in surprise, but he added: 'It is a secret. Don't speak about it and send him to me the minute he gets out of his carriage.'

I waited impatiently for my husband to come, keeping my good news secret from everyone except my son, Humbert.

This appointment caused much jealousy. Mme de Duras was furious. She had wanted the post for M. de Chateaubriand, for whom her attachment was then at its height. Adrien de Laval refused to be consoled, even when promised the embassy in Spain. On all sides there were accusations of corruption because my husband was also to retain his post at The Hague.

We held a family council and decided, to my great disappointment, that M. de La Tour du Pin should go to Vienna alone and that I would remain in Paris to arrange a marriage for Humbert. M. de La Tour du Pin wrote to Auguste, our son-in-law, who was already thinking of entering on a diplomatic career in his own country, and invited him to join him in Vienna as his private secretary, or even as an ordinary traveller, since he was no longer French, but once again a subject of the Netherlands. We thought that if M. de La Tour du Pin were to remain in Vienna after the Congress, it would not be difficult to persuade the King of the Netherlands to have Auguste attached to the staff of the Netherlands Legation there. Charlotte and I would then travel to Vienna to join them. These plans, like so many others, were overtaken by events, both personal and national. It was agreed, however, that I would accompany my husband as far as Brussels. There he would collect his son-in-law and I would bring my daughter and her child back to Paris. And that is what we did.

Humbert remained in Paris, and before I set out, I put Aymar to board with a tutor, M. Guillemin, in the Rue Notre-Dame-des-Champs. It was an establishment which had been very highly recommended to me. I had also particularly commended my son to the care of the lady of the house. I had every reason to think he would be well looked after, but you will see later how wrong I was.

Our return journey from Brussels to Paris passed most pleasantly, though I was very sad and disappointed not to be accompanying M. de La Tour du Pin to Vienna. However, there was nothing to suggest that his absence would last as long as it eventually did. And I had been assured that two special couriers would be sent every week from the Ministry of Foreign Affairs, so that I would receive regular and very up-to-date news of my husband.

We travelled by way of Tournai, where we paid long visits not only to the Cathedral, but also to two factories, one producing fine carpets and the other porcelain. We saw the magnificent chalice of St Eleuthera, which had been dug up not long before in a garden where it must have lain hidden since the days of the the very first Frankish invasion. When we reached Paris, we found news of our travellers. I settled into my own apartment and Charlotte took over her father's.

I took her to meet people of my acquaintance. Every day we went to call on the daughters of Mme de Duras—this was always the purpose of our morning walks—or passed our evenings with them. One, Félicie, had married young Léopold de Talmond; the other, Clara, lived at the Tuileries with her mother. My daughter Cécile was still too young, being not yet fifteen, to go into society. Her mornings were devoted to lessons and she only went out in the evening to come with us on a visit to our aunt, Mme d'Hénin, or to Mme de Duras when she did not have company.

Général Dupont continued to be most attentive to my interests and arranged for the Cross of the Legion of Honour to be awarded to Auguste in recognition of his good services as sub-Prefect in Amiens at the time of the Restoration. I sent the decoration on to him in Vienna, and it gave him great pleasure.

Properly speaking, he should have been awarded this decoration at the recommendation of the Abbé de Montesquieu, Minister of the Interior. But I was far from being in favour with him and it would have embarrassed me to seek his good offices in the matter. In any case, I was under no necessity to do so, for neither my husband, who was a diplomat, nor my son, who was a soldier, came under his Ministry. When M. de Montesquieu resumed his cassock, he also reverted to his ecclesiastical manner, but I could never quite forget that I had seen him at the theatre resplendent in a rose-coloured waistcoat, laughing heartily at the jokes of Brunet.[1] Remembering this, his new attitude seemed to me both ridiculous and insincere.

II

As I told you earlier, M. de La Tour du Pin had gone to Boulogne to welcome the King on his return from England. On his way through Abbeville, a Sub-Prefecture of his Department, he thought it his duty to tell the Sub-Prefect, André Dumont, that in view of certain notorious incidents in his past, he did not consider it possible to present him to the King. As Prefect, he considered that the rôle he had played at the Convention and his conduct when sent on special missions as the people's representative, constituted an insuperable barrier to presentation to the new sovereign. M. de La Tour du Pin therefore asked him—and if he refused to comply willingly, the request would have to be considered an order—to find some reason for being absent from Abbeville at the time the King was expected to pass through the town. His duties would be carried out temporarily by one of the Conseillers of the Prefecture.

André Dumont, of bloody memory, accepted this decision. By mutual agreement, it was to remain a secret between him and M. de La Tour du Pin. The King himself was unaware of what had happened. In spite of this, it roused a very bitter resentment in the regicide against his Prefect and immediately after M. de La Tour du Pin's departure for Vienna, he had a pamphlet printed pointing out the forbearance shown to other regicides and contrasting it with the ill-will shown him by my husband, whom he accused of injustice, abuse of power and even of fraud.

I heard from Amiens that this libellous pamphlet had been sent to Paris to be distributed there by M. Benoît, Chief Secretary of the Ministry of the Interior and a friend of Dumont. My son, Humbert, went to see M. Benoît, who received him none too warmly. He did not exactly try to justify Dumont, for that would have been impossible, but he set out to show that my husband's severity had been excessive.

I, in turn, went to see M. Beugnot, Minister of Police, to tell

[1] A comic actor.

him of the publication, which he might be able to stop. That would have been the best solution, for its contents were such as to prejudice M. de La Tour du Pin in his new appointment. It was certain that those who wished him ill would seek to use it.

M. Beugnot was very amiable and helpful, as he always was. The conversation turned to other matters, particularly the plottings of the Bonapartists. At Court and in Royalist drawing-rooms it was the fashion to deny their existence, but to the Minister of Police they were a constant anxiety. After I had talked with M. Beugnot for some time, he asked me if I saw my stepmother, Mme Dillon. I told him that of course I did, where-upon he said: 'Well, then, do her a service. Tell her that Mme Bertrand has no need of "embroidered bonnets".' I longed to know what it was all about, but he said that nothing more was necessary. So I took my leave.

The next day, I went with my daughters to call on my step-mother. She was already suffering from the illness which was to cause her death three years later. After talking of this and that, I said quietly to her as I rose to leave: 'My sister has no need of "embroidered bonnets".' After a startled exclamation, she cried: 'Lucy, who in Heaven's name told you that?' I told her it was M. Beugnot, whereupon she collapsed into her armchair muttering 'All is lost!'

Unfortunately, all was not lost so far as the conspirators were concerned, for everyone obstinately refused to believe in the conspiracy. At the Tuileries, in the Ministries, at the house of Mme de Duras or that of the Duchesse d'Escars, everywhere, the royalists vied with one another in ridiculing the fearful who saw Napoleon around every corner. They made music, danced and amused themselves like children on holiday from school. One evening about that time, Mme de Duras' guests happened to include two or three generals and their wives, the latter all very much be-jewelled. Maréchal Soult and his wife were among them. M. de Caraman, who was standing behind me, leaned over and murmured: 'The eyes of Notre Dame del Pilar are upon you.' There was, indeed, a rumour that the two enormous diamonds gracing the ears of Maréchale Soult had been taken from the miraculous statue of that name which was so greatly venerated throughout Spain. Such brilliant ornaments did not, however, prevent that extremely plain woman from continuing to look like a 'cantinière'.[1]

About this time, my poor Charlotte's daughter[2] died from a teething fever which carried her off within two days. She expired on my knee, and I wept for her as if she had been my own child, though with the added grief of realising her mother's suffering. I tried to distract my poor Charlotte by taking her to spend the next day with Mme d'Hénin while Humbert attended to the sad duty of burying the poor, pretty child whom we all mourned.

No sooner had Humbert joined us at Mme d'Hénin's house than my maid came rushing in, looking quite distraught, to ask him to return home as someone was waiting for him. The maid had spoken very quietly, but Charlotte had none the less heard that this courier was from Vienna, from M. de Liedekerke. Both she and her brother immediately felt the same dread, that something had happened to their father. They hurried down to the courtyard and were away in Humbert's cabriolet before I had any idea of what was happening.

Their fears, thank God, were unnecessary. My husband was in good health, and all that had happened was that the special courier for the week happened to be our son-in-law, Auguste, who had arrived with dispatches. Since he could not stay more than two days, he had hurried to find his wife.

Charlotte's despair at the loss of her baby was so intense that I thought it best to send her to Vienna with her husband. As her father loved her dearly, her presence there would be a great happiness to him too. I had an excellent travelling barouche and undertook to buy and pack everything necessary for the elegant toilettes she would wear at the functions held during the Congress. I also gave her my own maid, a very clever woman. Nothing was lacking to her. Thanks to my usual despatch, it took only two days from the time of making the decision to have my daughter ready to set out, and she was able to leave with her husband. He was carrying despatches from M. de Talleyrand who was still in Paris.

1 Women cooks who travelled with the armies. (T)
2 Marie de Liedekerke Beaufort, born early in 1814.

I was left with my little Cécile, who was then fifteen, and my two sons, Humbert and Aymar. Not long afterwards, Aymar almost died from a pleurisy due to his tutor's negligence. It was my custom to visit him twice a week, on Sundays and Thursdays. On one of these visits, towards the end of November, I was told when I arrived that he had a cold. When they took me to the infirmary, I began to feel anxious. The infirmary was a gloomy room on the ground floor, facing north, and opening on to the courtyard. I was horrified to see that the window and doors were open, the excuse being that the chimney was smoking. I found my son with a high temperature and symptoms which filled me with alarm. I asked to see the doctor of the establishment. He was not expected until the following day. Hearing this, I did not hesitate, but climbed back into my carriage and went to fetch my own doctor, Auvity. He lived in the Rue Duphot, a long way from the Rue de Notre-Dame-des-Champs. Luckily, I found him in, and although anxious about his own young wife, he agreed to come with me.

By the time we reached the school, more than two hours had elapsed and Aymar was worse. Auvity, shocked at finding him in such a miserable room, told me: 'Madame, if you wish to save your child's life, you must take him away from here.' He rolled him up in the bed covers, carried him to the carriage and took us home. For several days, the illness continued to get worse. Auvity came three times a day. On the sixth day, he asked to call in his father[1] and M. Hallé,[2] the leading doctor of the day, for a consultation. They told Humbert he must prepare me for the loss of his brother, saying 'he would not last out the night'. Then, having pocketed a napoleon each for pronouncing sentence, they left, never to return.

But Auvity refused to be discouraged. He sent for a cantharidine waistcoat[3] from the only chemist in Paris who prepared them. It was applied to Aymar's poor little eight-year-old body, already so wasted, and covered it entirely, except for the arms. Mustard poultices were applied to his feet and renewed every quarter of an

---

[1] Chevalier Auvity, Surgeon to the Children of France during the Empire.
[2] A former Physician-in-Ordinary to the Emperor's Household.
[3] A plaster jacket impregnated with cantharidin, used for raising blisters. (T)

hour. Every two minutes, he was given a teaspoonful of some refreshing, nourishing drink. The following day, his body was one large sore, but the fever had gone and Auvity pronounced the words so sweet to a mother's ear—'He is safe now'.

He had a long convalescence. By the time the doctor recommended fresh air and exercise, the weather was so bad that I could not take him out. Then I thought of asking for an artist's pass in order to take him to the museum. Through M. de Duras, I got permission to take him every day, with his nurse. There he could run about as much as he liked. Six weeks later, when the weather had improved sufficiently for it to be safe to take him walking in the Tuileries, he missed the museum and its pictures, of which he knew both the titles and the names of the painters by heart. I have no doubt that those long hours in the museum laid the foundation of Aymar's taste for the arts, and provided him with his first education in that field.

III

Once relieved of anxiety for my son's health, I went out a great deal into society that winter. I used to collect every possible piece of news, all the 'on-dits', and even mere tattle to put into the letters I wrote regularly twice a week to M. de La Tour du Pin. They went by Foreign Office courier and as I lived very near the Ministry, I did not need to seal them until the very last minute —which meant when M. Reinhardt, who had charge of the courier service, sent his messenger to collect them. If these letters had not later been burned, they would have given more point and interest to my memoirs. Now that so many years have passed and old age is upon me, my memory is much dimmed and I feel that many facts and details escape me.

How did I spend my days after the restoration of the monarchy? Firstly, I went to the Tuileries, where the King received the ladies once or twice a week. As a former Lady-in-Waiting to the Queen, I had certain privileges. Instead of mingling with the crowd of ladies in the first salon, that of Diana, to wait for the King to be wheeled into the Throne Room—he could not walk— I went with the other ladies who enjoyed the same privilege straight to my place on the Throne Room benches. There, we always found a number of gentlemen who also had the *entrée* and we would sit comfortably chatting together until the time honoured formula 'The King' brought us to our feet, and forced us to assume a reasonably correct and respectful attitude. Then we passed in turn before the royal chair.

The King always had something amusing or amiable to say to me. For instance, on the feast of St Louis there was a 'grand couvert'[1] in the Gallery of Diana. A barrier was set along almost the entire length of the room to form a passage for all those who wanted to see the horse-shoe table at which the royal family sat. The King sat alone at the head of the table, facing the stares of the curious; on one side of him sat the Duc d'Angoulême and his wife and, facing them, the Duc de Berry and, perhaps, the Duc d'Orléans, though I am not sure about the latter. Behind the King stood the high officers of his Household and the ladies, standing in tiers. On that particular day I had chosen to remain with the crowd in order to walk past the barrier with my daughters. The King saw me among the people and called out: 'It's just like Amiens!' That brought me considerable respect from the good people about me.

During that winter, the Duc de Berry gave two balls to which he invited all the leaders of Bonapartist society: the Duchesses de Rovigo, de Bassano and so on. They did not dance and appeared to be in very bad tempers, despite the attentions of the Prince and his aides-de-camp. Mme de Duras and I took Albertine de Staël to these balls. We had achieved a metamorphosis in her dress, managing at last to persuade her mother—herself always very carelessly and unsuitably dressed—to allow us to use our own taste. It was an enormous task, for it meant re-making everything, even to her chemises. But the change was acclaimed as such an improvement that she renounced there and then her former English styles. The Duc de Broglie was much in love with her, and I think I am right in thinking that it was at one of these balls that he decided to ask her mother for Albertine's hand in marriage.

Since I have mentioned Mme de Staël again, this is the place to tell you that when she returned to Paris shortly after the Restoration, I resumed my old acquaintance with her. I had seen her

[1] A formal dinner which the King and the Royal Family ate in public. ('T')

earlier, when I returned from England in 1800 shortly before Napoleon obliged her to leave Paris, and again at various other times. On 18 Fructidor, when still closely associated with Benjamin Constant, she had been very revolutionary. But her ideas changed during her stay in England and she came back from there a royalist. She entertained brilliantly, and with much kindness, all the notables from European countries who flocked to Paris during the winter of 1814–1815.

I happened to be in Mme de Staël's drawing-room on the evening the Duke of Wellington arrived in Paris. A hundred other persons were gathered there, all as eager as I to see this already famous man. My own acquaintance with him went back to childhood: we were of much the same age and his mother, Lady Mornington, had been a very great friend of my grandmother, Mme de Rothe. We had spent many an evening together, the young Arthur Wellesley, his sister, Lady Anne, and I. In later life, I had met Lady Anne in England, at Hampton Court, when I went to visit the Prince of Orange, the old Stadtholder. The Duke greeted me as an old friend, and was delighted to find someone in that large salon who could understand and answer his questions, for he knew no one and was the cynosure of every eye.

Among those presented to him was a man who longed to speak to the hero of the day: none other than M. de Pradt, the former Archbishop of Malines. Mme de Staël introduced them, and when M. de Pradt had made sure that the Duke spoke perfect French, he began to explain Europe and France to him. He talked for half-an-hour without stopping. The Duke himself was barely allowed time to insert a word, and whenever he did manage to do so, the Archbishop took it for granted that it was one of admiration. M. de Pradt's prodigious conceit often carried him beyond the limits of taste: for example, when speaking of the Emperor, he had the audacity to say: 'And one day, my Lord, Napoleon said to me: "There is only one man who can prevent me becoming master of Europe . . ." '—and while everyone waited for him to continue '. . . and that man, my Lord, was you', they heard him saying instead: '. . . and that man, my Lord, was I'!

IV

M. de Blacas lived in considerable state. His overweening complacency did not allow him to admit the smallest possibility of a plot. He shrugged his shoulders and laughed contemptuously at those who were inclined to think that Napoleon might not be far away.

One day, Humbert came in with a very worried face. On his way back from the headquarters of the Mousquetaires, he had met two generals—I cannot remember their names, but one of them was a mulatto—whom he had known quite well at Sens. They had invited him to lunch with them at the Jardin Turc and Humbert had accepted. After oysters and champagne, these gentlemen had begun to sound him on the progress the government was making, the general discontent, and expressed their regret at being no longer in the Emperor's service. Then, their tongues loosened by the champagne, they made certain very indiscreet remarks which startled Humbert and made him very anxious. He was far from suspecting Napoleon's audacious landing on the French coast, but the conversation of his two companions at lunch had shown him very clearly that a summons to the Emperor's standard was being prepared. These two generals were by no means prominent men, but it was easy for Humbert to guess the identity of the real leaders of the conspiracy—Queen Hortense in particular, at whose house the Comité Directeur Bonapartiste (Bonapartist Committee of Direction) held its meetings. He told Mme de Duras about this luncheon and what he had heard. She, too, thought it very disquieting and told her husband. He in turn told the King, but M. de Blacas was there to soften the anxiety and ridicule those who believed that the Emperor would return.

One evening in early March, I was in the apartment of Mme de Duras at the Tuileries, at a large gathering which included Général Dulauloy and his wife. My curiosity was aroused by two or three almost imperceptible signs I had observed passing between the General and his wife which seemed to mean: 'No, they know nothing.' Mme Dulauloy looked rather fearful and seemed anxious to take her leave. This was especially evident when M. de Duras passed through the salon on his return from the King's 'coucher' (retiring). Her colour rose, and she got up to leave, taking her husband with her. I remained until the last, waiting for Mme de Duras to return from her husband's room, for she had followed him there. When she appeared I saw that she was very troubled and she told me: 'Something terrible has happened, but Amédée will not say what it is.' I returned home with Humbert and, as is so often the case, we guessed at all the possible causes except the right one. Next morning, news of the landing in the Golfe Juan spread through Paris, brought by Lord Lucan. He had left the previous evening for Italy and several stages from Paris had met the courier arriving from Lyon with the news. He returned immediately to Paris and made it known.

The consequences of that landing belong to history, so I will only tell you how it affected me, personally.

I had too thorough a knowledge of the Court on the one hand and of the strength of Napoleon's supporters on the other to doubt, even for a moment, the efficacy of the measures which would be taken.

Although M. de La Tour du Pin was one of the four Ambassadors of France to the Congress of Vienna and was dealing temporarily with the diplomatic affairs of France in Austria, he was still French Minister in Holland. I decided that I could not remain in Paris when Napoleon might arrive at any minute, and thought it best to go to Brussels or The Hague. My plans were submitted to the King by M. de Jaucourt, Deputy Minister for Foreign Affairs. The King approved my decision, so I began making my preparations.

From the moment it was decided that the King would leave, Humbert had to remain at the headquarters of the Mousquetaires. As a result, I had to make all the arrangements for the journey completely on my own, and would be accompanied only by my daughter Cécile, who was sixteen, and my son Aymar, who was eight.

I remember that there were many petty difficulties and that I overcame them with my usual calm. So many years have passed since then that they are no longer of interest, but there is one incident about which I must tell you. I had called on the Minister of Finance during the evening to collect my husband's salary, wishing to take it with me. The King was to leave the same evening at midnight. I had known the Minister fairly well for a long time and when I reached his office, I found him in a terrible rage: 'Look,' he said, showing me about a hundred small casks similar to those in which anchovies are sold. 'I have had these casks made especially and they each contain ten to fifteen thousand francs in gold. I meant to give one to each member of the body-guard accompanying the King, but those fine gentlemen refuse to take them, declaring that such tasks are not among their duties.' While he was telling me this, he signed my receipt and I went immediately to collect the money. I took it to my man of business to have it changed into gold. I had asked M. Louis to give me one of the casks of gold in his office, but he had absolutely refused. It was after nine o'clock when I left my man of business, and he told me to come back at eleven o'clock, when he would give me the gold he would meantime have procured. I went to say goodbye to Mme d'Hénin, who had also decided to leave. I found her with M. de Lally, in a state of indescribable confusion: packing, gesticulating urging on her portly friend.

I returned to the Rue Saint-Anne on the stroke of eleven and was given twelve thousand francs in piles of napoleons. I had hired a cabriolet and as I got back into the carriage, told the coachman to take me home. I was living at 6 Rue de Varenne. We wanted to take the road through the Carrousel, but on account of the King's departure, it was shut. The coachman drove me along the Rue de Rivoli and just as he was about to cross the Pont Louis XVI, he heard midnight strike. He stopped dead and told me that not for anything in the world would he go one step further. He said he lived at Chaillot, that the gates had to be shut at midnight, asked for his fare and said I could continue my journey on foot.

In vain did I use all the eloquence of which I was capable, promising him a magnificent reward if he would take me even as far as a fiacre. but he refused. I had to get out, and was terribly afraid. Fortunately, just at that moment, I heard the sound of a carriage. It was a fiacre and, thank Heaven, empty. I rushed towards it, offering the coachman a generous fee to take me home.

As soon as I reached the house, I sent for post horses. Despite the fact that my journey was official and despite the Minister's signature on the permit, I had to wait until six o'clock for the two miserable animals to be harnessed to the small barouche which was to carry me, Aymar, my beloved Cécile and a small Belgian maid whom I had brought up and kept in my service.

I spent the long hours of waiting at the window, listening for the sound of the horses arriving. Never have I been more impatient. Men passed continually beneath the window, all walking in the same direction. Most of them were soldiers, recognisable under the street lamps by the gleam of the waxed cloth which covered their shakos. The weather was fine, but they were using this means of hiding their white cockades, and the coverings, decorated with a small cluster of violets, had become a rallying sign.

V

Our journey passed without incident. All we saw was a regiment of cuirassiers cantering in disorderly fashion across the highway near Péronne or Ham. They shouted 'Long Live the Emperor' as they passed.

We arrived safe and sound in Brussels, where I took a very small lodging in the Rue de Namur, in the house of a lawyer named Monsieur Huart. I believe that later on, in the reign of King Leopold, he became a Minister.

I was very impatient for news from Vienna. It was probable that the Foreign Office courier service had been interrupted and although I had written to tell both my husband and Charlotte that I had gone to Brussels, I had many reasons to fear that it would be a long time before news reached me there. And in the event, it was so.

In Brussels I found all my friends, both Belgian and French. Everyone welcomed me warmly, except such Bonapartists as the families of Trazegnies and Mercy.

The King of Holland was in Brussels. I called on him and he received me with every courtesy. As we sat on a sofa in what had once been M. de La Tour du Pin's office, he turned to me and said: 'In this salon I try to discover means to be as well loved as your husband was.' Alas, the poor prince never succeeded. I spoke to him with some insistence about my son-in-law's future. He was a subject of the King, and I think it may have been this conversation of ours which paved the way for his diplomatic career. I should like him to remember that.

Mme de Duras, too, had come to Brussels with her daughter, Clara, and her mother Mme de Kersaint. A few evenings after our arrival, Mme de Kersaint—already in her dotage—was stricken with a sudden apoplexy.

Shortly before this sad happening, Mme de Duras and I were spending the evening together when we were told that a 'gentleman' of our acquaintance wished to speak to us. It was added that he did not dare to present himself in our salon as he was not correctly dressed. At that time, strange happenings did not surprise us, so we went out on to the landing of the Hôtel de France. There, we found a servant bespattered with mud, whom Mme de Duras recognised immediately. The servant opened the door of one of the rooms for us, and on entering we found ourselves in the presence of the Duc de Berry. He told us that the Colonel of a 'corps franc', in other words of a band of brigands, had stolen his baggage, pillaged his carriage and taken everything, even his shirts. As I knew Brussels very well, I undertook to find him a new wardrobe. I immediately put him in touch with good Mme Brunelle, and was delighted to be able to put such a profitable occasion in her way.

Shortly afterwards, my dear daughter Charlotte arrived from Vienna, travelling alone with her maid and her father's servant. She brought me news that the Congress had dissolved on learning of Napoleon's landing at Cannes. Everyone had rushed away at top speed and the allies, who had all been on the verge of becoming enemies, had buried their differences in the face of the common danger. They had only one idea: to make France pay dearly for her welcome to the hero who, by making her powerful and very glorious, had roused so many enemies against her.

In the southern provinces, the Dauphin[1] had gathered a measure of support which, led by someone else, would have been a force to reckon with. Someone was needed to carry to this

[1] The Duc d'Angoulême. He did not actually become the Dauphin until 1824, when his father succeeded to the throne as Charles X.

prince an assurance that the allied powers were united in their determination to wipe out Napoleon. M. de La Tour du Pin, always prepared to answer the call of duty, agreed to go to Marseilles and join the Dauphin. He set out, and was accompanied as far as Genoa by my son-in-law, who left him there and then returned to Brussels to bring me news of my husband. There, young de Liedekerke was reunited with his wife and I was able to tell him that I had secured for him a place in the service of his King.

Translator's Outline of the French Revolution

The eighteenth century saw a widespread quickening of political, social and religious thought, marked by three main principles: universality of outlook, the judgement of religion, government and social customs by the criterion of humanity, and a critical, often hostile attitude to established Churches. In England, the movement was led by such men as Hume, Locke and Gibbon; in America, by Benjamin Franklin; in France, by Voltaire, Montesquieu, Diderot and Rousseau. Parallel with this philosophical movement was another, also very important—that of the economists: Adam Smith in England; Quesnay, Mirabeau (father of the member of the States-General of 1789) and others in France.

The new ideas were combined with resentment at the heavy burden of taxation everywhere to pay for the wars which had bedevilled the history of the century in the search for a balance of power. For all these reasons, there was unrest in most western countries.

In 1774, against this background, Louis XVI succeeded to the throne of France. His accession was welcomed, for he was not unsympathetic to the need for change and he shared many of the humanitarian hopes of the day. He presided over a sincere effort to reduce privilege, eliminate corruption and devise fairer taxation. But the monarchy remained absolute and the nobility and clergy continued to enjoy their very considerable degree of privilege. This did not correspond with the growing belief in the right of the people to share in government.

The English system of constitutional monarchy was much studied by the French and, led by the Marquis de La Fayette, they took a very active part in the struggle of the American colonists for the right to govern themselves. They became increasingly convinced that similar constitutions and freedoms could be won at home.

But involvement in the American War of Independence greatly aggravated the financial problems of France. Attempts to solve them by economies, by the elimination of corruption and by careful administration failed, and in 1787 the King, who alone had the power to impose taxation, summoned the Assembly of Notables (nobles and clergy) to seek their help. He hoped they would propose the taxation of their own orders, for privilege absolved them from most taxes. But they did not, and advised the King to call the States-General. Next, the King tried to use his right to impose taxation on them, but was prevented by a ruling of a court of law known as the 'Parlement' of Paris.

The King then had no alternative but to summon the States-General, an ancient, advisory body representing the three Estates: Nobles, Clergy and Commons, which had not met since 1614. The representatives gathered at Versailles in May 1789: 285 Nobles, 308 Clergy and 621 Commons. M. Necker, Director General of Finance, and the equivalent of a Prime Minister, had led the movement for double representation of the Commons to reflect the greater number of people of that Estate, and he did so largely in the hope of enabling the Commons to force the imposition of taxes on the other two Estates.

The first task of the States-General was to decide procedure, and here the Commons won a major victory. They refused to accept the old system of three separate chambers with a vote for each Estate, and insisted on a single chamber with a vote for each representative. They also determined to take a large part of the government of the country into their own hands and to assume an appropriate title. On the 17th of June, they decided to call themselves the National Assembly. The next step was to frame a constitution, so the name was soon changed to National Constituent Assembly. Although dominated by the Commons, this Assembly included many representatives of the other Estates.

Discussion so far had centred around everything but finance, and meanwhile taxes went unpaid, poverty and hunger were rife, the harvest was bad, trade was poor and unemployment widespread. There was discontent and growing disorder in town and country. The Court blamed M. Necker for the mounting unrest, and the King dismissed him on the 11th of June 1789. To the people of Paris, this looked like an attempt to prevent reform, and they prepared to assert their independence. For the first time in their long history, they began to organise a municipal government and to create a civic Garde Nationale to defend their rights and property. It was to get arms for this new Garde that the crowd marched on the Bastille on the 14th of July 1789. The Governor of the small garrison surrendered.

Militarily, the victory was of little importance, for the King still disposed of enough loyal forces to crush the rising. But he made no attempt to do so, partly, perhaps, from indecision, but also from sincere humanitarian feeling. Politically, the consequences were immense: the municipal government of Paris was established; on the 15th of July, command of the Garde Nationale was given to the Marquis de La Fayette who ordered the destruction of the Bastille, that symbol of centuries of autocratic rule; M. Necker was re-instated and on the 17th of July, the King paid an official visit to the new Municipality. There, the Marquis de La Fayette presented him with a tricolour cockade—the white of the Monarchy flanked by the colours of Paris, blue and red—in token of reconciliation.

But the mood of Paris was more dangerous than ever. While agitators fomented unrest in the countryside, political newspapers and clubs sprang up in Paris. There was mistrust of the Court, particularly of the Queen and the King's brother, the Comte d'Artois, and a growing demand that the King should move to Paris, away from its influence. There was as yet no disloyalty to the King himself, only a determination that the people should share in the government. On the 5th of October 1789, the people of Paris, angered by a trivial incident at a banquet,[1] marched on Versailles demanding food and the return of the King to Paris. The following day, the King yielded and was escorted with his family, to the Palace of the Tuileries in the heart of Paris. The Assembly followed and from that day, Paris became not only the centre of government, but also the focal point of the Revolution.

Emigration increased. Led by Princes of the royal blood[2] large

---

[1] Description on page 125 of text.
[2] Only the Comte de Provence, the King's brother, and, after the Dauphin, heir to the throne, did not leave France until 1791.

numbers of the nobility left the country. Some regarded the King's concessions with contempt and fear, others refused to live in a France dominated by principles they detested. In the German towns where the Princes settled, small courts were set up and all the talk and planning was of an imminent overthrow of the Revolution. Nothing could have been more disastrous for the Monarchy.

While all this was going on, the Assembly drew up its Declaration of the Rights of Man, which was adopted on the 1st of August 1789. On the 4th of August, feudalism was declared abolished. Next came the political reconstruction, greatly influenced by Montesquieu's theory that the executive, legislative and judicial elements in the State should be separate and counterbalancing. The King, as head of the executive, appointed the chief officers of the Army, and the Ministers of State, but as these Ministers were not allowed to hold a seat in the Assembly there was an unbridged gap between the representatives of the people and the Ministers of the King.

Legislative power was entrusted to a single Chamber of 745 members. The franchise was limited by a property qualification, so that the Assembly remained essentially a middle and upper-middle class body.

The judicial system was re-modelled and judges were elected. The jury system was introduced.

The old system of local and provincial government was abolished. In place of the proud, historic provinces came 83 soulless 'departments'.

Finally, the National Constituent Assembly turned its attention to the Church. In 1790, tithes were abolished and the Church had to surrender all its wealth to the impoverished State. In return, the State undertook to pay salaries to the Clergy. The Assembly then proposed to alter the government of the newly 'established' Church by instituting the election of bishops and priests. This proposal was referred to the Pope, who refused it and threatened to excommunicate anyone putting it into effect. The Assembly retaliated by enforcing on all clergy an oath of obedience 'to the King, the Law and the Nation'. Some priests accepted (Constitutionalists), others refused (Dissidents). The

State continued to pay them all. But this oath divided the French people in their attitude to the Revolution and for the first time it became openly civil war. The King had more or less accepted the Revolution, but he was by nature a strongly religious man and he signed the Church laws only for fear of the storm his refusal would bring. At Easter 1791, he tried to go to his palace at St Cloud to avoid receiving Communion from a constitutional priest, but a suspicious and hostile crowd forced him to return to the Tuileries.

For some time the King had been wanting to get away from Paris to revise and alter the Constitution, particularly that part of it affecting the Church. The Marquis de Mirabeau, the most clear-sighted and conservative of the popular leaders, had strongly urged him to go openly to nearby Rouen, the very prosperous capital of Normandy. There, to summon the Assembly to his side and to make certain changes in the Constitution; but to do all this in such a way that his loyalty to the main principles of the Revolution should remain unquestioned. Unfortunately, neither the King nor the Queen trusted Mirabeau, and his death in April 1791 destroyed the last chance of the plan being carried out. The King decided instead to escape, with the Queen and the Dauphin, to his armies in the north-east, commanded by Général Bouillé, in the hope that they would support him in imposing the alterations he wanted. But at Varennes he was recognised and brought back to Paris.

At this point, some urged a change of dynasty, with the Duc d'Orléans replacing Louis XVI on the throne. The Assembly decided, instead to suspend the King from his royal functions until the new Constitution was completed. Then, if he accepted it, he would be reinstated; if not, a successor would have to be found. For the first time there was serious talk of a republic.

In September 1791, the King accepted the new Constitution and the National Legislative Assembly came into being on the 1st of October 1791. It lasted less than a year. The King's Ministers were of the Right, the Assembly became increasingly of the Left and the people of Paris grew daily more revolutionary and egalitarian.

The appeals of the émigré Princes to foreign powers for help in putting down the Revolution had always been a serious cause of annoyance and danger to the King, and his own flight had aroused great fear of foreign intervention. But none of the European states, not even Austria, wanted a war with France. The Emperor Leopold II, brother of Queen Marie-Antoinette, hoped that something might be done for the French royal pair by diplomacy, threatening a war he had no intention of waging. He arranged a meeting with the King of Prussia at the Castle of Pillnitz, near Dresden, on the 27th of August 1791. From there they issued the so-called Declaration of Pillnitz, stating that the restoration of order in France was a matter that concerned all European states and that, provided other European states would co-operate with them, they would be willing to interfere to secure better conditions for Louis XVI and Marie-Antoinette. Leopold knew that Britain had no intention of co-operating and that the apparent threat was thus nullified. But the French did not know this and saw the Declaration as a threat by all the monarchies of Europe to interfere in their domestic affairs.

At this juncture, the Girondins came into power. Radical, wanting an eventual republic, they felt a foreign war would be a useful way of rousing republican enthusiasm and overthrowing the monarchy. Readiness for war spread. There were hopes of alliances with Britain and Prussia and a speedy victory. The Royalists, too, welcomed the idea of war, hoping it would strengthen the Executive, headed by the King. In March 1792, when negotiations with Austria were already very strained, the Emperor Leopold II died and was succeeded by the inexperienced Francis II. Certain demands made by the French Foreign Office were refused. On the 20th of April, 1792, Louis XVI went to the Assembly and, with tears in his eyes, declared war on Francis, not as Emperor, but as King of Hungary and Bohemia.

French hopes of alliances failed. Britain stood aloof for a time, Prussia joined Austria. France attacked the Austrian Netherlands, where she hoped to find sympathetic support from local revolutionary movements but her campaign was a humiliating failure. In Paris, the Ministers and the people saw this failure not as a consequence of insufficient preparation, but of the treachery of the King.

The way was clear for the resolute minority of Jacobins, the most fanatical in their devotion to the Revolution and to France, to overthrow the throne and seize the government of the country. Power had now passed from the preponderantly conservative and royalist middle classes to the Parisians, notably to the 'sans culottes', for the homespun striped trousers of the workers had become the symbol of revolution and 'culottes' or breeches represented reaction.

The Prussian Duke of Brunswick led the combined Austrian and Prussian armies into France and threatened Paris with total destruction if any further insult were offered the King. The fervour and excitement of the Parisians became more aggressive. On the 10th of August, they invaded the Tuileries, both the Assembly and the Palace. The King and his family took refuge with the Assembly, but it felt powerless before the Commune of Paris and the rioters and decided to pass a decree that very day inviting the French people to elect a National Convention to draw up a new Constitution. It provisionally suspended the King from his functions and three days later handed him over to the newly-appointed Commune of Paris, dominated by Robespierre.[1] At the latter's demand, the Commune became the authority for the examination of crimes against the State, and a Committee of Supervision was appointed for the purpose, led by Marat, able but vicious. As the war news grew worse, the excitement mounted. Danton, Minister of Justice, was given power of house search, to seek out the enemies of the Revolution. Thousands of suspects were seized, tried summarily, often in batches, and condemned to death or even just murdered as they left the tribunal. Those found innocent were sent back to prison. This frenzy culminated in the September Massacres, when many hundreds of people, particularly clergy, were killed in Paris in the three days between the 2nd and 4th of September.

The National Legislative Assembly dissolved itself on the 21st of September 1792, and the new National Convention, elected by universal suffrage, met later in the same day. The authority of the King and his Ministers had already been reduced

[1] M. de La Fayette tried to raise armed protest among his forces, failed, and had to leave the country.

to nothing and on the following day, the 22nd of September 1792, by a unanimous vote, the Monarchy was abolished and France declared a Republic. The Convention was determined that the King should face trial. On the 11th of December, he was charged with plotting against the nation, paying troops raised by the émigrés abroad and attempting to overthrow the constitution. The Convention voted individually in an open ballot and declared the King guilty. By a majority of one vote, it was decided to execute him immediately, and on the 21st of January 1793, he was guillotined in the Place Louis XV, which was re-named the Place de la République. Today, it is the Place de la Concorde.

Early in 1793, England, Holland and Spain joined Prussia and Austria in their war against France. Dumouriez, commander of the French armies in the North, was suspected—like La Fayette before him—of treating with the enemy, and had to leave the country. Inside France, the western province of La Vendée rose in rebellion against the Paris Government's demands in men and money. And thus, military danger and doubt closed the ranks of Frenchmen who might otherwise have protested at the actions of the Convention.

With the death of the King, executive authority ceased to exist and for three years—the most violent of the Revolution—there were bitter personal and party struggles for this power. Effective executive power lay with the Committees, particularly the notorious Committee of Public Safety, which at one time sent its representatives out on missions all over France. The faction which controlled this Committee dominated the police and also exercised judicial power through the Revolutionary Tribunal set up by the Convention in March 1793, at the instance of Robespierre. This Tribunal had the right to arrest and imprison without any proof of guilt. The prisons were crowded, acquittals were rare and the guillotine the only penalty. In October 1793, Queen Marie-Antoinette faced this Tribunal and was sentenced to death. On the 6th of November, Philippe, Duc d'Orléans, a champion of the Revolution, was also sentenced to death because of his connection with Dumouriez.

There were sporadic revolts throughout the country, notably in

Lyon and Toulouse, and the Vendean rebellion assumed the proportions of a civil war, but the Government in Paris—in effect, the Committee of Public Safety—was strong enough to put them down and it inflicted terrible punishment. Though brutal and ruthless, it was efficient and energetic.

The direction of the war was put into the able hands of Carnot. He infused a new energy into the army, gave it improved weapons, better discipline and new ideas in tactics and strategy. By September 1793, this new French army, largely officered by men from the ranks who were ardent supporters of the Revolution, had begun to win its battles. Not the least spur to success was the danger of the guillotine for a general who lost a battle.

In the summer of 1794, the Reign of Terror reached its peak. It culminated in the execution of Robespierre in July and then quickly subsided. Robespierre's death was a victory for the National Convention over the forces of violence working through the Committees. The Convention regained its self-confidence, and authority and power passed at last from the factions in Paris to the elected representatives of the nation. The latter, horrified by the excesses of the preceding few years, became rather more conservative in outlook.

In the spring of 1795, the National Convention turned again to the task for which it had been elected: the making of a constitution, and this time it was determined that there should be safeguards against extremists. This new Constitution was completed in August 1795 and the Convention dissolved itself a month later.

Meantime, in June 1795, the Dauphin had died in prison and the Comte de Provence (later Louis XVIII) had become heir to the throne.

France now entered the period of the 'Directoire' (Directorate). Again there was separation of the powers: executive power was in the hands of a body called the 'Directoire', which consisted of five Directors who presided in turn; legislative power was entrusted to the two Chambers of the 'Corps Legislatif' (Legislative Body). One Director and one-third of the members of each Chamber were re-elected annually.

At first the Government reflected the resurgence of conservative, even royalist feeling in the country. Relief at the return to legality, revulsion from the excesses, both political and religious, of the Robespierre period made a return of the monarchy seem imminent. At this, the Jacobins took fright and when, by 1797, they had gained control of the Directorate they called on the Army, under the command of General Bonaparte to help them arrest deputies hostile to their policies. Napoleon Bonaparte was thenceforth a figure to be reckoned with in political life and when, in 1799, the corrupt, discredited Directorate was again in trouble, people looked to him to get for them the honour and security they sought. In conjunction with his brother Lucien, President of the Council of Five Hundred (one of the two legislative chambers), Siéyès and others, a measure was forced through entrusting provisional government to three Consuls: Bonaparte, Siéyès and Roger-Ducos. A new Constitution was drawn up by Bonaparte promulgated in December 1799 and approved by the nation in a referendum. The Consuls proclaimed that their Constitution marked the end of the Revolution—it certainly marked the end of France's first experiment in democracy.

From 1799 until 1814, the supreme authority in France was Napoleon Bonaparte, in the beginning as First Consul, then as Consul for Life (1802) and finally as Emperor (1804). At each step, he obtained national approval through a plebiscite or a referendum. In practice, the majority of Frenchmen probably supported Napoleon until towards the end of his reign, for despite the demands of his wars, he was tremendously admired for his military and administrative genius and his internal policies were of the greatest importance in the development of the administrative and legal systems of the country.

Appendices

Appendix I

————◆————

*The Story of Monsieur and Madame de la Tour du Pin
from 1815–1853, by Aymar de Liedekerke Beaufort*

The Memoirs of Madame de La Tour du Pin end with the return
of Napoleon from Elba in March 1815. But she lived until 1853,
and from the account written by her great-grandson, Colonel
Comte Aymar de Liedekerke Beaufort in the Preface to the
original edition, we can follow the remainder of her story:

At the time of Napoleon's return to France, Madame de La
Tour du Pin was living, as she herself tells us, in Paris, but thought
it prudent, since her husband was Minister to the Court of the
Netherlands to withdraw to Brussels, where the Court was.
M. de La Tour du Pin was in the Austrian capital, for he was also
one of the Ambassadors Plenipotentiary of France to the Congress
of Vienna. He signed the famous declaration of the Congress on
the 13th of March, 1815 outlawing Napoleon and then went,
with the approval of M. de Talleyrand, the Foreign Minister, to
Toulon to try to stiffen the loyalty of its Governor, Maréchal
Masséna,[1] to the King.

He went next to Marseilles to confer with the Duc de Rivière.[2]
His mission, after that, was to join the Duc d'Angoulême[3] whom
the King had ordered to Nîmes. But while still in Marseilles,
M. de La Tour du Pin heard of the Duc's surrender at Pont
Saint-Esprit and after taking, with the Duc de Rivière, certain
essential measures, he chartered a ship to carry him to Genoa,
meaning to return by that route to Vienna.

However, bad weather, or, more likely, the ill-will of the
Captain forced him to go to Barcelona. From there, he travelled

[1] Formerly one of Napoleon's Marshals. (T)
[2] A close supporter of the Comte d'Artois, brother of the King. (T)
[3] Eldest son of the Comte d'Artois and husband of the only daughter of Louis XVI.
He renounced his rights to the throne in 1830, when his father, then Charles X,
abdicated. (T)

by way of Madrid to Lisbon, where he took ship for London. During the twenty-four hours he was there, he was received by the Duchesse d'Angoulême to whom he gave an account of the situation in France. He left that night for Dover and travelled by way of Ostend to rejoin Louis XVIII at Ghent. After the Battle of Waterloo, he set out for Paris at the same time as the King.

In August 1815, M. de La Tour du Pin took part in the general election, serving as Chairman of the constituency of the Department of the Somme. On the 17th of the same month, the King made him a peer of France[1] and, in October he went to Brussels to present his credentials to King William I of the Netherlands and to attend his coronation.

Returning shortly afterwards to Paris to take his seat in the Chamber of Peers, M. de La Tour du Pin was present at the trial of Maréchal Ney,[2] in the early days of December. It had been decided that the vote could take into account how much of the penalty was to be exacted. M. de La Tour du Pin therefore voted for the death penalty, but made at the same time the following statement: 'I condemn Maréchal Ney to the penalty decided upon by the Procureur-Général,[3] but as I am far from considering him solely responsible for the miseries of this terrible period, I find him deserving on many grounds of the King's mercy and I would avail myself of the power given me in Article 595 of the Code of Criminal Justice did I not think it more to His Majesty's advantage to leave the guilty man to his justice, his clemency and perhaps to his judgement which must be dictated by our present circumstances (see Appendix II), but a few days afterwards he any other.' This appeal to the King's mercy was, as we know, disregarded.

Several weeks later, on the 28th of January, 1816, M. de La Tour du Pin lost his eldest son, Humbert, in distressingly tragic circumstances (see Appendix II), but a few days afterwards he returned to The Hague to resume his duties as Minister Plenipotentiary to the Court of the Netherlands.

[1] An hereditary member of the Chamber of Peers. (T)
[2] One of Napoleon's generals—the 'bravest of the brave'. He was made a peer of France by Louis XVIII, but rejoined Napoleon when he landed in 1815 and fought with him at Waterloo. He was condemned to death by the Chamber of Peers and shot. (T)
[3] Equivalent to the Attorney-General. (T)

During the following year, a fresh tragedy befell Monsieur and Madame de La Tour du Pin: on the 20th of March, 1817, their youngest daughter, Cécile, died at Nice.

In September 1818, the Duc de Richelieu[1] summoned M. de La Tour du Pin to act as his assistant at the Congress which was meeting at Aix-la-Chapelle to settle the terms for the evacuation of foreign troops from French territory. As soon as the Congress was over, he returned to his post at The Hague.

At the end of 1819, M. de La Tour du Pin went to Paris to take his seat at the opening session of the chamber of Peers and was still there on the 13th of February, 1820, when the Duc de Berry[2] was assassinated.

Shortly afterwards, in April 1820, M. de La Tour du Pin was appointed Ambassador in Turin. He took up the appointment immediately and, except for a visit of four months to Rome in 1824, remained there without a break until January 1830, when he retired.

While living in Turin, Monsieur and Madame de La Tour du Pin sustained another very grievous blow. On the 1st of September, 1822, Charlotte, their only surviving daughter, who had married the Comte de Liedekerke Beaufort, died at the Château de Faublanc, near Lausanne. She was on her way from Turin to join her husband in Berne, where he was Netherlands Minister to the Swiss Republic.

In January 1830, M. de La Tour du Pin travelled to Paris and soon afterwards, troubled, tired and very unhappy over the course events were taking, went to live in Versailles. He was there when the revolution of 1830 broke out.[3] On the 2nd of August, at three o'clock in the morning, he set out from Versailles and travelled towards Orleans, thinking that the King—Charles X—

---

[1] Président du Conseil.
[2] Second son of the Comte d'Artois. Shot in Paris as he left the Opéra. It was the crime of an unbalanced individual, not a political assassination. (T)
[3] Since his accession in 1824, the ultra-reactionary Charles X had been challenging the moderate assembly which represented the general feeling of the country. The struggle came to a head in 1830, and the King abdicated in favour of his grandson, the Duc de Bordeaux, son of the assassinated Duc de Berry. But the people put Louis Philippe d'Orléans on the throne. It was a victory of the middle classes over the aristocracy, most of whom, like M. de La Tour du Pin, remained faithful to the allegiance they had sworn to Charles X. (T)

after withdrawing by way of Rambouillet, would take the Orléans road to Tours to fall back on forces in the south, and above all in the Vendée, and that he would be able to join him there.

The following day, learning of the King's abdication and departure for Cherbourg, M. de La Tour du Pin decided to go to Le Bouilh, near Saint-André-en-Cubzac. From there, he wrote to the Chamber of Peers protesting against the proposal that the Duc de Bordeaux should replace his grandfather on the throne.

The events of that month also brought to an end a mission to the King of Sardinia which M. de La Tour du Pin had undertaken. Free, therefore, from all commitments, he spent the last part of 1830 peacefully on his estates at Le Bouilh.

However, fresh anxieties soon arose. In 1831, Aymar, his only surviving child, was carried away by a generous enthusiasm for the legitimist cause[1] and joined a movement which was forming in the Vendée. He was arrested and imprisoned and his father, not wishing to be separated from him, spent the four months of his sentence in prison with him, both in Bourbon-Vendée and at Fontenay.

In April 1832, Aymar de La Tour du Pin was freed, but he soon set out again for the Vendée to rejoin the Duchesse de Berry. The failure of their attempt is well known and after the arrest of Madame de Berry, Aymar de La Tour du Pin had to go into hiding. In November 1832, he reached Jersey. For his part in the rebellion, Aymar was condemned to death in his absence. M. de La Tour du Pin, too, was fined and imprisoned for three months in the Fort du Hâ for defending his son in public against accusations he considered outrageous. Madame de La Tour du Pin remained with him throughout his imprisonment.

Since the sentence passed on his son meant that his only safety lay in exile, and in order to escape persecutions directed against himself, M. de La Tour du Pin decided to live abroad.

When he came out of prison in March 1833, he went to live in Nice,[2] where his wife and son joined him. For political reasons, however, he could not remain there, and moved to Turin and

---

[1] That of the Duc de Bordeaux—a movement led by his mother, the Duchesse de Berry. (T)
[2] Then in Piedmont, a part of the Kingdom of Sardinia. (T)

then to Pignerol, where he stayed until the 28th of August. A number of very urgent matters then required his presence in France, so he and Madame de La Tour du Pin returned. They remained scarcely a year and then went abroad again, intending to settle in Lausanne. They arrived there towards the end of November 1835 and it was there, on the 26th of February, 1837, that M. de La Tour du Pin died. He was seventy-eight.

The story of Madame de La Tour du Pin was always very closely linked with that of her husband. She accompanied him to The Hague and later to Turin. She even shared his imprisonment in the Fort du Hâ, and afterwards went with him to Italy and Switzerland, sharing the exile he had voluntarily imposed on himself in order to share that of his son, Aymar. She was in Lausanne with M. de La Tour du Pin when he died and some time later left for Italy, accompanied by Aymar, her only surviving child. She settled at Pisa, in Tuscany, where she lived until her death on the 2nd of April, 1853, at the age of eighty-three. Her death removed one of the last remaining traces of the 'haute société' of pre-Revolutionary days. Those who knew her said it was rare to find such strength combined with so much charm, such serenity with such conscientiousness, such steadfast devotion to duty with such kindliness.

It is probable that she wrote the Memoirs over a period of years, and at long intervals. In fact, although the first part is dated 1st of January, 1820, there are indications in the Memoirs themselves that the last pages of the first part were not written until some time between 1839 and 1842. If they were written earlier, they were certainly not finally corrected until then.

As for the second part, the first draft—or the copy of it—was not begun until the 7th of February, 1843.

The Marquise de La Tour du Pin died before she could finish the work she had undertaken. After her death, the manuscript passed into the hands of her son, Aymar, Marquis de La Tour du Pin. He bequeathed it to his nephew, Hadelin, Comte de Liedekerke Beaufort[1] who, shortly before his death, entrusted it in turn to one of his sons, Colonel Comte Aymar de Liedekerke Beaufort, to whom we owe its publication.

[1] Son of Charlotte de La Tour du Pin. (T)

Appendix II

Aymar de Liedekerke Beaufort's Account of the Death of Humbert de La Tour du Pin in a Duel

A detailed account of the tragic circumstances of Humbert's death is given in the Preface written by Colonel Comte Aymar de Liedekerke Beaufort when the Memoirs were first published.

Humbert de La Tour du Pin was twenty-six years old when he was killed. During the last years of the Empire, he became Sub-Prefect of Florence and later of Sens. At the Restoration, he was given a commission in the Mousquetaires Noirs and later became aide-de-camp to Maréchal Victor, Duc de Bellune.

At the time of his appointment to the staff of the Duc de Bellune, one of the other aides-de-camp was Major Malandin, an officer who had risen from the ranks, a rough and ready, uneducated man, daring, courageous, honest and loyal, but oversensitive on points of honour, a man whose every promotion had been won on the Emperor's fields of battle.

On the very day that Humbert de La Tour du Pin joined the Marshal's staff, he went to the aides-de-camps' room and met there a number of other officers on the staff, including Major Malandin. Hardly a minute later, this Major was making joking, but vulgar and unseemly remarks to the newcomer on some unimportant detail of his uniform.

The remainder of the incident is best described in an account written by a descendant of the Duc de Bellune, who had the story directly from the Marshal's eldest son:[1]

'Hearing himself spoken to in this fashion, M. de La Tour du Pin coloured to the roots of his hair and was about to retort when the Marshal arrived to see how their work was getting on. He gave the Major a commission to the Minister of War, and the Major left immediately, with the dispatch customary in someone used to carrying out orders promptly.

[1] Taken from the *Supplément Littéraire du Petit Journal* of the 4th of January, 1880.

'The Marshal himself left a few minutes later, and it was not long before M. de La Tour du Pin did likewise.

'He went straight to the house where his family was living, trying to control the anger which flamed in him, and went immediately to his father's study.

' "Father," he said, "this is what has just happened to a young officer whose circumstances are exactly the same as my own." And he described in detail, but with sufficient calm not to awaken any suspicions in the old gentleman, the scene which had just taken place in the staff room. "This officer," he went on, "is, if not one of my friends, at least one of my equals, and what touches his honour touches mine also. What ought he to do?"

' "Challenge the aggressor," said the old man.

' "And if he is offered an apology?"

' "Refuse it . . . Your companion should be the more zealous in defence of his good name in that he, unlike the man who has insulted him, has not had to pay in blood for the insignia of his rank."

' "Thank you, Father." And the young officer went off.

'That same evening, he demanded that Major Malandin should offer him satisfaction with weapons.

'There was great agitation among the Marshal's staff. The Marshal charged his own son to use his good offices in arranging the conditions of the meeting. It was at this point that the rare qualities hidden deep in the good Major's soul came to light. He offered, without any false pride, to admit his fault and the baselessness of his remarks.

'The challenger refused to accept an apology in any form and since Malandin's skill with the pistol was notorious, the seconds suggested sabres. This met with a fresh refusal. Swords were then proposed, but again without success. Finally, the challenger's obstinate insistence on pistols forced the seconds to give way and they arranged for the duel to take place the following morning in the Bois de Boulogne. The conditions were that the adversaries should stand twenty-five paces apart and exchange shots until one of them should be too badly wounded to continue.

'That evening, a deep gloom pervaded the Marshal's house for, understanding all the delicacy of the quarrel, he could do nothing more, except shut his eyes to it. Major Malandin's friends showed him by their silence, how much they regretted the unfortunate situation he had so heedlessly provoked and he himself, for the first time in a very long while, forgot to drink after dinner that half-bottle of rum which he always maintained was essential to his digestion.

'As for M. de La Tour du Pin, he spent the evening with his family, outwardly calm and even gay. In a perfectly normal voice, and before them all, he gave instructions for his horse to be saddled very early next morning, saying he had promised to ride with some friends.

'Before going to his rooms, he kissed his mother goodnight with scarcely a tremor, firmly setting his lips against a longing to tell her all that was in his heart.

'The next day, on a calm, sunny, but chilly morning, one group of three riders and another of four made their separate ways towards the Porte Maillot, then the principal entrance to the Bois de Boulogne. Four of the riders were in undress uniform, one wore the insignia of a military surgeon and two were in civilian dress, though it was obvious from their bearing that they were more accustomed to wearing uniform.

'When they reached the clearing which had been decided on as suitable for a duel, the riders dismounted and tied the bridles of their horses to the nearby trees. The two groups then approached one another. The seconds had brought with them their principals' saddle holsters containing their weapons. Lots were drawn and the choice fell on the pistols of M. de La Tour du Pin. They were loaded and handed to the adversaries, who had taken up their stand at the agreed distance.

'From the moment he arrived in the clearing, Major Malandin had been feverishly twisting his moustache and before the signal to fire had been given, he indicated that he wished to speak. In a loud, but not quite steady voice, his gaze fixed and his face very pale, he made the following declaration:

' "Monsieur de La Tour du Pin, I feel it is my duty to state once more, in the presence of these gentlemen, that I regret my unfortunate jest. Two good men should not kill one another on such an account."

'M. de La Tour du Pin hesitated a moment, then walked slowly over to the Major. Hearts beat fast and everyone felt secretly relieved at this respite. But when the young man reached his adversary, instead of holding out his hand, he raised his arm and struck Malandin across the forehead with the butt of his pistol, saying through his teeth: "Monsieur, I think that now you will not refuse to fight."

'And he went back to his place.

'The Major's expression changed: a flash of what could only be called madness lit his eyes; it was not anger, but the startled bewilderment of a lion suddenly spat upon by a gazelle.

' "He is a dead man," he said, drawing himself up.

'To such a scene, only one end was possible and it was essential that it should come as quickly as possible. The signal was given. M. de La Tour du Pin fired first. His adversary then raised his arm, and was clearly heard to murmur: "Poor child—and his poor mother!"

'The shot was fired, and the young man, spinning round, fell face downwards to the ground. The bullet had gone straight to his heart.'

Appendix III

Madame de La Tour du Pin's Brief Historical
Account of the Dillon Regiment

At the end of 1688, Theobald, Viscount Dillon, Irish peer and head at the time of the illustrious family of that name, raised on his Irish estates and equipped at his own expense, a regiment to serve King James II. During 1690, this regiment passed into the service of France, under the command of his second son, Arthur Dillon. It formed part of a body of 5,371 Irish troops who landed at Brest on the 1st of May, 1690, given by King James II to Louis XIV in exchange for six French regiments.

After the fall of Limerick in 1691, the number of Irish troops who passed into the service of France was considerably increased, amounting in all to more than 20,000 men. From then until the French Revolution, they were known as the Irish Brigade, and served with most outstanding distinction in all the wars in which France was engaged.

Arthur Dillon, first Colonel of the Dillon Regiment, became a Lieutenant-General at the age of thirty-three, being promoted exceptionally from the rank of Brigadier-General[1] in recognition of his brilliant service. He was for a long time Commander in Dauphiny and Governor of Toulon. On the 28th of August, 1709, near Briançon, he defeated General Rehbinder, Commander of the troops of Savoy, who was attempting an invasion of France. Arthur Dillon ended a glorious career in 1733, aged 63, leaving five sons and five daughters.

In 1728, Arthur Dillon had given his regiment to Charles Dillon, his eldest son. Charles became the head of the family in 1737, after the death of his first cousin, Richard, Lord Dillon. He kept command of the regiment for a time and then gave it to his brother, Henry Dillon.

In 1741, Henry Dillon succeeded his brother Charles in the

---

[1] An approximate translation of the obsolete rank 'maréchal de camp'. (T)

family titles and property, but he none the less retained command of the Regiment and led it until 1743. Until shortly before the Battle of Dettingen,[1] the English had only supported the Austrian cause; now they took the field against France. To preserve his Irish peerage and to prevent the confiscation of his property, Henry, Lord Dillon found himself obliged to leave the service of France. He did this with the consent, and even on the advice of Louis XV.

The third brother, James Dillon, a Knight of Malta, was then promoted Colonel of the Regiment. He was killed while leading it at Fontenoy in 1745.

On the field of battle, Louis XV appointed the fourth brother, Edward Dillon, to be Colonel of the Regiment. But in 1747, he too was killed, leading the Regiment at the battle of Lawfeld.

Only the fifth brother, Arthur-Richard, remained, but he had recently entered the Church. He died in England in 1806, as Archbishop of Narbonne.

After Edward Dillon's death at Lawfeld, Louis XV was most strongly urged to dispose of the Regiment, on the ground that there was no Dillon to command it. But the King replied that 'Henry, Lord Dillon had recently married and he could not consent to this family losing a possession so closely theirs by virtue of the blood they had shed and the excellent service they had given, so long as there was any hope at all of seeing the con nection revived'. The Dillon Regiment was, therefore, commanded successively by a Lieutenant-Colonel and two Colonel Commandants until command was given to the Honorable Arthur Dillon,[2] second son of Henry, Lord Dillon, on the 25th of August, 1767 when he was seventeen years of age.

At the time of the French Revolution, the Irish Brigade found itself reduced to three infantry regiments: those of Dillon, Berwick and Walsh. In 1794, the remains of these three regiments, including most of the officers (who had emigrated to England) passed into the pay of His Britannic Majesty. The Dillon Regiment, or the remaining fragment of it which England was willing to call

[1] The English army was commanded by George II—the last occasion when an English Monarch led his army in Battle. (T)
[2] Father of the writer. (T)

by that name, was given to the Honourable Henry Dillon, third son of Henry, Lord Dillon and brother of Arthur Dillon, the last Colonel of the Regiment during its service in France, who had died on the scaffold in 1794. This new Regiment filled the gaps in its ranks by recruiting in the same region from which its first soldiers had come in 1688. Shortly afterwards, it sailed for Jamaica, where it lost so many men that it was released from service. The flags and colours of the Regiment were returned to Ireland and carefully handed over to Charles, Lord Dillon, head of the family and eldest brother of the Colonel.

Index